THE IMPACT OF BUDDHISM ON
CHINESE MATERIAL CULTURE

BUDDHISMS:
A PRINCETON UNIVERSITY PRESS SERIES
EDITED BY STEPHEN F. TEISER

A list of titles in this series appears at the back of the book

THE IMPACT OF BUDDHISM ON
CHINESE MATERIAL CULTURE

John Kieschnick

:TON UNIVERSITY PRESS · PRINCETON AND OXFORD

Copyright © 2003 by Princeton University Press
Published by Princeton University Press, 41 William Street, Princeton, New Jersey 08540
In the United Kingdom: Princeton University Press, 3 Market Place, Woodstock,
Oxfordshire OX20 1SY

Library of Congress Cataloging-in-Publication Data
Kieschnick, John, 1964–
The impact of Buddhism on Chinese material culture
p. cm.   — (Buddhisms)
Includes bibliographical references and index.
ISBN 0-691-09675-9 (alk. paper) — ISBN 0-691-09676-7 (pbk. : alk. paper)
1. Buddhism—China.   2. Material culture—China.   I. Title.   II. Series.
BQ626 .K54 2003
294.3'0951—dc21   2002072258

British Library Cataloging-in-Publication Data is available

This book has been composed in Sabon and Caslon Open Face
Printed on acid-free paper. ∞
www.pupress.princeton.edu

Printed in the United States of America

3 5 7 9 10 8 6 4

ISBN-13: 978-0-691-09676-6 (pbk.)

ISBN-10: 0-691-09676-7 (pbk.)

For Regina

CONTENTS

ACKNOWLEDGMENTS

A FULL LIST of all who have helped in the writing of this book would tax the patience of my publisher and of all but my most sympathetic readers. Suffice it to say that the book would have been much weaker, contained more inaccuracies, and been much duller had it not been for the generous assistance of friends and colleagues, as well as specialists whom I know only through correspondence, but who have without exception replied to my queries with information, suggestions, and encouragement.

I have published earlier versions of three sections of what follows. Namely, "Buddhism and the History of the Chinese Bridge" in *Economic History, Urban Culture and Material Culture.* Papers from the Third International Conference on Sinology, History Section (Taipei: Academia Sinica, Institute of History and Philology, 2002), pp. 1–25; "The Symbolism of the Monk's Robe in China" in *Asia Major,* Third Series, vol. 12, part 1 (1999), pp. 9–32; and a Chinese version of my discussion of Buddhism and the history of the chair as "Yizi yu fojiao liuchuan de guanxi" in *The Bulletin of the Institute of History and Philology, Academia Sinica,* vol. 69, part 4 (1998), pp. 727–61. I am grateful to the editorial boards of these journals for permission to print revised versions of these articles here.

THE IMPACT OF BUDDHISM ON
CHINESE MATERIAL CULTURE

INTRODUCTION

WHEN Buddhism began to influence Chinese culture in the first century A.D., it brought with it a vast array of new concepts, doctrines, and beliefs. Detailed conceptions of heavens and hells, a new pantheon, belief in reincarnation, and the doctrine of karma all eventually worked their way into the fabric of Chinese life as Buddhist ideas took hold and spread. Buddhism brought with it as well new types of behavior: forms of seated meditation, the practice of making offerings before images, Buddhist rites of consecration and confession, and even the new gesture of palms pressed together. By exposing Chinese to foreign missionaries and through the translation of foreign texts, Buddhism made contributions to the Chinese understanding of their own language and to the language itself; many expressions common in modern Chinese originated in Buddhist texts, and the recognition of the distinctive characteristics of the Chinese language, such as its dependence on tones, was also sparked by scrutiny of the Indian language in which Buddhist texts were couched.

In addition to all of this, however, Buddhism also altered the material world of the Chinese, introducing new sacred objects, new symbols, buildings, ritual implements, and a host of other objects big and small, as well as new ways of thinking about and interacting with these objects. The impact of Buddhism on Chinese material culture began immediately, with the first evidence we have of Buddhism in China in the first century, and continued long after the twelfth, when Buddhism ceased to be a major cultural force in India. Objects, ideas about objects, and behaviors associated with objects came with Buddhism to China, where they continued to change and evolve in response to new environments and the demands of a dynamic society with an immense capacity to manufacture, employ, and discard material things. Today in all areas where Chinese culture is present, Buddhism continues to hold a prominent place in local material culture. This book attempts to give an overview of these developments by focusing on the histories of a number of objects that are representative of the major themes in the history of the influence of Buddhism on Chinese material culture. But before discussing the histories of particular objects, we turn first to trenchant Buddhist attitudes toward material things in general.

The Buddhist Critique of the Material World

Few religions have attacked the material world with the intellectual rigor of Buddhism. From the earliest strata of Buddhist texts to the present day, Buddhist monks have espoused an austere ideal of renunciation of the world of things. In the first text of the *Dīrghāgama*, translated from Sanskrit into Chinese in the fifth century, Śākyamuni explains that like the six previous buddhas that came before him, he too was born a prince, and was raised for a life of ease and abundance in a luxurious palace. When his father suspected that his son was leaning toward the life of a renunciant, he attempted to seduce the boy into staying at home by appealing to his "five senses," supplying him with skilled, beautiful women and augmenting the already lavish adornments of the palace. But in the end, like similar acts of renunciation by the six buddhas that had preceded him in earlier eras, Śākyamuni secretly left the palace by chariot late at night, removed his "precious garments," donned the robes of an ascetic, and ordered his charioteer to take his princely clothing and chariot back to the palace, while he wandered alone into the forest with nothing.[1] This first great act of renunciation, the model for all Buddhist monks, repeated in numerous texts and depicted in countless paintings and statues, involved more than just the rejection of physical objects: it also signaled the renunciation of pleasing music, sexual pleasure, and attachments to family. But the fact that Śākyamuni was born to a family of great wealth underscored his rejection of *material* pleasures, for the more one has, the greater the act of renunciation. Śākyamuni's act also implied a juxtaposition between material comfort and spiritual advancement. His biography makes it clear that he could not have achieved enlightenment had he continued to lead the luxurious life of a wealthy prince, surrounded by the extravagant accoutrements of the immensely rich.

This contrast between the material concerns of the wealthy and the spiritual quest of the monk appears frequently in Buddhist scriptures. In the *Madhyamāgama*, the Buddha announces that unlike merchants, warriors, and priests, all of whom seek material wealth, the monk seeks after truth.[2] Elsewhere the Buddha states that unlike kings who think only of war and covet treasure, or women who think only of men and covet jewels, the monk thinks only of the "four noble truths" and wants only to achieve

---

[1] *Chang ahan jing* (Skt. *Dīrghāgama*), T no. 1, vol. 1, pp. 1–10. There is no early continuous biography of Śākyamuni, but his renunciation of the life of a prince is common to most of what are considered the earliest references to his life. See Étienne Lamotte, *History of Indian Buddhism: From the Origins to the Saka Era*, pp. 648–62.

[2] *Zhong ahan jing* (Skt. *Madhyamāgama*), T no. 26, vol. 1, p. 660b–c.

nirvana.[3] Wealth is the petty obsession of peddlers who crave one another's belongings, and cannot free themselves of their lust for material
things.[4] Money and treasure, like women, are fetters that "bind hard and
fast" and "pollute the mind."[5] It was for this reason, the seductive dis-
tractions of a life surrounded by material comforts, that Śākyamuni left
a life of leisure in a palace for the hard life of the renunciant, and for this
reason that he insisted that his disciples follow his example and adopt a
life of poverty and restraint.

In any number of scriptural passages, the Buddha warns that the pursuit of material things is not simply a distraction from purer, more lofty
concerns; it is short-sighted, because in the long term, one is not rewarded
for collecting personal possessions. For "when one's life comes to an end,
one's treasures remain in the world."[6] And things that were not put to
moral use in life serve no purpose in death. The Buddha is equally unre-
lenting for those content simply to enjoy material possessions in this life.
Surrendering to even a modest desire for things is dangerous because, un-
restrained, our thirst for possessions can never be quenched: "Even were
one to obtain everything in the world, still he would not be satisfied."[7]

We attach ourselves to the material world, ignoring the horrendous
karmic consequences of the neglect of moral duties and unaware that such
craving brings only the most fleeting forms of pleasure—fleeting because,
in the end, the material world is a deception, a dream from which we must
awaken sooner or later. The Buddha tells his disciples that material pleasures are "like a man who dreams of a fine house with fine gardens and
sumptuous delights. Yet when he awakes all of it vanishes. Distinctions of
wealth and poverty, noble and common are like a dream."[8]

Buddhist thinkers in India were drawn to this conception of the material world as illusory, and attacked notions of conventional reality with
great enthusiasm. This was done by systematically breaking down all phenomena into their constituent elements. Even at a superficial level, all
experience can be divided into the "five aggregates" (Skt. *skandhas*): matter, feeling, cognition, impulses, and consciousness. Each of these aggregates can further be seen to contain distinct elements. The influential Indian scholastic work *Abhidharmakośaśāstra,* for instance, states that
matter is comprised of eleven basic elements (*dharmas*): the five sense or-
gans, the five types of objects and *avijñapti* (unexpressed matter). The *Ab-*

---

[3] *Zeng yi ahan jing* (Skt. *Ekottarāgama*), *T* no. 125, vol. 2, p. 714b.

[4] *Bie yi za ahan jing* (Skt. *Saṃyuktāgama*), *T* no. 100, vol. 2, p. 439b.

[5] *Za ahan jing* (Skt. *Saṃyuktāgama*), *T* no. 99, vol. 2, p. 338b.

[6] Ibid., *T* no. 101, vol. 2, p. 496a.

[7] Ibid., p. 495c1.

[8] *Fo bannihuan jing* (Skt. *Mahāparinirvāṇasūtra*), *T* no. 5, vol. 1, p. 161c.

hidarmakośa goes on to list the five types of objects: visible matter, sounds, odors, tastes, and tangibles. Of these, visible matter can be divided into colors, including blue, red, yellow, white, light, and darkness. Sounds are divided into eight categories, tastes into six, odors into four, tangibles into eleven,[9] and so on. Only the most basic elements (*dharmas*) can be said to exist independently, if only for the briefest of moments; the objects in the world around us only appear to exist as independent, distinct entities. A red vase seems to us to have an enduring, independent existence, but in fact it is only a temporary conglomeration of diverse, independent elements that change constantly as the delicate combination of light, color, density, and so forth alters from moment to moment. The enduring vase that seems to remain whole and unchanged from one day to the next is a trick of the senses, disguising a more fluid reality. When viewed in this way, the material world that surrounds us dissolves into individual, independent elements in a frantic, evanescent flux, temporarily coming together in particular configurations (a red vase, a mountain, a person), only to disappear after the briefest moment and reappear with other elements in yet another configuration.[10] As one text puts it:

> The ignorant hold that the ground and other such things exist, while the sage looks on with eyes of wisdom and recognizes that this is folly. It is like a child taking for real an image in a mirror, while an adult sees it as nothing more than a trick of the human eye. [In the same way], ordinary people see the concatenation of dust particles that form the ground and say that it is real.[11]

Not surprisingly, given these repeated condemnations of the material world as an illusory distraction, the monastic ideal, as laid out in the monastic regulations, also eschewed material wealth. The property allowed to a monk was limited to a short list of necessary items that could be carried on his person: a sewing needle, an alms bowl, sandals, and such. Monks are not to touch money. They are to wear only the simplest of garments and to eat the simplest of foods. In sum, whether in well-known sermons, technical ontological treatises, or monastic regulations, Buddhist teachings are suffused with a suspicion of sensual pleasure and a tendency to denigrate and renounce the material world.

[9] Louis de La Vallée Poussin, *Abhidharmakośabhāsyam*, pp. 63ff.

[10] For a clear, brief overview of the concept of *dharmas*, see "Dharma: Buddhist Dharma and Dharmas" in Mircea Eliade, ed., *Encyclopedia of Religion*. For more detail, see the introduction to de La Vallée Poussin, *Abhidharmakośabhāsyam*, and Th. Stcherbatsky, *The Central Conception of Buddhism and the Meaning of the Word "Dharma."*

[11] *Da zhi du lun* (Skt.*Mahāprajñāpāramitāśāstra*) 42, T no. 1509, vol. 25, p. 365.

OBJECTS IN SERVICE TO THE DHARMA

If, however, we leave the world of recondite doctrines and statements of principle and look instead at the way Buddhism has been practiced, we find material goods everywhere. Archaeological evidence suggests that in India monks owned personal property from the earliest times, and did in fact make use of money.[12] Chinese monks too have always owned personal property, ranging from religious objects like scriptures and devotional images to slaves, animals, and vast estates.[13] Some both within and without the Buddhist monastic order saw the contrast between an austere monastic ideal and a more comfortable reality as a sign of decline and hypocrisy, but others found ways of justifying the gap through recourse to well-accepted doctrines and texts. In the *Mahīśāsakavinaya,* for instance, the Buddha says that different regions have different standards of purity, and that if a given practice is not appropriate for a particular region, then it should be adapted to local mores, thus leaving considerable leeway in the interpretation of the monastic regulations.[14] Most, however, saw no need to justify the keeping of personal property by monks; it was taken for granted.

Even if we set aside evidence for the way Buddhism was actually practiced and remain in the realm of ideals, it is not correct to characterize Buddhist doctrine as entirely opposed to the use of material things. Far from expressing disinterest in objects, the monastic regulations dwell on monastic possessions at great length, carefully detailing the cut and hem of the monk's robes, the material from which his alms bowl was to be made, and the length of his walking staff. This was done in order to maintain a clear distinction between the objects associated with the austere Buddhist monk and those associated with other types of people devoted to the pursuit of money, goods, and material display. That is, objects were used to express the monk's disdain for the decadent world of those obsessed with personal wealth. Certain objects could be harnessed for the greater cause of the rejection of the material world, but to do so required

---

[12] Gregory Schopen, *Bones, Stones, and Buddhist Monks: Collected Papers on the Archaeology, Epigraphy, and Texts of Monastic Buddhism in India;* and Xinru Liu, *Ancient India and Ancient China: Trade and Religious Exchanges AD 1–600,* pp. 104–12. For evidence of monastic use of money and ownership of private property in the *Mūlasarvāstivādavinaya,* see Gregory Schopen, "The Good Monk and His Money in a Buddhist Monasticism of 'The Mahāyāna Period,'" pp. 85–105.

[13] Jacques Gernet, *Buddhism in Chinese Society: An Economic History from the Fifth to the Tenth Centuries.*

[14] *Mishasaibu hexi wufen lü* (Skt. *Mahīśāsakavinaya*), T no. 1421, vol. 22, p. 153a15.

meticulous attention to detail and adherence to codes of behavior in their manufacture and use.

More important still, although individual monks were not supposed to amass *personal* wealth, the *corporate* wealth of the monastic community was not restricted. Indeed it was the sacred duty of the laity to support the monastic community with material donations, an act for which they were compensated by happiness in this world and a better rebirth in the next. In the *Ekottarāgama*, the Buddha explains that, on their death, donors may be rewarded with rebirth in the heavens, in addition to which, five advantages accrue to one who gives: "In aspect he is noble, majestic and powerful; he obtains whatever he wishes, and brings every endeavor to fruition; if he is reborn among men, he is born to a wealthy family; he amasses a great personal fortune; and finally, he is eloquent in speech."[15] The inclusion of the reward of "a great personal fortune" is particularly telling. One of the ways one is rewarded for giving material things is by the easy acquisition of even more material things. Here we have strayed far from the heady rhetoric of abstention and renunciation and entered instead the realm of philanthropy and monastic solicitation of funds. The importance of giving to the monastic community is stressed repeatedly in Buddhist scriptures and buttressed by references to the fleeting nature of human existence and the relative unimportance of personal possessions in the greater scheme of things. In one story, repeated in various scriptures, a prosperous layman remarks:

> Although wealth is a source of pleasure, it is impermanent. One's treasure, divided [eventually] among the "five clans" [rulers, thieves, water, fire, and profligate sons], serves only to distract one's mind, to scatter one's thoughts and dissipate one's focus, like a monkey that cannot stop fidgeting for even an instant. Life passes as quickly as lightning. The body is impermanent, a reservoir of suffering. For this reason, it is right to give.

Then follows a long list of all manner of things—grain, oil, elephants, jewels, gold, and furniture—that the layman donates to the monastic community.[16]

Similar stories of fabulous gifts by generous laypeople abound in Buddhist texts, which describe in great detail the gold and precious gems donated to the sangha during the Buddha's lifetime. Just as early Christians could draw on the story of the three wise men who brought precious gifts to the baby Jesus, Buddhist donors (and the monks who encouraged their

[15] *Zeng yi ahan jing* (Skt. *Ekottarāgama*), p. 826a.

[16] In addition to giving these goods to monks, he also gives them to brahmans, an act for which the gods criticize him. *Da zhi du lun* (Skt.* *Mahāprajñāpāramitāśāstra*) 11, p. 142b. The story appears in a number of other, earlier texts as well. See Lamotte, *Le traité de la grande vertu de sagesse* pp. 677–88.

donations) could draw on stories from the scriptures of great laypeople who gave spectacular gifts to the Buddha's community of monks.[17] Further, even those familiar with the Buddhist ontology of matter were encouraged to give, while at the same time recognizing that their gifts "exist only as a conglomeration of causes and conditions, without a single *dharma* containing an inherent self. They are like fabric that is the result of the combination of various conditions. Outside of the silk and thread, there is no fabric."[18] In other words, one could at once recognize the ultimate emptiness of all things and still make provisional use of them for a greater good by donating objects to the Buddhist cause. With this solid base of precedent in well-known, authoritative scriptures, donors needed feel no compunction about giving even huge amounts of wealth to what was supposed to be an austere, otherworldly community.

The sociological basis of the promotion of giving in Buddhist scriptures is obvious: Monks relied on donations for much of their income and so drew attention to doctrines that rewarded donations to the monastic community, and propagated stories of generous donors of the past. Often, however, scriptures go beyond the straightforward need to feed and clothe monks. Although the Buddha has passed into nirvana, devotees are encouraged to continue to make material offerings to him. In the *Lotus Sutra*, the Buddha encourages the pious to make offerings to stupas with gold, silver, crystal, clam shell, and agate. They are also enjoined to make Buddha images out of nickel, copper, bronze, and precious gems.[19] Unlike gifts of food, robes, and cash, these ornaments are made not for the direct use of the monastic community but rather as ornaments for the glorification of the Buddha. Objects offered in service to the Buddha were not restricted in the ways that objects associated with individual monks and nuns were. Simplicity and restraint were seldom important ideals in Buddhist art; Buddhist images and devotional objects were instead intended to provoke awe and devotion through spectacular displays of grandeur.

Similarly, in Buddhist scriptures, detailed descriptions of the objects that surrounded the Buddha highlight his majesty and splendor. Take, for example, the opening lines of the *Avataṃsaka Sutra*, which describe the Buddha in the land of Magadha, sitting on ground made of diamonds and surrounded by various gems and banners, with jeweled nets hanging overhead. He sits beneath the tree of enlightenment, its trunk made of lapis

[17] For the Christian parallel, see Dominic Janes, *God and Gold in Late Antiquity*, p. 61.

[18] *Da zhi du lun* 11, p. 142a; Lamotte, *Le traité de la grande vertu de sagesse*, p. 676.

[19] *Miaofa lianhua jing* (Skt. *Saddharmapuṇḍarika*), *T* no. 262, vol. 9, pp. 8c–9a; English translation, Leon Hurvitz, *Scripture of the Lotus Blossom of the Fine Dharma* p. 39. For further discussion of precious stones in Buddhist literature and practice, see Liu, *Ancient India and Ancient China*.

lazuli, its branches of "marvelous gems."[20] The scene, in the text constructed of precious objects, marks the Buddha as a superior being, despite the fact that all Buddhists considered the Buddha a renunciant who
had transcended attachment to such material goods, just as in early Christian images, Christ, himself a poor man who renounced wealth, carries a
gilded cross embedded with precious gems.[21]

In the same way, the paradise of the buddha Amithāba, considered an
ideal place for good Buddhists to cultivate themselves, is filled with rare,
expensive material objects. The ground there is made of gold. Steps leading to terraces are made of gold, silver, and lapis lazuli. Multiple tiers with
railings and netting, all made of jewels, surround the paradise. Even the
trees are made of jewels.[22] Here, rather than deride the pleasures of material goods, they are used as a lure, a reward for the pious. We have already seen that those who give are rewarded with material wealth; in the
same way, laypeople who keep five lay precepts (not to kill, steal, commit
lascivious acts, cheat, or drink liquor) are assured that as a reward for
doing so, "their wealth will increase and never decrease."[23]

We see the same technique at work in descriptions of the Buddha, who
a number of texts note had skin the color of gold.[24] Far from distancing
the Buddha from secular, material values, Buddhist exegetes readily drew
on them, albeit at times in a self-conscious, sophisticated way. The
Mahāprajñāpāramitāśāstra, for instance, cites the theory that in fact the
color of the Buddha's skin depended on the values of the viewer. For those
who did not value gold, the Buddha's skin looked like lapis lazuli, glass,
or diamonds, depending on what the viewer admired most.[25] Perhaps the
suggestion here that the Buddha's appearance was essentially an illusion
was intended to soften the contrast between the shimmering jewels of the
merchant and the appearance of the great renouncer, emphasizing as it
does that the Buddha ultimately transcends the limits of regional aesthetics and material values. Nonetheless, even in this case, there is no reluctance to encase the Buddha in the opulent imagery of secular literature.
In every society the possession of rare objects is so fundamental as a mark
of distinction, their enticement so strong, that it is natural that objects are
incorporated into the art and ritual even of religions that embrace the ul-

---

[20] *Da fangguang fo huayan jing* (Skt. *Buddhāvataṃsakasūtra*), T no. 278, vol. 9 p. 395a.

[21] Janes, *God and Gold in Late Antiquity*, p. 123.

[22] *Amituo jing* (Skt. *Sukhāvatīamṛtavyūha*), T no. 366, vol. 12, pp. 346c–7a; English
translation in Luis O. Gómez, *The Land of Bliss: The Paradise of the Buddha of Measureless Light*, p. 146.

[23] *Chang ahan jing* (Skt. *Dīrghāgama*), p. 12b.

[24] One of the thirty-two marks of the Buddha. For references, see Hajime Nakamura,
Bukkyōgo daijiten s.v. sanjūnisō, pp. 472–3.

[25] *Da zhi du lun* 88, p. 684a.

timate transcendence of such values. Linking the Buddha, or for that matter a monastery, with precious gems and elaborate ornamentation had immediate resonance with people from all walks of life, expressing majesty,
distinction, and splendor, while at the same time giving expression to the
collective desires of donors and devotees for material well-being.

ATTITUDES TOWARD BUDDHIST OBJECTS IN CHINA

In the preceding discussion, I have drawn on Indian texts from different
periods and from different traditions within Buddhism. Specialists in Indian Buddhism may be able to distinguish shades of attitudes toward objects in different time periods of Indian Buddhism and to trace developments from one set of texts to another. But in China, Buddhist texts
arrived in a haphazard fashion and were never placed in their proper
chronological order, an arduous project that vexes even the most talented
textual scholars today. All of the texts I drew on above that quoted the
Buddha were translated into Chinese before the middle of the fifth century, and in China all were generally considered to represent authentic
records of the sayings of the Buddha. Hence, from early on Buddhism
both presented Chinese devotees with a strong tradition calling for the renunciation of material things and at the same time actively promoted the
use of precious and mundane objects in certain specified contexts. Both
strands of Buddhist thought left their traces on Chinese history.

Even before Buddhism entered China, frugality and restraint in the use
of objects were important ideals in Chinese thought. Confucius, warning
against the seductions of wealth, remarked, "In the eating of coarse rice
and the drinking of water, the using of one's elbow for a pillow, joy is to
be found. Wealth and rank attained through immoral means have as much
to do with me as passing clouds."[26] Zhuangzi makes an even stronger
case, not just against the glorification of rank, wealth, and status, but
against attachment to objects in general, when he entreats his audience to
"treat things as things and refuse to be turned into a thing by things."[27]

Throughout ancient Chinese history, those who displayed wealth in a
manner inappropriate to their station were reprimanded, and an ideal of
frugal restraint was promoted, for example, in burial rites.[28] At the same

---

[26] *Lunyu zhushu* (SBBY edn.) 7, pp. 3b–4a.; English translation from D. C. Lau, *The Analects*, p. 88.

[27] *Zhuangzi jiaozhu*, ed. Wang Shumin, 20, p. 720; English translation from A. C. Gra-
ham, *Chuang-Tzu: The Inner Chapters* p. 121. See also Stephen Eskildsen, *Asceticism in Early Taoist Religion* pp. 1–14.

[28] Mu-chou Poo, "Ideas Concerning Death and Burial in Pre-Han and Han China,"
pp. 25–62.

time, however, the persistent rhetoric calling for frugality and restraint in the use of wealth betrays the opposite tendency; material goods were commonly used to assert and improve social position and as a way of conveying a sense of splendor, prosperity, and affluence.

In the centuries following the arrival of Buddhism to China, Buddhist attitudes toward material things found their own niche in the Chinese repertoire of ideas about objects. Chinese monks were very familiar with the Buddha's injunctions to renounce material wealth as ephemeral, pretentious vanity. As we have seen, major texts espousing this ideal were translated into Chinese by the middle of the fifth century and were well known to literate monks. All Chinese monks were expected to have some familiarity with the texts detailing the monastic regulations, in which an ideal of austere simplicity is set forth at great length, and Chinese monks composed many works commenting and debating various aspects of the monastic regulations concerning personal property and the proper relations monks are to maintain with material things. Similarly, Indian Buddhist writings on the ephemerality and illusory nature of all material objects received great attention in China. The text I cited above, the *Abhidharmakośa,* treating the way in which the phenomenal world can be broken down into distinct elements, was a standard part of the training of a monk, and important Chinese monastic thinkers pondered the true nature of objects at length in their own writings.[29] Buddhist notions of the emphemerality of the world and the fundamental tension between sensuous enjoyment of things and spiritual pursuits were not limited to monks. Through much of Chinese history, refined literary men fantasized about a simpler life in a mountain monastery away from the material trappings of high society, and when Buddhism appears in Chinese narrative, it is often to critique the material decadence of the secular world.

At the same time, in China, Buddhist attitudes toward splendor (*zhuangyan*) and the importance of material expressions of piety were no less influential. Archaeologists and art historians have documented countless Buddhist images from all periods of Chinese Buddhist history of all sizes and shapes, commissioned by people from all walks of life. Great attention was always paid to the substance from which the images were made, and statues of precious metal are common. Indeed, the metal taken up by Buddhist images was so great that it was persistently coveted by the state. From medieval times up to the 1960s, the Chinese government repeatedly called for the melting down of Buddhist images to fill state cof-

---

[29] See, for instance, the comments of the monk Zongmi (780–841) on the "teaching of the phenomenal appearances of the dharmas," in Peter N. Gregory, *Inquiry into the Origin of Humanity: An Annotated Translation of Tsung-mi's* Yüan jen lun *with a Modern Commentary,* pp. 148–60.

fers or provide metal for construction or the military. One such instance is particularly revealing. In 845, during Emperor Wuzong's sweeping persecution of Buddhism, the emperor issued an edict forbidding the use of gold, silver, copper, iron, and gems in the making of Buddhist images. Buddhists were to make their images of clay and wood, which, the edict notes, "are sufficient to express respect."[30] There is an undeniable logic to the emperor's comment, but his efforts to transform the material expression of Buddhist piety in China had little success; immediately after the emperor's death, his orders were rescinded, and Buddhist devotees began once again to employ precious metals in Buddhist objects. Wuzong failed for two reasons. First, many did not feel that wood and clay could adequately express respect for Buddhist deities; just as the emperor required precious objects in accordance with his position, so too did buddhas and bodhisattvas. Secondly, Buddhist images were seldom if ever only channels of communication between individual devotees and the deities they worshipped; they were at the same time attempts to win or assert social prestige. In social context, there was an enormous difference between a small clay image that anyone could afford to make, and a large image of precious metal that demanded resources available only to the wealthy and powerful. For similar reasons, in addition to substance, size too was of great importance. Monumental images of Buddhist figures commissioned at great expense and taking huge amounts of time and labor still hold a prominent place in the Chinese landscape, as do countless stupas, monasteries, and other Buddhist structures spread throughout the country.

When Chinese Buddhist texts describe Buddhist art and architecture, they do so with the vocabulary of opulence and not with the vocabulary of austerity and restraint, which was reserved for descriptions of monks. The famous fourth-century monk Zhi Daolin, for instance, praises the "color and loveliness of purple and gold" in an image of Śākyamuni.[31] Elsewhere, stupas are described as "resplendent" (huali) and as "ornamented with gold to make them splendid and dazzling."[32] They are marked by their beauty and "splendor."[33] As a group of laymen explain in the biography of a seventh-century monk, "Meritorious things made in service to the Buddha must be spectacular."[34] This same tendency toward the ornate and elaborate extends even to the rooms where monks lived. In monasteries, "The Buddha Hall is exquisite, the monks' quarters resplendent."[35] Or elsewhere, "The Buddha Hall and monastic quarters

---

[30] *Tang huiyao* 49, p. 862.
[31] "Shijiawen foxiang zan," p. 195c.
[32] *Xu gaoseng zhuan* 1, *T* no. 2060, vol. 50, p. 428b.
[33] See *Fayuan zhulin* 12, *T* no. 2122, vol. 53, p. 379c.
[34] *Song gaoseng zhuan* 18, *T* no. 2061, vol. 50, p. 821.
[35] *Fayuan zhulin* 18, p. 420b.

were gorgeous, the carving sumptuous."[36] Nowhere do we find praise of plain, unadorned Buddhist images and inexpensive stupas, or descriptions of monasteries as simple, humble monastic dwellings. In Chinese Buddhism, such terms were simply not a part of the aesthetic repertoire. And the economic harvest of Buddhist philanthropy was applied to a large extent to ornament.

The contrast between the austere ideal of the monk and the material success of Buddhist monasteries was not lost on Buddhism's critics. A fifth-century monk-turned-critic questioned his former brethren, asking, "Why is it that their ideals are [so] noble and far-reaching and their activities still are [so] base and common? . . . [Monks] become merchants and engage in barter, wrangling with the masses for profit."[37] One sixth-century critic complained of the wealth and energy "squandered" to erect "elaborate temples." For "the teaching bequeathed by the Buddha called on his followers not to cultivate the fields and not to store up wealth or grain, but to beg for their food or clothing, and to practice the *dhūtaṅgas.* This is no longer true."[38] The criticism of what seemed rank hypocrisy continued into later periods. In the early seventh century, Emperor Gaozu, for instance, noted the contrast between the teachings of Buddhism that "give priority to purity, distancing oneself from filth, and cutting off greed and desire" and the "inexhaustible greed" of monks intent on "amassing ever-greater quantities of goods."[39] Or consider a famous eighth-century memorial by Xing Tipi submitted in protest to imperial support for monastic construction that, again, contrasted the "purity" and "self-denial" of Buddhist teachings with the "vast halls, lengthy corridors" and "elaborate ornamentation" of Buddhist monasteries.[40]

But if the contrast between Buddhist ideals of austerity and the opulence of Buddhist buildings and images was shockingly apparent to critics like Xing Tipi, within Buddhist circles the contrast usually slipped by unnoticed. Buddhist texts are replete with references both to the unbridled splendor of devotion and to ideals of renunciation, simplicity, and restraint. Normally, Buddhist writers felt little need to justify the opulence

[36] *Song gaoseng zhuan* 27, p. 882b.

[37] Objections cited by the monk Daoheng in the early fifth-century treatise *Shi bo lun* in *Hongming ji* 6, T no. 2102, vol. 52, p. 35b; translated in Eric Zürcher, *The Buddhist Conquest of China,* p. 262.

[38] *Dhūtaṅga* are ascetic practices. The comments are those of Xun Ji (d. 547) in *Guang hongming ji* 7, pp. 128c–31b; translated in Kenneth Chen, *Buddhism in China,* p. 187.

[39] *Jiu Tang shu* 1, pp. 16–7.

[40] The edict appears in the *Tang huiyao* 49, pp. 850–51, and the *Wenyuan yinghua* 698, pp. 3603–4, each of which gives different dates. The memorial is discussed in Gernet, *Buddhism in Chinese Society,* p. 330, n.110, and in Stanley Weinstein, *Buddhism Under the T'ang,* p. 50.

of Buddhist art and architecture. Take for instance the biography of the Tang monk Yize (773–830), a disciple of the prominent Chan monk Huizhong. The biography repeatedly emphasizes Yize's detachment from the material world. As a youth he "lived tranquilly, seeking after nothing." When he became a monk, he "abandoned all of his possessions." The biography quotes him as saying, "There is nothing in heaven or earth, nothing in the self. Although all is thus negated, neither was there ever anything [to negate]. This is to say, the sage is like a shadow; humanity,[41] a dream. Who is there to live or die?" After studying under Huizhong, Yize retires to a deserted area where he lives in a hut he makes of grass and leaves. "He lived a life of simplicity, drinking from mountain streams and appeasing his hunger with fruit." All of this fits the pattern of common descriptions of Buddhist ascetics. But what follows is equally typical. "Later, woodcutters saw him and spread the word. There were those who admired his teachings and said, 'This man of the Way has no disciples.' And so they led each other up the mountain, constructed rooms, painted images of buddhas, and installed monks, so that it eventually became a flourishing hermitage."[42] The biography, and others like it, expresses no uneasiness with the transition in the monk's environment from stark simplicity to a bustling monastic complex filled with Buddhist paintings; the two ideals were seen as complementary rather than contradictory.

Like notions of emptiness, Buddhist ideals of austerity certainly influenced the way Chinese monks and laypeople thought about material objects. These ideals lay behind the ascetic tendencies of many monks. Monastic concerns to limit the personal property of monks, and an insistence by some monks on a plain monastic uniform of drab, simple garments, and even vegetarianism, can all be traced in part to the emphasis placed on renunciation and self-restraint in Buddhist doctrine. Refined laymen too were drawn to an ideal of Buddhist simplicity. In their later years, even men of means, like for instance the great Tang poet Wang Wei, retired to simple lives of reflection and recitation, surrounding themselves with only a few basic objects.[43] But the pull of austerity did not lead monks to strip monasteries of ornamentation in the manner of Protestant

---

[41] *Baixing.* The *Jingde chuan deng lu* version of Yize's biography here reads "one hundred years" (*bai nian*). *Jingde chuan deng lu* 4, T no. 2076, vol. 51, p. 234a.

[42] *Song gaoseng zhuan* 10, p. 768b–c.

[43] According to one biography, later in life Wang Wei maintained a vegetarian diet and, after his wife died, did not take a second wife. "His studio contained nothing save a teapot, a medicine pestle, a table for scriptures, and a corded chair. After he retired from the court, he burned incense and sat alone, occupying himself with meditation and chanting." *Jiu Tang shu* 190b, p. 5052.

reformers, or to even consider the possibility. In practice, monks at times amassed considerable personal fortunes, managed extensive monastic estates worked by tenant farmers and slaves, and adorned themselves with expensive, elaborate monastic robes.

In sum, Buddhist thought as it developed in China allowed for a wide range of attitudes toward objects, from denigration of them as illusory tokens of decadence to embracing them as tools for devotion and understanding of Buddhist truths. One approach to the history of the impact of Buddhism on Chinese material culture would be to examine the works of Chinese Buddhist thinkers with an eye to their treatment of wealth and of objects in general. And in the pages that follow, I devote much attention to the ways in which Buddhist doctrines influenced the history of material culture in China. There is, however, a danger of giving too much weight to the role of ideas in the formation and development of material culture. Many things are employed according to traditions of religious behavior rather than as outgrowths of well-defined doctrinal precepts.[44] Moreover, at times internal developments in the history of objects provoke doctrinal changes, and not the other way around. To paraphrase Zhuangzi, it is often the objects that manipulate us rather than we who manipulate them. The point is easily missed in the study of religion, which we too easily interpret as an extension of a stable set of core doctrines.

When, instead of looking at broad, general attitudes toward wealth in Buddhist texts, we look at the histories of specific objects, we begin to catch a glimpse of the full range of the impact of Buddhism on Chinese material culture, a spectrum that ranges from objects intimately linked to monastic Buddhism like the monastery and the monk's apparel, to Buddhist objects in settings that have little to do with traditional Buddhist concerns—Buddhist rosaries adorning Qing court clothing, or Buddhist devotional objects in a county museum. Conversely, the histories of objects that seem at first glance to have nothing to do with Buddhism— bridges, or the tools of print technology—on closer inspection turn out to be intimately linked with Buddhist ideas and practices. This is the approach I take below: a collection of the histories of particular objects, attitudes toward them, and ways in which they were used over long stretches of time that, taken together, reveal the complex and subtle ways in which Buddhism changed the material life of a civilization. But before embarking on the details of particular objects, a few remarks on what the term *material culture* means and how it has been used by other scholars to study similar topics will help to clarify what follows.

---

[44] For a discussion of the problem, see William H. Walker, "Where Are the Witches of Prehistory?" pp. 245–308.

On the Term *Material Culture*

Scholars working with artifacts have proposed various definitions of material culture. Some have attempted to limit the term to objects people make and use in order to survive, thus excluding ritual implements, objects made for aesthetic enjoyment (i.e., "art") and even objects made for greater physical comfort, such as furniture.[45] Others have pushed the boundaries of the concept of material culture to include not only all manner of objects but even human language, since "words, after all, are air masses shaped by the speech apparatus according to culturally acquired rules."[46] Most have come down between these two extremes, defining material culture as "all data directly relating to visible or tangible things such as tools, clothing, or shelter which a person or persons have made."[47] This "data" includes both ideas about objects (icons are holy, bells are beautiful) as well as behavior associated with objects (devotees make offerings to icons, monks ring monastery bells at particular times of the day). Archaeologist Michael Brian Schiffer has given more precision to the concept by defining artifacts as "phenomena produced, replicated, or otherwise brought wholly or partly to their present form through human means," thus including a wide array of objects such as art, food, clothing, and gardens, while excluding material things like the stars, natural rivers, and wild animals, which he terms "externs."[48]

An even more subtle nuance in the term *material culture* is the relationship between material objects and culture. Scholars ordinarily view artifacts as reflections of culture. The nature of the construction of an ancient Chinese bronze vessel, for instance, can give us clues to the social structure of the people who made it, while the images on the vessel may disclose religious beliefs. Others emphasize that in addition to reflecting culture, objects also play an integral part in shaping culture. Without objects, individual and group identity, and virtually all forms of communication and expression, are impossible.[49] Humans do not interact naked and in the wild: we are always surrounded by objects that influence the way we see the world around us and the way we behave.

[45] Melville J. Herskovits, *Man and His Works: The Science of Cultural Anthropology* p. 241.

[46] James Deetz, *In Small Things Forgotten: The Archeology of Early American Life*, pp. 24–5.

[47] Cornelius Osgood, *Ingalik Material Culture*, p. 26. For a discussion of definitions of *material culture*, see Thomas J. Schlereth, "Material Culture Studies in America, 1876–1976," pp. 1–5.

[48] Michael Brian Schiffer, *The Material Life of Human Beings: Artifacts, Behavior, and Communication*, p. 12.

[49] Schlereth, "Material Culture Studies in America," pp. 203; Schiffer, Ibid.

But while appreciating the greater significance of objects in all aspects of daily life, it is useful to focus on the narrower area of the ideas, behaviors, and relationships that coalesce in order to manufacture and use certain objects. To return to the ancient Chinese bronze, the manufacture of the object involved negotiations between the eventual owner of the bronze and the artisans who made it, in addition to a set of cultural assumptions about the significance of the bronze and technical knowledge passed down over generations about how to make a bronze. These aspects of culture came into being expressly for the sake of the object. In other words, in addition to exploring the ways in which artifacts reflect culture and the role they play more generally in all cultural performances, we can also look more specifically at the cultural figurations that center on specific objects. This will be my focus throughout this book: What negotiations were involved in making Buddhist objects? What were the objects used for? What were people's attitudes toward these objects?

SCHOLARSHIP ON MATERIAL CULTURE

Unlike literary theory, sociology or even religious studies, material culture studies cannot easily be summarized as a genealogy of movements and key figures. It is closer to the field of textual studies in that material culture studies have developed independently in various fields relatively isolated one from the other. Collectors, scholars in the fields of archaeology, folklife, anthropology, history of technology, art history, and social history have all had to come to terms with objects in their own ways. It is only recently that the field has become self-conscious and that scholars have begun to pool techniques and data from diverse disciplines for insights into the study of the role of objects in culture.

Long before the term *material culture* gained currency, nineteenth-century anthropologists and archeologists gave great importance to objects. This concern grew in large measure from their overriding project of mapping out the evolution of human culture; artifacts are useful for categorizing and comparing different societies. By comparing the manufacture of implements and vessels in prehistory, human development could be seen, for instance, to progress from the Paleolithic to the Neolithic, from the Iron Age to the Bronze Age. Once the basic framework of development was established, contemporary cultures could be placed on the scale of development: Aztecs higher than Tahitians, Chinese higher than Aztecs, Italians higher than Chinese.[50] Other aspects of culture, from re-

[50] Edward B. Tylor, *Primitive Culture: Researches into the Development of Mythology, Philosophy, Religion, Language, Art, and Custom*, p. 27.

ligion to political organization, were factored into the evolutionary equation, but at the foundation of the system of classification was assessment of the material sophistication of the society in question.

Anthropologists soon came to recognize the weaknesses of the evolutionary approach. The prehistorical archaeological record often leaves gaps, telling us, for instance, much about the manufacture of pottery (which survives) but little about basket weaving (which usually doesn't). Differences in technology often tell us more about material resources than about cultural and technological sophistication: one cannot make exquisite gold jewelry without a gold mine.[51] Archaeologists too gradually abandoned a mechanical, unilinear evolutionary model as they discovered instances in which more sophisticated material remains were followed chronologically by less sophisticated ones.[52]

From very early on, growing up alongside the evolutionary model was the equally important model of diffusionism: the possibility that artifacts were not developed from previous objects independently in a given culture but rather entered the culture in mature form from elsewhere. In its extreme form, "hyper diffusionism," diffusionist theory attempts to trace all developments in material culture the world over to individual discoveries in a small set of core cultures from which all others borrowed.[53] Neither evolution nor diffusionist theory have been abandoned entirely, nor should they be. Objects remain valuable and even essential for classifying cultures and for tracing the development (i.e., evolution) of technology.[54] Bronze signals an important advancement over a previous culture ignorant of its use. And artifacts can tell us much about the relations between cultures. Archaeologists of colonial North America have shown, for instance that the houses built by free blacks in the seventeenth century share characteristics with West African houses and are distinct in structure from houses made by European-Americans built at the same time, indicating the degree to which African Americans at that early date consciously maintained a distinct identity.[55] All of these themes—development, diffusion, and cultural identity—are key in understanding the impact of Buddhism on Chinese material culture. Some of the objects I discuss below

---

[51] For an early critique of the evolutionary model, see Robert H. Lowie, *The History of Ethnological Theory*, pp. 10–8.

[52] William H. Stiebing Jr., *Uncovering the Past: A History of Archaeology*, pp. 254–5.

[53] Bruce G. Trigger, *A History of Archaeological Thought*, pp. 150–5.

[54] In the midst of a critique of the evolutionary model, Robert Lowie, in one of the earliest references I have found to the term *material culture*, concedes that "notwithstanding the qualifications cited, evolution is a positive fact in material culture and freely conceded by the most determined critics of its Victorian champions." *The History of Ethnological Theory*, p. 27.

[55] Deetz, *In Small Things Forgotten.*

originated in China. Others came to China with Buddhism from abroad. And in many cases, the associations between particular objects and their origins were of great importance in the way people treated them.

Increasingly, anthropologists and archaeologists see artifacts as more than clues to more central cultural concerns; artifacts are themselves key components of culture, present in all forms of behavior and communication. This realization has inspired increasingly sophisticated analysis of objects. They have shown, for instance, that things, like people, go through stages of development, from manufacture (birth), through use (life), and ending in discard (death). An old, broken object is treated differently than a shiny new one is; it means something else. Hence, it is useful to write the "biographies" or "life histories" of things.[56]

Like archaeologists and anthropologists, art historians can be said to have been studying material culture all along, well before the term came into common use. While most have stuck to more strictly aesthetic concerns of style and iconography, some have ventured into regions on the borders of their discipline. Michael Baxandall, to cite one instance among many, has drawn attention to the prices of certain pigments in fifteenth-century Italy, shedding light on the reaction of a fifteenth-century viewer to a painting; at that time, the eye was attracted first to large patches of color made from what everyone knew to be expensive pigment.[57] In the same work, Baxandall discusses the influence of the mercantile practice of packaging goods in barrels on the way paintings were perceived; at that time, educated men tended to measure volume according to the shape of a barrel.[58] More generally, attention to patronage and the social and political function of art has become standard practice among art historians. Sociologists and historians have also made efforts to place art history into a social context in which objects are used to define one's position in society, and not only in order to derive aesthetic pleasure.[59]

Historians have always shown at least a passing interest in the objects people of the past made and used. Herodotus was sure to include the pyramids in his description of Egypt, and Sima Qian was careful to detail the design and contents of Qin Shihuang's tomb. Nor did the fathers of modern historiography completely neglect the material. Writing in 1848, Macaulay began his history of England by vowing that in addition to treating political and military history, he would also "trace the progress of useful and ornamental arts . . . and not to pass by with neglect even the

---

[56] Igor Kopytoff, "The Cultural Biography of Things: Commoditization as Process," pp. 64–94; and William H. Walker, "Ceremonial Trash?" pp. 67–79.

[57] Michael Baxandall, *Painting and Experience in Fifteenth-Century Italy*, pp. 81–6.

[58] Ibid., pp. 86–94.

[59] See, for instance, Peter Burke, *The Italian Renaissance: Culture and Society in Italy*; and Pierre Bourdieu, *Distinction: A Social Critique of the Judgment of Taste*.

revolutions which have taken place in dress, furniture, repasts, and public amusements."[60] At the same time, across the Atlantic, William H. Prescott devoted long passages of flowing prose to the material world of the Aztecs, at one point noting that their "material civilization" placed them "above the rude races of the New World" but "below the cultivated communities of the Old," echoing the use of artifacts by his contemporaries in archaeology and anthropology.[61]

But it is only in the twentieth century that historians began to pay particular attention to the role of tangible things in historical development. In his massive, sweeping survey *The Structures of Everyday Life*, Fernand Braudel examines the history of all manner of objects; maize in prehistoric North America, African huts, eighteenth-century German wallpaper, and Spanish windmills are all given their due place in the development of civilization.[62] At the other end of the geohistorical scale, Le Roy Ladurie, in a classic example of microhistory, describes carts, roads, textiles, and tools in a fourteenth-century village.[63] Perhaps most successfully of all, historians of technology have detailed the rise and impact of the stirrup, the horse-drawn plow, and the camel saddle, to name just a few examples.[64] In short, while archaeologists may complain that historians have failed to fully incorporate archaeology into their work and remain reluctant to venture beyond texts, few historians would deny the importance of material objects to the course of history, and we can easily find examples of the histories of objects written by some of the world's most prominent historians.[65]

OBJECTS AND THE HISTORY OF RELIGION

The relative lack of attention to artifacts in historical studies is in large measure the result of practical difficulties: archaeologists and historians are trained in different departments and publish in different journals. Historians do not in general find artifacts irrelevant or trivial in the course of human development; they are simply unfamiliar with the material. Historians of religion, on the other hand, have expressly placed objects out-

[60] Thomas Babington Macaulay, *The History of England (1848–1861)*, pp. 52–3.

[61] William H. Prescott, *History of the Conquest of Mexico*, p. 330.

[62] Fernand Braudel, *The Structures of Everyday Life: Civilization and Capitalism 15th–18th Century*.

[63] Emmanuel Le Roy Ladurie, *Montaillou: The Promised Land of Error*.

[64] Lynn White, *Medieval Technology and Social Change*; Richard W. Bulliet, *The Camel and the Wheel*.

[65] For a critique of the dearth of archaeology in historians' work, see Serge Cleuziou et al., "The Use of Theory in French Archaeology," pp. 114–5.

side their field of inquiry. Writing in the 1920s, Johan Huizinga was a pioneer in the use of nontraditional sources for the history of the Middle Ages, including the use of artworks to explore the mentalities of French and Dutch people in the fourteenth and fifteenth centuries. But when it came to a discussion of religion, he found the presence of objects distressing and lamentable: "By this tendency to embodiment in visible forms all holy concepts are constantly exposed to the danger of hardening into mere externalism." And later, "It was inevitable that this pious attachment to material things should draw all hagiolatry into a sphere of crude and primitive ideas.[66] The assumption, inherited from the Reformation, is that religion is properly a spiritual pursuit ("holy concepts") carried out internally, without recourse to any sort of objects ("hard externalism"). Hence, to dwell on relics, icons, and holy water is to waste one's time on peripherals, epiphenomena better left to antiquarians than the specialist in religion.

In a survey of material culture studies and American religion, Colleen McDannell lamented the same bias. In the vast majority of research on American religion, at most, images and artifacts are used to illustrate points drawn from texts, and often objects are ignored altogether.[67] This reluctance to discuss the place of material things in religion is remarkably pervasive, and even crops up in works of specialists in Christian archaeology, in which authors give caveats explaining that their findings do not pertain to the essence of Christianity.[68]

The origins of this disdain for religious goods are diverse but can be traced in part first to Protestant reformers like Zwingli and Calvin, who railed against "externalism" and concern for "outward things," and called for a return to the scriptures as the source of spiritual insights and strength. In the field of religious studies, this tendency was reinforced in a less direct way by the writings of major scholars like Durkheim, Weber, and Eliade, who focused on the separation between the sacred and the profane and insisted that religion at its core constituted a separate, special realm.[69] This assumption was tied to the division between spirit and matter. With the exception of a select group of objects attributed with sa-

[66] Johan Huizinga, *The Waning of the Middle Ages: A Study of the Forms of Life, Thought and Art in France and the Netherlands in the Dawn of the Renaissance*, pp. 152 and 167.

[67] Colleen McDannell, "Interpreting Things: Material Culture Studies and American Religion," pp. 371–87; William Walker makes a similar case for the use of "ordinary objects" in ritual. See Walker, "Where Are the Witches of Prehistory?"

[68] See the remarks of Gregory Schopen on Charles Thomas, *The Early Christian Archaeology of Northern Britain*, and Graydon F. Snyder, *Ante Pacem: Archaeological Evidence of Church Life before Constantine*, in Schopen, *Bones, Stones, and Buddhist Monks*, pp. 10–2.

[69] Colleen McDannell, *Material Christianity: Religion and Popular Culture in America*, pp. 4–8.

cred power, most religious artifacts seem entirely too ordinary, too profane, to offer interesting insights into the nature of religion. Hundreds of
nearly identical icons packed into a temple, prayer beads fingered by crass
patrons or pious peasants, the robes worn by ordinary monks and nuns
all seem better left to archaeologists, historians of popular culture, or
economists than to mainstream historians of religion, particularly since
the study of such objects inevitably involves discussions of techniques of
manufacture and often economic negotiations between craftsmen and
client, both of which seem far removed from the search for distinctively
religious ideas and values.

Gregory Schopen has demonstrated the same reluctance to engage the
material in the study of Buddhism.[70] From the nineteenth century to the
present, specialists in Indian Buddhism have relied almost entirely on
texts, despite the fact that a large body of coins, art, and inscriptions have
direct bearing on the history of Indian Buddhism. In the rare cases where
scholars have engaged material remains, they have been too ready to im-
pose interpretations on objects from textual sources, imputing orthodox
motivations to donors listed in inscriptions, for instance, when the inscriptions themselves say nothing of motivation. When artifacts contra-
dict scriptural pronouncements, the tendency has been to suggest convo-
luted explanations for the objects rather than accept that doctrines laid
out in scriptures may not reflect the way Buddhism was practiced. More
commonly still, archaeological evidence is ignored entirely, even in areas
where it provides the only evidence we have, as in the case of the disposal
of the dead in early Buddhist monasticism. Again, material things have
seemed at best trivial and at worst a distraction from what is important
in religion. Yet religion, like all forms of communication, is intimately
linked to the material world. Not only do objects play important roles in
all forms of religious activity, but people who engage in religious activities in general recognize the importance of things and comment on them
at length, leaving behind a wealth of material for historians willing to explore the place of material culture in religion.

Our understanding of religion changes significantly when objects are
added to the picture. At times artifacts reveal that previous assumptions
based on textual evidence alone do not hold true. Archaeological remains
show that monks in ancient India did in fact own personal property, despite scriptural prohibitions to the practice.[71] Tombstones in New England reveal that Puritans continued to make religious images, despite the
strident iconoclasm expounded in contemporary Puritan texts.[72] Despite

---

[70] Schopen, *Bones, Stones, and Buddhist Monks*, pp. 1–22.

[71] Ibid., pp. 3–5.

[72] Alan Ludwig, *Graven Images: New England Stonecarving and Its Symbols, 1650–
1815.*

their sermons calling for rejection of the material, in practice nineteenth-century Protestant missionaries on the Gold Coast placed great emphasis on the material distinctions of clothing and housing that marked the Christian convert.[73] More generally, close attention to the way religious objects are arranged in homes shows that in their day-to-day lives, most people do not see the need to separate the sacred and the profane: a religious image, though hung on a wall next to a commercial calendar, remains religious.[74]

More than a tool to verify or discredit textual claims, a focus on material culture draws our attention to aspects of religion we might otherwise overlook. When we examine how the Bible was used, for instance, we see that in addition to its content, the Bible was also an important cultural symbol. Victorian paintings depicting a stern father reading the Bible to a large, attentive family express an ideal of the upright, harmonious family, symbolized by the act of reading the Bible, apart from which particular passage was being read or how it was understood. The object of the Bible itself evoked strong feelings and shaped behavior. Similarly, historians of medieval religion have looked to images not just for their content, for what they depict, but also for how they were used, how they fit into a culture of prayer in which it was important to have ready access to devotional images at all times, even when traveling.[75] A focus on material culture also reveals the extent of the impact of religious movements on culture. Material remains in the New World reflect the impact of Spanish missionaries on indigenous religions. The Crusades introduced profound, pervasive changes to the material culture of Europe. And traces of the Islamic occupation in the ninth century can still be seen in the food and architecture of modern Spain.

China provides an abundance of data for the study of Buddhist material culture. After the Cultural Revolution, few academic fields in China have developed as rapidly and with as much success as archaeology. Major Chinese archaeology journals appear monthly, packed with new finds, many Buddhist, from all parts of China.[76] Artifacts aside, poetry,

---

[73] Birgit Meyer, "Christian Mind and Worldly Matters: Religion and Materiality in Nineteenth-Century Gold Coast," pp. 311–37.

[74] McDannell, *Material Christianity*, pp. 4–8.

[75] Eugène Honée, "Image and Imagination in the Medieval Culture of Prayer: A Historical Perspective," pp. 157–74.

[76] "Material culture studies" has only recently begun to appear as a self-conscious methodology in modern Chinese studies. Unlike archaeology, the discipline of anthropology within China continues to be very weak, and even outside China, anthropologists working on Chinese society have given little emphasis to material culture. The methodology of Chinese archaeologists in modern times derives for the most part from Europe and North America. That being said, the study of "artifacts" (*wenwu*) has been a respectable scholarly vocation in China for centuries; a tradition there of material culture studies in a loose sense can be traced back at least to the eleventh century if not earlier.

novels, miscellaneous notes, and Buddhist texts of various types and periods all contain information on Buddhist objects. We also have a large body of artifacts and writings about artifacts from before the first century A.D. when Buddhism began to influence Chinese society, making it possible in many cases to determine what came to China with Buddhism and what originated in China independently. Similarly, non-Buddhist materials from later periods often allow us to determine the role of Buddhism, as opposed to other distinct traditions, in the history of individual objects.

The greatest difficulties in assessing the impact of Buddhism on Chinese material culture do not relate to scarcity of data but rather to how we interpret it. Perhaps the greatest danger is accepting the spirit/matter dichotomy, according to which the prevalence of material things in Buddhism is a sign of its decadence. China, the stereotype runs, has always been a fundamentally down-to-earth, materially minded culture, unable to accept the purer, more ethereal values of the more spiritual culture of India. This is an idea that is reinforced in part by Chinese Buddhists themselves who have always considered Chinese Buddhism a pale reflection of the golden age of Buddhism at the time of the Buddha; Chinese monks were always ready to lament the degeneracy of the monastic order in China.

This view of the history of Chinese Buddhism does not hold up to closer scrutiny. Buddhist monks in ancient India were no less "materialistic" than their Chinese epigones; many of the objects and attitudes toward objects discussed in this book came to China with Buddhism from India. More fundamentally, we need see nothing wrong with the presence of objects, and even wealth, in religious practice. A small group of erudite monks within the Buddhist tradition has championed the idea that the highest spiritual goals can only be pursued in isolation from the material world. But *we* need not adopt this position. Nor did most Buddhists ever adopt a radical rejection of the material world. For most, in China as elsewhere, objects render the sacred tangible and proximate. Things allow one to communicate with deities and sense their presence. Objects are often the most expressive means for conveying religious ideas and sentiments. In short, material culture is as much a part of religion as language, thought, or ritual. Hence, unless we appreciate the place of material culture in Chinese Buddhist history, our picture of this history remains skewed and incomplete.

Chapter One

SACRED POWER

CERTAIN Buddhist objects in China were believed to contain sacred power that would manifest itself in a variety of ways, depending on the object in which it inhered. A scripture might suddenly emit light in a dark monastic library, attracting the attention of the devout monk for whom it was mysteriously intended. The relics of a holy monk might multiply and sparkle in response to the entreaties of a pious layman. Wondrous stories have circulated throughout Chinese Buddhist history of statues that wept during times of religious persecution or spoke to the faithful in dreams. The worldview of those who accepted such accounts was not so radically different from our own. They recognized that the materials from which these objects were made—paper, bone, and clay—were normally inanimate; but at the same time they believed as well that, under certain unusual circumstances, such objects could be imbued with a supernatural power. Indeed, it was this rupture between the animate and the inanimate that made sacred objects special, and attracted people from all walks of life to their power.

Sacred objects played a key role in many aspects of the history of Buddhism. Buddhist missionaries and monks who wrote histories of Buddhism drew on stories of numinous Buddhist relics and statues as proof of the power of Buddhism. Many monasteries relied on the reputations of the sacred objects they housed to attract patrons and build prestige. And accounts of miracles provoked by sacred Buddhist things attracted the attention even of those who were not otherwise interested in Buddhist doctrines and rituals.

More pervasively still, sacred Buddhist objects were at the center of devotional activity for many monastic and lay groups. Images and relics allowed the ordinary person to experience Buddhism in a manner that was at once powerful and intimate, without the immediate intervention of learned intermediaries explaining what should be felt, what should be understood. Sacred objects, perhaps more than any of the other types of Buddhist objects that I will discuss below, rendered the religion tangible and proximate for any who wished it, from the most erudite of monks to the illiterate devotee. From ancient times, the main activity of visitors to a Buddhist monastery has been to lay offerings of flowers, fruit, and incense before images and relics. Without the sacred objects that were the recipients of these offerings, the history of Buddhist devotion would have been quite different in China, and may never have succeeded at all. It was the nature of these objects that allowed them to "receive" offerings. Sacred Buddhist objects are seldom simply symbols of the holy; they are holy themselves. That is, devotees perceive a presence, or power, within the objects.

The nature of this power, not so much in Buddhism as in "primitive religion," was once a central concern of scholars of religion, who placed the notion of numinous power at the core of religious experience.[1] Of particular importance was E. B. Tylor who, writing at the end of the nineteenth century, popularized the concept of "animism," the belief that a phantom-like soul inhabits all things. Tylor proposed that the concept arose when primitive humans attempted to understand how in their dreams they could travel to distant places and meet with others. Tylor argued that all primitives—whether in the primeval past of Europe and Asia or in primitive societies in his own day—explained their dreams with the belief that people have a soul or spirit that can wander away from the body. Subsequently, these findings were applied to animals as well, who were also attributed with animating spirits. Finally, and for our purposes most importantly, Tylor proposed that humans in their primitive state explained the presence of inanimate objects in their dreams by attributing souls to objects as well. According to this view, then, for primitive humanity the world was alive with countless souls, present in people, the birds, and beasts that surrounded them, and even in the senseless stones beneath their feet. This, Tylor continued, was a universal stage in religious development: at the earliest stage, all cultures began with animism.[2]

Tylor's views had an enormous impact on subsequent scholars of religion. Following on Tylor's ideas, R. R. Marett proposed a preanimistic stage of religious development that he termed "animatism." In this stage, the power attributed to all things was not a personal soul, but an impersonal power that, borrowing a Melanesian term, he referred to as "mana." Mana, Marett explained, is a "life-force" present in all things, including people, animals, plants, and inanimate objects. Marett's primitive human, like Tylor's, lived in a world alive with spiritual powers, but for Marett it was a single, nebulous life force from which all things drew, rather than countless individual souls. Only later, in the next stage of evolutionary development, was the impersonal life-force of animatism transformed into the personal soul of animism. For both Tylor and Marett, the

[1] Take for instance Rudolf Otto: "There is no religion in which it [the numinous] does not live as the real innermost core, and without it no religion would be worthy of the name." Otto coined the word *numinous* to refer to an impersonal, neutral sacred power, as opposed to "the holy," which is considered morally good. *The Idea of the Holy*, p. 6.

[2] Tylor, *Primitive Culture*, chap. 11, "Animism."

belief that inanimate objects contained sacred forces marked the boundaries of credulity; for both, the attribution of powers to rocks and ornaments is the strangest and most primitive of beliefs.[3]

While some subsequent scholars, most notably Mircea Eliade, continued to discuss the notion of sacred power more generally, the terms *animism, animatism,* and *mana,* and with them the attention to powers attributed to inanimate objects, gradually lost their appeal. This decline in interest in the sacred power of things came with the realization that the conception of animism as formulated at the turn of the twentieth century contains a number of flaws. Tylor's theory that animism originated in dreams can never be more than speculation, and most scholars now wisely shy away from such venturous inquiries into the ultimate origins of all religion. More importantly, the theory that all religion evolved from animism—a historical argument that can to some extent be tested—is unsupported by historical evidence. More fundamentally still, careful examination of contemporary cultures reveals that primitive religions do not in general posit an animating force present in *all* things. Rather, most believe that numinous power resides only in particular objects and is made manifest—what Eliade termed "kratophany"—only under special circumstances. Perhaps in an effort to mark a clear distinction between the vital world of *homo religiosus,* where there was a spirit in every rock, a demon in every tree, and the dreary, mechanical world of modern rationalists, proponents of animism as an explanatory theory overstated the case: religious belief seems never to have been so democratically all-inclusive.

Scholarship on the nature of the numinous involves much more than objects, but for the purpose of studying material culture, we can set aside the broader question of the nature of the sacred in space, time, ritual, and deities—if indeed there is anything that all of them hold in common—and concentrate instead on a limited number of objects believed to hold sacred power. In the case of Buddhist history, this entails looking at the way Buddhists have treated and thought about particular things they believed to be numinous, rather than attempting to reconstruct a general Buddhist theory of the sacred. In this way, it is possible to assess the impact of Buddhism on Chinese material culture by focusing on the repertoire of things commonly thought to contain numinous power, on the way in which this power was made manifest, and on reactions to such marvelous manifestations. But to do this we need some grounding in attitudes toward sacred things in Chinese religion during the period before Buddhism began to affect Chinese culture.

Surveys of ancient China have continued to assert a widespread belief

---

[3] Ibid., p. 477; R. R. Marett, *The Threshold of Religion,* p. 18.

in animism long after the term lost currency in studies of the religions of other regions.[4] As in other cultures, ancient China provides us with little evidence for such claims, and it seems unlikely that ancient Chinese believed either in an impersonal sacred power present in all things or that everything has its own personalized soul. We can, however, find isolated examples of a belief in a sacred force occupying objects in pre-Buddhist China. One famous example is the cult to a rock at Chencang first recorded by Sima Qian in the second century B.C. According to Sima, an unusual rock was discovered by Duke Wen of Qin in 747 B.C. The duke constructed a shrine for the rock and made offerings to it. "The spirit [that inhabited the rock] would sometimes not appear for a whole year, while at other times it would come several times in a year. It always appeared at night, giving off light like a shooting star, arriving from the southeast and coming to rest on the wall of the shrine. It resembled a cock and made a screeching sound to which the wild cocks would respond at night."[5] The *Han shu*, compiled some two hundred years later, notes that the cult to the "treasure of Chen" (*Chenbao*) continued to flourish and, after describing the number of times the spirit appeared in the rock, concludes that it is "an old cult to the *yang* ethers."[6] This reference suggests a belief in an impersonal force (*qi*) in the rock, but this suggestion is contradicted by personification of the force as something that comes and goes, looking and sounding like a cock. The power does not come from the rock itself, but rather descends upon the rock from the outside in a form that leads us to suspect that the cult was originally to the spirit of a cock.[7]

We move closer to an impersonal sacred force in stories of the "nine tripods" of antiquity, which were said to have been forged by the Great Yu during the Xia (ca. 2200–1700 B.C.), and then passed down from the Xia to the Shang and from the Shang to the Zhou as a hereditary royal treasure.[8] The *Mozi*, a text composed somewhere between the fifth and second centuries B.C., refers to the remarkable properties of these tripods: "They boiled [their contents] without fire, hid themselves away without

---

[4] See, for instance, Wang Jihuai, *Zhongguo yuangu ji sandai zongjiao shi*, pp. 13–7.

[5] *Shiji* 28, p. 1359; Cf. Burton Watson, *Records of the Grand Historian of China*, p. 18.

[6] The cult to the rock has continued to the present day. See Marianne Bujard, "Le joyau de Chen: culte historique—culte vivant," pp. 131–81.

[7] Edward Schafer, describing the "indefinable force" that he describes as emanating from all things in ancient China, writes, "To say that a tree stump contained spiritual power did not mean that it was the physical home of a ghostly being. It meant that the stump itself had an energy in it that could, in some mysterious way, affect other beings, like the electricity in a charged wire." The assertion testifies more to the extent of Tylor's influence than to evidence from ancient China. Edward H. Schafer, *Ancient China*, p. 57.

[8] For a brief survey of these legends, see Du Zhengsheng (Tu Cheng-sheng), "Yu Hua wu ji: ding de lishi yu shenhua," *Gugong wenwu yuekan*, pp. 6–19.

being lifted, and moved without being pushed."⁹ Writing in the first century A.D., the great skeptic Wang Chong questioned the suggestion that
the tripods contained divine power. After citing the belief that the tripods
could boil their contents and move of themselves, Wang dismissed the tradition as so much piffle:

> This is a vulgar, popular exaggeration, incorporated into the books of literati,
> suggesting that ordinary objects were divine [shen]. Is it really necessary to
> refute the assertion that the Zhou tripods were divine? The metal of the Zhou
> tripods came from a distant land as tribute, which Yu then used to forge the
> tripods. Many things were represented on the surface of the tripods.
>
> If the claim is that they were divine because their metal came from a dis-
> tant land, why should this be so?
>
> If the claim is that they were divine because Yu made them so, [this too is
> wrong]. Yu was a sage; he was not divine. If even the sage himself was not
> divine, then how can a vessel he forged be divine?
>
> Or is the claim that they were divine because they were made of metal?
> Metal is like stone and we know that stone cannot be divine, so why should
> metal be divine?
>
> Or is the claim that they were divine because they were inscribed with im-
> ages of a hundred things? This is similar to the Thunder Goblet¹⁰ which was
> covered with images of clouds and lightning. Clouds and lightning are in the
> sky and hence much closer to the divine than a hundred ordinary things.
> Now if even the images of clouds and lightning were not divine, how could
> the images of the hundred things be divine?¹¹

With this critique, written before the entrance of Buddhism to China, the
basic elements of the discourse over sacred things, which was to continue
in China up to modern times, were already in place. Later, once Buddhist
objects did enter China in great numbers, when addressing cases similar
to those discussed by Wang Chong, later commentators on Buddhist objects would ask: Were Buddhist objects considered sacred merely, as in the
case of the tripod metal, because they came from a distant, exotic land?
Was there something in the substance of the objects that made them numinous, or was it the shape they took that gave them power? Or was the
whole notion of animate things an absurd hoax, accepted only by the
gullible?

In the two sections that follow, I will argue that the practice of worshipping images of holy figures and of venerating their remains entered

---

⁹ *Mozi jiangu*, ed. Sun Yirang, 46, p. 256.
¹⁰ A sacrificial vessel used during the Xia.
¹¹ *Lun heng jiaoshi*, Huang Hui, ed., 26, p. 277. Cf. Alfred Forke, *Lun-heng: Part 1.
Philosophical Essays of Wang Ch'ung*, p. 506.

China with Buddhism. A key factor in these practices was the belief that a power was present in images and relics. This power was revealed when marvelous, supernormal events occurred. In Chinese terms, the "numinous" (*ling*) within an object "evokes a miraculous response" (*ganying*). The descriptions of these events, usually suffused with a sense of wonder, most often provide us with glimpses into how the Chinese understood the sacred power of certain special Buddhist things.

As we have seen, the notion that objects could acquire sacred power was not new to China with the introduction of Buddhism; what was new was the type of objects credited with this power and the vast and complex apparatus that propagated them. This apparatus—including a professional clergy, a rich liturgical and doctrinal tradition, and, in the early centuries, a rapidly expanding lay following—is as much a part of the story of Buddhist sacred objects as the objects themselves. This being said, when examining the history of sacred objects, it is useful to look not only at the social context that made such beliefs possible but also at the nature of the objects for clues to the factors that rendered them sacred. What was it about icons in China that gave them their power? And what, beyond tradition, made relics—bits of bone, teeth, and ash—objects of reverence, fascination, and devotion?

RELICS

Early Indian legends of the life of the Buddha state that seven days after his death, the master's body was cremated in a casket on a funeral pyre, according to instructions he had given his disciples. The fire "burned without leaving behind any of the skin, flesh, sinews, or fluid of the joints, or any ash and soot." But all was not lost. After the fire expired, some bones and teeth remained. Representatives of various regions asked for portions of these relics, and after some dispute the relics were divided into eight equal parts and distributed among eight regions where stupas were erected to house them. One account notes that years later the remains of the Buddha's disciple Ānanda were similarly divided between competing factions, each of which wanted them for their own stupas.[12] While it is difficult to assess the historical accuracy of these accounts, it is safe to say that the cult of relics goes back to a very early stage in Buddhism, and is perhaps as old as Buddhism itself.

Again according to tradition, several centuries after the death of the Buddha, the great king Aśoka collected all the relics of the Buddha avail-

---

[12] Edward J. Thomas, *The Life of Buddha as Legend and History*, pp. 154–9; Jean Przyluski, "Le partage des reliques du Buddha," pp. 301–68.

able and had them redistributed among eighty-four thousand stupas.[13] While this legend is certainly exaggerated, archaeological evidence suggests that the historical Aśoka may well have participated in the cult of the Buddha's relics. In 1898, a reliquary was discovered near the Nepalese frontier bearing an inscription that paleographers recognized as sharing similarities with inscriptions reliably attributed to Aśoka. The inscription notes, "This is the relic-treasury of the Lord Buddha of the Śākyas."[14] Beyond the activities of King Aśoka, archaeological evidence confirms that at least as early as the third century B.C., stupas containing relics of Buddhist figures, including but not limited to the Buddha, were being built all over India.[15]

Later, in Mahāyāna texts compiled in India in the first centuries of the Common Era, relics were used as a foil for the power of the scriptures. The *Perfection of Wisdom* scriptures assure us, for example, that reciting scripture is much more efficacious than worshipping relics. This is not to downplay the value of relics, but rather to underscore the power of the *Perfection of Wisdom* scriptures, which are *even more* powerful than relics.[16] That is, relics were taken as the standard against which claims for the numinous power of other objects were judged. Such passages reveal the extent to which relics were still a vital component of Buddhist devotion during the centuries when Buddhism first began to have an impact on Chinese culture, a point confirmed by records of the earliest Chinese pilgrims to India that comment on relics of various sorts on display throughout the Indian subcontinent.

The Buddhist cult of relics in ancient India is remarkable in part because in general, human remains were and are still today regarded as impure in Indian society and subject to strict taboos. Perhaps at some level it was precisely the fact that body parts were normally considered polluting that made Buddhist relics so powerful. In any event, the veneration of relics was a distinguishing feature of Buddhism, and is one among many factors accounting for its success; the portability of relics, a tangible way of transporting Buddhist devotional practices and concomitant religious doctrines to new regions, was well suited to the Buddhist proclivity for proselytizing.

Reasons to worship Buddhist relics were readily available. Descriptions of the Buddha's death say that before he died, the Buddha himself announced that worshipping his relics would bring merit to the devotee.

---

[13] John S. Strong, *The Legend of King Aśoka: A Study and Translation of the Aśokāvadāna*, pp. 109–18.

[14] Thomas, *The Life of Buddha*, pp. 160–1.

[15] David Snellgrove, *Indo-Tibetan Buddhism: Indian Buddhists and Their Tibetan Successors*, p. 35.

[16] Ibid., p. 38.

This merit could then assure one of a better rebirth or be transferred to a loved one—alive or dead—to help them to achieve rebirth in a pleasant destination. Further, relics were intimately linked to the practice of building and worshipping at stupas, the most important Buddhist devotional monuments. Relics, placed inside the stupa, were needed to consecrate the stupa, to render it sacred. Bowing down to a relic of the Buddha was a sign of respect for a revered figure, but relics have always been more than mute referents to holy men. Rather, relics are themselves repositories of sacred power, and much of the attraction of relics lay in the powers they were thought to contain. The presence of sacred power in relics meant that they were capable of answering prayers to heal illnesses or bring children to the barren. More generally, the numinous powers of relics attracted the curiosity even of those who otherwise showed little interest in Buddhism; for the miraculous exerts a general appeal unmatched by statements of doctrine or philosophical principle.

The Introduction of Indian Relics to China

While the cult of relics grew in ancient India with the emergence and spread of Buddhism, no comparable cult was practiced in pre-Buddhist China. Certainly the Chinese had lavished great attention on burial practices from as early as Neolithic times, and the remains of the deceased were carefully attended to. In a belief that shares some of the theoretical foundations of relic worship, some in ancient China held that the spirit of a person was preserved in the bones after death—the only sure way to avoid being haunted by an enemy's ghost was to crush the bones to powder and scatter them to the wind.[17] But there seems never to have been a sense that the bones of a great man were inherently superior to the bones of an ordinary man, and we find no records of disciples treasuring bits and pieces of, say, Confucius or Laozi. Indeed, when bones continued to preserve the spirit of the deceased, it was considered the sign of a violent or otherwise improper death, rather than a sign of spiritual attainments. In contrast, a few hundred years after the first tentative Chinese contacts with Buddhism, the empire was covered with stupas (or "pagodas") containing human remains thought to be from India, as well as relics produced in China itself.[18] This dramatic change was the result of the persistent efforts of missionaries, pilgrims, rulers, and ordinary devotees to seek out, distribute, and extol Buddhist relics.

[17] Li Jianmin, "Zhongguo gudai yanci lisu kao," pp. 319–42.

[18] The Chinese word for stupa, *ta*, is an abbreviated transliteration (from *tapo*) of the Sanskrit *stūpa*. The origins of the word *pagoda* are obscure. It first appears in Portuguese as *pagode*. The Portuguese may have borrowed the word from a Dravidian language. In any event, in modern usage the words *pagoda* and *stupa* refer to the same thing.

One of our earliest records of the arrival of Buddhist relics to China comes in a biography of Kang Senghui, a monk of Sogdian descent who grew up in Jiaozhi (in present-day Vietnam), later traveling to China, where he eventually earned a place as one of the most prominent early Buddhist missionaries.[19] According to the biography, in 248, when Kang Senghui reached the capital city in Jianye (present-day Nanjing)—the first monk ever seen there—he "built a hermitage, set up images and carried out rituals." Suspicious local authorities had the foreigner brought in for questioning. When the ruler, Sun Quan, asked him what proof of divinity (*lingyan*) he could produce, Kang replied, "Since the Thus-Come-One passed away, a thousand years have passed. Yet the bones and *śarīra* [*sheli*, in Chinese, usually referring to small, crystalline relics] that he left behind shine divinely, without measure." The skeptical Sun then gave Kang seven days to prove himself, saying, "If you can produce *śarīra*, I will build a stupa for them. But if you are lying, you will face the punishments established by the state." After two failed attempts to produce relics, Kang's entreaties were answered when *śarīra* miraculously appeared in a vase. "They emanated five brilliant colors that radiated out of the opening in the vase. Sun Quan picked up the vase and poured them into a copper bowl. As soon as the *śarīra* struck the bowl, they smashed it to bits." After several experiments, all of which showed the relics to be indestructible and harder than any known substance, Sun kept his promise and had a stupa constructed for them, along with the region's first Buddhist monastery.[20]

This story is most likely a fanciful legend composed in the fourth or fifth century rather than an accurate account of events in the third. Nonetheless, the authors of the legend were quite right to give importance to relics in the early propagation of Buddhism in China. A late-Han tomb mural contains a depiction of a group of globular objects on a plate, beneath which are the characters *sheli*, or *śarīra*, indicating that from the very beginnings of Buddhism in China, the religion was linked to its relics.[21] Sun Quan's demand of proof of the miraculous powers of Buddhism reflects a general interest during the early phase of Buddhist propagation to China in material signs of Buddhism's worth. It was not enough to introduce concepts, rituals, and beliefs; whether it was holy images or holy relics, skeptics and devotees alike wanted *tangible* evidence of the efficacy of the new religion.

Chinese pilgrims responded to this thirst for relics by traveling to India,

---

[19] Erik Zürcher, *The Buddhist Conquest of China: The Spread and Adaptation of Buddhism in Early Medieval China* pp. 51–5.

[20] *Gaoseng zhuan* 1, T no. 2059, vol. 50, p. 325b.

[21] Wu Hung, "Buddhist Elements in Early Chinese Art," pp. 264–73.

seeing as many relics as they could and bringing samples back to China. In his account of his travels in India in the fifth century, the Chinese pilgrim Faxian carefully describes a shrine in Nagarahāra believed to contain a skull bone of the Buddha: "The bone is of a yellowish white color, oval in shape, with a length of four inches, and a convex upper side."[22] Faxian carefully notes how the relic is presented and the way offerings were regularly made to it. Later, wherever he traveled, Faxian was careful to record stupas and local legends about relics of the Buddha and his disciples. Travel accounts of subsequent pilgrims are similarly filled with meticulous descriptions of relics and records of legends associated with them.

Pilgrims brought back more than stories; they also acquired in their travels actual relics. In addition to bringing back hundreds of texts and seven statues of the Buddha, Xuanzang also brought back "more than a hundred grains of *śarīra*."[23] Similarly, the seventh-century pilgrim Yijing returned to China with "three hundred grains of *śarīra*."[24] As late as 979, a Chinese monk was dispatched to India on imperial edict to retrieve relics that were then placed in a stupa in China.[25] Besides these relics transported by famous monks, there must also have been a steady stream of relics—of varying degrees of authenticity—brought to China by merchants along the silk road.[26]

Indigenous Relics

When the efforts of missionaries, pilgrims, and merchants could not meet the demand for Indian relics, devotees could find them at home in China. I mentioned above the widely known Buddhist legend that the great Buddhist king Aśoka had collected all the relics of the Buddha and distributed them throughout his empire in eighty-four thousand stupas. In China it was thought that some of these stupas had been built on Chinese land during the Zhou dynasty (ca. 1000–256 B.C.) but eventually, through centuries of neglect, fell into disrepair and ruin, leaving behind relics of the Buddha, forgotten beneath the earth. Once this legend gained currency in

---

[22] *Gaoseng Faxian zhuan*, T no. 2085, vol. 51, p. 858c14; English trans. from H. A. Giles, *The Travels of Fa-hsien*, p. 16.

[23] *Da Cien si sanzang fashi zhuan* 10, T no. 2053, vol. 50, p. 279a; English trans. by Li Rongxi, *A Biography of the Tripiṭaka Master of the Great Ci'en Monastery of the Great Tang Dynasty*, p. 343

[24] *Song gaoseng zhuan* 1, p. 710b.

[25] See "Yanqing sita ji," by Zhu Lin, 7, pp. 11a–12b. See also Huang Zi, "Zhejiang Songyang Yanqing sita gouzao fenxi," pp. 84–7.

[26] Relics believed to be the teeth of the Buddha were particularly popular. See *Hōbōgirin*, vol. 3, s.v. "Butsuge," pp. 203–5; Chen Yuan, "Foya gushi," pp. 305–14.

China, Chinese devotees periodically announced the discovery on Chinese soil of ancient, long-forgotten pieces of the Buddha's remains.[27]

Inscriptions for other stupas and reliquaries claimed that they held the relics of pratyekabuddhas (buddhas who achieved nirvana but, unlike Śākyamuni, did not preach) or even of Dīpaṃkara, a buddha of the distant past who preceded Śākyamuni.[28] Both are of such prodigious antiquity that there was no need to establish an immediate history tracing them to India: they came from a time of different political boundaries and peoples thought to be beyond the historian's grasp.

While relics of the Buddha never lost their special cachet, they were supplemented by the relics of eminent Chinese monks. Biographies of prominent Chinese monks often conclude with a description of the śarīra that remain after their cremation and of the stupa that is erected to house them. As in the case of the relics revealed to Kang Senghui, relics of eminent monks disclosed their numinous powers to the attentive by emitting strange light. Take, for instance, a story recorded in the Song *Biographies of Eminent Monks* about the bones of a monk named Mucha:

> In the fourth year of the Zhonghe era [830], the father of Prefect Liu Rang who was a palace aide, dreamed one night of a monk in purple vestments who said to him, "A disciple of mine named Mucha is buried to the west of the monastery. He has been there a long time. You can unearth him now." The monk then indicated the burial site. At first, the palace aide paid no attention to the dream, but when he had a second dream the same as the first showing him the place, he decided to excavate the spot. When he discovered a family living on the plot, he purchased it from them. After digging about three feet down, he uncovered a casket. When he opened it, he saw that on top of the bones were śarīra which emitted light. He had [the bones] burned, after which more than eight hundred śarīra grains were recovered. He then submitted a memorial reporting these things to Emperor Xizong, who sent down an edict ordering that an image of the monk be made with the ashes.[29]

In this account and others like it, relics are proof of the attainments of a great monk, for the bones of a buddha or an eminent monk are not like

---

[27] One such incident occurred in 980. See *Song gaoseng zhuan* 23, p. 862a. For a survey of earlier "discoveries" of Buddha relics supposedly distributed by Aśoka, see Zürcher, *The Buddhist Conquest of China*, pp. 277–80, and Tang Yongtong, *Han-Wei Liang Jin Nanbeichao fojiaoshi*, pp. 4–5.

[28] For examples of relics of pratyekabuddhas, see *Nittō guhō junrei gyōki* (*Ru Tang qiufa xunli ji jiaozhu*), Bai Huawen et al., eds., 3, p. 282; English translation in Edwin O. Reischauer, *Ennin's Diary: The Record of a Pilgrimage to China in Search of the Law*, p. 235, and Shandong Liaocheng Diqu Bowuguan, "Shandong Liaocheng Bei Song tieta," pp. 124–30. For Dīpaṃkara, see Chang Shuzheng and Zhu Xueshan, "Shandong sheng Huimin xian chutu Dingguangfo sheliguan," pp. 60–2.

[29] *Song gaoseng zhuan* 18, p. 823b–c.

those of an ordinary person. First, at appropriate times they may emit light. And second, when burned, they leave behind hard relic grains (*śarīra* or *sheli*). The remarkable qualities of these marvelous remains were attributed to the cultivation of the man to whom they had belonged. "Relics result from the cultivation of the precepts, concentration and wisdom," writes one scripture, while miracle stories circulated in China of monks whose tongues did not burn during cremation because they had chanted the scriptures with great sincerity.[30] There is even an account of a parrot that left behind grains of crystalline *śarīra* because it had been taught to repeat the name of a buddha.[31] All of these cases drew on the belief that Buddhist practice transforms the body in a way that is often only apparent at death.

As powerful objects, containing in some sense the essence of holy men of great spiritual attainments, relics were capable of producing miracles. For instance, when the monk Huihai (550–606) delivered relics to a monastery in Haizhou, a man who had been "lame and diseased" for years was carried to the relics. When he repented for his faults, he suddenly found that he could walk again.[32] Few miracle stories dwell on the curative properties of relics, either because such beliefs were not common or because the focus of relic stories was on the objects themselves rather than their effects on others. More commonly, it is the light that relics emit, or the fact that they remain at all after a monk's cremation, that is remarked upon as a source of awe and wonder.

Thus far I have focused on teeth, bits of bone, and the hard crystalline *sheli* left over after cremation. At times, however, Chinese Buddhists worshipped corpses of eminent monks that had been mummified in their entirety, in a practice that seems to have been a Chinese innovation on traditional Buddhist mortuary practices.[33] The earliest example of a corpse worshipped in toto comes from a record of a third-century monk whose body remained intact after an attempt was made to cremate it.[34] Similar cases of self-preserving corpses appear in later sources as well. At the end of the seventh century and into the eighth, references begin to appear of disciples *intentionally* mummifying the corpses of their masters, usually through the use of lacquer. Prominent Chan masters such as Daoxin and Huineng were carefully preserved in this manner,

[30] The scripture is the *Jin guang ming jing* (Skt. *Suvarṇaprabhāsa[uttamarāja]sūtra*), p. 354a. Biographies of monks contain many examples of tongue relics, including the tongue of the prominent translator Kumārajīva. *Gaoseng zhuan* 2, p. 333a.

[31] *Song gaoseng zhuan* 19, p. 830c.

[32] *Xu gaoseng zhuan* 11, p. 510a.

[33] Robert H. Sharf, "The Idolization of Enlightenment: On the Mummification of Ch'an Masters in Medieval China," pp. 1–31.

[34] *Gaoseng zhuan* 10, p. 389a.

their bodies covered with lacquered cloth, as were a number of famous wonder-workers.[35]

Mummified monks were worshipped with offerings of incense and flowers in the same manner as icons or relic pellets.[36] As late as the seventeenth century, the gilded mummy of what was said to be the tenth-century monk Wenyan was still worshipped by "gentlemen and commoners from near and far. They prayed for rain or clear skies, in numerous instances receiving assistance [from the mummy]."[37] Unlike relic pellets, mummies and ash icons were accorded human qualities, at times sweating or announcing to their disciples in dreams that they had not been properly lacquered.[38] Here the classification of different types of relics—hard, shiny pellets or icons that looked like men—is useful. Icons, whether made of clay or of human remains, were attributed with human qualities not because of what they were but because of what they looked like. Śarīra, impersonal relics radiating light and pulsing with sacred power, were another matter.

The history of the spread and development of the cult of relics in China could be read as a process of the democratization of the sacred. That is, what was originally a cult restricted to those with the rare opportunity to visit the sites of the relics of the Buddha in India eventually became available to most everyone at local stupas containing the relics of a buddha brought back from India by a pilgrim, or of a holy Chinese monk. In the end, it made little difference, since the relic of a monk could emit light and produce miracles as readily as the tooth of a buddha or the nail clippings of one of his disciples. But in China, as elsewhere, more was involved in the cult of relics than the pious pursuit of the divine, or even the more mundane wish to heal a bum leg: relics were contested, stolen, fabricated, and manipulated for an assortment of purposes as varied and intricate as the web of interaction that binds any complex society.

The Uses of Relics

We have already seen that relics were objects of cult, worshipped by devotees in order to acquire religious merit and elicit miracles. The value ac-

[35] See Sharf, "The Idolization of Enlightenment," pp. 9–10, and Bernard Faure, *The Rhetoric of Immediacy: A Cultural Critique of Chan/Zen Buddhism,* pp. 151–3, for references.

[36] See, for instance, the case of the eighth-century monk Yuanshao, whose corpse was worshipped after it was discovered intact inside his stupa, having been encased there three years previously. *Song gaoseng zhuan* 13, p. 784c.

[37] *Yunmen si chongzhuang Kuangzhen zushi jinshen bei ji,* written in 1687 by Yuancai and included in Cen Xuelü, comp., *Yunmen shan zhi* 9, in *Zhongguo fo sishi zhi huikan,* p. 196.

[38] *Song gaoseng zhuan* 30, p. 899a; 22, p. 852b.

corded relics is reflected in the contention they provoked among the faithful. Recall that various factions were said to have contended for the relics
of the Buddha soon after his death. In China as well, groups and individuals went to great lengths to procure relics. One seventh-century account
tells, for instance, of men from rival villages fighting over the corpse of a
recently deceased monk. The dispute was only resolved when they re-
signed themselves to dividing the sacred corpse between them.[39] As in medieval Europe, in China the theft of relics was not uncommon.[40] Indeed,
accounts of relics stolen by foreigners suggest an international trade in
holy body parts in East Asia equivalent to the trade in relics in Europe,
though the Chinese sources are in general silent on any possible economic
motives for stealing relics. Accounts of theft and struggle show how loose
the connection between Buddhist ethics and Buddhist devotional practice
was. If the purpose of theft was to revere the relics, even violence and deception, it seems, were justified.

Accounts of bodies ripped apart and relics snatched away at night disclose that more was at stake than merit and devotion. After all, if the villagers in the preceding story only wanted to reverence the remains of a
holy monk, they could just as easily do so in the neighboring village, or
they could have erected a stupa between the two rival villages. The same
can be said for relic thieves, intent on taking relics back with them rather
than worshipping them in situ. More than simply an opportunity to worship relics, devotees wanted to *possess* them, both for the power they contained and for the prestige possession brought.

The skull bone of the Buddha in Nagarahāra described by Faxian was
worshipped daily by the local king as well as the "elders of the merchant
class." Faxian continues, "In front of the gate to the shrine there will be
found, regularly every morning, sellers of flowers and incense, so that all
who wish to make offerings may buy of all kinds. The kings of the countries round about also regularly send envoys to make offerings."[41] Un-
derstandably, such accounts do not dwell on specifics of payment for incense and flowers, but they are detailed enough to suggest the economic
implications of relics as magnets for pilgrimage and patronage. The same

---

[39] *Xu gaoseng zhuan* 27, p. 680c.

[40] The most famous account of relic theft is the story of the attempt to steal the head of
the Chan master Huineng. See Sharf, "The Idolization of Enlightenment," p. 10 and Faure,
The Rhetoric of Immediacy, pp. 163–4. The repeated thefts and relocations of a relic of the
Buddha's tooth supposedly brought to China in the fifth century are equally fascinating. See
Chen Yuan, "Faxian foya yinxian ji," pp. 469–71. Chinese accounts of relic theft cannot,
however, compare with the wealth of information from medieval Europe, where accounts
of stolen relics became a set genre. See Patrick J. Geary, *Furta Sacra: Thefts of Relics in the
Central Middle Ages*.

[41] *Gaoseng Faxian zhuan*, p. 858c; Giles, *The Travels of Fa-hsien*, pp. 16–7.

held true in China. In his travels through China, ninth-century Japanese pilgrim Ennin had opportunity on several occasions to worship relics. At one point, he notes the history of a particularly popular relic:

> At the entrance to the mountain was a small monastery called Shimen, in which there was a monk who for many years had been reciting the *Lotus Sutra*. Recently, some Buddhist relics were revealed to him, and everybody in the whole city came to make offerings. The monastery was overflowing with monks and laymen. . . . The noble and lowly, and the men and women of Taiyuan city and the various villages, and the officials, both high and low, all came and paid reverence and made offerings.[42]

Because of their portability and their nondescript nature, relics were easily manipulated for less than pious ends; though relics seem in outward appearance pristine and unadorned, it is precisely this raw, unembellished quality that left them open to manipulation. In general, the worth of a Buddhist statue is readily apparent in the substance from which it is made, from its size and level of craftsmanship. The value of a given relic, on the other hand, is less obvious. When modern archaeologists examine relics uncovered beneath old Chinese stupas, they often turn out to be horse teeth, charred bits of bone, coral chips, pebbles, and such.[43] If these objects are to elicit feelings of awe and devotion, context is essential. In addition to ornate reliquaries and sumptuous ceremony, a key component of the physical context of relics has always been the stupa that houses them.

The Buddhist stupa seems to be at least as old as the cult of relics. And in fact, the origins of the stupa as a commemorative monument go back to pre-Buddhist times.[44] Extant stupas from approximately the second century B.C. at Bhārhut and Sañcī were large domed monuments, topped with parasols. Later stupas were built as taller, more narrow towers. It was in this form that the stupa became popular in China. Considerable attention has been paid to the symbolism of the stupa, which scholars have interpreted as representing the *axis mundi* or as a symbolic microcosm.[45] But, like icons, stupas were not primarily symbols. Their most basic function has always been to preserve and honor relics.[46] In India, relics were at times placed at the top of the stupa, a practice that was con-

---

[42] *Nittō guhō junrei gyōki* 3, p. 323; Reischauer, *Ennin's Diary*, pp. 271–2.

[43] Chinese archaeological journals contain many such references. See for instance, Lianyungang shi Bowuguan, "Lianyungang Haiqing si Ayuwang ta wenwu chutu ji," pp. 31–8, or Liu Youheng and Fan Zilin, "Hebei Zhengding Tianning si Lingxiao ta digong chutu wenwu," pp. 28–37.

[44] Lamotte, *History of Indian Buddhism*, p. 312.

[45] The two most influential such interpretations are those of Paul Mus, *Barabudur: Sketch of a History of Buddhism Based on Archaeological Criticism of the Texts*, and Adrian Snodgrass, *The Symbolism of the Stupa*.

[46] See Peter Skilling's review of Donald Swearer's *The Buddhist World of Southeast Asia*, pp. 579–80.

tinued in a few Chinese stupas. In general, however, the Chinese placed relics in a subterranean chamber (*digong*), sometimes called the "dragon cave" (*longku*), at the base of the stupa.[47]

The early history of the stupa in China is sketchy, in part because before the Tang most stupas were made of wood and have not survived. The earliest textual reference to a stupa appears to be the story we have already heard of Sun Quan building a stupa to house the relics revealed to Kang Senghui. In the sixth century, in accounts of eminent monks and more directly in the *Record of Buddhist Monasteries in Luoyang*, we begin to get enough reliable textual references to verify that the stupa had by that time become a common sight in China.[48] It is safe to assume that most if not all of these stupas contained relics. The *History of the Liang*, for instance, notes that in 531, when work was being done on a stupa in the capital, workers discovered a few feet below the stupa a reliquary (in a "dragon cave") containing "four *śarīra*, as well as hair and finger nail clippings."[49] Modern excavations of later stupas confirm that stupas in China almost always contained relics buried in a compartment beneath their base.

Given the seeming centrality of relics for the efficacy of a stupa, we would expect descriptions of stupas in China to give prominent place to the provenance and power of the relics they contain. This, however, is not the case. The *Record of Buddhist Monasteries in Luoyang*, for example, describes the famous Yongning Stupa, built in 516 by the empress dowager Ling. Nine stories high, the stupa could be seen far away from the capital.

> There were nine roofs, one for each story, with golden bells suspended from the corner of each one, totaling 120 in all. The stupa had four sides, each having three doors and six windows. Painted in vermilion, each door had five rows of gold nails, altogether there were 5,400 nails on twenty-four panels of twelve double doors. In addition, the doors were adorned with knockers made of golden rings. The construction embodied the best of masonry and carpentry. The elegance of its design and its excellence as an example of Buddhist architecture was almost unimaginable. Its carved beams and gold door-knockers fascinated the eye. On long nights when there was a strong wind, the harmonious jingling of the bejeweled bells could be heard more than ten *li* away.[50]

[47] Li Yumin, "Zhongguo zaoqi fota suyuan," p. 85.

[48] For discussion of early pictorial evidence for the stupa in China, see, in addition to Li Yumin, Marylin Martin Rhie, *Early Buddhist Art of China and Central Asia*, vol. 1, pp. 21–2.

[49] *Liang shu* 54, p. 791.

[50] *Luoyang jialan ji jiaoshi*, ed., Zhou Zumo, 1, pp. 20–1; English trans. by Yi-t'ung Wang, *A Record of Buddhist Monasteries in Luoyang*, p. 16.

Relics appear nowhere in this elaborate description despite the scrupulous attention to ornament and style. Miracles and merit are passed over in favor of minute description of the "elegance of its design." The same holds for the book's descriptions of other stupas in the capital: the emphasis is almost always on the sumptuous ornamentation of the stupa or the circumstances of its construction. Taken together, these descriptions reveal that the stupa was more than a repository for sacred objects, and more even than a place of worship. A magnificent stupa was often the mark by which a monastery was known. And the modern function of stupas as tourist attractions has roots stretching back at least to the sixth century. The description of the Yongning Stupa built by Empress Dowager Ling alerts us as well to the fact that, as one of the few types of public, monumental architecture in and around the capital and other major cities, stupas could help secure prestige and fame for the prominent officials and members of the imperial family who financed their construction.

The historical record makes frequent reference to the use of stupas and relics for equally mundane ends by various rulers, stretching from Aśoka in ancient India to Chairman Mao in the twentieth century. The first Chinese ruler to incorporate relics into his agenda on a broad scale was Sui Wendi (r. 581–604). Said to have been born in a Buddhist monastery, Yang Jian (Wendi was his posthumous imperial name) rose in the ranks of the Northern Zhou administration until, in 581, he wrested the throne from the ruling family and declared himself emperor. Previously, the Northern Zhou had governed North China, while the south was ruled by the rival Chen dynasty. Intent on governing all of China, Wendi in 589 led a successful campaign to conquer the south, thus bringing all of China under single rule for the first time in three hundred years.[51]

In an effort to hold together an empire that had been separated politically, militarily, and culturally for three centuries, Wendi instituted a number of reforms, introducing a new, uniform administrative structure throughout the empire, and tying north to south with waterways. Another part of this program of cultural unification was the new emperor's campaign to distribute officially sanctioned Buddhist relics. On three separate occasions, Wendi gave orders for the dispatch of commissions to deliver Buddhist relics to various sites in his empire where stupas were to be erected to house them. The instructions for the first distribution of relics are given in detail in an edict of 601 that states that the emperor invited thirty monks "versed in the Dharma and capable as proselytizers" to distribute relics to various prefectures. Each of the thirty monks was to be accompanied by two attendants and one secular official. Each was supplied with 120 catties of frankincense and five horses. Each monk was to

<hr/>

[51] Arthur F. Wright, *The Sui Dynasty: The Unification of China*, A.D. 581–617.

supervise the construction of a stupa at his assigned prefecture, where locals were to be encouraged to contribute to the worship of the stupa,
though individual contributions were not to exceed a modest, set amount
to be used in part for a vegetarian feast to be held in honor of the relics.
All was to be prepared by noon of the fifteenth day of the tenth month,
when the relics in each of the thirty locations were to be placed in their
reliquaries and enclosed in the stupas at precisely the same time. Regional
civil officials were to suspend all administrative activities for a period of
ten days in honor of the event.[52]

Two aspects of the edict in particular point to the latent political agenda
of the distribution: the relics and the commissions that accompanied them
were dispatched from the capital, and the final placing of the relics in stupas was to occur throughout the empire at exactly the same time. The unification of time and event highlighted the new unification of the empire,
centered on the person of the emperor, and resonated with the distribution of relics by Aśoka that were also believed to have been placed in stupas simultaneously.[53] The distribution also signaled the new emperor's
concern for the welfare of his people, and underlined his close ties to the
sacred as well as the secular powers that shaped the day-to-day affairs of
the empire.

Curiously, the edict makes no mention of the provenance of the relics.
Presumably they were thought to be relics of the Buddha, but the edict
does not explain just how the emperor came to possess them. Another
source states that the relics appeared spontaneously to the emperor and
in the quarters of the palace women.[54] If any questioned the authenticity
of the relics, they left behind no record of it. This is not surprising. Monks
certainly had much to gain from the campaign, giving all but the most fastidious little reason to question points of detail, and for any official to
challenge the authenticity of the relics at the heart of a campaign redolent
with the symbolism of political unification would have bordered on
sedition.

Apparently Wendi's first distribution of relics to thirty prefectures was
considered a success; for it was followed by a second, similar operation
in 602 including fifty-three more sites, and a third operation in 604 involving another thirty sites. As in the previous case, in both 602 and 604
the relics were encased in stupas at locations throughout the empire at the

[52] *Guang hongming ji* 17, p. 213b. Cf. Wright, Ibid., pp. 134–36; see also Du Doucheng,
"Sui Wendi fen sheli jian ta de yiyi ji qi youguan wenti" in his *Bei Liang yijing lun*, pp. 282–
91.
[53] Du Doucheng has drawn attention to a passage in *Fayuan zhulin* (38, p. 585a) that
states that Aśoka had the eighty-four thousand relics placed in stupas simultaneously. See
Du Doucheng, *Bei Liang yijing lun*, p. 284.
[54] *Xu gaoseng zhuan* 26, biography of Daomi, p. 667c.

same time. Soon after the relics were distributed, enthusiastic reports reached the throne of miracles that occurred when the relics were installed. It was said, for instance, that when the monk Daomi accompanied some of the relics to Zhengzhou and placed them in a stupa in 604, wild birds circled the stupa, only dispersing when the ceremony was complete. In addition, three golden flowers wafted up into the air, emitted light, expanded, and circled the stupa three times.[55]

Stories of the marvels that accompanied the distribution of relics, proof of Sui Wendi's sacred resonance with the forces of nature, were collected by the court historian Wang Shao, vilified by later historians as a sycophant and charlatan. In the words of a seventh-century historian, Wang Shao "loved strange stories and valued devious and misleading talk. His written style was base and vile, the organization of his work confused; he brought dishonor upon the [historical] tradition."[56] But while later writers criticized Wang's collection of accounts of miracles provoked by the emperor's distribution of relics, in Wang's day they were apparently well received. And though Wang Shao's collection has not survived in full, it exerted an influence on Buddhist historical works where large sections from it were quoted.[57] Although members of the imperial family and other lesser rulers before Sui Wendi had made use of relics and stupas for the prestige and legitimacy they offered, the scale of Wendi's carefully orchestrated, elaborate campaign reflects the degree to which relic worship had become incorporated into Chinese political as well as devotional spheres by the beginning of the seventh century.

The combination of relics, faith, political propaganda, and attempts by various individuals, including court favorites and monks, to capitalize on the imperial fascination with the cult of relics was not limited to Sui Wendi's campaign. Throughout the Tang dynasty, emperors paid reverence to relics of the Buddha housed in monasteries in the capital, most notably a tooth relic and a relic said to be the finger bone of the Buddha.[58] Emperors of later periods continued to express interest in Buddhist relics, celebrating their discovery and actively seeking them out.[59]

Given the widespread belief in the numinous power of relics, the role

[55] Ibid., p. 668a.

[56] The comments are those of Wei Zheng. *Sui shu*, 69, p. 1613, trans. in Wright, *The Sui Dynasty*, p. 19.

[57] See Koichi Shinohara, "Two Sources of Chinese Buddhist Biographies: Stupa Inscriptions and Miracle Stories," pp. 212–4.

[58] See references listed under "relics" in the index to Weinstein, *Buddhism under the Tang*.

[59] In the early years of the fifteenth century, for instance, the Yongle emperor dispatched an emissary to Korea on several occasions to obtain Buddhist relics. See Frederick W. Mote and Denis Twitchett, eds., *The Cambridge History of China*, vol. 7, *The Ming Dynasty, 1368–1644, Part 1*, p. 268.

of the emperor as arbiter of the sacred, and the flexibility of imperial religious belief, the imperial use of relics is readily understandable. More surprising is the political use of a relic of the Buddha's tooth in 1955 by Chinese authorities who were otherwise hostile to Buddhism. At that time, a tooth relic, which had supposedly come to China in the fifth century, was sent together with a delegation to Burma, where it was greeted by government dignitaries, including then president of Burma, Ba U.[60] The tooth was then taken on a procession through the streets of Rangoon and worshipped by a large and enthusiastic crowd. The mission created a favorable impression on the Burmese, and President Ba U thanked Chairman Mao, Zhou Enlai, and the Chinese people for the gesture. Three years later, in hopes of achieving similar results in Ceylon, the Chinese government sent the tooth there as well, though, in part because of the importance in Ceylon of a tooth relic kept in Kandy and also because of questions about the authenticity of the Chinese tooth, this second mission was not as successful as the first.[61]

These two last cases are particularly useful for setting the parameters of attitudes toward relics by leaders who made use of them. The attitudes of Mao Zedong and Zhou Enlai toward Buddhism and religion in general are quite clear, and we can safely assume that they did not believe that the tooth relic of the Buddha contained sacred power. Indeed, when the Burmese ambassador first broached the idea of borrowing the relic, Zhou is reported to have said dismissively, "Take it—we have no use for it."[62] Later, when Zhou and other Chinese authorities recognized the diplomatic value of the relic, they amended "take" to "borrow." During roughly the same period, the Chinese and Burmese governments cooperated to root out anti-Communist Chinese guerrilla troops supported by the Guomindang government and based in Burma near the Chinese border. Mao and Zhou employed the relic for the purely political purpose of improving international relations, divorced entirely from traditional Buddhist concerns of devotion and merit-making. In earlier cases, attitudes of rulers to relics were more complex. Sui Wendi, for instance, was a devout Buddhist, who openly expressed his Buddhist beliefs on many occasions. Further, Chinese concepts of religious orthodoxy were loose enough so that even rulers who did not express particular devotion for Buddhism

[60] For an attempt to reconstruct the early history of the tooth, supposedly brought to China in the fifth century, see Chen Yuan, "Faxian foya yinxian ji." A photograph of the tooth can be found in Cheng Ling et al., *Shijiamonifo zhenshen sheli*, p. 43.

[61] Holmes Welch, *Buddhism under Mao*, pp. 180–4. The tooth was sent from China to Burma once again in 1994. Like the 1955 mission, this event was also closely tied to political concerns in China and Burma. See Juliane Schober, "Buddhist Just Rule and Burmese National Culture: State Patronage of the Chinese Tooth Relic in Myanma," pp. 218–43.

[62] Welch, *Buddhism Under Mao*, p. 181.

could still believe in the power of relics. Rulers were attracted to relics both because of the widespread belief in their power and because of their portability: encased in impressive reliquaries, tiny bits of teeth and bone could be sent off to distant provinces and foreign countries with a small escort and a powerful political-religious message.

While the maneuvers of emperors and high officials to assert their authority through carefully arranged movements of relics are the most amply documented, it is safe to assume that lesser figures—monks at prominent monasteries, leading local families—made similar efforts to link themselves and their institutions with sacred bits of the Buddha and his most eminent disciples. In the Tang, the Famen Monastery was known chiefly as the home of the finger bone of the Buddha, rather than as, say, the home of a particularly prominent monk or well-stocked library. The same is true for later periods—and indeed up to the present—in which the reputations of many monasteries were based on the relics they contained. As in the related case of stupas, relics were useful not only for the revenue a monastery received from pilgrimage and the donations of prominent patrons, but also for the general sense of pride and self-worth that possession of important relics conferred on a monastery, the monks who lived there, and the laypeople who supported it.[63]

Skeptics and Critics

Although belief in the numinous power of Buddhist relics was widespread, covering both all geographic areas of China and all social strata, a few mavericks applied the same skepticism to Buddhist claims for the sacred power of relics that Wang Chong had applied to sacred vessels in ancient times. The most famous critique of a Buddhist relic in Chinese history was that of Han Yu, revered in Chinese letters for his spare, vigorous writing style, who in 819 submitted a memorial criticizing the emperor for supporting a procession that brought a finger bone of the Buddha from a monastery outside the city walls into the capital. Han focused his attack on the foreign origins of the Buddha, a perverse ascetic unversed in Chinese ways, who would not, according to Han, have commanded respect at the capital had he come in person. "How much the less," Han continued, "now that he has long been dead, is it fitting that his decayed and

[63] Relics were also at times used for purposes of geomancy, since stupas were thought to "stabilize" the surrounding landscape. The focus in this practice was, however, on the shape and position of the stupa rather than the relics, and stupas built for geomantic purposes did not even necessarily have to contain relics. Seventeenth-century writer Qu Dajun once complained that the Guangdong region was covered with stupas built to alter geomancy, a practice he insisted was not in keeping with the Buddha's intention. *Guangdong xinyu* 19, in *Qu Dajun quan ji*, vol. 4, p. 455.

FIG. 1. "Decoy relic" for finger bone of the Buddha. 40.3 mm in height.
Photograph courtesy of the Shaanxi Famensi Museum.

rotten bone, his ill-omened and filthy remains, should be allowed to enter
in the forbidden precincts of the Palace?"[64] Annoyed by Han's comments,
the emperor promptly had him banished from his beloved capital. Note,
however, that even here, Han assumes that the bone in question is in fact
the finger bone of the Buddha. Reliquaries containing four bone-like relics

[64] Edwin O. Reischauer, *Ennin's Travels in T'ang China*, p. 223.

were discovered by archaeologists in 1987. Three are believed to be "decoy relics" (*yinggu*) intended to divert attention from the true relic (*linggu*), in all likelihood the very bone that Han Yu disparaged.[65]

I know of no tests on these objects to determine if they are in fact human finger bones or to assess their age or place of origin. It is very unlikely that any are in fact the relics of the historical Buddha—a claim that could never be proven in any event. These relics do at least look like finger bones to the untrained eye. Other examples of relics, however, as noted above, included horse teeth and bits of coral. The unusual appearance of such relics did not disturb the faithful; on the contrary, it was to be expected that the remnants of the Buddha (or other holy men) would differ from those of ordinary men.[66]

In an essay on the Buddha's teeth, twelfth-century scholar Cheng Dachang, another critic of relic worship, conceded the point, writing, "The world reveres the Buddha in large measure because of his marvels. They say that Chinese and foreign people grow according to the same principles. Yet relics of teeth and bones are as much as twice the size [of normal teeth and bones]. In addition, unlike desiccated bones, in color they are red and shiny. If they are not from the Buddha, they would not be so."[67] Cheng, however, goes on to point out that according to a record of a giant in the early Chinese text *Zuo zhuan,* there had been cases of less-than-holy figures of enormous size in the past. Further, he points out (apparently without intended irony) that the bones of diseased animals may retain a reddish hue. Again, the point is that the remains of the Buddha, though unusual, are not proof of his sanctity. Like Han Yu before him, Cheng did not question the pedigree of relics said to be those of the Buddha.

The Song writer Wang Pizhi describes yet another skeptic, the eleventh-century official Yu Qing. In the 1040s, a stupa burned down and relics were discovered at its base. These were then submitted to the palace and were said to emit light. Plans were then made to build a new stupa. At this point, Yu Qing complained that if the relics could not even protect their own stupa, they surely did not contain any special power. "Even ordinary,

[65] The "decoy relics" have continued to play an important role in the history of the relic, as most of the published photographs have been of one of the decoy relics (figure 1) rather than of the "true relic." The only photograph of the "true" relic that I have found is in Cheng, *Shijiamonifo zhenshen sheli,* p. 64, a catalog prepared for the exhibition of the relic in Taiwan in 2002. Like the other incidences of relic distribution and display discussed above, the display of this relic from the P.R.C. in Taiwan was rife with political and economic implications. The four finger relics found at Famensi look more or less the same.

[66] Liu Xinru points out that authenticity in such cases was judged on the basis of whether or not the objects came from India, rather than what they looked like. *Silk and Religion: An Exploration of Material Life and the Thought of People, AD 600–1200,* p. 44.

[67] *Yanfan lu zhengxu* 6, p. 164.

rotting grass emits light," he continued. "Balls of crystal or other jewels emit light at night. This is not particularly remarkable." After hearing Yu's comments, plans to rebuild the stupa were scrapped.[68] Here again, skepticism is directed at the power of the relics (dismissed as ordinary bones) rather than at their claims to be linked to holy men.

The earliest example I have found of a direct challenge to the historical authenticity of relics rather than claims for their sanctity is from the unlikely source of a catalog of plants and animals by the sixteenth-century writer Li Shizhen, who writes for his entry on the tapir (mo): "The tapir is similar to the bear. It is light yellow in color. Its teeth and bones are extremely strong. If one attempts to break them with blade or ax, the metal breaks. Nor can they be destroyed by fire. Some pretend that they are the teeth or bones of the Buddha in order to deceive the vulgar."[69]

As recently as 1998, relics of the Buddha were reverenced in a massive display of devotion when a tooth said to be that of Śākyamuni was brought to Taiwan from Thailand.[70] In this case, the authenticity of the relics *was* challenged by scholars in journals and newspapers. Tellingly, the effects of these challenges on the Buddhist community seem to have been negligible, and the relic was visited and reverenced by thousands. One scholar who questioned the authenticity of the tooth relic claimed that an article he submitted to a prominent newspaper was pulled at the last minute under pressure from the powerful Foguangshan Buddhist order, the organization responsible for bringing the relic to Taiwan.[71] The stakes were high, in part, perhaps, because of revenues brought in with the display of the relic, but more importantly for the public humiliation and loss of cultural capital if the relic could be shown to be a fake.

All of these critiques were made from the outside, by critics either overtly hostile to Buddhism or at least writing from a non-Buddhist perspective; there was never a strong tradition of monastic criticism or skepticism of relic worship or of the notion that certain relics contained holy power. Even in the modern era, there have never been substantial campaigns to root out relic worship from Buddhist practice. Biographies of monks at times note that just before his death, the monk in question ordered his disciples to scatter his remains and make no fuss over them.[72] But this was more a mark of humility than a critique of the practice per se, and in any event had little impact on practice—despite such requests,

---

[68] *Shengshui yan tan lu,* "Dang lun" (CSJC edn.) 1, p. 4.

[69] *Ben cao gang mu* (SKQS edn.) 51A, p. 10b.

[70] For a description of the event, see Chen Guangzu (Chen Kuang-tsu), "Foguangshan suoying de bu shi 'di san ke ya,'" pp. 88–105.

[71] Jiang Canteng (Chiang Ts'an-t'eng), "Guanyu foya sheli zhenwei zhi bian," pp. 68–73.

[72] Faure, *The Rhetoric of Immediacy,* pp. 144–7.

the disciples of some of these monks went ahead and had stupas made for the relics of their master anyway.[73] And Chan monks might in their sermons list the relics of the Buddha as subject to the ephemerality of all things, even the most sacred, but again the critique was muted and had no discernible influence on practice.[74] Rhetoric opposing the worship of relics or challenging their sanctity has until this century been weak, and was always marginal to the Buddhist tradition.

The Allure of Relics

Whether used to firm up diplomatic relations, demonstrate an organization's ability to command first-rate Buddhist artifacts, or attract tourists, relics were useful tools. But this practical side of the allure of relics is perhaps secondary to a more basic attraction: if devotees were not interested in the relics to begin with, relics could not be manipulated for other ends. What, then, was the attraction?

In large measure, the allure of relics sprang from the intimate connection they provided to otherwise remote holy figures—an attraction in some ways similar to the modern penchant for celebrity autographs. It is one thing to read the words of the Buddha, another to stand in his presence—or at least in the presence of a part of him. This sense of connection to the past permeates much of the literature on relics, and our brief survey of critiques of relic worship reveals that even in the writings of skeptics, the *authenticity* of relics, as remnants of prominent monks or the Buddha himself, was seldom questioned. As we will see in the next section, one interpretation for why sacred powers were attributed to images was because they capture the human form in what are normally lifeless pieces of rock, metal, and wood. It is in part the ambiguity of the relationship between the living and the lifeless that makes images compelling. In a provocative article titled "On the Allure of Buddhist Relics," Robert Sharf has made a parallel argument for relics. Stressing that relics are discovered or procured and in this respect fundamentally different from sacred objects like images and stupas, which are manufactured, Sharf argues that the power of relics "lies in what they are—their corporeal

---

[73] See for instance the biography of Wuran, *Song gaoseng zhuan* 23, pp. 855c–856b.

[74] Faure, *The Rhetoric of Immediacy*, pp. 144–7. Faure notes the comments (p. 144, n. 40) of Qu Dajun (1630–1696), who objected to a stupa supposedly containing Huineng's hair because, according to Qu, the act of tonsure signifies that the Buddha considered hair unclean, in addition to which the worship of human remains runs counter to the doctrine of the ephemerality of the self. While this theory is consonant with mainstream Buddhist doctrine, Buddhist thinkers did not as a rule make this argument. Qu's own attitude toward Buddhism was ambivalent. He became a monk as a youth but later returned to lay life and even wrote an essay ("Gui Ru shuo"), explaining why he had renounced Buddhism. For his comments on Huineng's stupa, see *Guangdong xinyu* 19, p. 456.

essence—rather than in their representational or iconic qualities."[75] That is, the fascination with relics—whether by medieval Buddhists or modern scholars—stems in part from an uncertainty about the relationship between corporeal embodiment and animating life force. Sharf sees the same dynamic at work in modern society, in which, for example, great efforts are made to recover bodies after plane crashes, though the underlying motivation for these efforts is never made explicit. The morbid fascination with bodily remains is perhaps in part an outgrowth of this uncertainty about the boundaries of consciousness: Where does the power of a holy man, or of any person, go after death?

The danger of a general theory of relics is the false assumption that everyone in every instance responds to a sacred object in the same way or for the same reasons. If the driving force behind the fascination with relics was the mystery of the source and destination of a life force, we would expect accounts of relics to devote great attention to the person from whom the relics came as well as to descriptions of relics as body parts. But this is not the case. Relics of the Buddha, for instance, did refer to the Buddha; it mattered that they were connected to this particular holy figure and not to another. Yet even in the case of relics of the Buddha, the focus is usually on the objects themselves. Thus, when Xuanzang recounted the relics of the Buddha that he had seen in India, he focused on a description of the objects at hand. "There is a tooth of Buddha about an inch long, and about eight or nine tenths of an inch in breadth. Its color is yellowish white; it is pure and shining." Those who have the greatest faith in the tooth, he continues, see it "emitting a radiance of glory."[76] His descriptions of other relics are similar. At most he traces a relic back to the original distribution of relics on the Buddha's death. Nowhere does he take the viewing of a relic as an opportunity to reflect on the life and teaching of the Buddha, the figure whose power was, supposedly, concentrated in the relic.

In many accounts of relics, the origins of the relics—whose body they came from—are not known. Recall the story of Kang Senghui, who, in order to prove the efficacy of Buddhism, prayed for the miraculous *appearance* of relics. As we have seen, Buddhists in China had recourse to various strategies when attempting to establish the authenticity of relics. The miraculous appearance of relics in Kang Senghui's vase tells us, however, that the fascination with and demand for relics were so great that questions of authenticity and provenance were seldom raised. Whose relics were they? How did they come to appear in the vase? And what in

[75] Robert H. Sharf, "On the Allure of Buddhist Relics," p. 89.

[76] *Da Tang Xiyu ji* 1, *T* no. 2087, p. 872c; Samuel Beal, *Si-yu-ki Buddhist Records of the Western World*, pp. 45–6.

the end were they good for? Such questions rarely merit mention in Chinese accounts of Buddhist relics. For all their detail, historical accounts of Sui Wendi's distribution of relics say nothing about where the relics came from or to whom they once belonged. The emphasis instead is on the numinous manifestations of these wondrous objects rather than their origins or function.

Just north of the spot where he viewed one of the Buddha's teeth, Xuanzang saw a large stupa. "It encloses a sacred relic, and at times this also reflects a divine splendor."[77] Did the "sacred relic" come from the Buddha, Ānanda, a holy monk? If Xuanzang bothered to ask, he received no definitive reply. The same indifference to the provenance of relics appears in biographies of monks. Like Kang Senghui before him, the Kashmirean missionary Dharmamitra prayed for *śarīra*, whereupon a single, impersonal relic appeared in a vessel, "emitting a light that filled the room."[78] Elsewhere, relics suddenly appear in boxes or fall from the sky, all in response to the entreaties of sincere monks.[79] A biography of the great seventh-century exegete Kuiji notes that when he picked up his writing brush and began work on one of his commentaries, "fourteen kernels of *śarīra* fell from its tip."[80] In this example, it is not clear just what the relics are. Here, the sacred pellets seem more auspicious omens than bodily parts that can be traced to a particular holy figure.

In a similar vein, two medieval accounts survive of men who consumed relics, one in a dream, the other in fact. In both cases, the relics are described as magical, medicinal pellets.[81] Here, as in the cases of relics appearing in bottles or on the tip of a brush, the relic is not a referent to a holy figure, or indeed to any once-living person; it is instead a potent, numinous object in its own right, regardless of its origins. The appearance of *śarīra* received at least as much attention as their provenance. Monks described the tiny pellets as "solid, hard, and without defect."[82] Great attention was paid to their color: "bright white," "vibrant red," or "five-colored."[83] The surface is smooth and fine.[84] And most importantly, they sparkle and shine.[85] Taken together, such descriptions reveal an aesthetics of relics, admired, like fine jade, for their "delightful" qualities.[86]

[77] *Da Tang xiyu ji* 1, ibid.; Beal, Ibid., p. 46.
[78] *Gaoseng zhuan* 3, p. 342c.
[79] *Song gaoseng zhuan* 14, p. 790b; 19, 834c; 14, 796a.
[80] Ibid. 4, p. 726a.
[81] *Dongpo zhilin*, by Su Shi (1036–1101) (CSJC edn.) 1, p. 12; *Song gaoseng zhuan* 6, p. 741a–b.
[82] *Song gaoseng zhuan* 25, p. 870a.
[83] Ibid. 6, p. 742a; 12, 779a; 11, 776b.
[84] Ibid. 7, p. 750a; 26, 886c.
[85] Ibid. 11, p. 776b; 17, 814b; 26, 873a.
[86] The term *delightful* (*keai*) comes from a description of the relics that appeared to Kuiji.

This careful scrutiny of relics reflects a general fascination with the strange, often the primary preoccupation of those who commented on relics. Take, for instance, the first-hand account of the eleventh-century figure Shen Kuo, who records his observation of a relic of the Buddha's tooth in some detail:

> During the Xining era (1068–1077) I paid a visit to Xianping. At that time, Liu Ding Zixian was the administrator of the district. We visited a Buddhist monastery there. Liu Ding said to me, "There is a Buddha's tooth here. It is a great marvel." After purifying myself, I removed it (from its reliquary) and examined it. The tooth suddenly produced *śarīra* [i.e., pellets] like a man perspiring. They wafted away in countless numbers, some flying up into the air and others falling to the ground. When we tried to catch them in the hand, they passed through to the other side, landed on the bed with a thud and passed through it as well. They sparkled brightly, filling the eyes with light.
>
> When I arrived back at the capital they circulated among ranking officials there who passed them among themselves. Later, someone else had some brought to the capital, and an executive official took them into the offices of the East Administration. They then circulated among the homes of the official class. Many marvels occurred, beyond number.
>
> An imperial edict had the relics brought to the Da Xiangguo Monastery, where a wooden stupa was built to house them. This is the Western Stupa of the Xiangguo Monastery of today.[87]

Here Shen makes no mention of religious merit, and no supplications before the relic, though his act of purification (*zhaijie*) suggests at least a pretence of reverence. We detect no political or economic motivations behind his visit. The relics he sees were not the property of the state. He does not charge others to see the relics he acquires. Nor does he pause to reflect on the Buddha or the nature of life and death. Rather, like so many who wrote on relics, his visit was inspired by the allure of the sacred as exotic. By his own account, he went to see the relic in the first place because another official told him it was a "great marvel" (*shen yi*). And others passed them around "among their homes" for the same reason, with no assumption that handling and observing relics need take place in a Buddhist environment. Similar accounts can easily be found in the writings of Ming and Qing authors. In short, regardless of where relics came from or what they could be used for, the objects themselves were out of the ordinary, the stuff of breathless tales told to friends and intimates—wondrous objects abruptly intruding on the monotony of day-to-day routine.

It is a relatively simple matter to sketch a general picture of the history of relics in China. The practice of worshipping the remains of revered fig-

---

[87] *Xin jiaozheng Mengxi bitan* 20, pp. 199–200.

ures was introduced to China along with Buddhism in the first centuries
of the Common Era. In subsequent centuries, the steady supply of relics
brought from abroad by monks and merchants was supplemented by the
relics of holy Chinese monks as well as foreign monks who died in China.
By the sixth century, and probably much sooner, relic worship was widespread, and stupas—the most important form of Buddhist reliquary—
were a common sight throughout China. Buddhist relics continued to be
an important component of Chinese religion into modern times. Participants in the cult of Buddhist relics included members of diverse social status—from peasant to emperor, from illiterate laymen to the most learned
monks—and from all geographic areas of China. The practice attracted
the criticism of a small number of skeptics who questioned the supposedly numinous power of relics, but before the later half of the twentieth
century, such criticisms were never powerful enough to seriously affect
relic worship.

When we turn from a description of the importance of relics to an
analysis of the social and psychological forces behind relic worship, however, the picture becomes considerably more complex. Aside from a rare
case such as the transparent attempts by Mao and Zhou Enlai to capitalize on relic worship in order to improve relations with Burma and Ceylon, most of those who have made use of Buddhist relics did so for a combination of reasons: to acquire religious merit, in hopes of miracles, in
order to attract pilgrims and patronage, or to assert imperial authority.
Often, accounts of relics reflect a general fascination with the marvelous
rather than religious convictions or a political agenda. At times the allure
of relics may have arisen from puzzlement over the limits and nature of
life, deriving as they did from holy human beings, but it is difficult to detect the presence of such subtle psychological factors or to weigh their relative importance in the stew of motivations beyond noting that no doubt
more was involved in the cult of relics than textual descriptions state outright. We can say, however, that Buddhist texts persistently promoted the
worship of Buddhist relics in part because relic worship was a distinguishing characteristic of Buddhist devotion that no other religious tradition could match. The same is true for Buddhist images, the objects to
which we now turn.

ICONS

The Place of Icons in Chinese Buddhism

Over the course of nearly two thousand years of Buddhism in China, Chinese sculptors, painters, metal workers, embroiderers, and potters manu-

factured countless images of buddhas, bodhisattvas, and assorted other Buddhist figures. We now know that the practice of worshipping icons did not become an important component of Buddhism until the early years of the Common Era, that is, just before Buddhism began to have an impact on Chinese civilization; our earliest examples of Indian Buddhist art seldom include anthropomorphic representations of the Buddha. But Chinese Buddhists were not aware of this fact until modern times, and accepted the legend that the first image of the Buddha was made with his approval when he was still alive.[88] As in the case of medieval Christians, some of whom thought their images of Mary were based on an original portrait made during her lifetime by Luke, Chinese Buddhists thought that they had access to accurate portraits of the Buddha, and even of the future buddha, Maitreya, whose portrait had been made long ago in a heaven.[89] In other words, Buddhists in China saw their art as a part of a long and continuous tradition stretching back at least as far as the time of the Buddha.

In China, Buddhism was always closely linked to Buddhist images. According to an early legend, until modern times accepted as true, the beginnings of Buddhist history in China were marked by the arrival of emissaries who returned from India with Buddhist books and an image of the Buddha.[90] Indeed, a common epithet for Buddhism in Chinese texts is the "teaching of the icons" (xiangjiao). And images never ceased to be a central feature of Chinese Buddhist devotion. The same can be said for Buddhism in other parts of the world as well; having earned a place in Buddhist devotional practices in first- and second-century India, icons maintained this position wherever Buddhism spread. The incorporation into Buddhist practice of the cult of images had an enormous impact on the material culture of all of Asia. From Sri Lanka to Japan, every Buddhist monastery contains images of buddhas; and innumerable Buddhist images of a wide assortment of materials, styles, and sizes are displayed

---

[88] In this legend, when the Buddha slipped away to the thirty-third heaven to preach to his mother (who had died shortly after his birth), one of his most devoted patrons, King Udayana, became so despondent that his ministers made an image of the Buddha out of sandalwood to cheer him up. This inspired another patron, King Prasenajit, to make a similar image of gold. *Zeng yi ahan jing* (Skt. *Ekottarāgama*) 29, pp. 705–06. For a discussion of this and other versions of the legend, see Paul Demiéville, "Butuzō" in *Hōbōgirin*, pp. 210–1.

[89] Various legends suggested that this image found its way to China and Japan—either as a copy of the original or as the original itself. See Michel Strickmann, *Mantras et mandarins: le bouddhisme tantrique en Chine*, p. 168. For legends of the portrait of Mary by Luke, see Hans Belting, *Likeness and Presence: A History of the Image before the Era of Art*, pp. 47–77.

[90] *Mingxiang ji* quoted in *Fayuan zhulin* 13, p. 383b.

FIG. 2. Scene in a tenth-century painting of the judgment of the dead in the
netherworld. The two men at the bottom are being led off to punishment for
their sins, while the woman at the top, holding an icon, will be rewarded with a
good rebirth. We are perhaps intended to understand that she is being rewarded
for her devotion to the icon when she was alive. Stein Painting no. 80.
Reproduced by permission of the British Museum.

outside the monasteries as well. The making of Buddhist images is almost
always a social rather than an individual activity, always involving negotiations between patrons and craftsmen, and often requiring the participation of monks and nuns as well.[91] Certain networks of relationships
and modes of interaction between disparate social groups would never
have developed were it not for the need to create Buddhist images. As one
modern historian of the Buddhist art of Dunhuang puts it, the creation of

[91] On the role of monks and nuns in the making of Buddhist steles in the fifth and sixth
centuries, see Hou Xudong, *Wu liu shiji beifang minzhong fojiao xinyang*, pp. 91–5, 255–
8. For the participation of monks in the making of Buddhist art at Dunhuang, see Sarah E.
Fraser, "The Artist's Practice in Tang Dynasty China," Ma De, *Dunhuang gongjiang shiliao*
pp. 29–30, and Ma De, *Dunhuang Mogaokushi yanjiu*, pp. 165–7.

Buddhist art "tied official and subject, nobleman and commoner to the same rope."[92] After a Buddhist statue was made, it continued to inspire and facilitate material culture. For most devotees, images were and are the chief point of contact with Buddhism, the point at which the faithful enter the presence of a buddha or bodhisattva, offer gifts, and ask for assistance. And once again, the communities formed on pilgrimages or even on short trips to a local monastery are a part of material culture, centered as they are on the object of the icon.

The evidence is too fragmentary to trace the introduction and spread of Buddhist images across China with any precision, but certainly by the sixth century they were common in all parts of China, and have continued to be so ever since. Buddhist images were not confined to monasteries. Throughout Chinese Buddhist history, images of buddhas could be found everywhere, from the palace to a bell-maker's workshop, as Buddhist devotion crept into the everyday lives of laypeople from all walks of life.[93]

Yet the importance of images for the laity did not overshadow the central place of images in the lives of monks and nuns. That is, images were not a monastic concession to lay piety. Indeed, a strong case has been made that monks and nuns played a leading role in the introduction of the image cult to Buddhism in ancient India.[94] This same attention to images carried over into the lives of monks and nuns in China. A list of the essential eighteen possessions of a monk in an influential text that was probably compiled in Central Asia or China includes "statues of buddhas and images or statues of bodhisattvas."[95] In China, images were important for monks in a number of common rituals. Monks, for instance, often confessed their faults before Buddhist images. Images were also used as tools for visualization practices in which adepts would spend long periods of time contemplating an image of a buddha until they could visualize a living buddha in all of his glory without recourse to props like images.[96] In short, soon after their introduction to China, Buddhist images became an integral part of the devotional life of all Buddhists—monks and nuns, laypeople, patrons rich and poor.

---

[92] Ma, *Dunhuang gongjiang shiliao*, p. 30.

[93] For example, a large gilded bronze buddha was installed in the Daming Palace by Emperor Daizong in 765. See Weinstein, *Buddhism under the T'ang*, p. 88.

[94] Gregory Schopen, *Bones, Stones, and Buddhist Monks*, pp. 238–57.

[95] *Fanwang jing*, T no. 1484, vol. 24, p. 1008a.

[96] For discussion of the use of images in confession rituals, see Kuo Li-ying, *Confession et contrition dans le bouddhisme chinois du Ve au Xe siècle*, pp. 41, 146–67, and Bernard Faure, *Visions of Power: Imagining Medieval Japanese Buddhism*, pp. 244–5. For the use of images in visualization practices, see Stanley K. Abe, "Art and Practice in a Fifth-Century Chinese Buddhist Cave Temple," pp. 1–31.

The prevalence of Buddhist images in clay, stone, wood, bronze, and gold exerted a profound influence on the development of Chinese sculpture, painting, and aesthetics in general, and continues to influence Chinese artists today. Monumental sculpture, cave reliefs, murals, and metal statuary all evolved in China primarily through the making of Buddhist images. Yet at the same time, Buddhist art was approached differently from secular art. In general, Buddhist art developed independently from the art of literati, and when literati art critics on rare occasions commented on Buddhist art, they did so as outsiders unfamiliar with Buddhist doctrine and interested chiefly in aesthetic considerations like brush stroke and composition.[97] Buddhist sources seldom apply aesthetic criteria to Buddhist images, and when they do, it is only with vague terms, such as we saw in the introduction, like *splendor, magnificence,* and *beauty.*

The manufacture of Buddhist images was not chiefly the product of the pursuit of beauty so much as it was the product of the pursuit of the sacred. At times Buddhist art was used for didactic purposes (as in Figure 2), and some served as ornament.[98] But Buddhist images were seldom purely decorative; they were objects of worship, repositories of powers capable of rewarding the pious and punishing the disrespectful. Even in modern China, art historians and archaeologists must contend with farmers, townsfolk, and other local devotees for access and use of Buddhist art. Devotees decorate images of buddhas, bodhisattvas, and other Buddhist deities—ancient as well as contemporary—covering them with cloth and paint, and making offerings of fruit and incense before them. They add new images at ancient sites and bring newly discovered old images into new temples. All of this is done in the hope that prayers for pregnancy, cure from sickness, success in an examination or business venture, or general well-being will be granted in return. None of this is new. Buddhist images were considered sources of sacred power from the earliest times.[99]

One way of interpreting such images, whether from modern or premodern times, is as representations or symbols of Buddhist figures. An image of Śākyamuni *reminds* us of the historical Buddha and encourages

[97] See Erik Zürcher, "Buddhist Art in Medieval China: The Ecclesiastical View," pp. 1–20.

[98] In "Religious Functions of Buddhist Art in China," T. Griffith Foulk cautions that in addition to their use as icons (my focus here), Buddhist images served also as decoration, sources of merit, platforms for unrelated texts, repositories of sacred objects, and as talismans. In Marsha Weidner ed., *Cultural Intersections in Later Chinese Buddhism,* pp. 13–29.

[99] Marylin Martin Rhie suggests, for instance, that depressions in the stone carvings at Kongwangshan, site of some of the earliest Buddhist images in China, were probably used to hold candles or lamps placed in offering to the images or, more properly, the deities they contained. Rhie, *Early Buddhist Art of China and Central Asia,* pp. 36–7.

us to imitate him. As the bodhisattva Guanyin is omnipresent, one could just as easily pray to her at home, but praying before an image of Guanyin at a temple allows one to concentrate one's thoughts and make offerings in an atmosphere of greater piety. This sort of detached symbolic interpretation of Buddhist images would, however, have struck most devotees throughout Chinese history as bizarre and counterintuitive. Devotees made offerings to images of the Buddha in part as a sign of reverence, but more importantly in hopes of deriving benefits from the act. Further, they did not pray to an image of Guanyin because it symbolized the deity, but rather because Guanyin was *present* at the site of the image. That is, Buddhist images were believed to contain the numinous power of the deities they depict. More than lifeless representations, images manifested a higher reality. That being said, the nature of this power is not as obvious as one might assume, and is seldom clearly articulated, whether in the doctrinal writings of leading monks or in the ritual practice of ordinary believers. This is the topic that I will focus on here: What was the nature of this sacred power, what function did it serve, and how did icons get it?

The concept of the sacred icon seems to have secured a prominent position in Chinese religion under the impetus of Buddhist influence from India. Icons are extremely important in contemporary Indian religion and were common there in medieval times as well, though the origins of the ideas that icons contain divine power and that the deity can be introduced into an icon through ritual are obscure. The Vedas make no mention of religious icons, suggesting that icons were no more important in ancient Vedic religion than they were in early Buddhism. It has been suggested that sacred icons became important in India through Greek influence, though the evidence is far from conclusive.[100] In any event, textual evidence suggests that beliefs in the sacred power of icons were held in India by at least the fifth century, and we can conjecture that they arose some centuries earlier, though just how the numinous icon came to such central prominence—a position it holds as well in Hinduism today—is far from clear.[101] We can at least assert that sacred icons were an important part

---

[100] Strickmann, *Mantras et mandarins*, pp. 165–75, and Alexander Soper, *Literary Evidence for Early Buddhist Art in China*, pp. 243–52.

[101] Images existed in India much earlier. The point in question here is when we have evidence for the belief that images contained sacred power. The practice of consecrating images is alluded to by the fifth-century Indian Buddhist exegete Buddhaghosa in his *Samantapāsādika*. Trans. in N. A. Jayawickrama, *The Inception of Discipline and the Vinaya Nidāna, Being a Translation and Edition of the Bāhiranidāna of Buddhaghosa's Samantapāsādika, the Vinaya Commentary*, p. 39. Buddhaghosa also refers to the practice in the *Mahāvamsa*, Wilhelm Geiger, ed., p. 34. These references are given in Richard Gombrich, "The Consecration of a Buddhist Image," pp. 23–36, in which, in addition to citing classical evidence, Gombrich describes a ceremony in Ceylon that he witnessed in which an image was consecrated.

of Buddhism at the time when Buddhism began to have a major impact on Chinese civilization.

Later texts as well as extant statues tell us that the making of Buddhist images flourished in India in the first centuries of the Common Era. Monks, nuns, and laypeople quickly accepted the practice. The vinayas of various schools mention images in a matter-of-fact way, advising, for instance, that monks should not take Buddha images to the privy.[102] Such references suggest that by that time, images were a common part of the daily life of practicing Buddhists. The production of icons was further encouraged by a number of scriptures that speak enthusiastically of the merit that accrues to a devotee who makes or venerates Buddhist images.

Yet even after the manufacture and worship of images became a common part of Buddhist devotional practice, Buddhist thinkers in India continued to express discomfort with the concept. The monastic regulations of the Sarvāstivādin school, for instance, contains a passage in which a rich patron (Anāthapiṇḍada) asks the Buddha for something to remember him by when the Buddha is away preaching. He asks first for strands of hair and nail clippings, which the Buddha grants him. Later in the same passage, the donor states, "As we are not to make images of the Buddha's body, I hope that the Buddha will allow me to make images of attendant bodhisattvas." The Buddha grants him this permission. Elsewhere in the same passage, when asked if patrons can paint murals, the Buddha replies that devotees can make all manner of murals with the exception of those depicting men and women in sexual union.[103] In the first passage, the reference to a prohibition on making Buddha images may be a vestige of an older, more commonly accepted taboo on representing the Buddha. In the second passage, on the other hand, the need to ask permission to paint murals seems to suggest a hesitancy about making representations of any sort. In both cases, monks felt the need to produce a quotation from the Buddha specifically granting permission to make images.

Evidence for sacred icons in China before the entrance of Buddhism is as sketchy as it is for sacred icons in pre-Buddhist India. There were, of course, statues in human shape in China very early on. From the late Shang we have evidence of the practice of burying clay figures with the dead—a custom that continued all the way up into the Ming period.[104] The most spectacular example of the practice is the massive terra-cotta army of Qin Shihuang, but many images on a smaller scale exist from other periods as well. During the pre-Buddhist period, such images were

---

[102] *Si fen lü* (Skt.*Dharmaguptakavinaya*), *T* no. 1428, vol. 22, p. 711c. Other references to Buddha images in the vinayas are discussed in Zürcher, "Buddhist Art in Medieval China", and in Demiéville, "Butsuzō," pp. 210–3.

[103] *Shi song lü* (Skt.*Sarvāstivādavinaya*) 48, *T* no. 1435, vol. 23, pp. 351c–352a; the passages are discussed in Zürcher, "Buddhist Art in Medieval China," pp. 5–7.

[104] For a general survey, see Cao Zhezhi, gen. ed., *Zhongguo gudai yong.*

usually believed to come to life in the afterworld, where they would serve
the deceased, or in some cases take the deceased's place in performing
unpleasant duties there, such as corvée labor.[105] Deep inside long-sealed
tombs, these humble surrogates had little impact on the daily lives of the
living, and do not seem to have been the focus of worship. Above the
ground, ancestor worship centered on tablets rather than anthropomorphic representations of the deceased.

We must search the early historical record carefully to uncover references to statues of deities in ancient China. The *Records of the Historian*
recounts a story of a decadent Shang king who made statuettes, calling
them "heavenly gods" and ridiculing them.[106] Yet even this example does
not indicate reverence for sacred icons, suggesting instead quite the opposite. Most importantly, shrines in China before the entrance of Buddhism almost never contained images of deities.[107] Recall that in the
account of the "treasure of Chen," the cock-like deity inhabited a nondescript rock rather than a statue of a cock. In other words, although images existed in ancient China, they were rarely attributed with divine
power. And the peculiar idea that a powerful deity could be induced to in-
habit a man-made likeness was not common, if it existed at all. As we will
see, just a few centuries after the arrival of Buddhism, all of this changed
dramatically, as the countryside was quickly populated with images that
not only represented deities but were also deities themselves, capable of
profoundly affecting the lives of those around them.

Animating Icons

The most systematic means of manipulating the numinous power of
icons is through ceremonies carried out to consecrate or "establish" (Skt.
pratiṣṭhā) new images, a practice with roots in Indian Buddhism. Par-

[105] Mu-chou Poo, *In Search of Personal Welfare: A View of Ancient Chinese Religion*,
pp. 172–4.
[106] *Shiji* 3, p. 104; English trans. in William H. Nienhauser ed., *The Grand Scribe's
Records*, vol. 1, p. 49. The Qing scholar Zhao Yi, in a brief discussion of the history of images in China, makes the point that images existed before the entry of Buddhism, and provides a number of citations of classical texts in support. "Su xiang" in *Gaiyu congkao* 32,
pp. 692–3.
[107] See Fu-shih Lin, "Chinese Shamans and Shamanism in the Chiang-nan Area during
the Six Dynasties Period," p. 91 in which Lin shows that one of the most significant differences between shrines in the Six Dynasties and in the Han is that shrines in the Six Dynasties contained images. Lin also gives a few possible exceptions, that is, Han images that may
have been worshipped. The finds in Sichuan at Sanxingdui, dated tentatively to the end of
the Shang, are as mysterious as they are spectacular. These masks and other images may well
have been believed to contain divine power, but in the absence of any context for these images, we can only speculate as to their original function. See Sichuansheng Wenwukaogu
Yanjiuso, ed., *Sanxingdui jisi keng*. In any event, allowing for a few exceptions, it is safe to
say that the worship of images was not common in China before the entrance of Buddhism.

ticularly revealing is the ceremony in which the eyes of the image are
"opened." When a Buddhist image is almost complete, the craftsman
often carries out a final step to convert a lifeless piece of clay, wood, or
metal into the receptacle of a god. In all cultures where Buddhism is practiced, this is done in a ceremony in which the eyes of the deity are dotted
or otherwise completed. This done, the image is born, and a living entity
now present within the inanimate exterior. The person performing the ceremony approaches the task with great caution, in many cases taking care
not to look directly at the image when its eyes are first opened, instead
dotting the eyes indirectly, with the help of a mirror.[108] Images treated in
this way are more than reminders or symbols of the Buddha (or bodhisattva); rather, they contain in some way the power of the Buddha. The
extent to which we are dealing here with the power *of the Buddha* (who
in theory has long since left the world and entered nirvana) is open to interpretation, and a question to which we will return.

In China, our first glimpse of the ceremony in which a statue is invested
with sacred power through the opening of the eyes comes in a brief inscription for an image made in 524 by one Du Wenqing that states: "We
have opened the vision (*kaiguang*) of this marvelous image. Who could
say this is not good? Who could say it is not numinous (*ling*)?"[109] The inscription is too terse to allow us to reconstruct a theology of icons, but it
tells us at least that the ritual had made its way to China at this time, and
that through this ceremony, ordinary pieces of stone and metal became
sacred.

Early inscriptions reveal that by the sixth century, the practice of dotting the eyes was fairly widespread in China. In general, the inscriptions
provide us with little more than a title: "Head [of the Ceremony] of Opening the Vision" (*kaiguangzhu* or *guangmingzhu*), followed by a name,
usually the name of a layman.[110] This would at first seem to indicate that
laypeople, rather than craftsmen or monks, conducted this crucial ceremony. The fact that some of these laymen are listed as "deceased," however, indicates that they did not themselves perform the ceremony of dotting the eyes.[111] This assumption is supported by reference to a similar
ceremony conducted in Japan in 752, presumably modeled closely on
contemporary Chinese practice.[112] The ceremony, which took place at

[108] Gombrich, "The Consecration of a Buddhist Image," pp. 23–36.
[109] "Du Wenqing deng zao Tiangong xiang ji," in *Lu Xun jijiao shike shougao*, comp.
Lu Xun, case 2, vol. 1, p. 131, cited in Liu Shufen, "Wu zhi liu shiji Huabei xiangcun de fojiao xinyang," vol. 63, no. 3 (1993), p. 527.
[110] For examples, see ibid., p. 527.
[111] Ibid., p. 528; Soper, *Literary Evidence*, p. 137.
[112] William George Aston, *Nihongi: Chronicles of Japan from the Earliest Times to A.D.
697*, part 2, pp. 297, 423. See also Bernard Frank, "Vacuité et corps actualisé: Le problème

Tōdaiji, states that the actual dotting of the buddha's eyes was carried out by an Indian monk, while financing for the elaborate ritual was supplied by a number of prestigious donors. Hence, the sixth-century Chinese images were probably also consecrated by monks, while the men listed as "Masters of the Ceremony of Opening the Vision" were either donors who funded the proceedings or were intended recipients of the religious merit generated by making a Buddhist icon.[113] In other words, while laypeople were concerned that their images be consecrated and were willing to finance the operation, the actual manipulation of sacred power was left to monastic specialists.

Setting aside the inscriptions and moving forward in time, the primacy of the ritual specialist (usually a monk) in the ceremony of opening the eyes is asserted in a ritual manual translated into Chinese by the Indian monk Dānapāla at the end of the tenth century. At one point in this scripture, the Buddha proclaims, "All rituals of offering [related to the opening of the eyes] must proceed according to the instructions of the ācārya [i.e., presiding master]. In this [the participants] must not be lax if the patrons are to receive great benefits [from the ceremony]."[114] The text is adamant that the ceremony must be performed for an icon to be effective. At one point in the text, the Buddha says, "If an image has been completed for some time and one does not carry out the joyous ceremony of installation [i.e., the dotting of the eyes], the results will be inauspicious, and those who make offerings to the image thereafter will never receive any benefit from it."[115] This emphasis was important both for the self-preservation of the manual itself—since in effect one needed the manual in order to make an image sacred—and for the monks versed in its mysteries; without the ritual and a specialist to perform it, one's icon would never be more than a lump of clay. In other words, without doubting the sincerity of the participants in such rituals, the manipulation of sacred power here touches on more mundane concerns as well: through the ritual of dotting the eyes, monks were paid for their services and accorded prestige as specialists in a necessary ritual.

Scholars discussing this ceremony in other cultures at other times have disagreed about whether the numinous force directed into the icon is maleficent or benign. They have also disagreed about who plays the key

---

de la présence des 'Personnages Vénérés' dans leurs images selon la tradition du bouddhisme japonais," pp. 53–86.

[113] Here I follow Liu Shu-fen, "Wu zhi liu shiji Huabei xiangrun de fojiao xinyang," p. 528.

[114] *Yiqie rulai anxiang sanmei yigui jing*, T no. 1418, vol. 21, p. 933c. This text is discussed in Strickmann, *Mantras et mandarins*, pp. 198–202.

[115] *Yiqie rulai anxiang sanmei yigui jing*, p. 933b.

role of carrying out the ritual: monk or craftsman.[116] Both, of course, may depend on time and geography; there is no reason that all Buddhists must understand and carry out the ritual in the same way. As we have seen, what little evidence we have in China suggests that there the ritual was chiefly in the hands of monks rather than craftsmen. And in China, the powers channeled into an image during the ritual were in general benign. In none of the Chinese material, whether inscriptions or references in ritual manuals, are the powers directed into a newly made icon explicitly referred to as dangerous, though they are certainly powerful.

In addition to the dotting of the eyes, yet another way of bringing life to a Buddhist image was to incorporate sacred relics into the image itself. The use of bone and ash was usually reserved for images of monks, rather than images of buddhas or bodhisattvas. For instance, the ninth-century work *A Record of Monasteries and Stupas* records the case of a monk who burned himself to death as an offering. After his death, the faithful collected his ashes and made an image of the monk from them, which was then placed in a monastic hall and worshipped.[117] A number of medieval ash icons have been discovered by archaeologists in modern times, indicating that the practice was widespread in the Tang.[118] Similarly, according to his tenth-century biography, when the influential Sillan thaumaturge Musang died in China, his ashes were also used to make an image of him. Later, when a huge bell was moved to Musang's monastery, the workers found the bell strangely light. When the work was complete, someone noticed that the portrait of Musang was perspiring. Only then did they realize that it was he who had moved the bell through his divine power.[119] In both cases, the images of the monks were not merely reminders of the monks or signs of a place of worship: the spirits of the deceased monks were present in the images. According to a similar logic, several old statues of buddhas have been found to contain scriptures, usually including spell texts, considered powerful in themselves.[120] The logic

---

[116] Stanley Tambiah, discussing the consecration of Buddhist icons in Thailand, has objected to Gombrich's reference to the "evil influence" of the "dangerous" power that emerges from an icon when its eyes are dotted. Tambiah prefers to characterize the power of the newly consecrated deity as too great for the ordinary person to withstand, but not necessarily evil. See Stanley Tambiah, *The Buddhist Saints of the Forest and the Cult of Amulets*, pp. 256–7. On the question of whether the monk or the craftsman dots the eyes of the icons, see Strickmann, *Mantras et mandarins*, pp. 451–2, n. 36.

[117] *Sita ji, T* no. 2092, vol. 51, p. 1023c; also recorded in *Song gaoseng zhuan* 23, p. 857b.

[118] Li Jianchao, "Sui Tang Chang'an cheng Shiji si yizhi chutu wenwu," pp. 314–7.

[119] *Song gaoseng zhuan* 19, pp. 832b–833a. For more on this practice, see T. Griffith Foulk and Robert H. Sharf, "On the Ritual Use of Ch'an Portraiture in Medieval China," pp. 149–219.

[120] Yuan dynasty scriptures were discovered in 1984 in the statue of a buddha in Beijing.

in these practices is more direct than that of dotting the eyes of a new image; rather than coaxing or summoning a numinous presence into the image through ritual, the sacred force, already present in another object—whether a text or a relic—is placed directly in the image. The end result, however, is much the same: an image was not complete unless it was invested with the sacred power that made it come alive.

Living Images

Despite the prominent position of monks as ritual specialists in the creation of sacred images and the insistence of certain Buddhist texts on the importance of monks for consecrating images properly, in practice, images became holy with or without monastic assistance. Most Buddhist images do not contain sacred scriptures or the bones of famous monks. And most inscriptions on Buddhist images make no mention of the ceremony of opening the eyes.[121] Nonetheless, countless stories in Chinese Buddhist literature testify to the belief that even images that had undergone no consecration ceremony or other ritual were still thought to be alive and powerful.

Take for instance, the following story about an unfinished buddha recounted in a Tang collection of miracle tales:

At the end of the Northern Qi a sramana of the Lingshi Monastery in Jinzhou, one Senghu, . . . vowed to make an eighteen-foot stone image. The monks all marveled at his boastfulness; but later on in a valley north of the temple a rock some eighteen feet long was found lying on its side; sculptors were hired, and in time they fashioned a buddha. It was worked all around but the face and abdomen were only blocked out, and it still lay on its back on the ground. They tried to haul it upright with all the equipment they had, but it would not move; then during the night it rose lightly of itself, and was so discovered, to everyone's delight, on the morrow. Then it was worked over, and transferred to the Buddha Hall.[122]

See Xu Huili, "Beijing Zhihuasi faxian Yuandai zangjing," pp. 1–7, 29. For a Ming example, see Herbert Franke, "Einige Drucke und Handschriften der frühen Ming-Zeit," pp. 55–64, cited in Strickmann, *Mantras et mandarins*, p. 181. Strickmann cites as well a number of examples of the practice from medieval Japan (pp. 178–81). Textual references to the practice go back to the fourth century, and the hollows in several extant early images may well have been for relics. See Rhie, *Early Buddhist Art of China and Central Asia*, p. 83, no. 127–8, and p. 133.

[121] Among the hundreds of inscriptions at Dunhuang, for instance, only one, in Tibetan, refers to the ceremony. The Tibetan inscription is in Cave 365 (Ma De, personal communication).

[122] *Ji Shenzhou sanbao gantong lu* B, compiled by Daoxuan, *T* no. 2106, vol. 52, p. 420b; trans. from Soper, *Literary Evidence*, p. 115.

Later in the story the image continues to exhibit human qualities, sweating profusely in nervous apprehension when soldiers begin looting the monastery, and complaining in a devotee's dream that its fingers are in need of repair. Of particular interest here is that the statue's life began even before the carving was complete. There is no mention of a ritual of consecration, which would not in any event have been carried out before the statue was completed. And as the image was made of stone, it would not have contained sacred relics. For the author of the story and presumably his readers, ritual animation was not required for the image to come alive; the longing to animate sacred images could not be contained by formal ritual.

In the literature, icons respond primarily to the sincere supplications of the faithful, emitting beams of light in recognition of the accomplishments of great monks, and healing the sick when they pray before them or finance their repair.[123] While these stories cannot be pinned to the spread and development of a specific ritual of consecration, it would be wrong to argue conversely that the ritual was created chiefly as a liturgical concession to popular belief. Rather, both the ritual of consecration and legends of the miracles of images are outgrowths of a more fundamental reaction to images made in human form. That is, there is something about artistic representation itself that encourages the attribution of sacred powers to inanimate objects.[124]

To appreciate how readily images were imbued with a sacred presence, we must take into consideration the context in which icons were displayed in premodern times and the distance that separates us from them. I emphasized earlier that Buddhist images were common in monasteries and could be found as well outside of monastic contexts. That being said, the prevalence of images of all kinds in premodern times can in no way compare with the prevalence of images today. Indeed, one of the most significant ways in which modern society differs from the world of premodern China is in our exposure to images. Images have become so prevalent, whether in photographs, billboards, or television, that we accord them a status no different from other everyday objects that surround us.[125] In medieval China, however, when a peasant, or even a literatus, came be-

[123] In the section that follows, I draw on ideas put forth in Glen Dudbridge, "Buddhist Images in Action: Five Stories from the Tang," pp. 377–91. Hubert Delahaye's "Les antécédents magique des statues chinoises" contains a number of anecdotes of animate icons from various periods. pp. 45–54.

[124] This is a major theme of David Freedberg's, *The Power of Images: Studies in the History and Theory of Response.*

[125] For an influential formulation of the problem of the "decay of the aura" of art in modern times, see Walter Benjamin, "The Work of Art in the Age of Mechanical Reproduction," in his *Illuminations: Essays and Reflections.* See also Bernard Faure, "The Buddhist Icon and the Modern Gaze," pp. 768–813.

fore a Buddhist image in a monastery, the experience was novel: they had most likely not seen such a lifelike representation since the last time they had come to a religious site; and it was the lifelike nature of images that they knew to be made of stone, metal, or clay, "the raised eyebrows," and "vivid eyes" that "look so true" that struck them.[126] This disturbing combination of a lifelike presence and the knowledge that the image was made of lifeless material accounts in part for the attribution of supernormal powers to images. Buddhist doctrine and practice provided the impetus and framework for these beliefs to develop. In addition to the efforts of ritual specialists discussed in the previous section, Chinese pilgrims like Faxian and Xuanzang related legends of powerful Buddhist icons in India, and laymen and monks in China told stories of animate icons on Chinese soil.

Further, the context in which Buddhist images were viewed contributed to their sacred aura. While China eventually created a strong tradition of figure painting, images of beings outside of a religious context were seldom accessible to any but a small minority of the population until recent times. In modern times, even with the proliferation of images—some much more realistic and grand than anything a monastery can muster— images in monasteries are still different: they are encountered on sacred land, in special halls reserved for prayer and offering, redolent with the smell of incense and the sound of chanting monks.

If ordinary laypeople entered into a special relationship with a Buddhist icon when they knelt down and made supplications before it, the relationship between monks and icons was at times even more intense. As we have seen, in a practice that goes back to the early stage of the *Mahāyāna*, monks would go before an image, attempt to systematically visualize the buddha represented by the statue, and through this visualization attain a state of *samādhi* (i.e., meditative absorption). In addition, in confession rituals, monks were to confess their faults before an image of the Buddha. Through these rituals, involving contemplating an icon for an extended period of time, monks (and some lay devotees as well) developed a more personal relationship with the icon. The ninth-century monk Weize, known for making Buddhist statues, described his approach to icons as follows:

> Images are a powerful means of persuading others to goodness. For this reason, we must create them in great numbers. When one first looks [at a Buddha image], it seems like a stern father. Next one finds that one's mind is calm. Then one perfects the skill of contemplation, and in the end all is thusness, a great expanse. At this point *samādhi* must as a matter of course man-

[126] The quotations are from the poem "Yong jin'gang," by Tang poet Jiang Yigong, in *Quan Tang shi* 870, p. 9871.

ifest itself. For this reason, when promoting the transformation of the deluded, we base ourselves on [images].[127]

Here, after first giving a practical justification for images—persuading
others to do good—the monk turns to the importance of images in ritual
in which it appears first as a father figure before eventually becoming
something more abstract and transcendent. Whether the icon is transformed into a spectacular deity through visualization and the state of
samādhi, or whether he becomes a "stern father" judging one's faults,
there is inevitably slippage between the icon and the deity it represents. In
this atmosphere of reverential attention and wide-eyed expectation, it is
not surprising that when many rise from their knees before a Buddhist
image and look into its face, the image stares back. This reaction is fos-
tered by the way icons are made. Artisans in China created a wide variety of forms of buddhas and bodhisattvas. At times bodhisattvas look rev-
erently at a buddha standing between them. The central buddha may at
times look down in contemplation, or off to the side. But in general, the
central deity looks straight out at the viewer. We return again to the importance of eyes we have already encountered in consecration ceremonies.[128] In the most basic form of the Buddhist icon, a buddha squarely
faces us, staring straight out in an expression that facilitates an unnerv-
ing exchange of gazes between icon and devotee.

But who, precisely, is it that stares out of the animate icon? In the story
above of the unfinished statue that rose up by itself, the image is referred
to as a "buddha." More specifically, the image would probably have been
of Śākyamuni, or perhaps Maitreya or one of several less popular candi-
dates. But in what sense was a buddha acting through the image? In theory, the last buddha, Śākyamuni, has left the cycle of life and death and
so no longer acts in this world, while the next buddha, Maitreya, has yet
to appear. Modern scholars have invoked this notion as an explanation
for the absence of buddha images in early Buddhist art.[129] Some Buddhist
thinkers solved this problem of agency through reference to the "*dharmakāya,*" or "body of the Law," the transcendent aspect of "Buddha"
that is made manifest in human figures that appear among us as individual buddhas. Hence, just as the *dharmakāya* appeared as Śākyamuni Buddha, so too it may appear in a statue made in his image. This explanation

[127] *Song gaoseng zhuan* 27, p. 880c.

[128] David Freedberg notes perceptively that eyes are often the primary target when images are defaced; for "[e]veryone senses that to deprive the image of its eyes, in particular,
is to deprive it effectively of its life." *The Power of Images,* pp. 415–6.

[129] Richard F. Gombrich, *Precept and Practice: Traditional Buddhism in the Rural High-
lands of Ceylon,* p. 112; David L. Snellgrove, ed., *The Image of the Buddha,* pp. 23–4. Susan
L. Huntington has objected to this explanation. Huntington, "Early Buddhist Art and the
Theory of Aniconism," p. 1.

FIG. 3. Buddhas from Dunhuang, Cave 322. Early Tang. Photograph courtesy
of the Dunhuang Research Academy.

appears on occasion in Chinese inscriptions. One inscription for a Buddhist stele containing depictions of Buddhist figures completed in 535 explains, for instance:

> The ultimate principle is empty and pure; without great wisdom it cannot be expressed in words. The body of the Dharma (i.e., *dharmakāya*) is concentrated and tranquil; without marvelous faith, its image will not respond. . . .

[B]right it is and sacred; it shines without attachment. Supremely tranquil, supremely marvelous, clear and blissful, it has no [constant] image, no [constant] language. Its form and name appear in response to [the needs of] the world.[130]

In other words, it is the mysterious power of the *dharmakāya* that animates the image. In stories about the miracles of Buddha images, however, no reference to such erudite doctrines was necessary, and the precise identity of the buddha is seldom important. This tendency is clearer when we look at the personality of the statue as revealed in the second half of the story cited above, when the image sweats nervously at the approach of soldiers. One searches accounts of the life of Śākyamuni in vain for stories of the Buddha perspiring with anxiety, or complaining about injured fingers—such behavior is entirely too mundane for Śākyamuni or any other buddha. Nor do sweating and whining seem suitable manifestations of the sublime *dharmakāya*.

In other words, setting aside the knotty buddhalogical problem of whether or not a buddha who has entered nirvana continues to appear and act in the world, the actions of statues of buddhas described in miracle tales are often at variance with the generally accepted personality of the Buddha. Statues frequently emit rays of golden light—something we might imagine the Buddha to do—but the story above of the "buddha" sweating and complaining about his fingers points to something else. In any number of miracle stories, Buddhist images shout, bleed, gripe, and moan. More strikingly still, images frequently punish those who mistreat them or their patrons. In the story above of the image at Shiling Monastery, for instance, when a bandit steals the banners used to ornament the image, the statue appears to the bandit in a dream and threatens to punish him unless he return the banners immediately. In this story, the reader shares sympathy with the icon-protagonist, but in other stories the buddha statue turns vicious. In one sixth-century account, for instance, when a patron, one Hou Qing, had a bronze image of a buddha made, he originally planned to have it covered in gold leaf, but ran into financial difficulties and so used the money for other purposes. In response, the buddha appeared to Hou's wife in a dream and explained that in compensation for their failure to gild him, the statue would take their only son. The next morning, the son took ill and died, victim of the "buddha's" jealousy.[131]

Taking these stories together, one can only conclude that in general Bud-

---

[130] "Dong Wei Tianping er nian Songyang si shamen tonglun Yanzun fashi deng zao qi ji fota tiangong ji baiyu xiang ji," p. 28.
[131] *Luoyang jialan ji jiaoshi* 4, p. 162; Wang, *A Record of Buddhist Monasteries in Luoyang*, p. 189.

dhist images were thought of as independent, living entities with distinct personalities, rather than as emanations of the transcendent Buddhist figures described in Buddhist scriptures or the even more abstract force of the *dharmakāya*. At times the images respond violently to the threats of persecutors, striking blind those who slander or destroy Buddhist images, and in one case going so far as to kill the craftsmen who were ordered to melt down a Buddhist statue.[132] Such stories can be read at least in part as a form of proselytizing or even political propaganda, intended to warn those with plans to destroy or expropriate monastic property. One might argue that these stories of vengeful icons are the product of the efforts of a small monastic elite to protect their interests, and did not have resonance in society at large. But stories of the miracles of icons are so common that we can safely assume that they sprang from a widespread belief in the power of religious images, rather than from any one specific group.

Iconoclasts

The preceding discussion, with its dual focus on rituals for drawing deities into statues and on the large corpus of stories relating the miracles of Buddhist icons, points to a widespread understanding of the nature of religious images as living, acting presences. This belief in the animate power of icons appeared in China with the entrance of Buddhism, eventually spreading to all parts of China and to all levels of Chinese society. But this is only a part of the story. Rising up alongside this tradition of pious reverence was a movement in opposition to it, expressing skepticism and even hostility toward the Buddhist icon.[133]

The sixth-century *Biographies of Eminent Monks* relates a legend said to have taken place in the third century under the reign of Sun Hao. When a Buddhist image was unearthed from the palace grounds, Sun had the image moved to a privy, where he urinated on it in a ceremony he jokingly called "bathing the Buddha," much to the amusement of his courtiers. Soon afterwards his body broke out into boils, while the offending member in particular caused him great pain. Only after Sun repented and acknowledged the truth of Buddhism was his illness cured.[134] This anecdote reads like a piece of Buddhist propaganda—a warning to those who would desecrate Buddhist icons—and we have no way of knowing if the

---

[132] *Song gaoseng zhuan* 26 (biography of Zijue), p. 874b, and 26 (biography of Huiyun), p. 874b–c.

[133] For this section I draw in part on Faure, *Visions of Power*, pp. 264–74. For a concise survey of iconoclasm in Chinese Buddhism, see Paul Demiéville, "L'iconoclasme anti-bouddhique en Chine," pp. 17–25.

[134] *Gaoseng zhuan* 1 (biography of Kang Senghui), p. 326a; Soper, *Literary Evidence*, p. 6.

historical Sun Hao did in fact urinate on a Buddhist image.[135] The story and others like it do, however, reflect the resistance to the Buddhist theology of icons that many must have felt as the country was flooded with Buddhist images. That is, even if the story is a pious legend, it was created to counter real attacks by those who rejected the sanctity of Buddhist images.

The most important of these attacks were carried out in campaigns launched by the state. All of the most famous state persecutions of Buddhism involved the destruction of Buddhist images. As a part of the first great persecution of Buddhism in Chinese history, an edict promulgated by Emperor Zhou Wudi in 574 called for the "burning and destruction of Buddhist images."[136] The extent to which the edict was actually carried out is difficult to assess, though the wealth of extant Buddhist images from the period suggests that it was not implemented effectively. In contrast, according to a wide variety of sources, the destruction of Buddhist images ordered by Emperor Wuzong of the Tang in the 840s was devastatingly effective, causing the melting down of countless images in the space of a few years.

Opponents of Buddhism in modern times have also singled out Buddhist images for destruction. In the name of rooting out superstition, Buddhist images were destroyed in sporadic actions immediately following the revolution in 1949.[137] And more widespread destruction took place during the Cultural Revolution (1966–76), when Red Guards targeted Buddhist statues as examples of superstition and the "four olds" (old customs, old habits, old culture, and old thinking). The most concerted attacks on Buddhist images during the Cultural Revolution were carried out by young Red Guards in 1966 when Buddhist images at the Biyun Monastery, the Wofo Monastery, the Summer Palace, and other shrines, temples, and parks around Beijing were smashed and replaced with portraits of Mao Zedong. At approximately the same time, many Buddhist images at Longmen, an important Buddhist site outside Luoyang, were destroyed. Similar attacks took place in and around major cities throughout China.[138]

Whether modern or premodern, these campaigns to destroy Buddhist images were in general carried out either for the symbolic significance of

[135] Erik Zürcher discusses the remote possibility of a historical core to the legend. *The Buddhist Conquest of China*, p. 52.

[136] *Guang hongming ji* 6, p. 135c; Chen, *Buddhism in China*, p. 189.

[137] Welch, *Buddhism under Mao*, p. 163.

[138] Gao Gao and Yan Jiaqi, *Wenhua dageming shinian shi* p. 58; Wang Nianyi, *Da dongluan de niandai*, p. 70. It is at this time difficult to assess the overall damage to Buddhist sites during the Cultural Revolution. Soon after the appearance of the two books I draw on here, publication of research on the Cultural Revolution was banned in the P.R.C.

the act or for economic reasons. Because Buddhist images were one of the most visible manifestations of the religion, when officials railed against Buddhism as a foreign aberration that had brought China nothing but waste and corruption, they called for the destruction of Buddhist images as a powerful expression of their disdain. At times the symbolism of the act of smashing Buddhist images is particularly apparent. For instance, in 844, in a move that hinted at the widespread persecution of Buddhism that was soon to follow, Emperor Wuzong of the Tang announced that Buddhist statues in the Palace Chapel were to be demolished and replaced by Daoist images.[139] The destruction of Buddhist texts and monasteries, as well as the defrocking of hundreds of monks followed soon after, but the smashing of buddhas in the Palace Chapel signaled from the outset the depths of the emperor's contempt for the "teaching of the icons" and his intention to give whatever resources had been allotted to Buddhism to Daoism instead. In the same way, the replacement of images of buddhas with portraits of Mao signaled a clear transfer of reverence from one symbolic referent to another.

More concretely, the fact that Buddhist statues were often made of valuable metals made them attractive targets for vocal critics of Buddhism. Not only could the state deal a fierce symbolic blow to corrupt monks and superstitious peasants by smashing their most sacred icons, but the state could at the same time fill its coffers with copper, gold, and silver by melting down the bits that remained. At the height of Wuzong's persecution in the ninth century, a decree announced that all Buddhist images made of copper were to be turned over to the state to be minted into coins. Iron images were to be melted down and used for agricultural implements, while images of gold, silver, and other precious metals were to be turned over to the Ministry of Revenue.[140] Archaeological evidence confirms that the primary target of Wuzong's iconoclasm was metal images; wooden statues were left alone.[141] Similarly, in 1958, during the Great Leap Forward, monks were pressured into contributing Buddhist icons to the scrap metal drive.[142] And during the Cultural Revolution, more than 117 tons of metal from old artifacts (including many Buddhist statues) were turned over to forgeries in Beijing to be melted down and put to other uses.[143]

All these incidents presuppose a rejection of the divine power of Buddhist images. Anti-Buddhist memorials to the throne and the edicts they inspired speak matter-of-factly about the destruction of images, nowhere

---

[139] Weinstein, *Buddhism under the T'ang*, p. 125.
[140] Ibid., p. 133.
[141] Luo Zongzhen, "Tangdai Yangzhou simiao yizhi de chubu kaoxi," pp. 359–62.
[142] Welch, *Buddhism under Mao*, p. 163.
[143] Wang Nianyi, *Da dongluan de niandai*, p. 70.

suggesting that images might be inhabited by powerful deities. Those who called for the destruction of Buddhist icons never expressed concern that they might suffer reprisals from the deities contained in the images, though certainly *Buddhists* consistently claimed that this would happen. Nor do figures like Zhou Wudi and Wuzong of the Tang seem to have thought the deities inhabiting Buddhist images *relatively* less powerful. Rather, they dismissed the notion that deities inhabited the images at all. For Buddhism's detractors, Buddhist images were sterile symbols of the Buddhist religion and its accoutrements, and at the same time a treasure of valuable metals wasted on the foolhardy and better put to other purpose.

Thus, while the attention that rulers hostile to Buddhism paid to icons testifies to the importance they attached to them as representative of Buddhist beliefs and practices, as well as to the economic value of icons, none of the incidents I have discussed so far reveal iconophobia in a strong sense of the term. Anti-Buddhist rulers destroyed Buddhist icons along with texts and monasteries as a part of general campaigns to reform or dismantle the Buddhist clergy. They justified orders to destroy Buddhist images with reference to the foreign origins of Buddhism, the degeneracy of the clergy, and the sap that Buddhist institutions put on the economy. The theoretical foundations of these instances of image destruction are only iconoclastic in a superficial sense, in that the perpetrators were not opposed to the notion of erecting icons in itself. One critic of Wudi's plan to destroy Buddhist images was closer to the truth than he realized when he complained that "the images and statues themselves are not to blame."[144] The focus of criticism was always on what the images represented socially and economically rather than the numinous forces they contained; the state seems never to have found disturbing the Buddhist claim that icons were alive with sacred power worthy of veneration. It was a claim to be dismissed or ignored rather than challenged or rooted out.

In contrast, true iconophobia involves a preoccupation with the inadequacy of physical representation of the divine.[145] Jewish, Islamic, and to a lesser extent Christian doctrines all contain strong currents of iconoclastic thought holding that attempts to represent the divine are doomed to failure. More than inadequate, such idols are dangerous, for they may lead an unsuspecting devotee into false worship, whether this means worshipping a heterodox deity or simply expressing sentiments for pieces of clay that should be reserved for something more sublime. Elsewhere these notions have had an enormous impact on material culture, pushing Islamic artisans toward the decorative rather than the anthropomorphic

---

[144] *Guang hongming ji* 8, p. 135c.
[145] Christopher S. Wood, "Iconoclasm and Iconophobia," pp. 450–4.

and stripping Protestant churches of representative art. Even in the United States in the late twentieth century, concerns about the dangers of "realistic" representation of religious figures haunted debates on the nature of religious art in modern American cathedrals.[146]

Similar strands of thought appear in the writings of Buddhist thinkers, who often express reservations about the use of images to convey higher truths. The Buddha is not represented in the earliest Indian Buddhist art. In places where we would expect to see the Buddha, we see instead an empty throne or the Tree of Enlightenment. This was not simply a technical problem: the same sites contain many skillfully executed human figures. It was instead a choice, reflecting a reluctance to represent the Buddha in human form.[147] Evidence from this period is so sparse and so difficult to date that we cannot reconstruct a theology of icons for early Buddhism. The general assumption is that ancient Indian Buddhists did not make images of the Buddha because of philosophical objections, but it is impossible to determine just what these objections might have been or how commonly they were held.

More important for their influence on Chinese Buddhism, Mahāyāna texts both extol the inconceivable merit accruing to those who make and worship Buddhist images and on the contrary stress the illusory nature of Buddhist images. "The icon of the Thus-Come-One is devoid of consciousness and knowledge, and so are all phenomena—they too are devoid of consciousness and knowledge. The icon is just a name [i.e., a conventional referent], and so too are all phenomena—they too are just names. Their inherent nature is empty and non-existent."[148] Or again, as

[146] Colleen McDannell, *Material Christianity*, ch. 6, "Christian Kitsch and the Rhetoric of Bad Taste."

[147] The prevalence of what has been termed *aniconism* in early Buddhist art has been the subject of debate. Susan Huntington has argued that in the majority of cases, the artisans were not attempting to depict scenes from the life of the Buddha with symbols taking the place of the Buddha. Instead, she suggests that the artisans depicted scenes of devotees, well after the Buddha's death, worshipping actual things associated with the Buddha. Further, even in these scenes she considers it a mistake to think of relics of the Buddha (a wheel, a throne, a stupa) as representing the Buddha. They were instead considered powerful objects in their own right. Her thesis has been attacked on two fronts: first with arguments that aniconism was in fact a dominant principle in early Indian Buddhist art, and secondly that objects such as wheels, footprints, and stupas depicted in early Buddhist art were seen as symbols intended to evoke the presence of the Buddha. See Susan L. Huntington, "Early Buddhist Art and the Theory of Aniconism," Michael Rabe's comments in *Art Journal*, pp. 125–7, Vidya Dehejia, "Aniconism and the Multivalence of Emblems," pp. 45–66, and finally Susan L. Huntington, "Aniconism and the Multivalence of Emblems: Another Look," pp. 111–45.

[148] *Da bao ji jing* (Skt. *Mahāratnakūṭa*) 89, *T* no. 310, vol. 11, p. 513c; Zürcher, "Buddhist Art in Medieval China," p. 11.

74 CHAPTER ONE

the bodhisattva Dharmodgata explains to the bodhisattva Sadāprarudita in the *Aṣṭasāhasrikāprajñāpāramitā*:

"After the Buddha's nirvana, someone made an icon in the Buddha's image. When people saw this icon in the Buddha's image, they bowed down and worshipped it. The icon was well-formed and an exceptionally good likeness, no different from the Buddha himself. Everyone made offerings to it of flowers, incense and cloth. Tell me, friend, was the spirit of the Buddha inside of the icon?" Sadāprarudita replied, "It was not inside. Buddhist images are made only so that people can derive merit from them."[149]

Here the sanctity of the image is directly refuted. Whatever the average believer may think, according to this text, Buddha images are reverenced only as symbols of the Buddha, the worship of which creates merit; the spirit of the Buddha is not inside. None of this constitutes a severe form of iconophobia (Sadāprarudita does not call for the destruction of Buddhist images), but such pronouncements did lay the foundation for a persistent mistrust of Buddhist images by Buddhists themselves. One of the concerns among Chinese Buddhists, as among medieval Christians, was that images of the Buddha be executed properly. Above we saw how one Buddhist text emphasizes the essential role of the liturgical specialist for animating icons. Other texts that claim to have been composed in India, but were probably written in China, emphasize the importance of making a statue correctly, with all the necessary marks. A Buddha image must have all of the thirty-two marks of a buddha, insists one text, though in practice this was rarely carried out.[150] Even to neglect to make nostrils for a Buddha image, or to make them too long after the image has been completed, is forbidden.[151] How, such passages seem to suggest, can one accurately represent something as majestic and transcendent as a buddha? Even the slightest iconographic error results in a faulty, improper image.

This same anxiety surfaces in Chinese inscriptions to Buddhist images, which frequently begin with a line or two justifying the need for representation. The inscription on the back of a Buddha image completed in 494 begins by explaining, "The ultimate way is empty and tranquil; its principles do not manifest themselves. Yet, if images are not erected, the true countenance would not be revealed. Without a profusion of words, the far-reaching doctrines would not be clarified."[152] Or again in the in-

[149] *Daoxing banruo jing* (Skt. *Aṣṭasāhasrikāprajñāpāramitā*) 10, T no. 224, vol. 8, p. 476b.
[150] *Jinguan jingfu jing*, cited in *Fayuan zhulin* 33, p. 540a; discussed in Zürcher, "Buddhist Art in Medieval China," p. 8.
[151] *Mulian wen jielü zhong wu bai qingzhong shi*, T no. 1483, vol. 24, pp. 973b and 984c; Zürcher, "Buddhist Art in Medieval China," p. 8.
[152] Now in the Nelson Gallery. Jin Shen, ed., *Zhongguo lidai jinian foxiang tudian*, no. 58.

scription to an image made in 543, "True enlightenment has no words, but without language one cannot interpret its essence. Although manifestations [of the Truth] appear in response to [sublime] stimuli, without images there would be no way to express its appearance. Therefore, for release from suffering, nothing surpasses devotion to images; and for cultivating goodness, there is nothing better than reverence for scriptures and icons."[153] Examples like these could easily be multiplied. Again and again, ultimate truth is juxtaposed with language and icons, both of which were seen as weak symbols, feeble approximations of something infinitely more subtle and profound.

In the late Tang and into the Song, Chan monks picked up on these themes, emphasizing in their writings the limitations of language, images, and other forms of mediation between mundane reality and ultimate truth.[154] In the *Bodhidharma Anthology*, for instance, in response to a question about "false notions," a Chan master replies:

> It is as if in front of the garden at your house there were a great rock. Should you fall asleep on it or sit on it, you would be neither alarmed nor fearful. One day, you decide to make an image, and so you have someone paint a buddha image on it. Now, because your mind interprets it as a buddha, you are afraid to commit a sin [in its presence], and do not dare to sit on it. It is the same rock it originally was; it is your mind that has made of it something else.[155]

This sort of interpretation runs counter to the mainstream understanding of Buddhist images; whether in scripture or in everyday devotional practice, a rock with a buddha image on it was, for most, fundamentally different from a rock without one, because, as we have seen, it was sacred, containing in some sense the presence of the buddha and for that reason warranting respect and, at times, fear. The "mind" of the devotee has nothing to do with it. It was this conventional understanding of images that maverick Chan monks challenged.

This same Chan suspicion of images asserts itself in the *Platform Scripture*, perhaps the most influential Chan text of all. Originally, the story goes, the "Fifth Patriarch" Hongren commissioned a painter to paint illustrations of the *Laṅkāvatāra Sutra*. But when he found a verse by his leading disciple, Shenxiu, on the wall extolling the pristine nature of the mind ("The body is the Bodhi tree, / the mind is like a clear mirror. / At all times we must strive to polish it, / And must not let the dust collect"),

[153] "Bei Wei xiaochang san nian Jiang Boxian zao Mile xiang ji," no. 23253, in the collection of the Fu Ssu-nien Library, Institute of History and Philology, Academia Sinica.

[154] This theme is treated in depth in Faure, *The Rhetoric of Immediacy*.

[155] *Daruma no goroku. Zen no goroku* 1, ed., Yanagida Seizan, p. 226. Cf. Jeffrey L. Broughton, *The Bodhidharma Anthology: The Earliest Records of Zen*, p. 43; Bernard Faure, *Le traité de Bodhidharma: Première anthologie du bouddhisme Chan*, pp. 55, 133.

Hongren changed his mind, announcing to the painter, "I will give you thirty thousand cash. You have come a long distance to do this arduous work, but I have decided not to have the pictures painted after all. It is said in the *Diamond Sutra:* 'All forms everywhere are unreal and false.' It would be best to leave this verse here and to have the deluded ones recite it."[156] The episode demonstrates the connection between the philosophical reservations in Mahāyāna scriptures and more concrete manifestations of these anxieties in Chan narrative. Given the empty, ephemeral nature of material representations, the passage suggests, perhaps it would be better to avoid Buddhist art altogether.

By far the most famous instance of Buddhist iconoclasm is the story of how the Chan monk Danxia Tianran (739–824) burned a Buddha image. According to the earliest account of what was to become a popular, oft-repeated legend,

> While at the Huilin Monastery, on a cold day Danxia burned a wooden buddha to stave off the cold. When the head monk of the monastery criticized him for this, the Master said "I am cremating it, in search of relics."
>
> "It's only wood. How could it contain relics?" asked the head monk.
>
> Danxia replied, "If that's the case, then what are you complaining about?" When he approached Danxia, the head monk's eyebrows suddenly fell out. [Later] someone once asked Grand Master Zhenjue, "It was Danxia who burned the wooden buddha. What did the abbot do wrong?" The Grand Master replied, "The abbot saw only the buddha." The disciple then asked, "And what about Danxia?" "Danxia burned only wood," replied the Grand Master.[157]

If this were an accurate account of a historical incident, we could see in it the elements of true iconoclasm: a monk recognizes the limitations of representation (the Buddha is not, in fact, present in the wood), and responds by destroying the profaning image, not in order to attack Buddhism or to recover precious metal from the image, but because, from a doctrinal standpoint, images are false. But the passage is closer to a parable than it is to a historical account; the point is not that one should go about burning Buddhist images, but rather that one should not look for ultimate truth through external mediation, images included.

Similarly, after calling on his followers to burn images, the prominent Chan monk Linji (d. 866) is said to have explained, "When you can see the emptiness of causes and conditions, the emptiness of the mind, the emptiness of all phenomena, when the mind is every instant completely

---

[156] *Tanjing jiaoshi,* ed., Guo Peng 5, pp. 11–4; English trans. in Philip B. Yampolsky, *The Platform Sutra of the Sixth Patriarch,* p. 130.

[157] *Zu tang ji,* Wu Zeshun, ed., 4, pp. 96–7.

calm, far removed and doing nothing, this is burning the sutras and images."[158] Here again, the call to burn images is a rhetorical ploy. The Chan monk shocks the reader at this apparent attack on a revered object of devotion, only to explain, once the initial shock has subsided, that he is referring to the state of enlightenment in which one recognizes the emptiness of all things. The destruction of "images" is a metaphor for the destruction of delusion. Nowhere do Chan monks seriously call on Buddhists to destroy all Buddhist images. In practice, Chan monks continued to stock their monasteries with images, and pilgrims continued to flock to these images and to make offerings to them. Patrons continued to commission statues and paintings in Chan monasteries, and monks continued to use them in monastic ritual. More telling still, even portraits of Chan monks were often considered to contain sacred power and were prayed to for miracles.[159] Chan iconoclasm never made the leap from a rhetorical trope to a concerted program dedicated to removing images from Buddhist practice.

Just such a leap from philosophical speculation to the destruction of actual images was made not by Buddhist monks but by Confucian thinkers and statesmen. Confucian thinkers beginning with Zhu Xi (1130–1200) questioned the practice of representing Confucius and his disciples with statues in Confucian shrines. Fifteenth-century scholar Qiu Jun returned to this issue and composed an essay attacking the practice and suggesting that images in Confucian shrines be replaced by spirit tablets. Images, he argued, are inherently inferior because they can never perfectly represent the figures they imitate, suggesting to the viewer imperfections that did not exist in the sages themselves. Significantly, both Zhu Xi and Qiu Jun recognized, quite accurately, that the practice of representing Confucius in a shrine as a three-dimensional statue was the result of Buddhist influence; ancient, pre-Buddhist Chinese texts make no reference to any such practice. Unlike the Buddhist case, the philosophical and historical objections of Confucian thinkers eventually translated into action; for images were destroyed or removed from Confucian shrines in the sixteenth century, an indignity Buddhist images were spared.[160]

These final comments on the limitations of iconoclasm in Chan underline the primacy of the icon in Chinese Buddhism. That is, while the ele-

---

[158] *Zhenzhou Linji Huizhao chanshi yulu*, T no. 1985, vol. 47, p. 502b; English trans. from Burton Watson, *The Zen Teachings of Master Lin-chi*, p. 75. Commenting on the Danxia story, the thirteenth-century Japanese monk Dōgen specifically explained that the story was not meant to be taken literally. See Heinrich Dumoulin, *Zen Buddhism: A History, vol. 2: Japan*, p. 99.

[159] Foulk and Sharf, "On the Ritual Use of Ch'an Portraiture in Medieval China."

[160] See Deborah A. Sommer, "Images into Words: Ming Confucian Iconoclasm," pp. 1–24, and Huang Jinxing (Chin-shing Huang), "Huixiang yu shengshiji," pp. 1–8.

ments of a "hard iconophobia"—particularly the belief that images distract from more profound soteriological goals—were present in Mahāyāna scriptures and revived in Chan writings, such pronouncements always remained abstract and tentative. We find no Chinese equivalent to the removal of icons from churches that took place during the Reformation in the belief that worship of such images constituted idolatry.[161] And when emperors hostile to Buddhism or twentieth-century rationalists called for the destruction of Buddhist images, it was as a more general campaign to eradicate a pernicious foreign religion, or to stamp out superstition, rather than to salvage a higher Buddhist truth from desecration. The difference between Chinese Buddhist and European Christian iconoclasm most likely stems from the different religious milieus out of which the two religions sprang. Early on, Christians were concerned to distinguish their worship of icons from the practices of Roman pagans for whom icon worship was central.[162] The same can be said of attitudes toward religious art in Judaism and Islam, both of which were surrounded by strong divergent traditions of devotion to images. The same dynamic crops up in post-Tang China, when Confucian thinkers attempted to define their doctrines and practices against those of a thriving Buddhism. In contrast, when Buddhism entered China in the first centuries of the Common Era, because images were not commonly used in ancient Chinese religion, Buddhism was defined in part precisely by its use of images rather than its opposition to them. Recall the epithet "Teaching of the Icons" used for centuries to describe Buddhism in China. Hence, for Buddhists to attack religious images in general was to weaken one of the areas in which Buddhism far excelled its competitors.

Once we set aside the subtle philosophical poses of a handful of Chan monks and occasional misgivings of the more erudite exegetes, Chinese Buddhists in general have always accepted the sacred character of icons. From the earliest Buddhist texts translated into Chinese until modern times, Buddhists have encouraged devotees to make offerings to Buddhist images. Conversely, whatever their detractors say, Chinese Buddhists have always held that those who destroy Buddhist images risk reprisal, whether it be the vengeance of an angry icon or assignment to hell after death.[163]

---

[161] Although I here focus on differences between Buddhist and Christian attitudes toward icons, the similarities—a belief that icons were inhabited by spirits, the means of consecrating them, and the controversies they provoked—are striking. For an overview of icons in the West, see Belting, *Likeness and Presence.*

[162] Belting, Ibid., p. 7.

[163] For an important early text on the merit of making Buddhist images, see *Zuofo xingxiang jing* (Skt. *Tathāgatapratibimbapratiṣṭhānuśaṃsā*) *T* no. 692, vol. 16; English trans. by Robert H. Sharf in Donald S. Lopez Jr., ed., *Religions of China in Practice*, pp. 261–7; and *Zeng yi ahan jing* (*Ekottarāgama*) 28, p. 708b. For injunctions against destroying im-

For Buddhist devotees, images were revered not only as symbols of great deities but as repositories of sacred power. Comparison to other religions discloses that, in general, this is the norm.[164]

I have paid little attention to the aesthetics of Buddhist images not only because my focus in this chapter is on the sacred character of icons but also because in the creation and use of Buddhist images, aesthetic considerations were in general secondary to liturgical ones.[165] One can find scattered references to people who appreciated Buddhist images for their beauty, divorced from their function as devotional objects, but these were rare exceptions. It is only in modern times that this tendency to consider Buddhist images valuable, *even if they do not contain sacred power,* has come to the fore. During the Cultural Revolution, quick-thinking local caretakers of Buddhist images argued with Red Guards (itching to knock off a few Buddha heads) that ancient images represented not the superstition of the "four olds," but rather "cultural relics" (*wenwu*) valuable as aesthetic artifacts and useful for understanding the past. This sort of defense was entirely new and would have seemed quite foreign to Buddhists in premodern times.

The charge of "superstition" still presupposes that images have at least a quasireligious function. Now, even this charge has faded, and the chief forces threatening Buddhist images are forgery, commercial theft, and vandalism, none of which involve a respect for the numinous power of icons or a belief that they are in any way alive. We could lament this modern development as another sad chapter in the history of the disenchantment of the world, but we need not do so. Vandalism and theft aside, the aestheticization of Buddhist icons allows even those who do not accept their sacred character or participate in Buddhist ritual to derive pleasure from them and to use them in new and interesting ways.

More in keeping with the theme of this book, the removal of some Buddhist images to museums and a string of antisuperstition campaigns have not overwhelmed the traditional devotional function that Buddhist images have played in Chinese society since their introduction two thousand years ago: the pious continue to contribute to the manufacture of Bud-

---

ages, see *Zheng fa nian chu jing* (Skt. *Saddharmasmṛtyupasthānasūtra*) 15, *T* no. 721, vol. 17, p. 85c.

[164] Freedberg, *The Power of Images.*

[165] Here, again, there are exceptions. Even in Buddhist ritual, not all images were believed to contain sacred power. For instance, in the Inner Altar of the *shuilu* ritual, placards were believed to contain sacred power, while the paintings adorning the walls behind them were not. See Daniel B. Stevenson, "Text, Image, and Transformation in the History of the *Shuilu fahui,* the Buddhist Rite for the Deliverance of Creatures of Water and Land," in Weidner, ed., *Cultural Intersections,* p. 58.

dhist images, to make offerings to them, and to believe that their supplications are heard by a sacred presence inside the images before them.

Conclusion

With this overview of Chinese attitudes toward relics and Buddhist images, we can return to inquiries into the nature and function of sacred
objects raised in the introduction equipped with a more nuanced understanding of how the numinous power of sacred objects was perceived
over the course of Chinese Buddhist history. In the case of relic pellets
(*sheli*), sacred power was vague and impersonal, a living source of light
that could appear from nowhere and at times reproduce itself. Devotees
occasionally perceived other objects such as particular Buddhist scriptures, rosaries, or other belongings of holy figures as having this same
power, but these objects were not accorded sacred power as consistently
as relics were. This perception of the power of relics did not spring from
a more general belief in a sacred mana-like force present in all things; only
a very limited number of objects were conceived of in this way.

In the case of mummies and icons, animating power took the form of
human attributes, as images wept, bled, perspired, threatened, and complained. These attributes were not necessarily those of the figures depicted: some no doubt thought the image of a certain bodhisattva to be
inhabited by that particular bodhisattva, but accounts of miracles reveal
that, in general, icons were given their own personalities. For this reason,
familiarity with accounts of the life of Śākyamuni often contribute little
to understanding a particular statue of the Buddha known to have been,
say, effective at curing illness, or to have taken vengeance on one who did
not show it sufficient respect. Each image, in other words, has a history
of its own, distinct from the figure it was made to represent.

This distinction between the personal presence in objects that resemble
human beings and the impersonal presence in more abstract objects indicates that the distinction between what Marett termed "animatism" and
"animism" was not the result of stages of evolutionary development, but
grew instead from the way in which the appearance of certain objects
molds perception. It was in part the poorly defined appearance of relics
(bits of teeth and bone that were not supposed to look *like* anything) that
accounts for their peculiar visual allure. Accounts of the activities of icons
are more prevalent than those of relics, and icons make for more compelling characters in miracle stories. Yet icons were seldom scrutinized as
intensely as relics were, as generation after generation of devotee and
skeptic examined Buddhist relics in an attempt to determine just what
they were.

Whether in images or relics, the power inhering in objects was almost always thought to be benign, though sacred objects could on occasion turn vindictive and dangerous if threatened or treated with disrespect. In fact, the power of images and relics was often considered more a subject of idle curiosity—something to be marveled at in one's leisure or discussed among friends—rather than a terrible source of overpowering awe.

The notion that certain Buddhist objects contained sacred power was consistently challenged by opponents of Buddhism and the occasional skeptic. They argued the point on various fronts, questioning whether Buddhism, a foreign and hence inferior teaching, really had access to supernatural powers, as, for example, in Han Yu's critique of the bone of the Buddha. Although not explicit, the same dismissal of the belief that Buddhist images contained mighty powers is inherent in repeated campaigns by the state to destroy Buddhist statues, whether as a symbol of contempt for Buddhist teachings or for the more down-to-earth desire for precious metals. While such dismissive attitudes certainly had a quantitative impact on the history of Buddhist sacred objects—persecutions in premodern times and especially in the twentieth century resulted in the destruction of countless images—they did not undermine the belief in sacred objects of monks or Buddhist devotees, who persistently accepted the divine nature of certain objects and promoted devotion to them. The same holds true for suspicion of the historical accuracy of relic claims, that is, whether certain relics were in fact the remains of the Buddha rather than coral, glass, or the bones of some other figure or animal. Even today, when reliable knowledge of the history of Buddhism is more readily accessible than ever before, few within the Buddhist community openly challenge the authenticity of even the most dubious Buddhist relics.

Similarly, while critiques of icons and relics were common among outsiders, few Buddhists ever openly questioned the belief that sacred power adhered in certain things. Strains of Buddhist thought that could have been harnessed to eliminate the worship of relics and icons were employed in passing in the rhetoric of some monks, but were never applied to Buddhist practice systematically or used to fuel a social movement against these practices. It is, perhaps, for this reason that iconoclastic campaigns by the state created only temporary setbacks for cults to Buddhist images and relics; when the external pressure faded, relic and image production have always quickly returned to previous levels.

In other areas, belief in the sacred power within these objects did influence behavior. Images and relics were believed to be capable of effecting miracles, most often involving healing. Accounts of miracles associated with sacred Buddhist things were also useful for the cause of proselytizing; for they gave concrete proof of the extraordinary qualities of the Buddhist religion, evoking a sense of awe, wonder, and fear. This being said, if when discussing sacred objects we limit ourselves to the beliefs and psychology of the pious devotee imagined in a private devotional context of a one-on-one encounter with an icon or relic, we miss much of the story of the impact of Buddhist objects on Chinese culture. Chinese rulers consistently drew on the widespread belief in the sacred power of certain Buddhist objects and the respect these beliefs inspired. By commissioning monumental Buddhist art and distributing numinous relics, rulers signaled both their own intimate connections with sacred power and, at the same time, on a more mundane level, demonstrated their ability to muster material resources at a level of extravagance that no one else could match.

A similar dynamic was at work at lower social strata. The head of a wealthy family, by sponsoring construction of a stupa to house a sacred relic or commissioning an image, could, in addition to acquiring religious benefits from association with a holy object, at the same time assert his position as a leader of the community. Monasteries too benefited from possession of sacred objects, the focus of Buddhist pilgrimage and devotion, both directly through the revenue exhibiting such objects brought in and less directly for the general prestige accorded monasteries known to have a famous relic or a particularly efficacious statue. Critics of Buddhism railed against the waste in expenditure on lavish images and extravagant ceremonies for spurious relics, but within the Buddhist community there was no sense that there was anything wrong in groups and individuals deriving worldly benefits from cults to sacred objects as long as these benefits were confined to laypeople or the monastic community as a whole and did not include the enrichment of individual monks.

In sum, in addition to the personal, emotional world of the individual devotee, the material culture of Buddhist images and relics encompassed a wide array of elements and relationships, including negotiations between patron, monk, nun, and artisan, the public display of sacred objects and the role such objects played in the larger community, the economics of pilgrimage, and the manipulation of sacred objects for political ends. When placed in this context, the allure of the sacred appears less mysterious than the first generations of scholars of religious studies would have us believe. There is, however, still room for much puzzlement and speculation. Beyond more readily understandable cravings for social prestige and physical well-being, there seems to be a more complex psychological dynamic at work in the desire to depict divinities; across cultural and geographic boundaries, images have always had a power over us, disturbing us with their cold, penetrating stare. Relics too continue to thwart simple explanations, and bones of the dead continue to trouble and fascinate us, eliciting psychological and physical responses that at once reveal our aspirations and our anxieties.

Chapter Two

SYMBOLISM

I MAGES in stone reliefs, tomb paintings, and burial goods of the Eastern Han (A.D. 25–220) provide us with our first glimpse of the impact of Buddhism on Chinese material culture. Most of these images and artifacts are firmly rooted in Han iconography. The walls of Han tombs are typically painted with images of Xi Wangmu, "Queen Mother of the West," and Dong Wanggong, "King Father of the East." Burial goods discovered in these tombs include objects such as the "Money Tree"—a traditional Chinese burial object—and mirrors decorated with dragons.[1] All of this is quintessentially Chinese, and betrays no trace of foreign influence. Embedded in this forest of symbols, however, are images that disclose the entry of Buddhism to China. For instance, two Eastern Han tombs in Sichuan include images of a figure holding up his right hand with palm facing forward. The figure has a protuberance on his head which is in turn surrounded by a disc. Those familiar with Buddhist iconography will immediately recognize the figure as a buddha: his hand makes the gesture of "fearlessness" known as the *abhaya mudrā* (Ch. *wuweiyin*), the bump on his head is an *uṣṇīṣa*, one of the essential marks of a buddha, and the ring around his head a halo, a sign of a buddha's sacred aura. All are distinctive iconographic features of a buddha.

Similarly, the wall paintings of a Han-era tomb at Helingeer in Inner Mongolia contain a white elephant and a depiction of ball-shaped objects heaped on a plate. The elephant in itself need not indicate Buddhist influence. But a common episode in the Buddha's biography is his conception, which took place when his mother dreamt of a white elephant, and a line in the "Rhapsody on the Western Capital" (*Xijing fu*) by the Han poet Zhang Heng confirms that this story had indeed reached China in the Eastern Han, suggesting that the elephant may have carried Buddhist connotations for the tomb owner. The balls on the plate are easier to identify as Buddhist, since they are marked with the inscription "*sheli*," or "relics."[2] All such images can be interpreted symbolically, that is, as standing

---

[1] For a summary of early Chinese Buddhist art, see Wu Hung, "Buddhist Elements in Early Chinese Art," and more recently Rhie, *Early Buddhist Art*.

[2] Wu Hung, Ibid., pp. 264–73.

for something else. The elephant stands for the Buddha and, more specifically, for his miraculous birth. The relics on a plate refer to the Buddha's nirvana and suggest his continuous presence in the world. Evidence like this reveals that by the end of the Eastern Han, Buddhism had begun to impact the Chinese symbolic repertoire. When, however, we look at the full panoply of religious images at the end of the Han and try to pin down just which images were Buddhist, and in what sense they were Buddhist, the picture begins to blur.

In an article on Buddhist elements in Han art, Wu Hung suggests that in these tombs, Buddhist images and motifs are so well incorporated into non-Buddhist iconography that it may be misleading to refer to these symbols as "Buddhist" at all; that is, the artisans who made them, and probably the owners of the tombs as well, may have read the symbols as vaguely auspicious, rather than as belonging to a distinct system of belief.[3] Elephants, relics, and haloed figures may have been more lucky charms than indexes to episodes in the life of the Buddha and the doctrines inherent in his biography. Setting aside the delicate question of whether we moderns should classify such images and objects as Buddhist, the question of the attitudes of late Han people to such images is, considering the paucity of Buddhist material for the Han, as difficult to answer as it is intriguing.

In subsequent centuries, in the Six Dynasties period, we are on firmer ground when attempting to assign self-conscious Buddhist symbolism to images in tombs. Given the wealth of Buddhist literature in circulation at the time, as well as the number of clearly identifiable Buddhist statuettes from the period, we can with confidence identify haloed figures on tomb tiles as buddhas, and assume that they were seen as such by most people of the day. Similarly, figures holding lotus flowers are almost certainly Buddhist devotees.[4] As we will see below, the identification of such imagery necessarily involves two of the key issues of iconology: the origins of symbols and the travails of their subsequent interpretation. It is one thing to identify the origins of a Chinese halo as Buddhist; it is another to determine the meaning of this symbol for a particular Chinese artisan, or to a particular devotee. Just as important as the meaning of a given symbol is the process by which one interpretation of a symbol predominates while others fade through neglect, accident, or suppression.

To continue with our overview of the introduction of Buddhist symbolism to China, in the Tang, along with new artistic techniques intro-

---

[3] Wu Hung, Ibid., p. 273. Rhie disagrees, arguing that depictions of the Buddha's nirvana and of a jataka tale at Kongwangshan must at some level have been seen as distinctly Buddhist rather than just generally auspicious. *Early Buddhist Art*, pp. 44–5.

[4] Wu Xiang, "Jiangsu Liuchao huaxiangzhuan yanjiu," *Dongnan wenhua*, vol. 115 (1997.1), pp. 72–96.

duced with Buddhism, such as illusionistic shading,[5] Buddhist symbolism became increasingly widespread, as symbols like the swastika and the Dharma wheel became well known. At times Buddhist symbolism in China reached great heights of complexity and sophistication, as in elaborate paintings of *maṇḍalas* or, for instance, images of the "Thousand-eyed Thousand-armed" Guanyin, in which each hand of the multiarmed bodhisattva contains a different implement. Such images were the subject of detailed description in ritual manuals which provided authoritative interpretations for the erudite monks who read them.

But when discussing the emergence of Buddhist symbols in China, we need not confine ourselves to the symbolism of Buddhist painting and sculpture. Various ritual implements, commonly used in day-to-day Buddhist liturgy, came to China laden with symbolism, much of it known only to liturgical specialists, but some of it known to interested laypeople as well. Even more prevalent were the articles used by monks and nuns, most of which were to some extent imbued with symbolism as these objects themselves came to represent the monastic ideal.

Symbolism pervades Buddhist ritual and art. Objects invested with symbolism became the locus of devotion for monks, nuns, and laypeople alike and a source for philosophical speculation and scholarly debate. Less obviously, Buddhist symbolic objects served as sources of identification. A monk could be readily identified as such by the garments he wore, just as an official was recognized by his cap, gown, and insignia of office; a layperson carrying a rosary could be identified as a Buddhist, just as a soldier was recognized by the sword hung at his waist.

Some Buddhist motifs, such as the long ears of a sage (originally of a buddha), were well incorporated into the Chinese symbolic vocabulary, while others, such as *mudrās* (symbolic hand gestures), remained distinctly Buddhist. Many objects and motifs fell somewhere in between, taking on the meaning ascribed to them by different social groups in different circumstances. Below, I focus on a number of portable objects that were invested with symbolic significance. Like most artifacts, the meaning of most of these objects was not inherent in their physical properties. Further, their iconographic value was never entirely fixed; that is, they meant different things at different times, and can best be understood in the context of the historical process of their development.[6] The first set of objects I discuss below ("the monastic uniform") was chiefly the preserve of monks, although these objects did earn a place in the minds of all Chinese as a part of the image of the monk. This section is followed by a dis-

[5] James Cahill, *Chinese Painting*, p. 15.

[6] For a general discussion of the issues involved, see Danny Miller, "Artifacts as Products of Human Categorisation Processes," pp. 17–25.

cussion of objects that, in addition to their value for monks, were also important to laypeople and even to those who were not Buddhists.

As we trace the introduction and development of Buddhist symbols in China, an overarching concern with the sinicization of Buddhism—how foreign ideas were adapted to Chinese customs and concerns—is too crude to be useful. As we will see, many objects underwent shifts in meaning not just from India to China but also from monk to layman, from one period to the next, and even from one group of non-Buddhists to another. It is the opportunity Buddhist symbols provide us for understanding this curious mechanism of interpretation and influence that is, I think, ultimately the most interesting aspect of the history of Buddhist symbols in China. But let us step back for now from the long-term trends in the history of Buddhist symbols and begin with the specific case of the symbolism of the monastic uniform. None of these objects are fundamentally symbolic: they all served functions that extended beyond the concrete expression of abstractions. Yet, all are examples of objects whose symbolism was discussed at length over the course of the history of Buddhism in China and illustrate that symbolism was important for the way many Buddhist objects were understood.

THE MONASTIC UNIFORM

In China, as elsewhere, the Buddhist monk was defined in part by his beliefs, his writings, and his oratory. But just as important to the monk's identity was the way he looked. Even when seen from a distance, monks and nuns in China have always been readily differentiated from other types of people. The most visible characteristic distinguishing monks and nuns from other sorts of men and women is the shaven pate. In traditional China, long hair was always the fashion, whether among men or women; except for monks and nuns, only criminals had shaven heads. Ancient and medieval medical texts reveal that long, shiny black hair was considered an important sign of health, and hair loss, regardless of one's age or state of health, a disturbing indication of old age and infirmity.[7] Hence, the decision to take the tonsure was a significant act of renunciation with clear social repercussions.

In similar fashion, other aspects of the monk's uniform were also symbolic of renunciation.[8] Extant versions of the monastic regulations reflect

---

[7] Xiao Fan (Hsiao Fan), "Changsheng sixiang he yu toufa xiangguan de yangsheng fangshu," pp. 671–726.

[8] For a discussion of the marks of monastic renunciation as reflected in Chinese Buddhist hagiography, see John Kieschnick, *The Eminent Monk: Buddhist Ideals in Medieval Chinese Hagiography*, pp. 16–32.

an ideal in which the monastic uniform (what a monk carried about with him) mirrored monastic property, since the ideal monk was only to own a few basic necessities, all of which could be carried with him during his life of wandering. The most common such set of possessions consisted of six objects, usually given as the three articles of clothing making up a monk's garment, the alms bowl, the water strainer (used to ensure that the monk does not consume insects with his drinking water), and a small rug on which the monk could sit.[9] The monastic regulations are not consistent on this point. Another list excludes the sitting rug but adds a needle, a razor, and thread—making for eight items. Yet another, apparently later list, adds a ring-staff, a censor, images of bodhisattvas, and a number of other items, bringing the number up to eighteen.[10] Careful study of the archaeological record reveals that even this expanded list represents only an ideal: Indian monks in fact possessed all manner of personal property.[11] In China, vast amounts of textual and archaeological evidence show that there too monks owned private property—from books and images, to gold, slaves, and even landed estates.[12] But regardless of the shared wealth of the monastery or even how much personal property individual monks possessed, the elements of a plain monastic uniform consisting of a few simple objects consistently played an important *symbolic* role in the life of the monk and the perception of the monk by those outside the Order. Below I focus on the two most symbolically prominent monastic possessions: the robe and the alms bowl.

Robes

The monk's clothing has always been an emblem of the profession, whether in ancient India or China. When biographers of Chinese monks note their subject's decision to "leave the family" and become a monk, they do so with the phrase "he cut off his hair and donned the black robes of the monk." Had it not been for the distinctive array of religious professionals in ancient India, or for the persistent attitudes of the Chinese toward clothing and nudity, the robe would not have acquired such importance.

Founders of the Buddhist monastic order had many options when determining proper attire for monks, ranging from elaborate gowns to no clothing at all. In ancient India, some Jains went completely naked—a

[9] Hirakawa Akira, *A History of Indian Buddhism from Śākyamuni to Early Mahāyāna*, p. 68; Foguang dacidian bianxiu weiyuan hui, ed., *Foguang da cidian* p. 1274.

[10] Kawaguchi Kōfū, "Kesa-shi ni okeru Dōsen no chii—ryokubutsu o chū shin ni," pp. 98–100.

[11] Schopen, *Bones, Stones, and Buddhist Monks*, pp. 3–5.

[12] Gernet, *Buddhism in Chinese Society*, pp. 79–93.

practice stalwart Jain ascetics have continued to this day—while other ritual specialists were expected to wear garments of great refinement.[13] The *Treatise on the Perfection of Great Wisdom*—a text now available only in Chinese but probably translated or at least based on a medieval Indian original—reflects the predominant Buddhist position on clothing in medieval India when it states: "The white-robed [brahmans] for the sake of pleasure keep various sorts of garments. In contrast, false religionists in the name of asceticism go shamelessly naked. It is for this reason that the disciples of the Buddha reject both extremes and practice a middle-way."[14] Passages like this disclose the need for distinction, for marking out a place for the monk in the social hierarchy of ancient India. Indeed, one of the reasons the monastic regulations give for forbidding monks to bathe naked was that they would risk being mistaken for non-Buddhist ascetics rather than Buddhist monks.[15] In other words, in India the monk's robe was a sign of prudent asceticism, placing the Buddhist monk neatly between the well-dressed brahman and the naked Jain.[16]

In China, the distinction between the Buddhist monk and the radical ascetic was never important. Chinese had from very early on shunned nudity, and there was no ascetic movement in China comparable to those in India strong enough to challenge the taboo. The prominent seventh-century Chinese monk Daoxuan gave a more immediate justification for clothing in his influential guidebook for monastic life, *Notes on Practice,* with the words: "As our body abides amidst the entanglements of the world, we must attend to comportment, and for shielding oneself from dust and stain, nothing surpasses clothing."[17] Later in the same text, a compendium of quotations from various versions of the monastic regulations organized by theme, Daoxuan returns to the essential use of clothing as a shield from the cold. For Chinese monks like Daoxuan, clothing

---

[13] See Paul Dundas, *The Jains.*

[14] *Da zhi du lun* 68, p. 538b.

[15] Mohan Wijayaratna, *Buddhist Monastic Life According to the Texts of the Theravāda Tradition,* p. 43.

[16] The history of the Christian priest's robe is similarly marked by a concern to avoid, on the one hand, the shabby garments of the destitute and, on the other, the fine garments of the decadent. See Louis Trichet, *Le costume du clergé: ses origines et son évolution en France d'après les réglements de l'Eglise.*

[17] *Sifenlü shanfan buque xingshichao* C1, *T* no. 1804, vol. 40, p. 104c. For a carefully annotated version of Daoxuan's discussion of clothing in this text along with a modern Japanese translation, see Kawano Satoshi et al., "Sō-i shiryō kenkyū: *Shibunritsu gyōji shō ni-i sōbetsu-hen hombun(shō) narabi ni yakkai ,*" *Bukkyōbunka* vol. 18 (1987), pp. 85–114, and vol. 19 (1988), pp. 74–86. For a concise survey of Daoxuan's views on monastic clothing, see Toriimoto Yukiyo, "Nanzan Dōsen no kesha kan ni tsuite, pp. 185–8. The prominent sixth-century monk Zhiyi made a similar case for the practical necessity of monastic clothing in his *Mohe zhiguan* 4, *T* no. 1911, vol. 46, p. 41c.

was taken for granted; the possibility of a naked clergy was not entertained. But while Chinese monks did not, like their Indian counterparts, have to negotiate a delicate balance between worldly decadence and excessive ascetic zeal, they still needed to distinguish themselves from other figures, religious and secular, in Chinese society.[18]

A biography of the great eighth-century exegete Zhanran describes his decision to abandon a promising career as an official for the life of a monk as a change of clothing, saying simply that he "removed his scholar's robe and registered as a monk."[19] In a similar case, the Tang monk Zhengong (740–829), after passing the civil service examinations, was on the verge of beginning a career as an official, "but before he had donned the official robes of office, he fell into a discussion of profound principles with a sramana, and decided to wear instead the robes of a monk."[20] Both passages presume the existence of an established rhetoric of clothing in China meant to mirror the social hierarchy; monks were one category of people among many—official, soldier, peasant—each marked by a distinctive uniform. Certainly there was more to distinguish a monk from a scholar-official than clothing, but when searching for the most concise symbol to mark the distinction, writers turned to the robes they wore. Just as a monk's robe—in Chinese jiasha from the Sanskrit kāṣāya—distinguished him from an official, variations in the robe also distinguished different types of monks. In India, monks belonging to different schools wore robes of different colors, ranging from red and ochre to blue and black, and in medieval China monks from different regions were recognized by the color of their robes—pitch black in the Jiangnan region, brown in the area around Kaifeng, and so on.[21]

In short, the monk's robes were just as important as a mark of distinction in China as they were in India. Chinese monks firmly wed to their Buddhist identity did not give up their robes without reluctance, and we have many accounts of monks who risked persecution rather than surrender their robes. Conversely, for enemies of Buddhism the monk's robe became a locus of criticism and ridicule. A telling case of the dangers of wearing the monastic robe is seen in the persecution of Buddhism during the reign of Wuzong of the Tang (841–46). In China, monks in general

[18] Bernard Faure's "Quand l'habit fait le moine: The Symbolism of the Kāṣāya in Sōtō Zen," pp. 335–69, in addition to providing analysis of the symbolism of the monk's robe in Japan, also contains useful information on the robe in India and China. I am indebted to this article for much of what follows.

[19] Song gaoseng zhuan 6, p. 739b.

[20] Ibid. 11, p. 775b.

[21] I draw here on the tenth-century work Da Song sengshilüe, T no. 2126, vol. 54, pp. 237c–38a. See also, Kieschnick, The Eminent Monk, pp. 29–32. In China, after the tenth century, the color of robes was gradually standardized. Now Chinese monks usually wear black or gray robes.

wore black robes; indeed, from at least the Tang on, monks were often referred to simply as the "black-robed ones" (ziyi).[22] During Wuzong's reign, because of a prophecy that "blacked-robed emperors" would one day rule the land, the color of monks' robes was cited as reason enough for the complete elimination of the monastic order.[23] Imperial representatives continued to pay particular attention to the robes of the monk, ensigns of the monastic life, in the persecution that followed. One imperial edict announced:

> The black clothing of the monks and the nuns of the land who have been returned to lay life should all be collected and burned by their respective prefectures and subprefectures. It is feared that the officials . . . have used their power to hide [monks and nuns] in their private homes and that *in secret [monks and nuns] wear their black robes.* These should be ruthlessly confiscated and all burned, and the matter reported to the throne. If after the burning there be monks or nuns who wear their black robes and have not given them all up and there be those who protect [monks and nuns] at the time of the investigation, they shall be sentenced to death in accordance with the Imperial edict.[24]

Given the importance attached to the monk's robe even by those outside the clergy, it is no wonder that leading Chinese monks devoted considerable attention to prescribing the proper form monastic robes should take. In theory, this was not a question of innovation but rather of correct interpretation of the admonitions of the Buddha, as recorded in the scriptures, which contained ample information on the robes of the monk. The ideal monastic garment propagated in Indian Buddhist texts is comprised of three robes: a rectangular piece of cloth wrapped around the waist so that it covers the lower body, another rectangular garment draped over the left shoulder, and a third rectangular garment draped over the other two (figure 4).[25] The inner robe (Skt. *antarvāsa*) was worn at all times, and could be worn without the other garments when working inside the monastery on hot days. The upper garment (*uttarāsanga*) was worn on most other occasions. The outer robe (*saṃghāṭi*) was to be worn when in public during alms rounds or when in the presence of high officials.[26]

---

[22] For examples, see Hanyu dacidian bianzuan chu, ed., *Hanyu dacidian,* s.v. "ziyi," p. 928.

[23] Reischauer, *Ennin's Travels in T'ang China,* p. 245.

[24] *Nittō guhō junrei gyōki* 4, p. 493; Reischauer, *Ennin's Diary,* pp. 384–5.

[25] See A. B. Griswold, "Prolegomena to the Study of the Buddha's Dress in Chinese Sculpture," pp. 85–130.

[26] Griswold refers to the three robes as respectively "undercloth," "robe," and "shawl." I follow instead Chang Kun's translations. See Chang, *A Comparative Study of the Kaṭhinavastu.*

FIG. 4. The three robes.

Despite the simplicity of the basic design—three rectangular pieces of cloth—the rules governing the composition of the robes are surprisingly complex. The outer robe, for instance, was made up of variously five, seven, nine, thirteen, fifteen, or more strips of cloth, with each strip divided into several segments (figure 5). Different texts provided different guidelines for the number and size of the strips. The *Dharmaguptaka-vinaya*, for instance, recommended a robe of five vertical strips (*tiao*) made up of ten square patches (*ge*), though it also allowed for robes of up to nineteen strips.[27] The *Sarvāstivādavinaya* divides robes into three types, with the "lowest grade" having nine, eleven, or thirteen strips; the "medium grade" fifteen, seventeen, or nineteen; and the "highest grade" twenty-one, twenty-three, or twenty-five, though the *Dharmaguptaka-vinaya* differs on this point, stating that a robe made of more than nineteen strips is unlawful.[28] There were also careful prescriptions for how to sew the hem of each robe, including the size of the hem and the type of stitching to be used. The patches and strips were not to be sewn with

[27] *Sifenlü*, 40, p. 855b; and 43, p. 878a.
[28] *Sapoduopinipiposha* (Skt.*Sarvāstivādavinayavibhāṣa*), 4, *T* no. 1440, vol. 23, p. 527b; *Sifenlü*, Ibid.

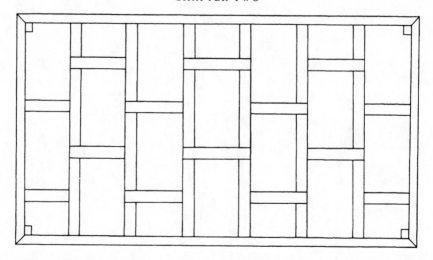

FIG. 5. The Outer Garment. This robe is comprised of seven strips (*tiao*) and twenty-one patches (*ge*).

straight lines, but rather in either a squared zigzag known as the horse-teeth stitch (*machi*) or in a triangular zigzag known as the bird's-foot stitch (*niaozu*).[29] The robe was to be made of heavy, coarse cloth donated by patrons in a special ceremony held at fixed times.[30] By the middle of the Tang dynasty, all the sets of the monastic regulations that were to affect Chinese monks had been translated into Chinese and were widely available, providing ample material for the investigations of learned monks.

For Chinese monks looking for a quick summary of the proper robe, works like Daoxuan's *Notes on Practice* provided a handy collection of prescriptions from the various monastic regulations on exactly how the robe was to be made. Yet even Daoxuan's work did not resolve the knottiest problems in the proper composition of the robe, and controversies continued to rage over colors, hemstitching and fabric. The Song monk Yuanzhao (1048–1116), for instance, defended Daoxuan's stance on the use of silk against a more recent detractor, while Zanning (919–1001) complained of Chinese monks who wore robes dyed pitch-black (*hei*)—a color he claimed was unsupported by the monastic regulations—rather than the more orthodox "gray-black" (*zi*).[31] In sum, much ink was spilled

[29] Ibid.

[30] For a careful study of texts in various languages describing this ceremony, see Chang, *A Comparative Study of the Kaṭhinavastu.*

[31] *Fozhi biqiu liuwu tu*, *T* no. 1900, vol. 45, p. 898a; *Da Song sengshilüe* A, p. 238a.

over what in retrospect seems at first the most trivial of matters. Of course, the fact that monks studied the composition of the robes with such intense scrutiny tells us that for them these matters were far from trivial. The impetus behind all of this meticulous attention to detail was more than a need for distinction. Nor can it be explained by an even more nebulous "force of tradition." To understand the full significance of the robe, we must appreciate its symbolism.

THE ROBE AS ASCETIC SYMBOL

The arrangement of three robes probably derived from indigenous Indian clothing, but monks were quick to discover specifically Buddhist symbolic implications in the number 3. The three robes, one monk insisted, represented abandonment of the "three poisons" (greed, anger, and ignorance), with the inner garment representing the elimination of "the greed of the body," the upper garment the "anger of the mouth," and the outer garment the "ignorance of the mind."[32] Elsewhere, the robes are said to symbolize buddhas of the "three times" (past, present, and future).[33] Or, with the monk's rug symbolizing the stupa, the monk's robe symbolizes the *dharmakāya,* or ultimate aspect of a buddha.[34] But there is an arbitrary quality to such pronouncements. Given the prevalence of numbers in Buddhist writings, it was a simple matter for a Buddhist exegete of even modest erudition to assign symbolic equivalents to the three robes when attempting to explain why monks wore what they wore. There is nothing inherent in the robe that suggests the "three poisons" or the "three times." These are conventional groupings of doctrinal concepts common throughout Buddhist literature. Commentators could just as easily have turned to the "three forms of being" (*sanyou*), the "three assemblies of the Buddha" (*sanhui*), the "three realms" (*sanjie*), or any of dozens of common sets of threes in Buddhist doctrine.[35] Nor need we give undue significance to the number 3: doctrinal correlates could just as easily have been found for four, five, six, or ten robes, since, owing perhaps to the origins of Buddhist doctrines in oral transmission, Buddhist literature teems with numbered concepts. In contrast to such off-the-cuff assignation of symbols, the notion that the monk's robes symbolized a life of

---

[32] *Guanzhong chuangli jietan tu jing,* by Daoxuan, T no. 1892, vol. 45, p. 816a. Daoxuan is probably drawing here from a passage in the *Flower Adornment Scripture. Da fangguang fo huayan jing* (Skt. [*Buddha] avataṃsakasūtra*) 6, p. 430c.

[33] *Sifenlü* (Skt. * *Dharmaguptakavinaya*) 40, p. 855b. In the *Fenbie gongde lun* 4, T no. 1507, vol. 25, p. 44c, the three robes are correlated with three seasons (winter, summer, and spring). See also, Faure, "Quand l'habit fait le moine," p. 338, n. 6.

[34] *Lüxiang gantong zhuan* T no. 1898, vol. 45, p. 881a.

[35] Nakamura Hajime's dictionary of Buddhist terms, *Bukkyōgo daijiten,* contains over a hundred doctrinal groupings beginning with the number 3.

mendicancy and austerity is apparent in the robe itself, in the way the fabric is cut, and the way the robe is worn. And unlike the symbolic interpretations mentioned above, this interpretation of the robe—as a symbol
of renunciation of wealth and comfort—appears persistently in various
types of writing throughout Buddhist history.

While I have emphasized the emblematic function of the monk's robe
as a marker of distinction, the robe was more than simply a sign of difference: the robe meant something much more specific. Made of ordinary
material, stitched together from rough rags and dyed a dull, staid color,
the robe was readily recognized as the minimal clothing of the sober ascetic.[36] For covering oneself, nothing could be simpler, nothing more
humble, than three drab rectangular pieces of cloth wrapped around the
body.

Textual evidence as well as early images of Chinese monks reveal that
the three-part robe was brought to China. But while this ideal uniform
continued to hold a prominent place in the minds of leading Chinese
monks for centuries, the history of the monastic robes in China is a history of adaptation and compromise. Modern Chinese monks and nuns in
general no longer wear the three robes, a custom that monks maintain in
countries in which Theravada Buddhism is practiced; Chinese monks and
nuns now wear sleeved robes, and often wear trousers as well. While still
a relatively simple type of clothing, the Chinese monk's sleeved robe and
trousers require a degree of design—pieces of cloth have to be cut and
sewn to fit, thus widening the gap between the ideal of a peripatetic, impoverished ascetic and a more comfortable reality.

This slow shift from the rectangular inner garments of medieval India
to the sleeved robes of modern Chinese monks began in medieval times.
In a detailed, passionate plea to Chinese monks to adhere to Indian
monastic practice in the cut and manner of wearing monastic robes,
seventh-century monk Yijing complained of the practice of Chinese
monks wearing garments with sleeves.[37] But Yijing's remonstrations did
not carry the day, and by the end of the Tang we can easily spot sleeves
beneath the outer robe in images of monks, as the sleeved robe gradually
took the place of the more cumbersome three rectangular pieces of cloth
that needed to be carefully wrapped, tucked, and held in place.

Nuns' robes were perhaps even more susceptible to innovation. According to Yijing's prescriptions based on canonical precedent, nuns
should have worn essentially the same garments as monks. But because

---

[36] Indeed, the Sanskrit word for "dull color" (kāṣāya) became synonymous with the
monk's robe. Nakamura, Ibid., s.v. "kesha," p. 298.

[37] Nanhai jigui neifa zhuan 2, T no. 2125, vol. 54, p. 214a–b; J. Takakusu, A Record of
the Buddhist Religion as Practiced in India and the Malay Archipelago, p. 67.

such robes are not firmly secured and run the risk of exposing the right breast, nuns were prone to feel "ashamed before men," and hence developed a more secure form of attire. As Yijing puts it, "The Chinese dress of the nuns is that of ordinary women, and the existing mode of wearing it is much against the proper rules."[38] Again Yijing's pleas were ignored, and nuns depicted in painting and sculpture from the medieval period on invariably wear either sleeved gowns or a high skirt that covers the breasts.

Yet the ascetic ideal persisted, and even after the Tang, monks and nuns continued to make regular use of the outer robe—worn over a sleeved robe or even a shirt and trousers. This outer robe continued to attract exegetical attention, even after the tripartite uniform had been replaced. If the symbolism of the three-piece robe as the ascetic's simple uniform had been lost, this symbolism could at least be maintained in the appearance of the outer robe. As we have seen, in China as in India, the outer robe was always made of several pieces of cloth, stitched together into a single rectangular garment. But what was the point of this practice? The modern scholar Mohan Wijayaratna has suggested that, when making their robes, Indian monks tore up the whole cloth in order to reduce its commercial value to a minimum; that is, they wished to render the fabric worthless.[39] Perhaps more important was the even more severe ascetic ideal to which the patched robe can be traced: the ideal monk's robe was pieced together from discarded rags—a clear gesture of renunciation of standard ideals of fine clothing. In practice, however, at least in China, this seems seldom to have been the case: most robes were prepared from new whole cloth that was cut into strips and then sewn together into the rectangular cloth that comprised the monk's outer robe. Again, despite the fact that this outer robe was not really a patchwork of discarded rags, it still conveyed an image of ascetic rigor. The Tang poet Zhang Ji (fl. 798), for instance, once praised a valiant monk who "practices the Four-part Regulations, and protects the purity of his robe of seven strips."[40] The strips are "pure" because they represent the uncompromising detachment of the monk from secular pursuits. The symbolism was heightened in the "robe of a hundred patches" (bainayi), made up of small patches of different fabrics and colors. Even more than in the case of ordinary, seven-strip robes, these robes were recognized by monk and layman alike as the mark of austere self-cultivation and renunciation.[41] Again, such robes were symbolic representations of poverty rather than a consequence of

[38] Nanhai jigui neifa zhuan 2, p. 216a; Takakusu, Ibid., p. 78.

[39] Wijayaratna, Buddhist Monastic Life, p. 36.

[40] "Song Min seng," Quan Tang shi 384, p. 4312.

[41] See for instance the poem "Du zhu seng" by the Tang poet Xu Ning, Quan Tang shi 474, p. 5380.

poverty itself: many such robes were especially made of fine material.[42]

We see the same sort of anxious compromise in the methods used to fasten the monk's robes. The simplest version of the three robes is held in place by tucking the robes in once they are wrapped around the body. At times a sash was used to secure the inner garment. The most visible device for securing the outer robe was a ribbon sewn to the part of the garment that draped over the back, which was tied to a knot or ring attached to the part of the cloth draped over the front (figure 6). As this was one of the most conspicuous parts of the monk's robe, it attracted the attention of monks and others concerned with the image of the monk. The chief concern was to show that there was canonical precedent for the ring. While at some point even leading Chinese monks had to admit that the three-part robe had given way to a sleeved garment over which an orthodox, rectangular garment was draped, these same monks could rest assured that there was precedent for the ring; the ring, they insist, is perfectly orthodox, and not another slip away from the ascetic ideal toward a more decadent form of attire.

Most monks justified ring and ribbon with stories drawn from various canonical texts, stating that originally monks did not make use of any device to secure their robes, but simply tucked their robes in around their bodies. Because of this, the robes tended to sag, becoming "disorderly." Critics, this apologetic goes, began to ridicule monks by saying that they looked like "lascivious women." At other times, the robes could even fall off entirely, forcing the monk to quickly set his alms bowl on the ground and scramble to reassemble the robe, prompting ridicule of the "sordidness" of the monk. For all of these reasons, the Buddha is said to have intervened and permitted the use of ring and ribbon (gouniu).[43] We sense in such discussions an anxiety over the ideals the robe represented. If monks could not win every battle in this struggle for symbolic equivalence, they could at least win the most visible ones. Daoxuan and others warned against the use of silver and other precious metals for the ring, though into the Song and beyond, monks of means continued to use silver and even gold for the ring, as the ascetic ideal persistently slipped from the control of the most exacting monks.[44]

[42] Very few old Buddhist robes are extant. For three spectacular examples of medieval robes from Japan but probably reflecting the style of Chinese robes at that time, see Shōsōin Jimusho, ed., Shōsōin hōmotsu, hokasō, vol. 1, pl. 24–9.

[43] Lüxiang gantong zhuan, p. 881a; Fozhi biqiu liuwu tu, p. 900b; Sifenlü (Skt. * Dharmaguptakavinaya), 40, p. 855c; Genben shuoyiqieyou bu pinaiye za shi, (*Skt. [Mūlasarvāstivāda] vinayakṣudrakavastu) 4, T no. 1451, vol. 24, p. 233c.

[44] In the Shishi yaolan, Daocheng cites a passage from the Mahāsāṃghikavinaya prohibiting the use of precious metals in the ring, but I have been unable to find the passage in the Taishō version of the text. Shishi yaolan A, T no. 2127, vol. 54, p. 270. For Daoxuan's comments, see his Shimen zhangfu yi, T no. 1894, vol. 45, p. 838c.

Twelfth-century figure Cheng Dachang cites the prevalence of silver robe-rings in his day

FIG. 6. Ming court painting, Yongle reign (1403–24). Note the ring used to affix the outer robe. The sleeved garments beneath the outer robe are in violation of the monastic regulations. Photograph courtesy of King's Art Collection, San Francisco.

In addition to the question of how one fastened the robe, monks also debated the proper material for the robe. Daoxuan, as we have seen, devoted considerable attention to the question of monastic robes, discussing them at length in his handbook on monastic regulations, and even composing a treatise devoted entirely to the subject of the monk's robes. A large section of this treatise discusses the use of silk to make monastic robes. In China, the manufacture of silk entailed killing the silkworms in order to extract the silk from their cocoons, yet the practice of wearing silk was common among monks in Daoxuan's day. As Daoxuan notes, "From the time China received the teachings [of Buddhism], monks have had nothing to do [with meat eating]. The system whereby meat is forbidden has long been in practice, yet prohibitions against silk have not been adopted."[45] That is, rules against killing for one's personal comfort were not applied consistently. Later in life, Daoxuan experienced a series of visions in which he conversed with Buddhist spirits. The topic of most of their conversation, duly recorded by Daoxuan, concerned the monastic regulations. At one point in this remarkable book, the spirits comment on how much they enjoyed reading Daoxuan's work on monastic robes. The spirits are particularly impressed with his admonitions against silk, and ask him how he came to this noble, correct view. Daoxuan replies that he first began to have suspicions about silk when reading a passage in the *Treatise on the Perfection of Great Wisdom* that remarks on the rough cloth of the Buddha's robe. Later, Daoxuan continues, he questioned monks from the West who told him that they did not wear silk.[46]

Whether a calculated fabrication or a genuine vision, the passage suggests that, however much the spirits might have approved of his stand, Daoxuan met with resistance among fellow monks, and that, consciously or subconsciously, he used his visions to vindicate his stance. Yijing, who was in his early thirties at the time of Daoxuan's death, was among those who objected to Daoxuan's rejection of silk. Indian monks had not dealt with the ethical implications of wearing silk in part because in India silk

---

in an essay entitled "Sengyi huan" in *Yanfan luzheng* 12, p. 343a. Cheng postulates that use of the ring originated as a mark of rank among Tibetan officials. While there is ample evidence that pre-Song monks fastened their robes with ribbon and knot, and Daoxuan complains of metal rings in his day, I have yet to find an example of a metal ring before the seventh century, when Tibetan official culture reached maturity. Hence, Cheng's hypothesis is not impossible. The earliest depiction of the robe ring I have found is from 629. See figure 9. Incidentally, Christian ecclesiasts fought similar battles against the use of gold and silver fasteners used to secure priest's robes. Trichet, *Le costume du clergé,* pp. 70, 85.

[45] *Shimen zhangfu yi,* p. 836a. Later in the same text, Daoxuan complains also of the practice of "robbing bees of their honey." Although in later periods some monks eschewed silk, few ever objected to eating honey.

[46] *Lüxiang gantong zhuan,* p. 879c. Daoxuan repeats the claim in *Xu gaoseng zhuan* 27, p. 684a–b.

strands were collected after the silk worms had gnawed through the cocoons. The Chinese method, on the other hand, produces a higher-quality
silk, but the worms must be killed before they damage the cocoon.[47] It is
not clear if Yijing was aware of the different method of making silk in
India. In any event, he approved of wearing silk, even in China. Yijing argued that silk was in many cases more readily available than other types
of fabric, and that it was improper for monks to be overly fastidious when
accepting gifts of robes from donors. "Why should we reject the silk that
is so easily obtained and seek the fine linen that is difficult to procure?"[48]
Further, the use of any kind of fabric, including cotton, at some level involved the taking of life, as worms and such are killed when the fields are
cultivated. Where, Yijing asks, does this excessively rigorous interpretation of the monastic regulations end? "If one attempts to protect every
being, there will be no means of maintaining oneself, and one has to give
up life without reason. There are some who do not eat ghee or cream, do
not wear leather boots, and do not put on any silk or cotton. All these are
the same class of people as are mentioned above."[49] Yijing's views on silk
seem to have found widespread acceptance. While it is true that some
monks in later periods eschewed the use of silk in monastic robes,[50] in
China avoidance of silk was never as prevalent as the vegetarian diet,
based on similar ethical concerns, and monks continued to accept gifts of
silken garments.

The debate over silk involved more than symbols; for a monk like
Daoxuan, silk was wrong because it entailed the taking of life. The silk
question involved complex quasi-legal issues of ethical culpability, and
not just the image monks projected to the outside world. This being said,
the ascetic impulse seems also to have played a role in the debate, with
Daoxuan intimating that, just as a monk renounces the pleasures of meat,
he should also renounce the pleasures of silk, and Yijing countering that
the renunciation of silk was hardly an ascetic act, since silk was in fact
easier and cheaper to procure than other materials.[51]

[47] Xinru Liu, *Silk and Religion*, pp. 50–51.

[48] Cotton only became commonly available in China after the tenth century. In the tenth
century, the price of fine cotton was about the same as the price for fine silk. See Eric
Trombert, *Le crédit à Dunhuang: Vie matérielle et société en Chine médiévale*, p. 122.

[49] *Nanhai jigui neifa zhuan* 2, pp. 212c–13a; Takakusu, *A Record of the Buddhist Religion*, p. 58.

[50] Some monks, for instance, wore robes of paper in order to avoid the use of silk. See
Tsien Tsuen-hsuin, *Paper and Printing*, p. 112. Once again there are Christian parallels, as
Christian priests were forbidden from wearing silk. Trichet, *Le costume du clergé*, pp. 60,
93–4.

[51] In his *Notes on Practice*, Daoxuan cites versions of the vinaya that emphasize that the
monk's robe is to be made of heavy, coarse material and not fine material like silk. See *Sifenlü
shanfan buque xingshichao* C1, p. 105b, and Kawano, "Sō-i shiryō kenkyū," p. 91. The de-

Lurking behind all of these debates, commentaries, and admonitions was an elusive ascetic ideal beyond the reach of all but the most determined monk. If scholarly monks like Daoxuan could not achieve an austere ideal of poverty and eremitic renunciation in practice, they could achieve it, to a degree, through careful attention to symbolism, both in their erudite treatises and in the very clothes they wore. Yet in China the monk's robe was not always a symbol of asceticism; on the contrary, some robes were marks of prestige and influence. This tendency is clearest in the curious history of the purple robe, to which we now turn.

THE PURPLE ROBE

According to an early legend, the monk Śāṇavāsin, one of Ānanda's disciples, was born wearing a monk's robe.[52] One tenth-century Chinese interpreter of the story remarked that Śāṇavāsin "was born wearing a robe which looked like a thin layer of skin but was not. When he was a child, it was like swaddling clothes; when he grew up, it covered his body. When he became a monk, this then served as his monk's robe. Only when he entered extinction and his body was cremated was the robe reduced to ashes."[53] Here, the "fetal robe" had clear symbolic associations: Śāṇavāsin was born to be a monk. In the same tenth-century work, two instances are recorded of Chinese monks who had been born wearing "monks' robes," which, according to the compiler of the text, were unusual placentas, though he still believed that they were signs that the infants were destined to become monks. Such stories underscore the importance of the robe as a sign of the monk's vocation. A minor detail of one of these accounts, the biography of Huileng, easily escapes the attention of anyone unfamiliar with the history of the monk's robe in China: unlike Śāṇavāsin's robe, Huileng's robe was purple.[54] By Huileng's time (the early tenth century), the *purple* robe signified that not only was its owner a monk, but that he was a monk of some distinction as well; for the purple robe had become a well-known badge of eminence.

The purple robe had become a sign of particular eminence because in the Tang, emperors began the practice of conferring a purple robe on monks of special merit. By the Tang, the color purple already had a long history of associations with nobility and high status in general. Rulers wore purple during the Warring States period, and after the Six Dynasties

---

bate over the use of silk in monastic garments underwent an interesting transformation in Japan. See Faure, "Quand l'habit fait le moine," pp. 346–52.

[52] See Foguang dacidian bianxiu weiyuan hui ed. *Foguang da cidian*, pp. 4407c–8b. On this and the "placenta robes" discussed below, see Faure, "Quand l'habit fait le moine," p. 363.

[53] *Song gaoseng zhuan* 11, p. 775b.

[54] Ibid. 13, p. 787a

period, the purple robe became a mark of high office more generally.[55] According to the tenth-century monastic historian Zanning, the first instance of a ruler conferring the purple robe on a monk was in 690, when Empress Wu Zetian awarded a purple robe to the monks who composed a commentary to the *Great Cloud Scripture*, a text that was instrumental in her campaign to establish her legitimacy to the throne.[56] Subsequent emperors continued the practice, granting robes to monks who performed well in debate before the throne, or when assigning prominent monks to important monastic positions, or, more generally, for a monk's reputation for virtue. At times a prefect or princess would memorialize the throne, reporting that they had recently discovered a particularly worthy monk who should be granted a purple robe.[57]

Monks were well aware that purple had been an important mark of high office in the Chinese bureaucracy from very early on,[58] and some Tang monks expressed discomfort at associating themselves with this secular symbol, seemingly at odds with the traditional symbolism of the dim-colored robe as a mark of sacred renunciation.[59] The purple robe even came in for ridicule by Song writers who scoffed at the hypocrisy of monks too busy scrambling for lavish purple robes to take time out for their alms rounds.[60] But for the most part, monks and laymen alike seem to have accepted the purple robe as a sign of prestige and imperial favor. For instance, when the seventh-century monk Huijing died, his cloister proudly displayed his purple robe together with his portrait. A pilgrim to the site would have instantly realized that the robe had belonged to a monk publicly recognized by the emperor for his virtue (in this case, chanting the *Great Cloud Scripture* for Empress Wu at the age of three).[61]

[55] See Hanyu dacidian bianzuan chu, ed., *Hanyu da cidian*, s.v. "ziyi" and "zifu," p. 815.

[56] Huang Minzhi (Huang Min-chih), "Songdai de ziyi shihao," collected in her *Songdai fojiao shehui jingjishi lun ji*, p. 444. My discussion of the purple robe relies heavily on this article. See also, Antonino Forte, *Political Propaganda and Ideology in China at the End of the Seventh Century*, p. 11.

[57] Here I draw from accounts in the *Song Biographies of Eminent Monks*, which contains dozens of references to the purple robe.

[58] *Da Song sengshilüe* C, p. 248c.

[59] Kieschnick, *The Eminent Monk*, pp. 31–2.

[60] Huang, *Songdai fojiao*, p. 450.

[61] *Song gaoseng zhuan* 24, p. 863a. Roderick Whitfield has suggested the same practice at work in the patched cloth in the Stein collection, which he argues may in fact be the purple robe conferred on the Dunhuang monk Hongbian in the ninth century. The cloth, like most of the other Dunhuang artifacts in the Stein collection, was discovered in Cave 17, which was originally a memorial cave for Hongbian. See Roderick Whitfield, *The Art of Central Asia: The Stein Collection in the British Museum*, vol. 3, pl. 9. The cloth, however, contains only two small patches that are actually purple. Further, at 107 centimeters, it is less than half the length of the robes in the Shōsōin. I suspect that, rather than being Hongbian's purple robe, the robe may in fact have been used to adorn a statue. According to one

Well before the first purple robe was granted, monks were at times awarded robes of other sorts. A biography of the great seventh-century pilgrim Xuanzang repeatedly notes gifts of robes from rulers, including one sewn by ladies in the harem, "so dexterously made that the stitches left no trace of sewing."[62] What distinguished the purple robe from such gifts is not the quality of the robe itself, but that an official system was established for its bequeathal, thus imbuing the robe with associations derived from a lengthy tradition of formal, official recognition of imperial favor. After Wu Zetian, the practice of bestowing purple robes was continued by emperors in the mid-Tang and into the Song, growing gradually in scope as a system developed of recommendations from local officials and review by the central authorities before a purple robe could be bestowed. As the number of requests for the robe increased—in the year 939 alone, 105 such robes were granted—criteria were established for just what sort of monk could receive the robe. Robes were given to reward monks for administering to the sick and for burying the dead in addition to robes given to monks for vaguer notions of virtue and sanctity. One indication of the value accorded the purple robe at the local level is the number of reports that reached the throne of bribery and cases of the robe reaching unworthy monks. These worrying reports in turn sparked periodic attempts to reform the system. From the standpoint of the state, instances of bribery and corruption threatened the efficacy of the policy, intended at some level to exert state control over the sangha.

In the eleventh century, a government in search of innovative ways of increasing revenue announced that purple robes could now be purchased from the state. In motive, the new policy represented a departure from the previous one, which had been intended to strengthen the moral character and social utility of the clergy; the purple robe was no longer a symbolic reward for moral eminence or virtuous service to the state—it had become instead a simple commodity, similar to other forms of currency.

By this point the severance of any connection to Buddhist ideals of ascetic simplicity and ethical purity was complete; funds derived from the sale of the robes were applied to various secular purposes, including even the training of imperial soldiers.[63] The policy of selling robes encountered problems similar to those of the practice of selling ordination certificates or, indeed, the issuing of state money: cases of forgery became common,

---

Dunhuang inventory, purple fabric was used in some such statue garments. (See Hou Ching-lang, "Trésors du monastère Long-hing à Touen-houang: Une étude sur le manuscrit P.3432," pp. 149–68.). In short, I do not believe that the Dunhuang robe is an example of a "purple robe."

[62] *Da Cien si sanzang fashi zhuan* 7, p. 258c; Li Rongxi, *A Biography of the Tripiṭaka Master,* p. 212.

[63] Huang, *Songdai fojiao,* p. 454.

forcing the state to issue a new style of robe embossed with the imperial reign mark, making it more difficult to copy. A long-standing ordinance requiring that the purple robe be returned to central authorities after a monk's death also helped to ensure the state monopoly on the robes.[64]

In sum, while originally a symbol of the renunciation of secular values, the monk's robe, at least in its purple variety, was absorbed into the hierarchy of these very values as Indian Buddhist symbolism was overwhelmed by Chinese imperial symbolism. Subsequently, the purple robe, relying on this imperial symbolism, became a valued commodity that, in addition to departing from traditional, canonical Buddhist prescriptions, extended beyond the reach even of the Chinese state, as individuals contended for a symbol disconnected from traditional Buddhist concerns and only tangentially linked to the imperial symbolic network.

Even after purple robes were made available to whoever could afford them, monks continued to receive purple robes from powerful patrons. But a purple robe obtained in these circumstances—purchased directly or through bribery—meant something different from a robe conferred by an emperor. Although still a mark of prestige, the robe had become an indirect symbol of vague connections to wealth and power, rather than a direct symbol of prestige conferred by the court, which, in principle, was decided on the basis of merit. A modern analogy would be the difference between winning a prestigious prize and the prestige that comes with owning an expensive watch. No single entity was in control of this slippery process of symbolic association: erudite monks made little effort to evaluate the purple robe on the basis of the scriptures, and even the emperor could not control the vagaries of the purple robe at the local level. In the end, the significance of the robe was decided in a haphazard fashion by any number of individual monks and their patrons. We can turn from this sort of loose, secular symbolism back to more specifically Buddhist concerns by taking up the rise and spread of the robe as a symbol of the highest, ineffable Buddhist truth—a symbolism embodied in the "Dharma robe."

THE DHARMA ROBE

In the early Tang, at approximately the same time as the purple robe was introduced as a symbol of imperial favor, the monastic robe was invested with yet another possible meaning: it became a symbol of the transmission of the Dharma, the essence of the eternal truths discovered by the Buddha.[65] Several legends circulating in the early Tang conveyed this notion of the robe as a sign of transmission. The most important of these

[64] On the purple robe in Japan, see Faure, "Quand l'habit fait le moine," p. 355.
[65] The discussion that follows draws heavily on Wendi Leigh Adamek's "Issues in Chinese Buddhist Transmission as Seen Through the *Lidai Fabao ji (Record of the Dharma)*."

was the story that just before his death, Śākyamuni bequeathed to his disciple Kāśyapa a "gold-embroidered robe" (given to the Buddha by his aunt) that Kāśyapa was to pass on to Maitreya, the next buddha. In the version of the legend told in Xuanzang's *Account of the Western Regions,* Kāśyapa eventually takes the robe with him when he enters into Cock's-Foot Mountain (the mountain closing behind him) and awaits the coming of the future buddha.[66]

The *Forest of Pearls in the Garden of the Law,* compiled by Daoshi (d. 668), contains a similar story, which it attributes to Daoxuan. In this story, Śākyamuni first receives from a tree spirit the robe worn by the previous buddha; as in the other legends, the robe is a sign of the transmission in a lineage of buddhas. Just before entering nirvana, Śākyamuni entrusts the robe to Ānanda, who is told to take it to a cave at Mount Qingliang (aka. Wutai) in China, where the bodhisattva Mañjuśrī resides.[67]

These stories suggested to the medieval Chinese reader not only that there was a robe passed down from one buddha to another from time immemorial, but that this robe had somehow found its way to China. These notions were adapted to several key early Chan texts and eventually incorporated into what would become one of the most beloved motifs of Chinese Buddhist narrative: the secret transmission of the Dharma from master to disciple. By far the most famous account of such a transmission occurs in the *Platform Scripture,* in which Hongren, the "Fifth Patriarch" of the Chan lineage, determines to transmit the Dharma not to his leading disciple, the learned Shenxiu, but instead to the illiterate but intuitively enlightened Huineng. After secretly calling Huineng to his quarters in the middle of the night, Hongren passes on a robe to Huineng, saying, "I make you the Sixth Patriarch. The robe is the proof and is to be handed down from generation to generation."[68]

While this version of the story became the most popular, texts discovered in modern times at Dunhuang provide us with further glimpses into the ways in which Chan monks in the Tang understood the symbolism of this robe of transmission. For instance, the *Record of the Jewel of the Law*

[66] *Da Tang Xiyu ji* 9, p. 919b–c; Thomas Watters, *On Yuan Chwang's Travels in India,* vol. 2, pp. 143–6. Curiously, the detail that the robe was made of "embroidered gold" contradicts the ideal monk's robe discussed above. Note also that while the Buddha was of course held to a different standard than ordinary monks, Daoxuan, as noted earlier, claimed to have first recognized the inappropriateness of fine silk robes when reading in the *Da zhi du lun* that the Buddha wore a coarse garment.

[67] *Fayuan zhulin* 35, p. 560a–c. The passage is discussed in Adamek, "Issues in Chinese Buddhist Transmission," p. 206, and, at greater length, in Koichi Shinohara, "The Kaṣāya Robe of the Past Buddha Kāśyapa in the Miraculous Instruction Given to the Vinaya Master Daoxnan (596–667)."

[68] Yampolsky, *The Platform Sutra of the Sixth Patriarch,* p. 133.

Throughout the Ages,[69] a Chan text compiled to lend support to claims of a particular Chan lineage in the late Tang, fleshes out the legend of the transmission of the robe, saying that the robe was passed down from Bodhidharma, the monk credited with bringing the Chan Dharma to China, or, in Chan parlance, the "First Patriarch." According to this legend, formulated in the Tang, at the moment when Bodhidharma passed the robe on to his disciple Huike, he said, "I have transmitted the robe for the sake of verification of the teachings. It is like the consecration of a Cakravartin King who obtains the seven true jewels and inherits the eminent kingly throne. Possession of the robe is the outward expression of the true inheritance of the Dharma."[70] The robe was then passed on from Huike, the "Second Patriarch," to his disciple and then from patriarch to patriarch until it reached Huineng, the Sixth Patriarch. At this point the account in the *Record of the Jewel* diverges from that of the *Platform Scripture.* According to the *Platform,* the transmission of the robe ended with Huineng. In the *Record of the Jewel,* however, the transmission continued when the robe was passed from Huineng to another monk, who passed it on to Empress Wu, who then passed it on to yet another monk, until the robe finally made its way to Sichuan, where the lineage responsible for the compilation of the *Record of the Jewel* was located.

The relationship between the accounts in these and other Chan texts—who borrowed from whom—is complex, and involves knotty problems of textual history with which Chan specialists continue to grapple. Setting aside the question of the precise historical development of the robe legends, we can still ask the more general question of what the compilers of relatively early versions of the legend made of the robe as a symbol. In these accounts, the robe is a mark of the authentic transmission of the Dharma. It signals a link with enlightened masters of the past and constitutes a "contact relic," that is, it is a relic by virtue of having come into contact with a holy man.[71] It is also a mark of legitimization that resonated with Chinese traditions of the legitimization of imperial reign through sacred talismans, stretching back to pre-Buddhist times.[72] As we have seen, some monks felt uncomfortable with the association of the monastic robe with imperial prestige. Chan monks were even more marked in their ambivalence toward the Dharma robe. In their case, it was not simply a symbolic association with prestige that made them uneasy, but the association between the Dharma, ultimate truth, and any mate-

---

[69] *Lidai fabao ji, T* no. 2075, vol. 51.

[70] Adamek, "Issues in Chinese Buddhist Transmission," p. 188. See also Adamek, "Robes Purple and Gold: Transmission of the Robe in the *Lidai fabaoji* (Record of the Dharma-Jewel Through the Ages), pp. 58–81.

[71] On the term *contact relic,* see Faure, *Visions of Power,* p. 159.

[72] Anna Seidel, "Den-e" to appear in *Hōbōgirin* (forthcoming volume).

rial object. For monks who emphasized the need for unmediated, direct enlightenment, to resort to any form of symbolic mediation was considered an embarrassing compromise.[73]

Commenting on the meaning of the robe, Shenhui, Huineng's most prominent disciple, wrote, "Although the Dharma is not in the robe, the robe symbolizes that the Dharma was transmitted from generation to generation. The robe is a mark of trust, so that propagators of the Dharma can receive something [to show to] students of the Way that they may know that the essence of the doctrine is not mistaken."[74] Shenhui's comments suggest that for some the Chan robe was not just a symbol representing the Dharma, but was in fact the embodiment of the Dharma, and that by possessing the robe one magically acquired the Dharma itself.[75]

It was this belief in the robe as a magical locus of the Dharma that Chan monks like Shenhui feared and spoke against so eloquently. We see the same idea challenged in the *Platform Scripture,* where, after Huineng takes the robe and the Dharma and leaves his master, he is pursued by a gang of murderous monks intent on killing him and taking back the robe. When one of these monks catches up to Huineng, the monk surprisingly asks not for the robe but for the Dharma, saying, "I have come this long distance just to seek the Dharma. I have no need for the robe."[76] Later, just before dying, Huineng himself makes a clear distinction between the Dharma and the robe when he announces that the robe, handed down from patriarch to patriarch beginning with Bodhidharma, will no longer be transmitted. In its place, he offers a series of verses also handed down from patriarch to patriarch beginning with Bodhidharma.[77] In this way, the less material symbol of the verses is substituted for the more material—and hence suspicious—symbol of the robe.

A more explicit statement of the secondary role Chan monks wished to ascribe to the robe, so central to their own legends, occurs in the writings of Shenhui, when he explains that the robe was not used as a sign of trust in India, where the monks are of higher attainments and the people pure and simple; the transmission robe is only necessary, he tells us, in places

---

[73] The problems created by the Chan propagation of unmediated enlightenment and the compromises entailed in such a claim are the subject of Bernard Faure's, *The Rhetoric of Immediacy.*

[74] *Putidamo nanzong ding shifei lun,* in Yang Zengwen, ed., *Shenhui heshang chanhua lu,* p. 29.

[75] As Bernard Faure puts it, the Chan transmission robe "is not just a symbol: like Huineng's other relics, including the *Platform Sutra,* it is the *embodiment* of the Chan Dharma," (*The Rhetoric of Immediacy,* p. 166), and elsewhere, "[T]he robe and other 'tokens,' which were at first included as proofs of enlightenment, tended to become its magical cause" ("Quand l'habit fait le moine," p. 343).

[76] Yampolsky, *The Platform Sutra,* p. 134.

[77] Ibid., pp. 176–8.

like China, where the people are "vulgar, seek after fame and fortune, and become involved in complicated disputes."[78] Shenhui provides us with an especially clear example of Chan ambivalence toward the robe; there is an uneasy tension between, on the one hand, the Chan fascination with the robe as a mark of legitimacy, and on the other, a wish to downplay any overt symbolism, regarded by some Chan thinkers as awkward and crass. That is, Chan monks felt it necessary to lard enthusiastic stories of robe transmission with erudite asides dismissing the robe as peripheral.

Radical iconoclasm is, perhaps, always doomed to failure; for without symbols of some sort, expression itself is impossible. And, taken together, Chan stories of contention for the transmission robe seem hardly more lofty in spirit than official documentation of bribery and payments received for the prestigious purple robe. What distinguishes the Chan literature, however, is the awareness of Chan monks to the problem. Not only were they conscious of the symbolism of the robe, but they were conscious as well of the problem of utilizing *any* symbol, however inevitable this sort of mediation between abstract truths and the everyday world may be. Constant vigilance was required. As in the famous Chan analogy, when pointing out the moon, there is always a danger that others will focus on the finger before them, rather than the moon in the distance.

The Alms Bowl

In many ways, the alms bowl provides a parallel case to that of the monk's robe. Like the robe, the bowl was considered, from the earliest texts, an essential part of the monk's uniform, and accorded much importance. The bowl is "the emblem of all the buddhas. How could one treat it lightly?"[79] A monk should protect his bowl "as he would his own eyes."[80] And like the robe, the alms bowl frequently carried symbolic associations with the life of the peripatetic Buddhist ascetic. In this respect, the symbolism of the bowl was even more direct than that of the robe, for the bowl was the central tool of the alms rounds on which the ideal monk was to rely for his sustenance. As Daoxuan put it: "The three robes of the sramana are an emblem of wisdom and of sanctity. The alms bowl is a vessel of one who has 'left his family,' and is not used by the secular. A monk should keep the three robes and an earthenware alms bowl, for this [is an expression] of the reduction of desire and activity."[81]

---

[78] *Putidamo nanzong ding shifei lun*, p. 849; Adamek, "Issues in Chinese Buddhist Transmission," p. 189.

[79] *Shi song lü* (Skt. *Sarvāstivādavinaya*) 39, p. 282b.

[80] *Pinimu jing* (Skt.* Vinayamātṛkā) 7, T no. 1463, vol. 24, p. 840a.

[81] *Sifenlü shanfan buque xingshichao* C1, p. 105a. Daoxuan is paraphrasing *Mohe sengqi lü* (Skt.* Mahāsāṃghikavinaya) 38, T no. 1425, vol. 22, pp. 528a, 468a.

THE ASCETIC'S BOWL

As in the case of the robe, Buddhist writers employed the symbolism of the alms bowl to position the Buddhist monk between, on the one hand, the "secular" (as we see in the preceding quotation) and, on the other, the radical ascetic of other religious groups. The *Dharmaguptakavinaya,* for instance, quotes the Buddha as forbidding monks from using alms bowls made of gold, silver, lapis lazuli, and other such precious substances, for such is the bowl of the decadent layman; at the same time, he also forbids monks from using bowls made of wood, for such are the bowls of followers of "other paths."[82]

In addition to the substance used, careful prescriptions were laid down as to number: just as a monk was not to keep more than three robes, so too he was not to keep more than one alms bowl. According to the *Dharmaguptakavinaya,* this regulation came about after monks who had received a large number of bowls from donors were ridiculed by outsiders for living in quarters that looked "like the shop of a pottery salesman."[83] In passages such as these, we return to the important symbolic significance accorded these basic monastic possessions. If monks writing on the robes felt compelled to lavish attention on the minutia of stitching, ribbons, and rings, when writing on the bowl they discussed in great detail the size of the bowl, how it was to be mended when broken, and how it was to be washed. According to the *Dharmaguptakavinaya,* the proscriptions concerning mending the bowl were established when it was discovered that an unscrupulous monk would intentionally break his bowl after only one use and then solicit a stylish new one from a donor.[84] For this reason, this and other vinaya texts state that the monk cannot solicit a new bowl until he has mended his old bowl at least five times. At the core of these concerns was the peripatetic, ascetic ideal: the ideal monk owned no property beyond the barest necessities.

This ideal and the importance of the alms bowl for it is reflected in China not only in writings by vinaya specialists like Daoxuan, who quote from scripture and discuss the acquisition and care of alms bowls at length,[85] but also in biographies of Chinese monks in which the alms bowl is prominent. We often read of monks who owned nothing more than the three robes and an alms bowl,[86] or ascetics like the ninth-century monk Shencou, who "ate from one alms bowl and slept on one bed. His cloak was sewn of coarse hemp, and he sat on a mat of thrushes."[87] Among the

[82] *Sifen lü* (Skt. *Dharmaguptakavinaya*) 52, pp. 951c–2a.
[83] Ibid., p. 621c.
[84] Ibid., p. 623a.
[85] See *Sifen lü shanfan buque xingshichao* B2, pp. 124–7.
[86] *Song gaoseng zhuan* 3, p. 720a "Baosiwei"; 4, p. 729b "Uisang."
[87] Ibid., 16, p. 807b.

ten vows by which the great Huayan thinker Chengguan was said to have lived was his vow to keep "only the three robes and a begging bowl, and own no other belongings."[88]

BOWL AS GIFT

As one of the few objects monks were permitted to own by even the most stringent observers of the monastic rules, the alms bowl was a popular gift to monks by Buddhist devotees. Ennin notes, for example, that each year the emperor sent vast quantities of clothing, incense, flowers, and alms bowls to the prestigious monasteries on Mount Wutai.[89] Impressed by the reputation of the monk Kezhou, the tenth-century ruler Prince Wusu granted him "a golden scepter and alms bowl, a purple robe, and the name Jingzhi Tongming ('Refined Ambitions and Perspicacious Knowledge')."[90] The *Biographies of Eminent Monks* contain many such references to imperial gifts of alms bowls to monks,[91] though unlike the case of the purple robe, most of these bowls do not seem to have been made of particularly precious material, and the conferral of an imperial bowl never took on the significance of a conferral of a purple robe. There were also instances of prominent laymen giving alms bowls to eminent monks.[92] It seems likely that such gifts, especially recorded, were more special than an ordinary donation of a bowl; even if the bowls themselves were not remarkable, the fact that they came from prominent figures imbued them with particular importance.

In one case, the alms bowl gift was special indeed, both because of the quality of its craftsmanship and because of the donor who gave it. This, one of our earliest extant alms bowls, was found in the stupa at Famen Monastery. From the inscription on the bowl we know that it was made for the monastery in response to an imperial edict issued by Emperor Yizong in 873.[93] Significantly, the bowl is made of pure gold, which, as we have seen, was in violation of monastic regulations. Yet another alms bowl, also found at Famen, is made of silver with gold inlay, again in violation of the monastic regulations that clearly state that alms bowls should not be made of gold or silver.

The inscription on the first bowl tells us that the bowl was made to "welcome the true relics" of the Buddha. In other words, the bowl seems to have been intended for a ritual involving a relic of the Buddha (in all

---

[88] Ibid., 5, p. 737c.

[89] *Nittō guhō junrei gyōki* 3, p. 296; Reischauer, *Ennin's Diary,* p. 249.

[90] *Song gaoseng zhuan* 7, p. 747c.

[91] For instance, Ibid. 8, p. 755a "Huineng"; 13, p. 787b "Quanfu"; 14, p. 793b "Daoan," and 18, p. 823b "Sengqie."

[92] Ibid. 28, p. 887a "Changjue."

[93] Shi Xingbang, ed., *Famensi digong zhenbao,* pl. 32, and Han Wei, "Famensi digong jinyinqi zanwen kaoshi," p. 72.

likelihood the relic of the Buddha's finger bone, which was found at the same site) and not for a monk's use. Nonetheless, if court artisans had wished to enter into the symbolic world of the monastic regulations, they would have either made the bowl of earthenware or iron (the most common, orthodox substances for a monk's bowl), or they would have made the bowl of stone, of which buddhas' bowls were said to be made.[94] Instead, as in the case of imperially made robes, the court artisans ignored monastic symbolic tradition and drew from the imperial tradition instead, creating exquisite bowls of the finest gold and silver.[95]

In addition to receiving bowls as gifts, because of the symbolic importance accorded the bowl by monks, prominent monks also made gifts of alms bowls to their benefactors, including even emperors.[96] Although, as we will see, some bowls were thought of as sacred relics possessing special powers, in other cases the gift of a prestigious monk's bowl seems to have been a more purely symbolic gesture as the gift of one of only a handful of objects lofty monks were expected to possess.

SYMBOL OF THE DHARMA

The alms bowl achieved a more specific symbolic meaning in some Chan texts, where it represented the Dharma and was a sign of the transmission of a master's highest teachings to his chosen successor. The bowl was not, in this respect, as prominent as the robe, but does on occasion appear alongside the robe as a symbol of transmission. In the *Lidai fabao ji,* a lay disciple inquires into whether or not the robe and bowl of the mysterious Chan monk Musang were transmitted to successors after his death.[97] Sometime after Huineng's death, the Chan monk Cangyong was said to "transmit" Huineng's bowl, although here the phrase seems to be a literary metaphor for Huineng's teachings, without implying that Cangyong possessed Huineng's actual bowl.[98] As in the case of robes, we cannot be certain that actual bowls were handed down from master to disciple as symbols of transmission in medieval China; the notion of a transmission of the bowl may be entirely a literary conceit.[99] We do, however, possess

---

[94] *Da zhi du lun* 26, pp. 252c–3b; Lamotte, *Le traité de la grande vertu de sagesse,* pp. 1674–81.

[95] Similar alms bowls have also been found in Song stupas. See Wenzhoushi Wenwuchu et al., "Wenzhoushi Bei Song Baixiangta qingli baogao," pp. 1–15, and Hebeisheng wenwu guanlichu, "Hebei Yixian Jingjuesi shelita digong qingli ji," pp. 76–80.

[96] *Song gaoseng zhuan* 29, p. 891a, "Chuntuo."

[97] *Lidai fabao ji,* p. 187c. For other examples of the bowl as a mark of Dharma transmission, see Faure, "Quand l'habit fait le moine," p. 353.

[98] *Song gaoseng zhuan* 15, p. 803a.

[99] In the case of robes, we do know, as Bernard Faure has pointed out, that Chinese and Japanese monks in modern times transmit a robe in ceremonies of ordination and Dharma transmission. Faure, "Quand l'habit fait le moine," p. 343.

one actual bowl owned by no less than Shenhui, the most prominent disciple of Huineng. The terra-cotta bowl was discovered in 1983 in Shenhui's stupa.[100] The symbolic meaning of this particular bowl is obscure. Perhaps it was a possession of the master and, as a "contact relic," stood for Shenhui himself. Given the importance attached to the alms bowl in the Chan tradition, it is not impossible that the bowl was a tangible symbol of transmission passed down to Shenhui from none other than the Sixth Patriarch, Huineng.

THE BUDDHA'S BOWL

Along with the Buddha's hair, teeth, and robe, the Buddha's bowl was one of the four principal relics left behind by Śākyamuni. According to a legend recorded in a number of early Indian texts, immediately after Śākyamuni's enlightenment, when two merchants offered him food, "four celestial kings" descended from the heavens and offered him four bowls.[101] According to some texts, the gods first offered the Buddha bowls made of gold and other precious substances, which, in keeping with the ascetic symbolism of the alms bowl, he firmly refused. Next the gods offered him four bowls made of stone. So as not to show preference for any one god, the Buddha accepted all four bowls and, miraculously, molded them into one.[102] Writing in the fifth century, the Chinese pilgrim Faxian noted that the bowl was still extant and worshipped in the kingdom of Fulousha (probably corresponding to Peshawar in modern Pakistan).[103] Later, Faxian claimed that while staying in Ceylon, he heard an Indian monk recite a scripture on the Buddha's bowl. According to this monk, the

> Buddha's alms-bowl was originally at Vāiśālī; it is now in Ghandhāra. After a great number of years . . . the bowl will be taken to the country of the Ephthalites of the west; after another similar period, to Khotan; after remaining there for another similar period, to Kara-shahr; after another similar period, it will go back again to China; after remaining there for a similar period, it will go back to Ceylon; and after another similar period, back to Central India. When it arrives there, it will be taken up to heaven; and Maitreya, the Bodhisattva, seeing it, will exclaim with joy, "The alms-bowl of Śākyamuni Buddha has come." . . . Then when Maitreya is about to become a buddha,

[100] Luoyangshi wenwu gongzuodui, "Luoyang Tang Shenhui heshang shenta taji qingli," pp. 64–7.

[101] My discussion of the Buddha's bowl is based on Françoise Wang-Toutain, "Le bol du Buddha. Propagation du bouddhisme et légitimité politique," pp. 59–82.

[102] A representation of this bowl, with four lines at the top representing the four bowls, can be seen at Gandhāra. See Wladimir Zwalf, ed., *Buddhism: Art and Faith*, p. 196, pl. 282, cited in Wang-Toutain, Ibid., p. 61.

[103] *Gaoseng Faxian zhuan*, p. 858b; Giles, *The Travels of Fa-hsien*, p. 14. The identification of Peshawar is from *Faxian zhuan jiaozhu*, Zhang Xuan, ed., p. 40.

the bowl will be divided into four bowls which will revert to their original
position on Mount Vinataka.

As soon as he has actually become a buddha, the four heavenly kings will
once again repeat the process of joining, in the name of Buddha, as in the
case of the former buddha. The thousand buddhas of this aeon of sages will
all use this bowl; and when it has gone, the Buddhist Faith will gradually die
out.[104]

In this schema, the bowl is more than a contact relic of Śākyamuni; it is
also a symbol of buddhahood itself, a sign of the transition from one buddha to the next, and proof of the legitimacy of the buddha-to-come. At
the same time, the bowl is a symbol, or rather a reflection, of the state of
Buddhism in general, for "when it has gone, the Buddhist Faith will gradually die out."

Françoise Toutain-Wang has uncovered traces of the prophecy of the
arrival of the bowl in China in various texts. Most notable of these is a
text "translated" by the Indian monk Narendrayaśas during the Sui dynasty (in 583), the *Scripture of Elder Śrīgupta*.[105] Perhaps in reaction to
the two persecutions of Buddhism he had himself witnessed, Narendrayaśas produced a scripture in which the Buddha is made to prophecy
that some time after his nirvana, when the Dharma is in decline, a great
king "of the kingdom of Sui" will appear to revive Buddhism. Some time
previous to this, the Buddha states, the Buddha's bowl will have arrived
in the kingdom of Sui, so that when this king arises, he will worship and
make offerings to the bowl.[106] Emperor Sui Wendi fulfilled the prophecy
admirably, providing ample support for various Buddhist projects. The
prophecy also fit nicely into Wendi's overall strategy of employing Buddhist texts, relics, and monks to buttress his claim to the right to rule all
of China. Wang-Toutain has in addition traced echoes of this prophecy in
later texts in which "China" was substituted for the more transparent
"Sui" of Narendrayaśas's text, and notes that after the Tang, the symbolism of the Buddha's bowl was seldom evoked, with the notable exception
of the efforts of Khubilai Khan in 1277 to retrieve from Ceylon what he
believed was the Buddha's bowl.[107]

---

[104] *Gaoseng Faxian zhuan*, p. 865c; Giles, Ibid., pp. 74–5.

[105] *Dehu zhangzhe jing*, T no. 545, vol. 14.

[106] Ibid. B, T no. 545, vol. 14, p. 849b20–28; Wang-Toutain, "Le bol du Buddha,"
pp. 75–78.

[107] The Buddha's bowl also appeared in the story of Hārītī, a demon the Buddha subdued by hiding one of her children under his bowl. The story was depicted frequently in Chinese art from the Tang on. See Julia M. Murray, "Representations of Hārītī, the Mother of
Demons, and the Theme of 'Raising the Alms-Bowl' in Chinese Painting," pp. 253–84.

Conclusion

Next to the robe and the bowl, the rug on which monks sat was the most essential part of the monk's uniform. The rug (Skt. *niṣīdana*) is discussed at length in the monastic regulations, where its dimensions, material, and use are carefully prescribed. Familiar with these discussions, Daoxuan distinguished the symbolism of the rug from that of the robe. One of Daoxuan's spirits informed him that in the past, monks carried their rugs draped over their shoulders, in part to secure their robes. But when one such monk was ridiculed for placing something he sat on above the robe, supposedly a symbol of the holy Dharma, the Buddha declared that monks were no longer to place the rug upon their robes; for if a monk is likened to a stupa, then his body is like the sacred relics contained in a stupa, while the rug is the base of the stupa.[108]

More intriguing than the rug is the curiously shaped ringed staff that monks carried with them when traveling. The ring-staff (Ch. *xizhang;* Skt. *khakkara*) consists of a central staff with two to four metal loops on top, from which metal rings hang (figure 7). Various versions of the monastic regulations state that the Buddha instituted use of the ring-staff for monks to frighten off spiders, snakes, and other dangerous beasts that they might encounter in their travels.[109] Shaking the staff can also alert a donor to a monk's presence when he arrives at the door to collect alms.[110]

The number of loops at the top of the staff and of rings attached to the loops varies. Three ring-staffs were uncovered at Famen Monastery, one with two loops and twelve rings, one with two loops and six rings, and another with four loops and twelve rings. Ever ready to assign symbolic meanings to numbers, and equipped with long lists of numbers of doctrines and principles, Buddhist scholars were quick to provide explanations for the proper number of rings on a ring-staff. One scripture, translated perhaps as early as the Eastern Jin, milked the Buddhist numerical lexicon for all it was worth, recommending four loops, variously symbolizing "the severance from the four types of birth, meditation on the four truths, cultivation of the four forms of equanimity, entrance into the four *dhyānas,* the purification of the four empty [regions], the clarification of the four areas of thought, the fortification of the four proper forms of diligence, and attainment of the four divine powers."[111] The same text recommends twelve rings, symbolizing the twelvefold chain of causation, twelve types of *dhyāna,* and so forth. It is difficult to determine if such

---

[108] *Lüxiang gantong zhuan,* pp. 880c–81a.
[109] *Shisong lü* (Skt. *Sarvāstivādavinaya*) 56, p. 417a; *Pinimu jing* 5, p. 826a.
[110] Ibid., p. 375a.
[111] *Dedao ticheng xizhang jing* T no. 785, vol. 17, p. 724c.

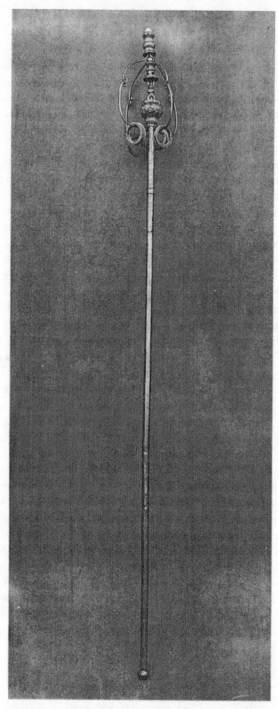

FIG. 7. Ninth-century ring-staff from Famensi. Photograph courtesy of the Shaanxi Famensi Museum.

willy-nilly enumeration had any resonance among medieval Buddhists, but the discovery of a staff with precisely four loops and twelve rings at Famensi suggests that when making such staffs, monks did pay attention to numbers. Other sources list six or eight rings, though we can only guess as to the symbolic meaning of these numbers.[112]

More generally, like the robe or the bowl, the staff appears as an emblem of the monk, and when referring to monks, poets wrote of "the tinkle of a golden ring-staff on a cold snow-covered path" or of a "ring-staff ascending to a monastery on high."[113] And biographies of monks use the phrases "picked up his ring-staff" or "planted his ring-staff" to signify that a monk set off on a journey or settled somewhere.

From medieval times to the present we can easily find images of Chinese monks wearing the outer robe, carrying an alms bowl or a ring-staff, or kneeling on a monk's rug. From early on in the history of Buddhism in China, these objects were emblems of the monk, signs that marked the monk as a distinctive type of person. The ascetic symbolism of the robe and alms bowl were also readily apparent to monk and layman alike. More precise symbolic interpretations of, for instance, the number of robes a monk wore, the substance from which a bowl was made, or the number of rings on a ring-staff were the preserve of sophisticated, well-read monks who could find answers to questions about the significance of these objects in commonly accepted canonical texts. We have also seen, however, that once we venture beyond the world of the erudite monk to the lay patron, and particularly to the imperial patron, the neat rules and categories of the monastic regulations give way beneath the pressures of imperial symbolism, as purple becomes an important color for the monk's robe and gold an acceptable substance for an alms bowl. Even within the monastic community, the symbolic interpretation of objects as fundamental as the robe and the bowl were subject to manipulation and dispute, as, for instance, Chan monks expressed new concerns through the traditional symbols of the robe and bowl, or as other monks shifted attention away from the two inner robes they had abandoned to minute details of the outer robe they continued to wear. Nonetheless, perhaps because of the importance of the monastic uniform to the image of the monk and the attention devoted to it in the monastic regulations, the symbol-

[112] Guanxiu (832–912), for instance, mentions the "six-ringed golden staff" in two of his poems—a description that matches one of the staffs found at Famen, except that the Famen staff is made of copper. See "Song Xinluo naseng," *Quan Tang shi* 836, p. 9418, and "Haijue Chanshi shanyuan," *Quan Tang shi* 837, p. 9437. Yijing writes that in India in his day, monks used staffs of either six or eight rings. *Nanhai jigui neifa zhuan* 4, p. 230b; Takakusu, *A Record of Buddhist Religion*, p. 191.

[113] "Song seng gui shan," by Liu Yanshi, *Quan Tang shi* 468, p. 5328; "Tianzhusi song Jian Shangren gui Lushan," by Bai Juyi, *Quan Tang shi*, 446, p. 5006.

ism of the uniform was remarkably stable, and for the most part the concern of monks alone. The rosary, the subject of the next section, on the other hand, provides us with a clearer example of how symbols translate both between cultures and between the religious and the lay.

THE ROSARY

A rosary appears early on in the great eighteenth-century novel *Dream of the Red Chamber,* when the young protagonist, Jia Baoyu, encounters the Prince of Beijing at a funeral for one of Baoyu's relatives. After chatting with the boy briefly, the graceful prince takes his leave, saying,

> "Today is our first meeting, but as it was an unforeseen one, I have not come prepared with a suitable gift. All I can offer you is this rosary made of the aromatic seeds of some Indian plant. It was given me by His Imperial Majesty. I hope you will accept it as a little token of my esteem."
>
> Baoyu took the rosary and turning back offered it respectfully to [his father] Jia Zheng, who made his son join him in formally thanking the prince for the gift.[114]

Later in the same novel, Baoyu's sister, an imperial concubine, makes a rare visit to see her family. The concubine brings with her an elaborate set of gifts for members of the family. Among the gifts to her grandmother are several *ruyi* scepters, a staff, satin, silk, a number of gold and silver medallions decorated with auspicious designs, and a rosary (of "putchuk beads").[115]

The presence today of a large number of rosaries in what was once the imperial collection (for instance, figure 8) demonstrates that in this episode, Cao Xueqin, author of the *Dream of the Red Chamber,* was quite accurate in his representation of court life: the rosary was indeed a common object in the Qing court. But beyond the basic fact of the prevalence of the object, the *meaning* of the rosary for these figures—what it was used for and what it stood for—is at first elusive. In the first instance, the prince was attending a funeral; perhaps then we are to assume that he brought the rosary to chant the name of Amitābha or some other buddha during the ceremony. Comparison with the concubine's case, however, suggests that the prince may just as likely have brought the rosary along as an ornament or as a potential gift. Baoyu's sister's gift to her grandmother is accompanied by goods with no religious connotations (silk, satin, auspicious medallions), and without suggestion that it is to be used

[114] Chapter 15. David Hawkes, trans., *The Story of the Stone,* p. 289.
[115] Chapter 18. Ibid., p. 372.

FIG. 8. 108-bead rosary with mother bead and reminder, from the Imperial collection. Made of "brown ivory" (*Huangqianya*). Reproduced by permission of the National Palace Museum, Taipei.

as a devotional object. All of this illustrates that in the final centuries of imperial China, the function of the rosary had, at least in some circles, drifted far from its origins in Buddhist ritual.

This is not to say that Qing Chinese did not use the rosary for devotional purposes or that those who exchanged such gifts were not aware of its liturgical function. The very word for rosary, *shuzhu*, literally, "counting beads," immediately betrays the function of the object as a de-

vice for counting prayers.[116] After citing a Tang reference to the rosary,
the eminent Qing scholar Yu Yue (1821–1907) concluded a brief essay on
the beads by noting, "Thus we see that there is a precedent for the practice of *people today* using beads to recite the names of buddhas."[117] For
this nineteenth-century scholar and for scholars of Buddhism today, the
primary function of the rosary is generally and quite rightly assumed to
be to count recitations. This is not surprising, since rosary beads are still
commonly used by practicing Chinese Buddhists for counting recitations
of the name of Amitābha.

But when we look more closely at the history of the rosary in China,
we find that the prince's use of the rosary as a gift to Baoyu that was in
turn given him by the emperor, the concubine's use of the rosary as a decorative object, Yu Yue's note on the devotional use of the object, and a
number of other uses of the beads in the Qing can all be traced back to
associations and functions the rosary accumulated in the long process of
its introduction and assimilation into Chinese culture. I will return to the
Qing at the end of this section; for now we begin with the origins of the
beads in ancient India.[118]

The Rosary in Indian Buddhism

We can safely assume that the rosary came to China with Buddhism: there
is no evidence of the use of prayer beads in pre-Buddhist China, and the
Indian origin of the Chinese rosary is undisputed.[119] But precisely when

[116] In addition to the word *shuzhu*, the rosary is also often referred to in Chinese as
nianzhu, "recitation beads," or more rarely, *chizhu*, "beads for keeping (recitations)." The
English word *rosary* derives from a Christian context in which it means either a particular
set of prayers or prayer beads. In Europe, the origins of the name *rosary* are as obscure as
the origins of the beads themselves. According to a legend popular in the fifteenth century,
the term was coined by a monk who was in the habit of weaving together garlands of roses,
which he used to adorn the Virgin Mary. These he later replaced with sets of Hail Marys.
Henk van Os, *The Art of Devotion in the Later Middle Ages in Europe 1300–1500*, p. 170.

[117] "Chizhu songfo," by Yu Yue, in his *Chaxiangshi sanchao* 17, p. 10a (BJDG edn.).

[118] Two studies on the rosary in Japan provide useful information on the rosary in India
and China as well. See the brief overview in E. Dale Saunders, *Mudrā: A Study of Symbolic
Gestures in Japanese Buddhist Sculpture*, pp. 174–7. For a more detailed discussion, see
George J. Tanabe Jr., "Telling Beads: The Forms and Functions of the Buddhist Rosary in
Japan" (unpublished manuscript). I am indebted to Professor Tanabe's article for a number
of the passages I cite below.

[119] Scholars have also suggested that the rosary used in Islam (from perhaps as early as
the eighth century) and in Christianity (from approximately the thirteenth century) can be
traced back to India. The evidence is slight, and most writing on the subject leaves open the
possibility that the beads developed independently in both Islam and Christianity. On the
rosary in Islam, see A. J. Wensinck, "Subha," p. 492, and Ignaz Goldziher, "Le rosaire dans
l'Islam," pp. 295–300. For Christianity, see Anne Winston-Allen, *Stories of the Rose: The
Making of the Rosary in the Middle Ages*, pp. 111–6.

the rosary first appeared in India is difficult to determine. The monastic regulations and the *Āgamas* (generally considered among the earliest Buddhist scriptures) make no mention of prayer beads, suggesting that the rosary entered Buddhist practice several hundred years after the establishment of a Buddhist monastic order.[120] This, together with the appearance of the rosary in one piece of early brahmanic art, has in turn led some to speculate that the rosary entered Buddhism from brahmanism, but the evidence is so slim and ambiguous that the search for the ultimate origins of the Indian rosary is probably a lost cause.[121]

The earliest datable textual reference to the rosary in any language is the *Mu huanzi jing*, a very brief scripture said to have been translated into Chinese in the Eastern Jin (A.D. 317–420), purportedly from an Indian original.[122] The text, literally the *Scripture of the Seeds of the Ariṣṭaka*, relates the story of a king from a troubled kingdom, wracked by bandits, disease, and famine, who comes to the Buddha for assistance, lamenting that his mind is so troubled by problems of state that he cannot practice Buddhism with a peaceful mind. The Buddha then tells the king,

> If you wish to eliminate the obstacles of affliction and bad karmic consequences, you should string together one hundred and eight seeds from the *ariṣṭaka*.[123] Keep this with you always. Whether you walk, sit, or sleep, always concentrate your mind, not allowing it to stray as you chant (*cheng*) the words "Buddha, Dharma, Sangha," after which you may pass one of the *ariṣṭaka* beads. In this way, gradually work your way through the *ariṣṭaka* beads. Do this ten times, twenty times, a hundred times, a thousand times, and even up to one hundred million times. If you can [chant through the

[120] Nor does iconography provide evidence for the rosary in early Buddhism. As far as I can tell, Sañci and Bharhut contain no examples of the rosary. By the seventh century, the rosary appears regularly in Hindu sculpture.

[121] See Mochizuki Shinkō, *Bukkyō daijiten*, s.v. "Juzu," pp. 2474a–7a, in which Mochizuki argues for a Brahmanic origin of the rosary on the basis of an image of what he claims is a brahman holding a rosary at Sahr-bohl. I have been unable to obtain a photograph of the image Mochizuki referred to. Works in various languages refer to the "origins of the rosary in Brahmanism," but Mochizuki seems to be the only one to have presented any evidence for this theory, attempting to explain what is probably an unresolvable problem.

[122] This text is not mentioned in our earliest Buddhist bibliography, the *Chu sanzang jiji*. As far as I can tell, the earliest reference to the text is in the catalog *Zhongjing mulu* (*juan* 3), completed in 594, where the title is listed. Hence the text may not have appeared before the sixth century. The text is quoted in Daoshi's *Fayuan zhulin* (34, p. 551b) completed in 668. Another version of the text was purportedly translated by Amogavajra in the eighth century, lending credence to the assumption that this was a translation of an Indian original rather than a Chinese work. See Ono Genmyō, ed., *Busshō kaisetsu daijiten*, vol. 11, p. 11d.

[123] Identified as *Sapindus Mukurossi* in Maku Takamaro, *Butsuden no shokubutsu*; Tanabe, in his "Telling Beads," gives "soapberry seed."

beads] two hundred thousand times then you will feel no confusion in body or mind, nor will you be swayed by flattery. When you give up this life, you will be born in the third heaven, realm of the *yāma* gods, where your clothing and food will be supplied naturally and you will constantly abide in tranquility, joyfully practicing [Buddhism]. If you can complete a full one million [rounds of the rosary], then you will cut off all hundred and eight forms of karma. Only then will you turn your back to the stream of life and death and head toward nirvana. Forever cutting off the roots of affliction, you will thereby achieve the highest reward.[124]

This early prescription for the use of the rosary tells us, first of all, that in contrast to the monastic symbols and emblems discussed above, the rosary was from very early on used by the Buddhist laity, in this case in order to gain merit by chanting the names of the "three jewels," that is, Buddha, Dharma, and Sangha. The text attributes a number of benefits to chanting. The Buddha insists that, as in other forms of Buddhist meditation, one is not to allow the mind to "stray" while chanting. The lines that follow suggest that the improved capacity for concentration developed through this practice will allow the king to think more clearly and hence to see through the deceit of unreliable advisers. On a higher level, chanting the names of the three jewels wins one a place in paradise and can even lead to nirvana, the loftiest goal of all. The scale by which this hierarchy of rewards is measured is based on the number of recitations, and the rosary is used to keep track of this all-important number. With the rosary one can know how many recitations remain before one can expect one's mind to finally clear, or before one's position among the gods is secure. In other texts, the rosary is variously used to keep track of recitations of spells, the names of bodhisattvas, or the names of buddhas.[125] As we will see below, however, in addition to its function as a counting device, the rosary is often assumed to have magical properties of its own. Not only did the rosary count recitations; a recitation marked with a rosary somehow counted more.

A part of what imbued the rosary with these special powers was its symbolic content. Already in this text we see one of the most enduring symbolic aspects of the rosary when the text instructs its reader to make the rosary with 108 beads, each bead representing one of the 108 afflictions. This number is repeated in dozens of descriptions of the rosary in later texts, most of which equate the number of beads with the number of

---

[124] *Mu huanzi jing, T* no. 786, vol. 17, p. 726a.
[125] *Jin'gangding yujia nianzhu jing, T* no. 789, vol. 17; *Da Biluzhe'na jing guangda yigui* C, *T* no. 851, vol. 18, p. 107c.

afflictions. Some, like the *Scripture on the Evaluation of Merits of the Rosary from the Spell Treasury of Mañjuśrī*,[126] translated from an Indian original by Yijing (635–713), provide for more flexibility, stating that if it is difficult to obtain 108 beads, one can make a rosary of half that number (54), half *that* number (27), or even of a mere 14 beads.

This concern for numbers discloses the close relationship between symbolism and sacred power. That is, the number of beads in the rosary is not simply a way of conveying information about the number of afflictions one must confront; rather, the proper number of beads is important for making the rosary effective—not just any string of beads will do. This tendency to emphasize the "efficacy" of a rosary not just for accurate accounting but for its magical power comes to the fore in discussions of the way rosaries were made and the stuff they were made of. Ritual texts, for instance, place particular importance on the act of consecrating or empowering (*jiachi*) the beads. This is usually done by chanting a special spell over the beads before their first use.[127] An Indian text translated into Chinese in the Song goes into the process of making the rosary in great detail, stipulating that once one has selected a potential tree as a source of beads for a rosary, one should first sleep beneath the tree and examine one's dreams before going ahead with its manufacture. Further, once the beads have been selected, they must be strung together by a virgin and then sacralized with a spell.[128]

Buddhist texts allow for use of various substances, in addition to the *ariṣṭaka*, when making a rosary. The text translated by Yijing lists nine substances, including iron, pearl, coral, crystal, and the seeds of a bodhi tree. These are arranged from least effective (iron) to most effective (seeds from a bodhi tree).[129] As the bodhi tree was the tree under which the Buddha achieved enlightenment, it is understandable that a rosary made of its seeds was considered supremely potent. The logic behind the hierarchical

[126] *Manshushili zhouzangzhong jiaoliang shuzhu gongde jing, T* no. 787, vol. 17. A different version of the same text was translated by Baosiwei, *T* no. 788.

[127] For instance, *Putichang suoshuo yizi dinglun wang jing T* no. 950, vol. 19, p. 202a–b; *Bai san'gai dafodingwang zuisheng wubi daweide jin'gang wu'ai dadaochang tuoluoni niansong fayao, T* no. 975, vol. 19, p. 400c.

[128] See the chapter on rosaries in Tianxizai's, *Da fangguang pusazang Wenshushili genben yigui jing, T* no. 1191, vol. 20, pp. 873a–4a.

[129] *Jiaoliang shuzhu gongde jing, T* no. 788, vol. 17, p. 727. A similar list is given in the *Jin'gangding yujia nianzhu jing, T* no. 789, vol. 17, p. 727, translated by Amoghavajra (Ch. Bukong). George Tanabe notes that the bodhi tree does not produce seeds large enough to be used for a rosary, and that usually the seeds used in a "Bodhi-seed rosary" are in fact from the Bodhici tree that grows in the Himalayan mountain region. See Tanabe, "Telling Beads."

placement of elements like coral, crystal, and pearl is less apparent, and relates, perhaps, to their availability in medieval India, or perhaps to the perceived purity of the various substances.

Tantric texts (in which rosaries frequently appear) at times prescribe different types of rosaries for different rituals (crystal for the "ritual of faith and love"; *ariṣṭaka* for the "ritual of wrath"), or for different categories of deities (seeds of a bodhi tree for deities of the "Buddha family," lotus seeds for deities belonging to the "lotus family," etc.).[130] Other Indian texts describe in detail the care one must take in selecting beads and making a proper rosary. The *Scripture of the Symposium of Dhāraṇīs*, for instance, advises:

> The Buddha said that one who wishes to make a rosary with the marks of the Dharma (*faxiang shuzhu*) should first call upon the services of a bead craftsman. Regardless of the price, the beads must be of good quality. If they are precious gems, they must never have been used for another purpose. Each bead must be clear inside and out, without crack or blemish. They should be round, clean, and sparkling. You may choose whichever size you wish.

Again, the attention to the quality of the beads and the proscriptions against using beads that had been previously used for another (presumably profane) purpose points to the special nature of the rosary as the powerful accoutrement of the ritual adept, distinguishing it from common jewelry and the tools of the accountant. The text goes on to describe a ritual of purification the bead maker must undergo, and concludes by explaining how the bead maker should supply a bead of gold for the mother bead (*muzhu*)—the large bead that marks the center point of the rosary. This is an important part of the rosary, since it alerts users that they have gone through the ring of beads once. The same text also prescribes making a "reminder" (*jizi*)—a tail of ten beads, attached to the mother bead—again to remind users that they have made one round of the rosary (figure 8).[131] Elsewhere, the mother bead is explained symbolically as representing Amitābha, while the string that hold the beads together represents Avalokiteśvara, and the remaining beads, the "fruits of the bodhisattva." When counting through the rosary, one is not to pass over the

---

[130] For the use of different beads for different rituals, see *Da beikongzhi jin'gang dajiaowang yigui jing* (Skt. *Hevajra[ḍākinījālasambara]tantra*) 5, T no. 892, vol. 18, p. 601a, trans. by Dharmapāla (Ch. Fahu) in the eleventh century (mentioned by the eleventh-century Japanese pilgrim Jōjin in his *San Tendai Godaisan ki* 1.4b, vol. 115, p. 147). For recommendations of different beads for different deities, see *Zhufo jingjie shezhenshi jing* C, T no. 868, vol. 18, p. 281c, trans. by Prajñā (Ch. Banruo) in the late eighth century, as well as T no. 866, vol. 18, pp. 248a–b; and T no. 894, vol. 18, p. 701a. On the notion of categories or "families" of deities, see Snellgrove, *Indo-Tibetan Buddhism*, pp. 189–98.

[131] *Tuoluoni ji jing* 2, T no. 901, vol. 18, p. 803a–b.

mother bead—a serious infraction—but is instead to reverse the direction of counting once the mother bead is reached.[132] In this reference to the mother bead "representing" Avalokiteśvara, and the injunction that one is not to pass over this bead, we see more clearly that the rosary was imbued with divine power that needed to be carefully attended to, for to pass over Avalokiteśvara's bead was to insult the bodhisattva himself.

In short, like the stupas, relics, and icons discussed in chapter 1, the beads themselves were thought to contain sacred power. At the very least, this notion laid the groundwork for the eventual use of the rosary as a talisman, and, while I have found no evidence directly pointing to this use in ancient India, it seems likely that the rosary was used as a talisman by some ancient Indians to fend off hostility and danger. We come close to this idea in a passage in the *Merits of the Rosary,* mentioned above, which states that even if one is incapable of chanting the names of the buddhas or *dhāraṇīs,* one can garner the same amount of merit simply by carrying the rosary on one's person.

Naturally enough, use of the rosary brings with it the rewards of recitation. The three most famous texts devoted specifically to the rosary all extol the value of chanting with the rosary for gaining merit and purifying oneself of faults.[133] The *Rosary from the Spell Treasury of Mañjuśrī* notes vaguely that the rosary brings benefit to oneself and others, and that through recitation with the rosary one can be born in one of "the various Pure Lands." As we have seen, the *Scripture of the Seeds of the Ariṣṭaka* similarly lists birth in a heaven as one of the rewards for practicing with the rosary. Other texts describe the use of the rosary in rituals that induce fertility in barren women or make charmed water to cure disease.[134]

In these last two instances, the one who is to hold the rosary is not the woman seeking a child or a sick man seeking a cure; it is instead the monk who orchestrates the ritual. The texts tell us little about whether such lay figures used the rosary, much less how they perceived it. Nevertheless, the presence of a layman at the center of our earliest datable description of the rosary alerts us to the possibility of widespread use of the rosary among Buddhist laypeople already in ancient India.[135]

[132] See *Jin'gangding yujia nianzhu jing,* p. 727c, translated by Amoghavajra. The passage is quoted in *Jin'gangding jing yizi dinglunwang yujia yiqieshichu niansong chengfo yigui, T* no. 957, vol. 19, p. 325b.

[133] The *Mu huanzi jing,* the *Jiaoliang shuzhu gongde jing,* and the *Jin'gangding yujia nianzhu jing.*

[134] The first is from the *Tuoluoni ji jing* 4, p. 819a–b, the second from the *Yiqie rulai wusenisha zuisheng zongchi jing,* trans. in the Song by Fahu, *T* no. 978, vol. 19, p. 408b.

[135] Similarly, in the absence of archaeological evidence, it is difficult to determine what materials actual rosaries were made of and, more importantly, just how widespread use of the rosary was. A compilation of texts translated into Chinese in the eighth century by Amoghavajra specifically states that for a ritual described in the text, "One does *not* resort

In sum, Indian Buddhist texts translated into Chinese in the early medieval period reflect the belief that the repetition of certain magical words and phrases brought great benefits, ranging from increased powers of concentration to rebirth in a paradise, or even attainment of nirvana. The rosary was used by monastic and lay alike for keeping track of the number of these recitations. But more than this, the rosary was also given symbolic as well as magical significance that increased the power of recitation. The relationship here between symbolism and magical power is particularly important. The 108 beads of the rosary, symbolizing the 108 afflictions, did more than convey information—it was more than a reminder to the adepts of the precise number of their potential problems. Precise symbolic criteria were necessary for the ritual of recitation to work.

The Introduction of the Rosary to China:
Fourth to Tenth Centuries

The earliest reference to the rosary in China is the same *Scripture of the Seeds of the Ariṣṭaka*, mentioned above, translated in the Eastern Jin (A.D. 317–420). At roughly the same time, during the Northern Wei (386–534), an image of a bodhisattva with a rosary dangling from his hand was chiseled in stone in a cave in what is now Gansu, at Mount Maiji.[136] While a number of texts translated into Chinese in the following centuries mention rosaries, before the Tang, references to *Chinese* people using rosaries or prescribing their use are scarce.[137] Iconography also presents a problem in that, while bodhisattvas are frequently depicted adorned with various sorts of beaded necklaces, it is at times difficult to determine if any of these were used as rosaries. Further, because most such images are positioned with their backs to the cave wall, very rarely is it possible to count beads draped around the neck—a useful method for separating rosaries from other types of necklaces. But strings of beads dangling from a figure's hand, which are clearly rosaries, can be found from the Northern Zhou (557–81) at Binglingsi, and from the Sui (581–618) at Mogaoku in Dunhuang, and at Tuoshan in Shandong.

---

to setting a limit [to the number of incantations] by counting one's beads," indicating that at least by this time the rosary was so common that if a ritual did not call for the rosary, it was necessary to specifically proscribe its use. See *Jin'gangding jing yujia shibahui zhigui*, T no. 869, vol. 18; English translation by Rolf W. Giebel, "The *Chin-kang-ting ching yü-ch'ieh shih-pa-hui chih-kuei*: An Annotated Translation," p. 198.

[136] In Cave 23. See Tianshui Maijishan Shikuyishu Yanjiusuo, ed., *Chūgoku sekkutsu: Bakusekisan sekkutsu*, pl. 65.

[137] In fact, I have yet to find a single pre-Tang textual reference to the use of the rosary *in China*.

In the Tang we begin to get richer evidence for the use of the rosary both in texts and in Buddhist art. Perhaps the rosary experienced a sudden growth in popularity at this time. It is just as likely, however, that the scarcity of evidence for the rosary from previous periods is the result of the relative scarcity of evidence on monastic life in general and private devotional life in particular. Prayers repeated quietly at home by anonymous laymen, or droned in a monastery by humble monks, were not the stuff of monumental sculpture. Hence, perhaps we should see continuity rather than innovation in a relief from 629 depicting a monk holding a rosary prominently in his left hand, and bearing the inscription "bhiksu monk Xiushan of the Zhenhai Monastery (figure 9)."[138] It is likely that monks like this one marked recitations with rosaries centuries earlier. Certainly by the seventh century the practice was common. The small individual stupas at Baoshan in Henan provide us with a number of seventh-century statues of monks and nuns with rosaries in hand.[139] The importance of the rosary in the lay image of the monk is reflected in a poem by Zhang Ji (c. 776–c. 829), dedicated to a monk, which ends with the line "I often hear from within his sleeves the sound of the rosary secretly fingered."[140] On a more concrete level, in a discussion of monastic property in an influential work on the monastic regulations, Daoxuan felt it necessary to determine the proper classification of the rosary, indicating that the rosary was a common part of a monk's equipment.[141] And the rosary appears in assorted Tang stories, such as an episode in the biography of the eighth-century monk Wuzhuo, who offers his rosary to a mysterious old man he encounters in the mountain mists of Wutai.[142]

It was at this time, in the Tang, that the position of the rosary as an emblem for the monk became firmly entrenched in the Chinese imagination. Two rather crude examples illustrate this point well. The first is a prose-poem by the Tang figure Bai Xingjian, younger brother of the famous poet Bai Juyi. The final lines of the poem—a lampoon of the sexual lives of monks and nuns—note suggestively, "The Buddha Law does not relieve [the nuns] of their thoughts, and they finger more than rosaries."[143] The

[138] In the Honolulu Academy of Arts. See Jin, *Zhongguo lidai jinian foxiang tudian*, pl. 251.

[139] See Baoshan, stupa no. 77, and Lanfeng, stupa nos. 38, 42, and 47 in Henansheng gudai jianzhu baohu yanjiusuo, *Baoshan Lingquansi*.

[140] *Quan Tang shi* 384, p. 4325.

[141] *Sifenlü shanfan buque xingshichao* C1, p. 115b; in the Song, Yuanzhao takes up the classification of the rosary as monastic property in more detail. *Sifenlü xingshichao zichi ji*, T no. 1805, vol. 40, p. 375a.

[142] *Song gaoseng zhuan*, 20, p. 836c.

[143] "Tian di yinyang jiao huan da le fu" in *Shuangmei jing'an congshu*, ed., Ye Dehui (1903 edn.) 1, p. 7b. I translated this passage slightly differently in *The Eminent Monk*, p. 20. It was also at this time that the rosary was established as a common iconographic

FIG. 9. Arhat, 629. Honolulu Academy of Arts, Gift of Mrs. Charles M. Cooke, 1928 (2608). Reproduced by permission of the Honolulu Academy of Arts.

other example is from a collection of anecdotes compiled in the Song, but which probably dates back to the late Tang. The story relates that when the eminent monk Guanxiu was riding alongside the prominent Daoist Du Guangting, Guanxiu's horse relieved itself on the road. Du, noting the balls of manure, turned to Guanxiu and joked, "Master, Master, your rosary fell on the ground." Guanxiu replied, "It is not a rosary; the horse

feature of the arhat (*luohan*). Images of arhats holding rosaries appear at the Kanjing Monastery at Longmen. See *Longmen shiku diaosu,* pl. 197, in Zhongguo meishu quanji bianji weiyuanhui, ed., *Zhongguo meishu quanji* 2, vol. 11.

is 'returning its cinnabar,'" a reference to Daoist alchemy in which cinnabar was a common ingredient.[144] Humor reveals widely held associations with rare precision; it is only because the authors of such pieces could assume that their readers would make associations between particular objects and their owners (the rosary and the Buddhist monk, cinnabar and the Daoist adept), and that these associations commonly evoked images of solemn piety, that the jokes worked.

In the Tang we also begin to get references to the rosary by leading Chinese monks. The *Further Biographies of Eminent Monks*, compiled in the early part of the seventh century, mentions a rosary in passing in a biography of a monk who lived at the end of the Sui.[145] Huizhao (fl. 710) notes in a commentary on a ritual text that the rosaries used in the ritual symbolize good fortune and wisdom.[146] In a study of the *Diamond Sutra*, Kuiji (632–82) notes that one of the "five improper ways for a monk to sustain himself" (*wu xieming*) is through ostentatious piety, "for example by chanting the rosary when sitting or standing" in public.[147] For monastic piety to be authentic, it had to be discreet. Rosaries, it seems, were to be kept in one's room or up one's sleeve. Feixi (fl. 742) went a step further, recommending against the rosary altogether. He writes: "Among men of the world, most make rosaries of crystal, vajra-seeds, bodhi-seeds, or *ariṣṭaka*. I use the inhaling and exhaling of my breath as my rosary. I chant the names of the buddhas in accordance with my breath. This is a very reliable method."[148] Such references tell us that by this time the rosary was so common among Chinese monks that some found its use crass and superficial. It is likely, though, that such monks were exceptions, so familiar with Buddhist liturgy that they felt comfortable introducing choice innovations.

The first great champion of the rosary in China was the charismatic monk Daochuo (562–645). An important figure in the history of Pure Land practice in China, Daochuo was known for encouraging his followers to chant aloud the name of Amitābha. His biography in the *Further Biographies of Eminent Monks* describes his tireless promotion of the rosary as follows:

> Daochuo encouraged others when chanting the name of Amitābha Buddha to use objects such as sesame seeds to keep track of the number of recitations. With each recitation of the name one was to move one seed. In this

---

[144] *Wudaishi bu*, by Tao Yue (SKQS edn.) 1, p. 14a.

[145] *Xu gaoseng zhuan* 29, p. 698c19, biography of Huiyun.

[146] *Shiyimian shenzhou xinjing yishu*, T no. 1802, vol. 39, p. 1009b.

[147] *Jin'gang banruo jing zanshu* A, T no. 1700, vol. 33, p. 126b. Ironically, when the Japanese pilgrim Jōjin visited China in the eleventh century, he observed a statue of Kuiji, depicted holding a rosary. *San Tendai Godaisan ki* 3, p. 57a.

[148] *Nianfo sanmei baowang lun*, T no. 1967, vol. 47, p. 138c.

way one can keep account of the recitations until one has filled millions of bushels. . . . In addition, one year [Daochuo] took to stringing together seeds from the *muluan*[149] as a method of counting. He gave these to the "four assemblies" [monks, nuns, laywomen, and laymen] and told them to chant.[150]

The reference here to the "four assemblies" is important because it suggests, once again, that use of the rosary was not limited to the "two assemblies" of monks and nuns, but extended to the other "two assemblies" of laymen and laywomen. The practice of using the rosary to chant the name of Amitābha, rather than, say, the three jewels as in the *Scripture of the Seeds of the Ariṣṭaka,* eventually became the norm.

The Buddhist canon, concerned primarily with translations of Indian texts and the ruminations of eminent monks, provides notoriously little information on the devotional life of lay Chinese Buddhists. Official sources like the Dynastic Histories, on the other hand, colored by the general disinterest of their compilers in Buddhism, do little to fill in this gap. In the case of the rosary, the problem is compounded by the fact that, as several of the references I cite above disclose, the rosary was closely associated with *private* devotion. And what was true for monks (the monk in Zhang Ji's poem chants with his rosary "secretly," while Kuiji criticizes monks who finger their beads in public) was equally true for laypeople. Nevertheless, scattered references slip through even sources such as these, revealing that Buddhist devotion was a part of the lives of laypeople during the Tang, and that the rosary played a role in this devotion. The official biography of the eunuch Li Fuguo (d. 762), one of the most powerful figures at Suzong's court, notes that Li was known both for his adept political machinations and for his Buddhist devotion. The biography states that Li "did not eat meat or unclean foods. He often conducted himself like a monk. Whenever he had a leisure moment, his hands would reach for a rosary. Everyone believed that this was a mark of goodness."[151] The phrase "conducted himself like a monk" seems to indicate that the rosary was seen chiefly as an emblem of the monk at this time, and not necessarily associated with Buddhist devotion more generally.

Other anecdotal evidence suggests, however, that use of the rosary by Tang laypeople was fairly widespread. For example, the *Queshi,* a Tang collection of anecdotes, contains a reference to a certain Layman Wang, clearly of more humble status than Li Fuguo. A devout Buddhist, Layman Wang "always held a rosary and chanted the names of the buddhas."[152]

---

[149] *Koelrevleria paniculata.*

[150] *Xu gaoseng zhuan* 20, p. 594a. Daochuo's only extant work, the *An le xing,* contains no references to the rosary.

[151] *Jiu Tang shu,* 134, p. 4759.

[152] *Que shi,* by Gao Yanxiu (BJDG edn.) B, p. 11b. The story is quoted in the *Taiping guangji* 84, p. 542. This is the story alluded to in the passage by Yu Yue cited above.

Similarly, the *Song Biographies of Eminent Monks* refers at one point to the prominent figure Wei Gao (746–806), saying, "In his later years, Wei Gao became a particularly devout Buddhist, always carrying a rosary about with him, and chanting the names of the buddhas. He even taught a parrot that he raised to chant scriptures."[153]

Images of laypeople with rosaries in pre-Song China are as rare as textual references to lay use of the rosary during the period. Again, this stems most likely from the association of the rosary with private devotion. Most of the images we have of lay Buddhists in medieval China are depicted together with others (usually donors who contributed to the art work in which they appear) in an act of public devotion. One exception is from Baoshan, where a seventh-century layman and laywoman are depicted holding rosaries.[154] A tenth-century drawing from Dunhuang provides us with another rare glimpse of a lay use of the rosary (figure 10) that was surely more common in real life than painting and sculpture might lead us to believe.

Thus far the history of the rosary follows a predictable path. Monks used the rosary in their personal devotions to keep track of recitations of names of buddhas or spells. Once introduced to China, Chinese monks used the rosary in their devotions, to the extent that it became a basic component of the monk's personal belongings and an emblem of the monastic life. Further, from very early on, whether in scripture, commentary, or in more public forms of proselytizing, monks encouraged laypeople to use the rosary when practicing recitation, including recitations of the three jewels of the Buddha, the Dharma and the Sangha, and, with Daochuo, including as well recitation of the name of Amitābha. At the same time, monks invested the rosary with symbolism, assigning meanings to the number of beads, the material used to make the beads, the mother bead that divided the rosary, the cord that strings the rosary together, and so forth. As time wore on, however, the rosary acquired additional uses, beyond its origins as a devotional tool.

Nondevotional Uses of the Rosary: Tenth to Seventeenth Centuries

One of the ways monks used the rosary was as a gift. To celebrate the occasion of a baby prince, whom the emperor had pledged would become a monk, having reached his first full month, the great Chinese pilgrim Xuanzang submitted a flowery letter together with a long list of gifts that included "one religious robe, an incense burner together with a table to

---

[153] *Song gaoseng zhuan* 19, p. 830c.

[154] Henansheng gudai jianzhu baohu yanjiuso, ed., *Baoshan Lingquansi*, Baoshan, no. 83; Lanfeng, no. 48.

FIG. 10. Layman with rosary. Ink drawing from Dunhuang, early to mid-tenth
century. Stein Painting 158 (detail). Reproduced by permission of the
British Museum.

place it on for burning incense, a bathing jug, a reading shelf, a rosary, a
staff with pewter rings, and a vessel containing bathing powder—all articles used by a monk—to express my personal exultation."[155] The key
to understanding the symbolic significance of the gift comes in the last
line, where Xuanzang notes that all of his gifts are "articles used by a

<hr/>

[155] *Da Ciensi sanzang fashi zhuan* p. 272b; Li Rongxi, *A Biography of the Tripiṭika Master,* p. 305.

monk." Here, then, the rosary is a gift from one monk to another (potential) monk, the baby prince. More often, however, the rosary is given from monk to layman, and is a symbol not of a shared monastic identity or even of devotion but is instead a token of friendship. In 838, during his pilgrimage to China, the Japanese monk Ennin met with a high official, who visited the monastery where he was staying. Eight days after the meeting, Ennin wrote in his diary, "We wrote a letter of thanks to the Minister of State for coming to the monastery and inquiring after us. We also gave him a few things—two rosaries of rock crystal, six knives decorated with silver, twenty assorted brushes, and three conch shells."[156] The Buddhist content of these gifts is not immediately apparent. Conch shells and knives were used in some Buddhist rituals, but there is nothing specifically Buddhist about "twenty assorted brushes," and one doubts whether a minister of state would have much use for equipment employed in complex Tantric rituals. Lumped together as it is with secular objects, the "rosaries of rock crystal" seem not be have been given for devotional purposes, or even for vaguer associations with Buddhist doctrine. Rather, like the fancy knives, brushes, and exotic shells, they were given primarily for their aesthetic appeal.

Just before his death, Amoghavajra, an eighth-century monk with connections much grander than those of Ennin, submitted to the throne "a rosary made of the seeds of a bodhi tree and crystal beads."[157] Again there is no indication that the emperor was expected to use the rosary to chant, although this possibility cannot be ruled out. Because monks were expected to keep a distance between themselves and material wealth—if only symbolically—they had only limited options when deciding on gifts to prominent figures. The rosary, made of exotic Indian wood or crystal, expertly carved, yet still carrying associations of pious devotion, was the perfect solution.[158] There is no indication that monks saw anything wrong with this. We hear no cries of "defilement" or "profanation" of what, in a private devotional context, was a sacred object charged with specifically Buddhist symbolism.

In these cases, even if the symbolism of the rosary has shifted from the elimination of afflictions to a token of friendship or respect, and even if it is removed from its devotional context, because it was the gift of a

---

[156] *Nittō guhō junrei gyōki* 1, p. 65; Reischauer, *Ennin's Diary,* p. 50.

[157] *Song gaoseng zhuan* 1, p. 713b.

[158] Other examples of monks giving and receiving rosaries can be found in various sources. The Song work *Meng liang lu,* for instance, records that the tenth-century monk Yongming Yanshou received a gift of golden thread for a *kāṣāya* and a purple, rock-crystal rosary from admirers of his in Korea. *Meng liang lu,* by Wu Zimu, in *Dongjing menghua lu wai sizhong* 17, p. 277. Jōjin mentions gifts of rosaries repeatedly in his eleventh-century travelogue. *San Tendai Godaisanki,* pp. 7b, 12b, 14a, 18b, 19b, 21a, 31a, 37a, 143a.

monk, the rosary still maintained some associations with monks and Buddhism, however faint. Other sources, however, indicate that at times the
rosary could not be contained by even these nebulous parameters. In a
collection of anecdotes, the Tang writer Feng Zhi tells the story of a brilliant disciple of the Tang official and religious aficionado Fang Guan
(697–763).

> Fang Cilü (a.k.a. Fang Guan) had a disciple named Jintu. When Jintu was
> twelve years old, Cilü questioned him about some matters in Ge Hong's tran-
> scendent writings (xianlu). The boy kept track with a crystal rosary, which
> he went through twice. He went through approximately two hundred items,
> chanting them fluently without stopping. Cilü rewarded him with a peony
> pear.[159]

Here the rosary is used to keep track not of recitations of the name of a
buddha but for recalling the Daoist writings of Ge Hong. Note that in the
story the boy went through the rosary twice, making for "approximately
two hundred items," indicating that the rosary may well have been composed of the traditional 108 beads. Yet there is not even a hint of Buddhism in the anecdote. The passage calls to mind another of Feng Zhi's
works, entitled Jishi zhu, meaning "Beads for Remembering Things," so
called because, as Feng explains in the work, when he was a young student, he would count the beads on a beaded curtain in his house to keep
track of what he had learned. In other words, although probably aware
of the Buddhist origins of the rosary, for Feng and the figures in his anecdote, the rosary could be used as a memory device without Buddhist connotations or any sense that the object was a sanctified, holy conduit for
devotion.

Similarly, the influential Northern Song thinker Cheng Yi (1033–
1107), who recommended controlling one's desires through reflection,
also offered advice on how to overcome an excess of reflection when trying to get to sleep. He gave a rosary to the prominent Song writer Shao
Bowen, who suffered from insomnia, "just so that he could use it to count,
in the same way the Daoists count their breaths."[160] Apparently, Cheng
used the rosary as a device for lulling himself to sleep—the Song equivalent of counting sheep. The key phrase here is "just so that he could use
it to count." In other words, Cheng had stripped the rosary of its Buddhist symbolism and concomitant sacred power, appropriating it for a
thoroughly mundane purpose. Perhaps there is a parallel between Cheng's
attempt to reduce excessive thinking and counting to concentrate the

---

[159] "Shuiyu shuzhu" in Yunxian zaji (SBCK edn.) 1, p. 4a. Feng is quoting from an earlier, no longer extant book, titled Tongzi tongshen ji.
[160] "Chengzi zhi shu: san" in Zhuzi yulei, 97, pp. 2491–2.

mind—as in the case of the king whom the Buddha encouraged to chant
with a rosary. But in place of achieving nirvana, Cheng simply wants to
get some sleep. We are here a long way from the rosary of Buddhist
scriptures.

A hundred years later, Lu You (1125–1210), describing the customs
of a southern, non-Han people, wrote that "[b]efore a male takes a wife,
he wears golden chicken feathers in his hair; before a female marries,
she hangs a rosary of seashells around her neck."[161] The reference to
seashells—unheard of in Buddhist descriptions of the rosary—suggests
that these necklaces bore no relation to Buddhist rosaries, and that for Lu
You, "rosary" (shuzhu) was simply another word for necklace. Residents
of the Southern Song capital at Hangzhou seem to have used the word
just as loosely. In his account of Hangzhou, Song writer Wu Zimu lists
various goods sold in the city's markets, at one point mentioning the merchants "along the sides of the streets hawking all manner of food for children," including baked biscuits, sugarcane, bitter sticks, lotus meat, and
rosaries.[162] We can only guess what exactly is meant by "rosary" here—
perhaps some sort of candied fruit strung together in a ring. Regardless
of the exact nature of the object, here we are far removed from the reverential, symbolically charged environment of Buddhist ritual texts or the
pious sermons of evangelical monks promoting Pure Land practice.

With the appearance of a body of literature on connoisseurship in the
Ming, this tendency to treat the rosary as an amusing aesthetic object
comes into clearer focus. Wen Zhenheng (1585–1645), in his *Treatise on
Superfluous Things* (*Zhangwu zhi*)—a compendium of pronouncements
on how a cultivated gentleman should tastefully select objects for his
home—discusses the proper assessment of studios, flowers, ornamental
rocks, painting, furniture, and so on.[163] In a section on "vessels and utensils," which includes discussion of lamps, mirrors, incense burners, lutes,
and pillows, Wen gives the following description of the standards by
which he judges rosaries:

> The most valuable type of rosary is made with vajra seeds,[164] ornate and del-
> icate. For a "reminder"[165] one should use a "Demon-subduing Vajra" made
> in the Song, or one of the "five offerings" made of jade.[166] Other substances

[161] *Laoxuean biji* 4, p. 22, in *Lu Fangweng quanji.*

[162] "Zhu se za huo," *Meng liang lu,* p. 245.

[163] Craig Clunas discusses this treatise at length in his *Superfluous Things: Material Culture and Social Status in Early Modern China.*

[164] *Jin'gangzi.* I have been unable to determine precisely what type of beads these were.

[165] *Zongji,* that is, a string of beads or other objects, extending from the mother bead,
to remind one that one has gone around the ring once (above referred to as *jizi*).

[166] The five offerings (*wu gongyang*) are incense paste, flowers, incense, foodstuffs, and
lamps.

such as skull bone, "dragon rock," jade, agate, amber, gold-amber, crystal, coral, and tridacna are all vulgar. Aloeswood or *qienan* aromatic wood can both be used. Substances that should be carefully avoided include Hangzhou bodhi seeds and perfumed wood (*guanxiang*).[167]

If we want to trace the sources for Wen's ideas about the rosary, rather than look to Buddhist scriptures, we must turn instead to writings in a similar style by other Ming connoisseurs.[168] Certainly Wen's preference for "vajra" seeds finds support in Buddhist scriptures, but the crystal and coral he disparages are both extolled in Buddhist scriptures, which say nothing about aloeswood or *qienan* aromatic wood. Unlike the ritual texts discussed above, the key distinction in Wen's assessment is not between numinous and mundane, much less between this or that deity or this or that ritual; the key distinction is instead between vulgar and elegant, categories of the Ming connoisseur that have nothing to do with Buddhism or religious values.[169] In the same vein, Wen cautions that certain substances are to "be avoided" (*ji*) for aesthetic rather than doctrinal or liturgical reasons.

In short, while monks and laypeople in the Ming continued to use the rosary for devotional purposes, at least some Ming literati at the same time approached the beads from an entirely different perspective. It may be going too far to say that they assigned different *symbolic* meaning to the rosary, but they certainly assigned it a different set of values. For a clear example of a community that did specifically assign new symbolic, or emblematic, meanings to the rosary, we turn briefly to the use of the rosary in the Qing court.

The Rosary at the Qing Court

One of the differences between paintings of court life in the Ming and in the Qing is the use by Qing royalty and certain Qing high officials of necklaces, which, on closer inspection, turn out to be rosaries, made up of 108

[167] *Zhangwuzhi jiaozhu*, Chen Zhi and Yang Chaobo, eds., 7, p. 288.

[168] In fact, most of what Wen says about the rosary is taken directly from the *Kaopan yushi* by Tu Long (1542–1605). See "Shuzhu," in *Kaopan yushi* (CSJC edn.) 4, p. 85. For a discussion on the relationship between Wen and Tu's texts, see Clunas, *Superfluous Things*, pp. 28–31.

[169] On the distinction between elegant and vulgar in Wen's work, see Clunas, *Superfluous Things*, pp. 82–3. Of course a familiarity and respect for the religious function of the rosary does not necessarily preclude an aesthetic appreciation of the beads as well. The Tang monk Jiaoran, for instance, composed a "Song to a Crystal Rosary" ("Shuijing shuzhu ge") in which he praises the beauty of the crystal beads "shimmering like the sun." Nonetheless, unlike the passage in Wen's work, Jiaoran's poem hinges on references to recitation of the names of the buddhas, nonattachment, emptiness, and other distinctly Buddhist concerns. (See *Quan Tang shi* 821, p. 9265). Marked by an exclusive concern with aesthetic matters, Wen's comments betray a clear break with the Buddhist tradition.

beads. The earliest example of a Qing court figure wearing a rosary seems to be an official portrait of the young Kangxi emperor (r. 1662–1722). But the connection between the rosary and the Qing imperial family probably goes back even further. A Qing collection of anecdotes reports that Nurhaci (1559–1626), consolidator of Manchu power and grandfather of the first emperor of the Qing, was known to count recitations with a rosary. This use of the rosary in the private devotions of members of the imperial family, it has been suggested, may be the origin of the practice of wearing rosaries at court.[170] Another scholar has proposed that the rosary came to the Qing court under the influence of Tibetan and Mongolian monks.[171] Indeed, we even have a court painting of one Qing emperor, Yongzheng, dressed as a lama, holding a rosary.[172] Nonetheless, while various sorts of rosaries continued to be used by members of the Qing court, the most visible type of rosary was used primarily not as a device for counting recitations but as a marker of social distinction, and soon became associated with an entirely new set of symbols. As a part of the meticulously regulated restrictions regarding court clothing, a set of regulations was also developed for rosaries, known as "court beads" (chaozhu). The emperor, for instance, was the only one at court permitted to wear a single rosary made of "Eastern Pearls," a highly valued kind of pearl produced in a particular section of northeastern China. The emperor's rosary, like those of other members of the court, was to have 108 beads, revealing the origins of the beads in the Buddhist rosary (figure 11). Compendiums of court ritual go on to describe regulations concerning the color of the thread running through the beads, the larger beads used to separate the smaller beads (here called "Buddha heads" [fotou]), the strings of beads called reminders (jinian), originally used to keep track of the number of recitations, and an innovation known as the "back cloud" (beiyun), a string of beads attached to the rosary running down from the back of the neck, which served to balance the weight of the beads hanging down the front.

The empress was permitted to wear a rosary made up of "Eastern Pearls" as well, but only in conjunction with two crossing rosaries made of coral. As a part of her court attire, the "Imperial Honored Consort" (the most esteemed secondary wife of the emperor) was allowed three rosaries, one to be made of amber and two of coral, while concubines were to wear one coral rosary with two amber ones. Lesser figures, while forbidden use of eastern pearls or any other type of pearl, were allowed to wear rosaries made of coral, agate, ivory, amber, and a number of other precious gems. In addition to the type of gem used for the beads, specific

---

[170] Wang Yunying, Qingdai Manzu fushi, p. 135.
[171] Schuyler V. R. Cammann, "Ch'ing Dynasty 'Mandarin Chains,'" pp. 25–9.
[172] See Nie Chongzheng, ed., Qingdai gongting huihua, pl. 18.13.

FIG. 11. Emperor Yongzheng. Reproduced by permission of the National
Palace Museum, Beijing.

regulations were laid down concerning the color of the thread. The right to wear court beads at all was a privilege granted only to select members of an elite group; only civil officials of the fifth rank and above, or military officials of the fourth rank and above, were permitted to wear rosaries at court.[173] Distinctions were further made between male and female, with men wearing rosaries with two "reminder" strings on the right and one on the left, and women wearing two on the left and one on the right.[174] The assignment of men to the right and women to the left is a ritual convention going back to pre-Han times. More specific symbolic associations were also made, asserting that the four large "Buddha head" beads represent the four seasons, and that the three remembrance strings stand for the three highest officers of state (*santai*).[175]

In addition to these large, 108-beaded "Court Bead" rosaries, many smaller, equally ornate hand-held rosaries from the Qing court survive as well.[176] The type of material used in these smaller rosaries—usually precious gems—and the meticulous craftsmanship of their design and execution indicate that they were admired as aesthetic objects. Nonetheless, it is possible that they were regularly used for keeping track of Buddhist recitations as well. The larger, court bead rosaries, on the other hand, are at times so ornate and complex, with multiple strings of beads hanging off the central strand to which were attached gems in various sizes, that they could have been used for recitation only with great difficulty. In Qing court beads, the reminders are no longer attached to the mother bead, but extend instead from the right and left sides of the string of beads, toward the top. Apparently, they were no longer used to keep track of the number of turns a devotee had taken around the rosary.[177] Although Qing figures were aware of the Buddhist origins and function of the rosary, they had clearly appropriated the rosary for very different purposes. At court the rosary was no longer an emblem for the Buddhist layman, much less the monk; it was an emblem of political status. Court ritual specialists went to great lengths to buttress the power of the rosary as a political emblem by making scrupulous distinctions between the rosary of the emperor, the empress, civil officials, military officials, and so on. At the same

[173] *Qingchao wenxian tongkao* 141, "Wangli" 17, p. 6074; *Qing huidian* 29, "Li bu," p. 242.

[174] Wang Yunying, *Qingdai Manzu fushi*, p. 136. Judging by Qing paintings and photographs, in practice this regulation seems largely to have been ignored.

[175] Ibid.

[176] For examples see Guoli Gugong Bowuyuan Bianji Weiyuanhui, ed., *Qingdai fushi zhanlan tulu*, pp. 133–43.

[177] In some Tibetan rosaries the reminder strings are also positioned on the side, supporting the theory that the Qing court beads originated in Tibet. See Lois Sherr Dubin, *The History of Beads*, pl. 70.

time, these same figures further strengthened the emblematic power of the rosary by ascribing to it various symbolic meanings, tying the rosary and its owner to a broader cosmology in a way that had little to do with Buddhism.

Over the long course of the history of the Buddhist rosary, the efforts of monks to define the rosary as a ritual implement met with mixed results. On the one hand, the rosary remains an important device in Buddhist recitation for monks, nuns, and laypeople to this day. Particularly note-worthy is the resistance to change of the number of 108 beads, which runs through references to the beads from the earliest texts through the Qing manuals of court etiquette. On the other hand, we have also seen that the monastic symbolism of the rosary was not strong enough to freeze its meaning. When Ming connoisseurs discussed criteria for the most taste-ful, elegant rosaries, they felt no compunction in ignoring the Buddhist meaning of the beads altogether. Similarly, when ritual specialists at the Qing court adopted the rosary as an emblem of court rank, they made no mention of Buddhist recitation and did not hesitate to redefine the signif-icance of the beads for their own purposes. Yet, to say that the rosary had a life of its own would be misleading. There was no primal significance to the rosary that continually asserted itself, despite attempts by others to change it. The beads by themselves mean nothing; it is only through the efforts of various social groups—be they monks, connoisseurs, or em-perors—to invest the beads with meaning that they become significant. Consequently, when the rosary moved from one group to another, its meaning changed from a sacred devotional object imbued with precise symbolic content, to an aesthetically correct curio, to a specific ranking in a neatly defined bureaucratic hierarchy.

THE *RUYI* SCEPTER

In his extensive comparative studies of religious symbolism, Mircea Eli-ade was drawn to instances of continuity between historically unrelated cultures separated by vast stretches of space and time. Similarities be-tween the symbolism of trees in the writings of Plato and in Icelandic folklore, parallels in the symbolism of water among the Karaja of Brazil and among Germans in late antiquity, continuities in popular interpre-tations of monoliths in ancient India and in twentieth-century France, all attracted his attention.[178] The seeming spontaneity of symbolic attribu-tions spoke to him of deep-seated affinities in the sensibilities of all peo-

---

[178] Mircea Eliade, *Patterns in Comparative Religion.*

ple. Eliade's research necessarily focused on basic, elemental objects found almost everywhere: monoliths, water, trees, stones, and so forth.

In the conclusion to the last section, I emphasized, on the contrary, the ephemeral nature of symbols; when an object like the rosary passes from one community to another, unless the meaning attributed to the object is rigorously monitored by a powerful social group, its symbolism may take any number of directions. While the enduring continuities of interpretation of, say, the moon across boundaries of time and culture suggests the unity of human perception and experience, the different interpretations given to the rosary—from sacred object, to emblem of political status, to entertaining curio—point to the variety of human needs for objects among different social groups in different environments.[179]

One could object, however, to my assertion that the rosary *in itself* meant nothing. Even if we cannot find one function of the rosary spanning all of Chinese history, the use of beads for counting—whether of the rosary to count recitations, beaded curtains to count books, or even the abacus as an accounting device—suggests itself naturally, as does, it seems, the ornamental function of beads, common in China already in the Neolithic. It does not surprise us that historically unconnected people used beads to count or wore beads as jewelry. In contrast, the case of the *ruyi* scepter considered in this section takes us a step further along the scale running from inherent to arbitrary symbolism. The *ruyi* is a curved, thin stick, usually made of metal or jade, and often embedded with various precious gems (figure 12). Old *ruyi* are a common sight today in antique shops in Taiwan and China, not to mention Western collections of orientalia. Like the rosary, they appear in the *Dream of the Red Chamber,* and were common in the Qing court, where they were considered attractive, auspicious objects, and tasteful gifts.[180]

It was in this context that Lord Macartney, British representative on

---

[179] Eliade is but one example of scholars who have focused on "natural" symbols. Jung, for instance, considered the cross and the maṇḍala to be natural symbols stemming from shared psychological traits of all humans. Mary Douglas has concentrated on symbols of the human body that transcend cultural boundaries. Others have discussed symbols that are more arbitrary, that is, that depend on interpretation and social convention for their meaning. Many scholars draw on the distinctions made by the nineteenth-century American philosopher Charles Peirce, who distinguished between "index" (what a lion's footprint is to the lion's passage), "icon" (something that resembles what it is intended to represent), and "symbol" (something that is arbitrarily assigned a referent, depending on habit or convention). For a review of the literature, see Raymond Firth, *Symbols Public and Private,* pp. 54–91.

[180] For much of what follows, I am indebted to Chen Xiasheng's introduction to *Jixiang ruyi wenwu tezhan tulu,* in which she clearly details the history of the *ruyi* and cites most of the important textual and pictorial sources for the history of the object. *Jixiang ruyi* (Taipei: National Palace Museum, 1995).

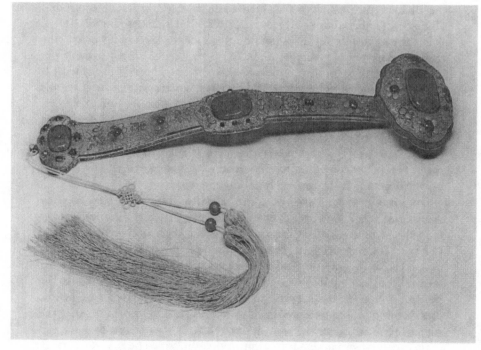

FIG. 12. *Ruyi* from the Qing Imperial collection. Reproduced by permission of
the National Palace Museum, Taipei.

embassy to China, first encountered the *ruyi* at the end of the eighteenth
century. During an audience with Emperor Qianlong, Macartney presented the emperor with a gold box containing a letter from the king of
England, and received in return a *ruyi* as a gift for the king. "It is a whitish,
agate-looking stone," Macartney wrote, "about a foot and a half long,
curiously carved, and highly prized by the Chinese, but to me it does not
appear in itself to be of any great value."[181] Macartney was also given a
ruyi for his personal use, and noticed the curious objects placed throughout the palace. Yet, he never seems to have acquired an appreciation for
the *ruyi*, remarking astutely on his exchange with Qianlong, "Those presents were probably, on both sides, less valuable in the estimation of the

---

[181] George Macartney, *An Embassy to China, Being the Journal Kept by Lord Macartney during His Embassy to the Emperor Ch'ien-lung 1793–1794*, J. L. Cranmer-Byng, ed.,
p. 122. Macartney's embassy is examined in James L. Hevia, *Cherishing Men from Afar:
Qing Guest Ritual and the Macartney Embassy of 1793*.

receivers than in that of the donors; but were mutually acceptable, upon the consideration of being tokens of respect on the one part, and of favour and good will upon the other."[182] Unlike the rosary, which, at least to a limited extent, betrayed its symbolism and function in its very shape, the meaning of the *ruyi* depended completely on the efforts of men and women to interpret it. With this as our starting point, let us look back and attempt to determine how this object that, in Macartney's words, "does not appear in itself to be of any great value" came to be "highly prized by the Chinese," and at the role Buddhism played in this process.

Origins

Scholars have proposed two basic theories for the origin of the *ruyi*. The first, commonly given in Buddhist dictionaries, is that the *ruyi* originated in India, where it was used by Buddhist monks who eventually brought the object to China. The term *ruyi*, literally meaning "as one wishes," appears frequently in Buddhist texts translated into Chinese in medieval times.[183] Most of these references, however, are either to the supernormal power (Skt. *ṛiddhi*) to do "whatever one wishes," including, for instance, the ability to fly through the air,[184] or to another important Buddhist symbol known as the *ruyi* gem, a fabulous jewel that gives to its possessor the power to accomplish "whatever he wishes," which appears frequently as a metaphor in Buddhist texts as well as in Buddhist iconography.[185]

A single reference in one Indian Buddhist text, translated into Chinese at the beginning of the fifth century, seems to refer to an ancestor of the object Macartney saw at Qianlong's court. The passage, in the *Dharmaguptakavinaya*, describes an incident during the time of the Buddha when a craftsman donated a number of exquisite ivory needle-holders (*zhentong*) to the assembly of monks. The donation was so expensive that the craftsman—whose piety was greater than his purse—was rendered penniless. On learning of this, the Buddha forbade monks from using needle-holders made of ivory, but conceded that the use of ivory to make a number of other items was acceptable. There follows a long, curious list of these items, which includes spoons, ladles, a bracelet clasp, a device for pulling teeth, a knife for scraping the tongue, a pick for cleaning one's

---

[182] George Staunton (based chiefly on Macartney's papers), *An Authentic Account of an Embassy from the King of Great Britain to the Emperor of China*, p. 233.

[183] For instance, Nakamura, *Bukkyōgo*, p. 1059d, Mochizuki, *Bukkyō daijiten*, p. 4130, Foguang dacidian bianxiu weiyuan hui, ed., *Foguang dacidian*, p. 2369c.

[184] That is, *ruyitong* (Skt. *ṛddhyabhijñā*), one of the "six supernormal powers."

[185] That is, the *ruyi baozhu* (Skt. *cintāmaṇi*), on which see Shiratori Kurakichi, "The Mu-nan-chu of Ta-ch'in and the Cintāmaṇi of India," pp. 2–54.

ears, and a *ruyi*.[186] Given the context, which includes devices for scraping and cleaning various parts of the body, scholars from the Song dynasty
on have suggested that the *ruyi* mentioned here was a back scratcher.[187]
The assumption then is that this monastic back scratcher, originating in
India, came to China with Buddhist missionary monks, at some point in
this process taking on the various other symbolic associations that I discuss below.

There is, however, scant evidence to support this assumption. We do
not possess a Sanskrit version of the *Dharmaguptakavinaya* and hence
cannot reconstruct the Sanskrit word the translators were attempting to
render with the characters *ruyi*.[188] Further, the translation of the *Dharmaguptakavinaya* was completed in the early fifth century, at a time when
the *ruyi* scepter was already common in China. It may be, then, that the
translators of the text simply used a Chinese term for back scratcher to
render the word for an Indian equivalent. The back scratcher is not a particularly ingenious device, and there is no reason to assume that the Chinese might not have developed it independently. In fact, the modern
scholar Ch'en Hsia-sheng has drawn attention to objects excavated from
what appears to be a late Warring States or early Eastern Han tomb—that
is, from approximately the third century B.C., well before Buddhism entered China. These scepter-shaped objects, with hands carved at the ends,
and (like the object described in the *Dharmaguptakavinaya*) carved from
ivory, may also have been back scratchers, though we do not know what
they were called and can only guess as to their function. These early
scepters suggest that, contrary to the standard description of modern Buddhist dictionaries, the *ruyi* may not have originated in India at all, or that
the *ruyi* may have been a felicitous meeting of similar implements in India
and China. The scanty evidence gives us no reason to choose one theory
over the other. In short, the origins of the *ruyi* are hopelessly obscure.

For our purposes, however, the interesting question is not where and
when the back scratcher came into use, but where and when it came to
take on symbolic significance. Unfortunately, evidence does not allow us
to determine if this transformation first took place in India or China.[189]

[186] *Sifen lü* 19, p. 694a.

[187] The eleventh-century monk Yuanzhao, commenting on the passage, states, "[T]he
ruyi is a stick used for scratching itches." *Sifen lü xingshichao zichi ji* B3C, p. 329a.

[188] Several Song texts give a Sanskrit equivalent for *ruyi*, reconstructed by Mochizuki as
anuruddha. *Bukkyō Daijiten*, p. 4130. The word *anuruddha* appears in Monier Monier-
Williams's *A Sanskrit-English Dictionary*, p. 37, but it is glossed as "checked, opposed;
soothed, pacified," rather than as an implement. The word may well be a back-translation
from the Chinese *ruyi*.

[189] J. LeRoy Davidson, arguing for an Indian origin for the *ruyi*, cites three texts. One is
a jataka tale that refers to a group of heretics who carried a branch of a tree that they planted
in front of them when they debated. Since the *ruyi* in China, as we will see, became an em-

The object does not appear in early Indian iconography, nor does anything clearly identifiable as a *ruyi* appear in pre-Buddhist Chinese art. Barring the discovery of further evidence that might allow us to trace the early development of the *ruyi*, the study of the *ruyi* as a symbolic object can begin only with the earliest Chinese references, which begin to appear in the fourth century.

The Ruyi *at Court*

The earliest reliably datable reference to the *ruyi* is in Wang Jia's *Shiyi ji,* completed in 370.[190] The reference occurs in an account of Sun Quan's first impression of his future wife, Lady Pan. When presented with a portrait of Lady Pan, made when she was melancholy, Sun Quan "was delighted at the sight of the portrait. He struck the table with an amber *ruyi*, breaking it, and exclaiming, 'This is a divine woman. Even when despondent she beguiles; how radiant she must be when happy!'"[191]

From this point, references to the *ruyi* become more common. Many of these references are connected to court life. For instance, the *Wei shu* records that when Emperor Xiaowen (r. 471–99) sent his son off to lead a military campaign, he gave him a *ruyi* "as an expression of his feelings."[192] In a biography of the powerful official Wang Dun (266–324), the *Jin shu* records that late in life, discouraged by court politics, Wang would drink heavily and sing a song about his misplaced loyalty, keeping time by rapping a *ruyi* on the side of a spittoon.[193] Examples such as these tell us that the *ruyi* was common among emperors and ministers, and indicate how the object was used. Other sources tell us that in addition to its use as a gift and to keep time to music, the *ruyi* was also used as a pointer by high officials directing their generals, and by at least one emperor to discipline an unruly princess.[194]

---

blem for debate, Davidson suggests that this passage may refer to an early form of the *ruyi*. The other two Buddhist texts refer to a "wishing tree," the name of which was translated by Chinese as *ruyi*. As Davidson himself notes, "[T]he evidence is slim." J. LeRoy Davidson, "The Origin and Early Use of the Ju-i," pp. 239–49.

[190] The Tang collection, *Youyang zazu* (SBCK edn. 11, p. 61), records the legend that the ruler of the kingdom of Wu, Sun Quan (182–252), unearthed a *ruyi* that had belonged to Qin Shihuang, first emperor of China. We have no way of knowing if the *ruyi* did in fact belong to Qin Shihuang, though the discovery of the early *ruyi*-like objects discussed above tells us that this is not impossible. Nor can we even be sure that Sun Quan discovered an object he believed to be Qin Shihuang's *ruyi*—the story may have been invented entirely during the Tang.

[191] *Shi yi ji*, by Wang Jia, ed. Qi Zhiping, 8, p. 181.

[192] *Wei shu* 21, p. 546.

[193] *Jin shu* 98, p. 2557.

[194] For an instance of a high official directing troops with a *ruyi*, see *Shishuo xinyu jiaojian* 24, no. 14, p. 415; English translation in Richard Mather, *A New Account of Tales of*

Evidently, the politically powerful kept *ruyi* about them and picked them up to wave about, make a point, or as a spontaneous gift. Taken together, anecdotes that mention the *ruyi* suggest that it was a part of the equipment of decision makers, a part, in a sense, of their uniform. This close association between the *ruyi* and governance is made clear in an anecdote from the *Wei shu,* which states that when the future Emperor Xuan Wudi (r. 500–515) was still a small child, his father, Emperor Gaozu, had a number of objects arrayed before his sons in an attempt to evaluate the princes' potential. Unlike his brothers, who all reached for frivolous toys, Wudi chose a *ruyi* made of bone, much to the delight of the emperor, who from that moment on began to train the child in the art of governance.[195] Whether the story is an accurate account of an incident at court in the early part of the sixth century or a legend recorded as fact by the late sixth-century compiler of the *Wei shu,* it tells us that by the end of the sixth century, not only was the *ruyi* common at court, but it had even begun to take on emblematic significance as the mark of a ruler.

Tang sources indicate that the *ruyi* continued to play a role in court life at that time. At several points in discussion of court ritual, the Tang codice *Tongdian* prescribes use of the *ruyi.* For instance, during a ritual in which the heir apparent inspects the imperial academy, one official is charged with the duty of holding the *ruyi.*[196] The prevalence of the *ruyi* at the Tang court is further evidenced in one of the murals from the tomb of the Tang princess Li Xianhui (685–701), which includes a depiction of a palace woman holding a *ruyi.*[197]

Below we pick up the history of the imperial use of the *ruyi* and carry it through to the Qing. For now, suffice it to say that the *ruyi* was a familiar sight at the Chinese court from the Three Kingdoms period through the Tang. Although, as we have seen, the *ruyi* was in certain contexts an emblem for political power, its associations were more diverse than the scepter in Europe, which immediately brings to mind images of kingship; in China, besides its use at court, the *ruyi* was also used by literati outside the court in much the same way as court figures used it.[198] In addition, the *ruyi* was a common sight in Chinese monasteries, the subject to which we now turn.

---

the World, p. 387. For the emperor who beat his daughter with an ivory *ruyi,* see *Nan shi* 60, p. 1489.

[195] *Wei shu* 8, p. 215.

[196] *Tongdian,* 117, p. 2997; see also 117, p. 2984.

[197] Yin Shengping and Li Xixing, *Tangmu bihua zhenpin xuancui,* p. 9.

[198] See especially the references to the *ruyi* in the *Shishuo xinyu* jiaojian 6, no. 41; 13, no. 4, 11; 25, no. 23; 30, no. 8; trans. in Mather, *A New Account of Tales of the World.*

The Ruyi *among Buddhists*

A Tang collection of anecdotes records an imperial gift of a *ruyi* to a scholar named Li Xun (d. 835), who spoke before Emperor Wenzong. "Li Xun lectured on the subtleties of the *Book of Changes* to the emperor's great satisfaction. This took place in the hottest part of summer. And so the Emperor ordered that Li be granted a crystal belt and a 'cool ivory *ruyi*.' When Li thanked the Emperor, the Emperor said, 'The *ruyi* may serve you as a lecture baton (*tanbing*).'"[199] This "lecture baton," whether it took the form of a *ruyi* or a fly whisk (*zhuwei*), was used by the lecturer to punctuate particular remarks and as a tool for gesture. One scholar, writing on the fly whisk—an object that gained popularity among adepts of "pure conversation" (*qingtan*) during the Six Dynasties period—compares the relationship between the lecturer and his fly whisk to the relationship between a soldier and his sword.[200] We see a similar sort of identification between discoursing and the *ruyi* in Buddhist texts, which reveal that the *ruyi* was a common implement among debating and lecturing Buddhist monks. A Tang biography of the monk Zhixi (556–627) notes that just before his death, the monk "sat upright in the lotus posture and, holding a *ruyi*, spoke on the Dharma with great logic and profundity."[201] A biography of the monk Huibu (d. 587) records that during a debate with the eminent monk Huisi, Huisi was so impressed by Huibu's discourse that he "struck a table with a metal *ruyi* and said, 'In the space of ten thousand miles, you will not find one to match this monk's wisdom.'"[202] Another account refers once again to Huisi's *ruyi* when it describes the monk holding a *ruyi* while assessing the abilities of one of his most prominent disciples, the Tiantai exegete Zhiyi.[203] Finally, an image dated 587 carved in stone at the Lingquan Monastery in Henan depicts two monks facing each other: one with palms joined (apparently listening), while the other, holding a *ruyi*, lectures.[204] Anecdotes and images like these indicate that, like the judge's gavel in present-day courtrooms, the *ruyi* had become both a tool of discourse and an emblem of author-

---

[199] *Duyang zabian* (CSJC edn.) B, pp. 17–8.

[200] He Changjun, "Shishuo xinyu zhaji," pp. 1–7. The origin of the *zhuwei*, thought by some to have come to China from India, is the subject of some dispute. Wang Yong reviews the evidence and the arguments in his "Shubi zakkō," (1987.11), pp. 73–89.

[201] *Fahua zhuanji* 3, T no. 2068, vol. 51, p. 60b.

[202] *Xu gaoseng zhuan* 7, pp. 480c–1a.

[203] Ibid. 17, p. 564b.

[204] See *Gongxian deng shiku diaosu*, pl. 215, in Zhongguo meishu quanji bianji weiyuanhui ed., *Zhongguo meishu quanji* 2, vol. 13, or Henansheng gudai jianzhu baohu yanjiusuo, ed., *Baoshan Lingquansi*, pl. 21.

146 CHAPTER TWO

ity. Monks continued to use *ruyi* at least up to the seventeenth century, when the late Ming figure Zhang Dai noted that he was led to see the abbot of a monastery by a monk carrying a *ruyi*.[205]

Because of its associations with lofty conversation and debate, the *ruyi*, like the rosary, was considered a suitable monastic gift to or from a monk. The biography of the prominent exegete Huiyuan in the *Liang Biographies of Eminent Monks*, for instance, relates a gift of a *ruyi* to the great monk from one of his admirers.

> [Huiyuan's] appearance was stern and grave, his behavior upright and dignified. Everybody who set eyes on him trembled with awe in body and spirit. Once there was a monk who held a bamboo *ruyi* which he wanted to present [to Huiyuan]. He came to the mountain and stayed over two nights, and finally he did not dare to show [his present], but stealthily left [the *ruyi*] at the corner of [Huiyuan's] mat and silently went away.[206]

Similarly, Huisi, an exegete who seems to have had a particular fondness for the *ruyi*, once gave an ivory *ruyi* to an aspiring student (while use of animal skins was often forbidden by the monastic regulations, monks seem to have felt no compunction at using objects made from their tusks).[207] One account of the sixth-century monk Zhiyi states that when he died, the great monk left behind a *ruyi* with his last testament.[208]

We know from Ennin that the practice of monks exchanging *ruyi* continued at least into the ninth century. In 839, while traveling in China, Ennin recorded in his travelogue, "I have passed on to the Student of History, Nagamine no Sukune, to take back to our country, the four letters and the black horn scepter [*ruyi*] entrusted to me at Chuzhou for delivery to Mount [Hi]ei by the Student Monk."[209] And from some typically spectacular examples in the Shōsōin collection we know also that some *ruyi* did in fact find their way to Japan.[210]

If the use and function of the *ruyi* among monks is well documented, the place of the *ruyi* among Buddhist laypeople is less clear. *Ruyi* similar in shape to those housed in the Shōsōin collection appear in a rubbing from a Buddhist stele engraved in 525 in Shandong commissioned by one Cao Wangxi.[211] According to the inscription, the other side of the stele depicted an image of Maitreya, though the rubbing that survives contains only the

---

205 *Taoan mengyi* (CSJC edn.) 6, p. 50.
206 Zürcher, *The Buddhist Conquest of China*, p. 245; *Gaoseng zhuan* 6, p. 359a.
207 *Xu gaoseng zhuan* 16, p. 557a.
208 *Sui Tiantai Zhizhe dashi biezhuan*, T no. 2050, vol. 50, p. 196a.
209 *Nittō guhō junrei gyōki* 1, p. 134; Reischauer, *Ennin's Diary*, p. 99.
210 Shōsōin Jimusho ed., *Shōsōin hōmotsu*, vol. 3, pl. 100–105.
211 *Beijing Tushuguan cang Zhongguo lidai shike taben huibian*, vol. 4, p. 181. A similar image of a *ruyi* from a stele made in 519 can be found in the same volume, p. 59.

part of the stele depicting a procession of devotees. The central figure, presumably Cao himself, is accompanied by attendants holding various objects, including fans, a parasol, and long, curved *ruyi*. Unlike the fan and parasol, used to fan and provide shade, the *ruyi* appears to be of entirely symbolic significance—it is too long to be conveniently used to scratch the back and is not broad enough to be used as a fan or for shade. Images of devotees in Chinese Buddhist art are often marked as such by the objects they hold, most notably a single lotus flower or a censer. The temptation, then, is to read the *ruyi* in this stele as an emblem of Buddhist devotion. The artisan who created the stele had at least some knowledge of Buddhist symbols; the lions at the top of the stele are almost certainly symbols of Buddhism.[212] Nevertheless, in this stele the *ruyi* seems, like the parasol, to have been provided for the devotee rather than for the Buddha. In other words, as in many of the examples we have seen above, the *ruyi* may here be an emblem of secular authority rather than religious piety.

Our earliest extant example of a *ruyi*—the elegant ninth-century silver *ruyi* discovered at Famen Monastery in 1987—has a similarly tenuous connection to lay devotion. This short-handled *ruyi* with a head variously described as "cloud shaped" or "bat shaped" carries an inscription on its back stating that it was made in an imperial workshop in 872 and listing the artisans and supervisors responsible for its manufacture.[213] Judging by the shape of the flattened head, the object would have made a poor back scratcher. But while recognizing that it must chiefly have served as a symbol of something else, it is difficult to pin down just what this symbolism was. The *ruyi* was given by the emperor to be installed in the stupa at Famen and hence was a devotional object. But did the object itself possess specifically Buddhist associations or symbolism, or was it, on the contrary, significant for its imperial associations and as a symbol of authority? In addition to this *ruyi*, the Tang inventory discovered along with the objects at Famen lists two other silver *ruyi*, each donated by a separate nun.[214] This easy blend at Famen between imperial, lay, and monastic offering is typical. When court figures became intimately involved in Buddhist devotion, the two sets of symbols—imperial and Buddhist—become difficult if not impossible to separate.

Mañjuśrī's Ruyi

After Kumārajīva's translation of the *Vimalakīrtinirdeśasūtra* in 406, the scripture, centered on a debate between the great layman Vimalakīrti and

[212] On the lion as a Buddhist symbol, see Edward H. Schafer, *The Golden Peaches of Samarkand: A Study of T'ang Exotics*, p. 30.

[213] Han Wei, "Famensi digong jinyinqi zanwen kaoshi," pp. 71–8.

[214] Xu Pinfang, *Zhongguo lishi kaoguxue luncong*, p. 437.

the bodhisattva Mañjuśrī, grew to a level of popularity in China that it seems never to have attained in India. In part because the central figure in the scripture is a layman, the *Vimalakīrti* enjoyed especial popularity among lay Chinese Buddhists; hence, it is no surprise that images of Vimalakīrti appear frequently in Buddhist art sponsored by wealthy lay figures. Depictions of the debate between Vimalakīrti and Mañjuśrī appear no less than ten times in engravings in caves at Longmen completed in the early part of the sixth century.[215] Typically, Vimalakīrti appears on one side, under a parasol, holding in one hand a fan or fly whisk, while Mañjuśrī appears on the other side holding a *ruyi*. Similar images can be found in mid-sixth-century steles from elsewhere.[216] Although it describes the great debate in some detail, the *Vimalakīrti* scripture itself makes no mention of the *ruyi*, suggesting once again that the origins of the use of the *ruyi* are to be found in China rather than in India. As we have seen, during the Six Dynasties period, the *ruyi* was commonly used during lecture and debate by monks and laymen alike. Hence it is easily understandable that the *ruyi* was taken into the iconography of the debate between Vimalakīrti and Mañjuśrī. Further, once the structural symmetry between Vimalakīrti's fan and Mañjuśrī's *ruyi* was established, the *ruyi* became a requisite iconographical feature, clearly identifying Mañjuśrī. In fact, Mañjuśrī continued to hold a *ruyi* in later representations of the deity, even when he is depicted alone and not engaged in debate.[217]

Medieval Interpretations of the Ruyi

Thus far we have seen four interpretations of the *ruyi*: as a back scratcher, as a symbol of secular authority, as a mark of the public speaker, and as an emblem of the bodhisattva Mañjuśrī. These interpretations can be adduced from anecdotal or pictorial evidence. Occasionally more deliberate attempts were made to interpret the scepter. Daoxuan, for instance, mentioned the *ruyi* in a work on regulations concerning the disposal of a monk's property on his death. Under the heading "Clothing and Trifles"

[215] Specifically in the Lianhua, Guyang, Dihua, and Yaofang Caves. See Longmen Wenwu Baoguan Suo et al., eds., *Longmen shiku*, vol. 1, pls. 53, 56, 61, 63, 64, 102, 168, 177, 203. See also Emma C. Bunker, "Early Chinese Representations of Vimalakīrti," pp. 28–52.

[216] See, for instance, the stele known as the "Shangguan Sengdu deng zaoxiang bei" completed in 563, housed in the Anhui Provincial Museum. *Gongxian deng shiku diaosu* in Zhongguo meishu quanji bianji weiyuanhui, ed., *Zhongguo meishu quanji* 2, vol. 13, pl. 122. See also the Eastern Wei stele (534–50) in the Metropolitan Museum of Art, U.S.A., in Guoli Gugong Bowuyuan Bianji Weiyuanhui, ed., *Haiwai yizhen: foxiang*, vol. 1, pl. 33.

[217] See, for example, the tenth-century woodblock prints of Mañjuśrī holding a *ruyi* and riding on a lion—another common iconographic feature of the deity—at Dunhuang. In Whitfield, *The Art of Central Asia*, vol. 2, fig. 142, 143, and 147 (Stein paintings 236, 237, and 239).

(fuwan), Daoxuan lists "small tables, satchels, *ruyi* lecture batons, various sorts of fly whisks, spittoons and such." Daoxuan then goes on to explain that such objects are frivolous and, in his judgment, not "tools of the Way."[218] As we have seen, the *ruyi* was not commonly discussed in Indian monastic regulations, appearing only once in the entire Indian Buddhist corpus. Hence, inclusion of the *ruyi* in Daoxuan's discussion of the monastic regulations was not driven by the prevalence of the object in Indian texts, but because *Chinese* monks owned them.[219]

While demonstrating that the object was common in Tang China, Daoxuan's comment also reveals that, despite the iconographic prominence of the *ruyi* as Mañjuśrī's most recognizable implement, Daoxuan did not give much weight to its symbolic significance, placing it as he did alongside tables and spittoons. Daoxuan was well aware of the use of the *ruyi* in debate, as his comment reveals. At the same time, as a specialist in the *Dharmaguptakavinaya,* he was also aware of the passage in that text in which the term *ruyi* is applied to a back scratcher. It was perhaps his familiarity with this passage that led Daoxuan to dismiss the *ruyi* as a trifle.

The modern scholar Erik Zürcher, struck by the disjunction between the lofty symbolic significance of the *ruyi* as a mark of wisdom and its use as a back scratcher, mused, "It is not clear how and why this humble instrument could become the most venerable attribute of the Buddhist priest, unless we assume that the *ruyi* came in some way to be associated with the *ruyibao,* the 'wish-fulfilling gem' (*cintāmaṇi*) which plays such an important role in Indian Buddhist and non-Buddhist mythology."[220]

At least one Song writer, the monk Daocheng (fl. 1019) was also puzzled by the gap between the symbolism and use of the *ruyi,* between Daoxuan's trifling back scratcher and Mañjuśrī's emblem of eloquence. In an entry for *ruyi* in his glossary, the *Shishi yaolan,* Daocheng writes:

> Ruyi: In Sanskrit it is called *a'nalü;*[221] in Chinese, *ruyi.* The *Manual*[222] states that it is an ancient back scratcher. It may be made of bone, ivory, bamboo, or wood. It is carved into the shape of a hand with nails; the handle is ap-

[218] *Liangchu qingzhong yi* T no. 1895, vol. 45, p. 842a.

[219] The assertion that the *ruyi* was common among monks in the late Tang is buttressed by a passage in a text discovered at Dunhuang, dated 972, which recounts that after a court debate the Six Dynasties monk Huiyuan was granted a series of gifts by the emperor, including "a *ruyi,* six rosaries, and a ring-staff." (Pan Chonggui, ed., *Dunhuang bianwenji xinshu* p. 1070.) It is not likely that this tenth-century account accurately reflects an actual imperial gift of the fifth, but it tells us at the least that in the tenth century the *ruyi* was still considered an appropriate possession for a monk, just as a rosary and a ring-staff were.

[220] Zürcher, *The Buddhist Conquest of China,* p. 407, n. 59.

[221] Sanskrit reconstructed by Mochizuki as *anuruddha* (*Bukkyō daijiten,* s.v. *nyo-i,* p. 4130), though, as I mentioned above, the word was probably coined by Chinese monks attempting to reconstruct what they presumed to have originally been a Sanskrit word.

[222] *Zhigui.* Apparently the name of a text, though I am unable to identify it.

proximately three *chi* long. When one's back itches and one can't reach the spot, one uses the *ruyi* to scratch it. Since this accomplishes one's wish it is called *ruyi* ["as you wish"].

I once asked the translator of scriptures Tripiṭika Grand Master Tongfan Qingzhao, and the philologist Grand Master Tonghui Yunsheng about the *ruyi*.[223] Both said that the *ruyi* is an expression of the mind, and that that is why the bodhisattvas hold it. In appearance it looks like billowing clouds, or like the character for mind (*xin*) in Chinese seal script. Although it can be used as a back scratcher, when one like Mañjuśrī holds it, how could it be used simply to scratch the back?

In addition, when lecturing monks hold the *ruyi* they often secretly write the words of passages or blessings on the handle so that they will not forget them. When they need the words, they pick up the *ruyi* and see them, just as they wish; hence it is called *ruyi*.[224]

Daocheng then follows with historical references to non-Buddhist figures who gave the *ruyi* as a gift, and ends by stating, "Based on this, we conclude that there are two types of *ruyi* [one used as a back scratcher and another as a Buddhist symbol]. Although the word is the same, they are different in function."

We see in this passage a valiant attempt to make sense of the complex, confusing development of the *ruyi*. First Daocheng tries to account for the origins of the *ruyi* in India and to supply a Sanskrit equivalent for the term. But as we have seen, there is in fact just as much evidence for a Chinese origin of the *ruyi* as there is for an Indian one. Next, while noting the use of the *ruyi* as a back scratcher and providing a folk etymology for the term, Daocheng attempts to locate the symbolism of the *ruyi*. Ignoring (or perhaps unaware of) the use of the *ruyi* at court as a symbol of authority, Daocheng turns to the symbolism of the *ruyi* in iconography of Mañjuśrī, which—with the help of two erudite monks—he interprets as a symbol for (the pure) mind. He then goes a step further by cleverly interpreting the distinctive shape of the head of some *ruyi* as having the shape of the Chinese character for mind, "*xin*," in seal script calligraphy.[225] Daocheng then skirts past the symbolic significance of the object in lecture and debate, and goes on to list its practical function as a sort of notepad for lecturing monks. Finally, he conveniently divides *ruyi* into two types: one a lofty symbol and the other a humble back scratcher.

[223] Qingzhao (fl. 982) and Tonghui were both prominent Song monks. Tonghui is better known as Zanning (919–1001), author of two important Buddhist historical works, the *Brief History of the Clergy* (*Sengshi lüe*) and the *Song Biographies of Eminent Monks* (*Song gaoseng zhuan*). For Qingzhao, see *Song huiyao jiben*, 200.2.6.

[224] *Shishi yaolan* B, p. 279c.

[225] For the shape he is probably referring to, see the *ruyi* discovered at Famen Monastery. See Shi, *Famensi digong zhenbao*, pl. 30.

Redolent of a relaxed medieval scholarship that did not require rigorous proofs and evidence, the passage represents an offhand attempt to bring order to what was and is an untidy historical record. Daocheng was not conducting an extensive review of historical evidence relating to the meaning of the *ruyi;* nor was he writing from within an oral tradition assured of just what the object meant. Rather, he looked at the words for the scepter, examined its shape, talked to fellow monks who had done the same, and proposed some commonsense interpretations. Although Daocheng recognized that the *ruyi* was a symbol, in contrast to more rigid iconographical traditions in which artisans and specialists are trained in the precise symbolism of specific images and objects, no one within or without the monastic community had ever firmly established a specific meaning for the *ruyi*, Buddhist or otherwise. Even more than in the case of the rosary, this ambiguity allowed for a wide array of interpretations and uses of the *ruyi* scepter.

Connoisseurs and Aficionados

In addition to an entry for the rosary in his *Treatise on Superfluous Things,* the Ming collector Wen Zhenheng also gives aesthetic criteria for evaluating *ruyi.* Wen writes:

> The *ruyi* was used in ancient times to give directions or to protect oneself from the unexpected. It was for this reason that it was made of iron, and not on the basis of strictly aesthetic considerations. If you can obtain an old iron *ruyi* inlaid with gold and silver that sparkle now and then, and if it has an ancient dull color, this is the best. As for *ruyi* made of natural branches or from bamboo and so on, these are all worthless.[226]

Concerned as usual with refined taste and distance from affected vulgarity, Wen was perhaps aware of some of the references to the *ruyi* in secular texts from the Six Dynasties period, but was unaware or uninterested in the symbolic use of the *ruyi* in debate, much less the more specific meaning assigned to the scepter as emblem of Mañjuśrī and symbol of wisdom. In the following entry in Wen's book, an entry devoted to the fly whisk, he notes that although the ancients used the fly whisk when engaging in "pure conversation," if one of his time were to "wave a fly whisk about in front of a guest, he would incur disgust." In other words, Wen recognized that had he been born a thousand years earlier, he would have employed the whisk in conversation, but as a literatus of the Ming, he saw it as a curio to be contemplated rather than as a tool of discourse to be

[226] *Zhangwuzhi jiaozhu* 7, p. 279.

used. The same probably applies to the *ruyi*. For laypeople, by the seventeenth century when Wen lived, the *ruyi* had lost its function as a debating baton and become instead a collector's item—merchandise for the leisured and the snobbish.

Paintings and textual sources reveal that Wen was not alone in late imperial China in his affection for the *ruyi* as an aesthetic object. Rare and elegant *ruyi* were a common pursuit of Ming and Qing collectors. The same fascination with the *ruyi* as an amusing curio carried over to the Qing court, where, as we have seen, it was a common sight. Some of the extant *ruyi* from the Qing imperial collection are decorated with Buddhist motifs, such as swastikas and, in one case, a passage from the *Diamond Sutra*. But other *ruyi* from the same collection are decorated with non-Buddhist symbols such as peaches, fish, and the eight immortals, and one suspects that the Buddhist elements, like these motifs, were considered merely vaguely auspicious and did not carry strong Buddhist associations.

In addition to auspicious ornaments, some *ruyi* in the Qing imperial collection are marked with the "double happiness" sign (*shuangxi*), a symbol of matrimony. These *ruyi* are products of the practice of newly betrothed couples exchanging *ruyi* in a Qing dynasty equivalent of the engagement ring. With the use of the *ruyi* as a symbol of marriage, we are a long way from its use as an emblem of Mañjuśrī, much less as an emblem of monastic sermons and debate. At the same time, while the origins of the *ruyi* are far from clear, the use of the *ruyi* by Chinese monks seems to have been borrowed from secular court use, where it maintained a strong tradition of use from at least the fourth century A.D. right up to the fall of the Qing in 1911, long after its Buddhist associations had faded. In other words, rather than an example of the Buddhist impact on Chinese material culture, the *ruyi* may well be an example of the impact of Chinese material culture on Buddhism. This being said, if we devote too much attention to the question of origins and whom to credit for influencing whom, we run the risk of missing the equally interesting and certainly more accessible question of the interaction between Buddhist and non-Buddhist symbols in China. Monks, Buddhist laypeople, and court officials all drew on the *ruyi* as a symbol of authority and eloquence. And once the symbolic importance of the object was firmly established in Chinese society, however vague the precise content of this symbolism might be, monks, devotees, Ming collectors, emperors, Buddhist artisans, and newlyweds were all attracted to the *ruyi* for personal, material, and aesthetic reasons. None of these groups seems ever to have attempted to fix a single interpretation of the symbolism of the *ruyi* for the others; in the history of the symbolism of this particular object, its development was largely unplanned and always open to innovation.

CONCLUSION

It would be easy to extend the list of symbolic objects introduced or some-how altered by the spread of Buddhism to China. Like the monastic uniform, other ritual objects brought to China from India were chiefly the preserve of monks. Certain rituals called for the use of small bells or the scepter-like object known as the vajra. Such objects were imbued with symbolic meaning in texts and in the practice of rituals. More intriguing is the "wooden fish," a piece of wood hung or supported from a rafter, that was struck to call monks to assembly. The origins of the wooden fish are as obscure as the *ruyi* or the fly whisk.[227] While there are records of a wooden chime that was struck to call monks to meals in ancient India, none of these records specify that it was shaped like a fish. But from at least as early as the Tang dynasty, monasteries in China used a wooden chime, shaped like a fish. The significance of the shape is hardly more clear than its origin. According to one tradition, the wooden fish symbolized vigilance, because fish never sleep, but the wooden fish seems to have persisted more because of the force of tradition than because of the resonance of a readily recognizable symbolism.[228]

A similar monastic symbol was the ever-burning lamp (*changming-deng*), an oil lamp kept in the monastery that in theory was never allowed to burn out. As with the case of the wooden fish, the origins of the ever-burning lamp are obscure. We have a number of documents testifying to its prevalence in monasteries in the Tang, ranging from poems and ornate prose to accounting records of oil used for the lamp at a Dunhuang monastery.[229] Precise references to the symbolism of the lamp are hard to come by. Prominent seventh-century Chan monk Hongren used the lamp as a symbol of the "mind of correct enlightenment" (*zhengjuexin*); more generally, the lamp seems to have served as a perpetual offering to the Buddha.[230] As in the case of other Buddhist symbols we have looked at, laypeople did not confine themselves to Buddhist interpretations of the

---

[227] What follows is based on Huang Zhaohan, "Muyu kao," *Shijie zongjiao yanjiu* (1987.1), pp. 28–38.

[228] Though often cited, the origins of this tradition are difficult to trace. See Huang Zhao-han, ibid., p. 37, n. 6.

[229] Poems include Zhang Hu's "Ti Xiushi yingtang," *Quan Tang shi* 511, p. 5837, and Liu Yuxi's "Xie si shuang kuai," *Quan Tang shi* 359, p. 4051. For a rubbing of a prose piece engraved on an ever-burning lamp in 688, see "Longfusi changmingdenglou songchuang" in *Beijing Tushuguan cang Zhongguo lidai shike taben huibian*, vol. 17, pp. 87–8. For an overview of the history of the ever-burning lamp see Hubert Durt, "Chōmyōtō" in *Hōbōgirin*, pp. 360–5.

[230] Durt, ibid. For Hongren's quotation, see *Guanxin lun*, *T* no. 2833, vol. 85, p. 1272a.

lamp; they were just as likely to see in the lamp a symbol of time, or to puzzle over properties of an old flame, as they were to reflect on the lamp as an offering or symbol of enlightenment.[231] Other cases of the shifting of Buddhist symbolic meaning can be found in motifs in Tang jewelry and Qing ceramics.[232]

This tendency toward symbolic drift alerts us to the tenuous nature of the relationship between a given object and its symbolism. All symbolism is, of course, the result of human projection; it is never entirely inherent in the object itself. Yet, some symbolic interpretations suggest themselves more naturally—for instance, the patched robe as mark of asceticism—while others are more strained—the *ruyi* scepter as a symbol of the mind. In the case of the *ruyi*, one suspects that in general the object was manufactured and used because of the force of tradition—the *ruyi* was simply the object one held in certain situations—and not in order to express any abstract truth. But even in this case, exegetes could not resist the symbolic impulse and so set out to discover and assign a symbolic meaning for the object. In other words, symbolism was invoked to explain the object and not the other way around. Regardless of its effect on objects themselves, the pull of symbolism is itself a constituent element of material culture, prominent in the history of Chinese Buddhism.

If we look for a general model that encompasses the history of Buddhist symbols in China, the notion of sinicization immediately comes to mind: How did the Chinese adapt and alter foreign symbols to their own culture? Any discussion of sinicization necessarily involves inquiries into origins, the focus of much of the preceding discussion. Yet, the results of my research on the origins of Chinese Buddhist symbols are admittedly seldom satisfying. We know that the Chinese Buddhist rosary originated in India, but whether it sprang from Indian Buddhism or the practices of brahmans remains a mystery. The origins of the *ruyi*, the fly whisk, the wooden fish, and the ever-burning lamp are even more puzzling; we cannot even determine if they began in India, China, or elsewhere. Even when we can locate the Indian origins of certain symbols, such as that of the monk's robe and the alms bowl, when these objects undergo changes in China, we are faced with the vexing question of just what is Chinese about these changes—and the vast stretches of time I attempt to cover here makes this particularly difficult. I referred, for instance, to the neglect of

---

[231] Liu Yuxi uses the lamp as a symbol for time in his poem "Xie si shuang kuai." In his *Du xing za zhi*, Zeng Minxing (d. 1175) reflects on the properties of the lamp's ancient flame (SKQS edn. 4, p. 2a).

[232] For Tang jewelry, see Sun Ji, *Zhongguo shenghuo*, pp. 107–21, in which he discusses the transformation of a particular type of necklace, from an Indian Buddhist symbol to a Chinese ornament of no symbolic significance. On Buddhist motifs in Qing ceramics, see F. Hitchman, "Buddhist Symbols on Chinese Ceramics," pp. 14–20, 207.

Buddhist symbolism when court craftsmen made an alms bowl of gold for
the Famen Monastery. But the practice of making implements of gold was
not common in ancient China, and the interest in gold utensils seems to
have arisen from the fifth century on under foreign influence.[233] The
adaptations to the rosary at the Qing court presents an even clearer case
of the difficulties of applying sinicization to the history of Buddhist symbols in China: even as a generalization, the concept is not flexible enough
to encompass the variety of forces at work in the spread of Buddhist
symbols to China since the Qing rulers were Manchu rather than Han
Chinese.

Mircea Eliade turned to a different model for interpreting the history
of various symbols, that of "degeneration," a pattern he saw repeated
over and over again. According to this model, what begins as a sophisticated attempt to comprehend ineffable sacred truth through the mediation of symbols inevitably undergoes degradation as lesser minds reinter-
pret religious symbols in their day-to-day lives. Diamonds, once emblems
of absolute reality, become talismans to protect from snake bites. Names
of holy rivers that once symbolized purity become part of a recipe to treat
constipation.[234] If we attempt to test this model against the history of specific objects in China, origins are again crucial. Unfortunately, the gene-
sis of Buddhist symbolic meaning leaves even fewer traces than the geographic origin of symbols, and speculation about the "original" meaning
of, say, the monk's staff is probably as hopeless as speculation about the
original teachings of the Buddha: such histories always begin in the middle. Happily, this better-documented "middle" history of Buddhist symbols, often far removed from their origins, is equally interesting, and it is
here that we can evaluate whether or not interpretations of symbols follow a particular direction. Commenting on the process by which symbols
are reinterpreted, Eliade noted that his purpose in studying symbols—a
central concern of his work—was "to show, on the one hand, the mani-
fold ramifications of the symbol, and, on the other, the processes of rationalization, degeneration and infantilization which any symbolism undergoes as it comes to be interpreted on lower and lower planes."[235]
Similarly, Eliade elsewhere refers to the "lowering of the metaphysical significance from the 'cosmological' to the 'aesthetic.'"

We can certainly see rationalization in interpretations of some of the
objects I have discussed. Recall, for instance, Daocheng's interpretation
of the *ruyi* as being shaped like the Chinese character for mind. We have
also seen that in several instances things were treated as aesthetic objects

[233] Sun Ji, ibid., p. 156.
[234] Eliade, *Patterns in Comparative Religion.*
[235] Ibid., pp. 443–4.

divorced from their Buddhist symbolism. Eliade's unfortunate use of the words "degeneration," "infantalization," and "lower planes," however, presents an easy target for criticism. Even if we accept the word *degeneration* as meaning cruder and less theoretical, new interpretations of the symbolism of the monk's robe by Chan monks were, if anything, more sophisticated and ethereal than earlier interpretations. Similarly, reinterpretations of the rosary at the Qing court were made with full knowledge of the earlier Buddhist symbolism of the beads and can hardly be characterized as "infantile" or as emerging from a "lower plane." Nor need we find such hermeneutic drift particularly distressing. The aesthetic interpretation of the rosary as a sensual object did not detract from its symbolic significance: it added to it. The monk's robe could be used both as an emblem of the ascetic and as a sign of imperial favor. Perhaps owing to China's rich literary tradition, the symbolism of a given object accumulated layer upon layer over the centuries. The history of Buddhist symbols in China is not, then, a history of degeneration in which a profound, pristine notion is slowly abandoned for a coarser more mundane one; it is instead a history of the growth and expansion of the potential of objects as conduits of expression.

Chapter Three

MERIT

IN CHAPTER ONE we saw how the notion that certain objects contain sacred power profoundly influenced the development of Chinese material culture. The potential of abstract ideas to shape the material world is even more apparent in this chapter as we turn to the principle of "merit" in Chinese Buddhism. From the entry of Buddhism in the Han until the present day, the manufacture and distribution of countless objects—from small images and charms to monumental buildings and statues—were driven in part by belief in the Buddhist notion of merit: the idea that there is an invisible moral order governing the universe, and that under this system one is rewarded in this life or the next for good deeds, including the production of certain specified types of objects.

In many early Buddhist texts, the Buddha presents various moral standards, the violation of which brings punishment, and the maintenance of which reaps rewards. One should not kill or steal or lie, for "a bad deed yields a bad reward," while "good deeds inevitably reap good rewards."[1] This, of course, is the foundation of karma; at some point in the never-ending cycle of life and death, every good deed will be rewarded and every bad one punished. This is a natural, spontaneous process often described with agricultural metaphors: with a good action, one plants a seed in a "field of blessings" (*futian*) and later harvests the "fruits" of these good actions. From comforts or pains in this life, to rebirth in a heaven or hell in the next, one's well-being depends in large measure on the morality of one's actions in this life or a previous one—that is, "fate" depends on one's store of merit.

What is interesting for our purposes here, however, are the instances when such basic Buddhist ethical concerns involve objects. According to a number of early Buddhist texts, in addition to gaining merit through refraining from killing, lying, and so forth, one can also gain merit through material donations. The Buddhist canon is replete with references to "giving," an act that is always richly rewarded, depending in degree on the donor, the recipient, the gift, and the mental state of those involved,

---

[1] This particular example is taken from the *Chang ahan jing* (Skt. *Dīrghāgama*) 6, p. 37a, but such exhortations can be found scattered throughout Buddhist literature.

among other factors. One famous passage states that not only are the generous donors rewarded during their life (they are well respected and loved by their contemporaries, etc.), but further, that when they die, they will be reborn in a heaven.[2]

What, specifically, is one to give, and to whom? In one of the Buddha's sermons, he explains to a potential donor that the lay can gain merit through seven acts: (1) building monasteries for the sangha, (2) furnishing monasteries, (3) providing monks and nuns with food, (4) providing clothing to protect monks and nuns from rain, (5) supplying monks and nuns with medicine, (6) building wells, and (7) constructing hostels for travelers.[3] The focus in this passage on gifts to the monastic community should not surprise us, since these texts were composed and propagated by monks who depended in some measure on the charity of the laity for their survival. Elsewhere, donors are encouraged to plant trees, build bridges, and provide ferries—material, charitable acts that benefit more than just monks.[4] We also know from both textual and archaeological evidence that Indian Buddhists also contributed to the manufacture of stupas, books, images, and precious stones used to adorn stupas and icons, all in the belief that such gifts would produce merit.[5]

Leading Indian monks devoted considerable attention to the problem of the mechanism of merit, and debated questions of the nature of the gift, the ethical problem of motivation, and the relative degree of merit accruing one who gives to, say, the sangha as opposed to the Buddha or to a stupa.[6] For instance, in a discussion of the purpose of material offerings, the *Abhidharmakośa* begins by asking how one can receive merit by giving offerings to "holy sites" (*caitya*) devoted to holy men who have long since died.[7] That is, why give offerings when there is no one there to receive the gift? The text responds by deftly explaining that the merit for such acts derives not from the physical gift but from the charitable state

<hr>

[2] From *Anguttaranikāya* 3, cited in Lamotte, *History of Indian Buddhism*, p. 415.

[3] *Zeng yi ahan jing* (Skt. *Ekottarāgama*) 35, p. 741c.

[4] Lamotte, *History of Indian Buddhism*, p. 72.

[5] For the role of Buddhist doctrine in the importation of Indian gems to China in ancient times, see Liu, *Ancient India and Ancient China*, pp. 104–12.

[6] André Bareau gives references to discussion of these problems in his *Les sectes bouddhiques du petit véhicule*, pp. 269–70. Erich Frauwallner suggests provocatively that one of the main motivations for monks to compose technical treatises on such subjects was the belief that by doing so they could derive merit; in other words, one could even gain merit by writing about merit. Erich Frauwallner, *Studies in Abhidharma Literature and the Origins of Buddhist Philosophical Systems*, p. 122.

[7] In some texts, the term *caitya* (Ch. *zhiduo*) covers all Buddhist holy sites, including stupas. Here the term seems not to include stupas, the distinction being that stupas contain relics and *caityas* do not. Hence, unlike stupas, holy men are in no way present at a *caitya*. The distinction between stupa and *caitya* is made in the *Mohe sengqi lü* (Skt. *Mahāsāṃghikavinaya*) 33, p. 489b.

of mind of the donor, and that this state of mind is achieved through the donation of offerings.[8] The wealth of discussion on gift-giving in early Buddhist literature testifies to the importance monks attached to the doctrine of merit and lay donations. Yet, precise details of exactly how merit worked eluded even the most persistent theoreticians. Certainly a donation of a large tract of land capable of supporting generations of monks was worth more merit than the gift of a single meal to an itinerant monk. But wasn't a small donation from a poor man worth more than a small donation from a rich one? And wasn't a gift to an accomplished holy monk more meritorious than a gift to an ordinary or substandard one? Such issues were open to interpretation on a case-by-case basis, and theories of merit and gift-giving no doubt took shape in the context of interaction between monks and potential donors, for merit-making was always an issue of immediate, practical concern.[9]

We can move from speculation about notions of merit in early Buddhism to concrete examples when we turn to the epigraphical evidence. We have, for instance, an inscription dated to the period between 210 and 200 B.C. in Ceylon, recording the gift of a cave from a Sinhalese princess to a local group of monks. The inscription reads: "The cave of the princess [Abi] Tissā, daughter of the great king Gāmaṇī-Uttiya, is given to the sangha of the ten directions, for the benefit of [her] mother and father."[10] The inscription fits well with the scriptural injunctions to donate places of residence to monks. It also illustrates the doctrine of the "transfer of merit": the belief that not only can one gain merit by donating certain objects to monks and nuns, but one can also transfer this merit to another. In general, the most common recipients of transferred merit in extant Indian Buddhist inscriptions are, as in the case of the princess, the parents of the donor.[11] Inscriptions also at times indicate that the merit for giving the gift is to be transferred to specific monks or even to the donors themselves. Moreover, from very early on (120–80 B.C.), in addition to laypeople, monks and nuns also made donations for the embellishment of sacred objects and sacred sites.[12] This last point illustrates how fully merit-making was integrated into Buddhist practice. As even monks gave in order to receive merit, the doctrine cannot be seen as simply a means

[8] *Apidamo jushe lun* (Skt. *Abhidharmakośaśāstra*) 18, *T.* no. 1558, vol. 29, p. 97a–b; de La Vallée Poussin, *Abhidharmakośabhāsyam*, pp. 702–3. The Tang commentary *Jushe lun ji* provides a clear discussion of the passage. *T* 1521, vol. 41, p. 286a–b.

[9] On the subject of merit in early Indian religion, see Torkel Brekke, "Contradiction and the Merit of Giving in Indian Religions," pp. 287–320.

[10] Schopen, *Bones, Stones, and Buddhist Monks*, p. 7.

[11] On this point, see Schopen, "Filial Piety and the Monk in the Practice of Indian Buddhism," ibid.

[12] Ibid., p. 30.

for monks to sustain themselves; rather, with rare exception, it was a standard part of the beliefs and practices of all Buddhists. The same point is highlighted by texts like those cited above that encourage donors to help the sick and to plant trees, neither of which directly benefits the monastic community.

In sum, in Indian Buddhism, the production and donation of large numbers of stupas, images, monastic buildings, and a prescribed set of other objects big and small were motivated in part by the belief that such gifts brought merit to the donors, which could, if they so desired, be transferred to one of their intimates. Hence, when Princess Abi Tissā donated a piece of her property, she gave the gift twice: once to a group of monks and once, in the form of merit, to her parents. This combination of earthly and religious merit was to prove enormously popular both in India and, as we will see, in China as well.

Turning to China, we find no comparable notion of religious merit before the entry of Buddhism. In recent decades, archaeologists have unearthed a wealth of artifacts from ancient Chinese tombs, including both everyday objects like pottery and cooking utensils, as well as various sorts of surrogate objects such as models of mansions, cattle, and servants.[13] From the Warring States period onward, objects were buried with the dead in the belief that these objects or the things they represented could be used by the deceased in the netherworld.[14] Burial goods were not exclusively for the dead; for in addition to the social prestige accruing to, for instance, a son capable of burying his father in style, geomantic manuals claimed that an auspicious burial would bring good fortune to the descendants of the deceased.[15]

But here we are far from Buddhist notions of merit, in which one earns credit for making objects that are either useful to the living (wells, bridges, etc.), contributions to the monastic assembly (monasteries, land), or more generally expressive of devotion to Buddhism (stupas, icons). In addition to burial goods, some early Chinese texts speak vaguely of rewards for the good and punishment for the bad. The *Book of Changes,* for instance, states that "A family that accumulates goodness will be sure to have an excess of blessings, but one that accumulates evil will be sure to have an excess of disasters."[16] But again, this is far from the precise, almost me-

---

[13] For an overview of the material, see Pu Muzhou (Poo Mu-chou), *Muzang yu shengsi—Zhongguo gudai zongjiao zhi xingsi.* Of course, more has been unearthed in the decade since the publication of this book.

[14] For an overview of beliefs in the afterworld in ancient China, see Poo, *In Search of Personal Welfare,* ch. 7.

[15] Ibid., p. 174.

[16] *Zhouyi zhengyi* 1, p. 7a, in *Shisanjing zhushu,* ed. Ruan Yuan; English trans. Richard John Lynn, *The Classic of Changes: A New Translation of the I Ching as Interpreted by Wang Bi,* p. 146.

chanical concept of karma, and nowhere is "accumulation of goodness" linked to the manufacture of specific objects as it is in Buddhist writings.

Buddhist doctrines relating to merit probably entered China in the first centuries of the Common Era along with Buddhist texts and devotional practices, though evidence for Buddhism in this period is sparse. Certainly by the fifth century, the doctrine was widespread. The *Biographies of Eminent Monks* devotes an entire chapter to monks who "elicit blessings" (*xingfu*), that is, make merit. In general, the method used to gain merit in these biographies is the construction of stupas, monasteries, and Buddhist icons. We read, for instance, of a monk named Huili, who "cultivated blessings" by erecting stupas, or of the monk Fayi, who "was fond of devoting himself to merit, and so erected fifty-three monasteries."[17]

Huijing, his biography tells us, was knowledgeable in the scriptures, but because he "took good works (*fu*) as his duty, never completely mastered exegesis. Wherever he went, he erected stupas and images in order to benefit the karma of all beings."[18] This account is particularly interesting because it concludes by noting that Huijing applied the merit he received for making stupas and images to his own karmic destiny: "In all of his good deeds, Huijing transferred (the merit) to the Western Paradise. On the day he died, his room was filled with a remarkable fragrance which lingered long after." In other words, when building Buddhist stupas and icons, Huijing made vows that the merit for doing so be used to send him to Amitābha's Pure Land upon his death. The fragrance that appeared when he died was proof of the efficacy of his vow. In this anecdote, as in others, the precise functioning of the mechanism of merit is not explained: we are not told just how Huijing's merit was accounted for and applied to his next life. Evidently such details were considered a hidden part of the natural order—like the arrival of seasons or the movement of the stars, attempts to explain such mysteries in full were thought futile.

The lines at the beginning of Huijing's biography stating that he sacrificed opportunities to master the scriptures in order to perform good deeds are also revealing. In Buddhist texts, doctrinal knowledge is often juxtaposed to pious works, with these works taking the place of (and often given precedence over) knowledge of the finer points of the scriptures. At the end of the chapter of the *Biographies of Eminent Monks* that is dedicated to monks who perform good deeds, the compiler of the text attempts to balance meritorious deeds and knowledge of Buddhist doctrine, stating that good works are "the foundation of wisdom," and that the two are like the two wings of a bird—each worthless without the other.[19] But as we will see in the pages that follow, many were willing to

[17] *Gaoseng zhuan* 8, pp. 410a and 8, 411a.
[18] Ibid. 8, p. 411b.
[19] Ibid. 13, p. 413b.

make do with "good works" alone, contributing toward the manufacture of images or other objects *in place of* knowledge of the scriptures. This tendency illustrates both the importance attached to detailed knowledge of Buddhist scriptures—if one didn't have it, some replacement was needed—and that one could get by with less erudition through piety and good works.

Archaeological evidence helps us to flesh out this picture of monks roaming the countryside soliciting funds and overseeing the construction of monasteries and Buddhist objects. In fact, judging by inscriptions on extant icons, the most common donors of Buddhist objects were not monks, but laypeople.[20] Among our earliest Chinese Buddhist images that can be dated with precision is a small stone stupa with an inscription dated 337, in which the donor, one Cheng Duaner, writes:

> Mid part of the sixth month of the second year of the Taiyuan era, in the year of *bingzi* [337]. Cheng Duaner, recognizing that his own blessings are few, that he was born in the final age [of the Dharma], and that he has not read Buddhist classics, has expended [his wealth] for the sake of his parents and his entire family in order to erect this stone stupa decorated with images. May the merit from this allow him to achieve the ultimate path and avoid the office of punishments. His young wife and valiant sons also join in this vow.[21]

The inscription contains the two basic elements of a standard Buddhist donation: it names the donor and indicates the people to whom the donor wishes the merit of the donation to go. The detail that Cheng Duaner "has not read Buddhist classics" once again points to the notion that material donations could take the place of familiarity with Buddhist texts.

As in this inscription of Cheng Duaner, most Chinese donative inscriptions employ the doctrine of transfer of merit, specifying to whom they wish the merit to go. Many such vows are elaborate, generously giving the merit to all beings, though usually specifying relatives first. Take, for instance, a seated Maitreya image dated to 423, one of our earliest such images from the Southern Dynasties. The inscription reads:

> Fourteenth day of the first month in the first year of the Jingping Era [423]. Disciple of the Buddha, Wang Shicheng, has respectfully made this image of Maitreya for the sake of his deceased parents and living wife, for the "four benevolent ones"[22] in the six paths of existence, and for all beings in

[20] See, for instance, statistics compiled by Hou Xudong for the fifth and sixth centuries in his *Wu liu shiji beifang minzhong fojiao xinyang*, p. 95.

[21] The image is now in the Jiuquan Museum in Gansu Province. Jin, *Zhongguo lidai jinian foxiang tudian*, pp. 2, 433.

[22] *Sien*. There are various sets of four. One of the most common is (1) parents, (2) sen-

the universe [*dharmadhātu*], that they may achieve the most marvelous reward.[23]

Hundreds of such images are extant from throughout Chinese history. The most frequent recipient of merit for making an image are the parents of the donor. But we also have examples of wives donating merit to deceased husbands, mothers for dead children, sisters for deceased brothers, and even one case of soldiers donating merit to a fallen comrade.[24] Occasionally, inscriptions specify that the merit is to allow deceased parents to be born in the Pure Land, or to protect a family from disease.[25] More usually, however, the inscriptions ask for generic "blessings" and "good fortune" for the donors, their family, and all sentient beings. At times we can identify the donor as a nun or as a mid-level official,[26] but in general we know nothing about the donors beyond their names—a reminder of just how limited and random the extant historical record is.

This leaves us asking just who was Wang Shicheng, the "disciple of the Buddha" who had a Buddhist statue made for the souls of his parents. What specifically did the sixth-century mother, a certain Han Xiaohua, believe would happen when she donated the merit for making an image to a dead child? Terse, usually formulaic inscriptions are frustratingly silent on such specific questions—like a legal contract, once the essential information has been given regarding the parties involved (donor and recipient) and the provenance of goods in question (including merit produced), further elaboration was superfluous. Nonetheless, even if the specific circumstances surrounding the gift of Wang Shicheng, Han Xiaohua, or countless other names recorded in stone and metal remain beyond the historian's grasp, the circumstances of meritorious acts by other individuals *have* come down to us, and taken together comprise a general pic-

---

tient beings, (3) rulers, and (4) the Three Jewels (Buddha, Dharma, Sangha). Another set is (1) heaven and earth, (2) teachers, (3) rulers, and (4) parents.

[23] Chang Qing, "Ji Yulin faxian de Liu-Song jintong foxiang," p. 92.

[24] For the wife, mother, and sister, see the stele of 529 and the stele of 536 reported on in Shandongsheng Qingzhoushi Bowuguan, "Qingzhou Longxingsi fojiao zaoxiang jiaozang qingli jianbao," pp. 4–15. For the image dedicated to a soldier, see Zhou Zheng, "Luo Sishen zaoxiang xiaokao," pp. 23–4.

[25] For examples, see the 570 image reported in Cheng Jizhong, "Hebei Gaochengxian faxian yi pi Bei Qi shi zaoxiang," pp. 242–5, and the 848 image of the Medicine King Buddha reported in Wang Xixiang and Zeng Deren, "Sichuan Zizhong Chonglongshan Moyai zaoxiang," p. 24.

[26] For nuns, see, for instance, the 536 image in Shandonsheng Qingzhoushi Bowaguan, "Qingzhou Longxingsi fojiao zaoxiang," or the Maitreya image of 660 reported in Liu Shanyi, "Shandong Chipingxian Guangping chutu Tangdai shi zaoxiang," p. 752. For one of the few donors who happens to appear in one of the dynastic histories as a mid-level official, see the 521 image reported in Zhongguo Shehuikexueyuan Kaogu Yanjiuso et al., "Hebei Linzhang Yecheng yizhi chutu de Beichao tong zaoxiang," pp. 741–4.

ture of how the idea of Buddhist merit exerted a sustained and powerful influence on Chinese material culture from its entry into China until the present day.

Many of the objects we have already seen were made in part in order to earn merit. This is particularly true for stupas and icons, both of which are frequently extolled as merit-making objects in scriptures, and have left behind a wealth of epigraphy testifying to the prevalence of this belief among Chinese Buddhists. Below I focus instead on three different objects—books, monasteries, and bridges—the histories of which were also guided by the Buddhist doctrine of merit. All three objects played prominent roles not just in the history of Buddhism but in the overall history of Chinese material culture as well.

Books

The Early History of Bookmaking in India and China

One of the reasons for the important place of books in the Chinese Buddhist tradition is the belief that one can gain merit by copying or printing Buddhist scriptures. The origins of this belief can be traced to India. From early on, Indian monks diligently applied themselves to a vast corpus of sermons purportedly preached by the Buddha to his disciples. This literature and the injunctions to propagate it belonged, however, to an oral tradition in which texts were recited from memory rather than read from written sources. Physical books were not an important element of the earliest phase of Buddhism, and, indeed, may not have been used at all. Thus, for the history of material culture, the eventual appearance of references to reading and copying physical Buddhist manuscripts, in approximately the first century A.D., marks an important development.[27] In particular, a number of prominent texts from this period state that the act of copying the scriptures brings religious merit. As we have seen, the notion of merit goes back to at least the second century B.C., but the idea that one can gain merit by copying manuscripts, a part of what has been termed the *cult of the book*, seems to have emerged in the first centuries of the Common Era in the body of texts now grouped under the heading of "Mahāyāna."

To give a representative example, one such text, the *Aṣṭasāhasrikā*, one of the *Perfection of Wisdom* scriptures, considered among the earliest of Mahāyāna scriptures, states that "where this perfection of wisdom has been *written down in a book,* and has been put up and worshipped . . .

---

[27] For a concise history of books in India, see Pratapaditya Pal and Julia Meech-Pekavik, *Buddhist Book Illuminations*, pp. 21–94. The authors note that as late as A.D. 400, books were still not widespread in India (p. 24).

there men and ghosts can do no harm, except as a punishment for past deeds."[28] Similarly, important Mahāyāna texts such as the *Diamond Sutra*, the *Lotus Sutra*, and the *Flower Adornment Sutra* all describe with great enthusiasm the merit to be gained from copying scriptures. Take, for example, the *Lotus*, which comments:

> [I]f there is a man who shall receive and keep, read and recite, explain, *or copy in writing* a single *gāthā* of the Scripture of the Blossom of the Fine Dharma [i.e., the *Lotus Sutra*], or who shall look with veneration *on a roll of this scripture* as if it were the Buddha himself, or who shall make to it sundry offerings of flowers, perfume, necklaces, powdered incense, perfumed paste, burnt incense, silk canopies and banners, garments, or music, or who shall even join palms in reverent worship of it, O Medicine King, be it known that this man or any other like him shall have already made offerings to ten myriads of millions of Buddhas in former times, and in those Buddhas' presence taken a great vow. It is by virtue of the great pity he shall have had for living beings that he shall be born here as a human being.[29]

Passages like these justify the expression *cult of the book*. Not only was the book a source of information, but it was also a physical object of worship to be venerated with offerings "as if it were the Buddha himself." Most importantly, texts like these insist that Buddhist scriptures were a source of merit—credits for a better life and a higher rebirth.

These early Mahāyāna texts are notoriously difficult to date beyond a general assignment to the first centuries of the Common Era, and specialists in Indian Buddhism have yet to provide a detailed account of where, when, and how books rose to prominence in Indian Buddhism. Gregory Schopen has, however, proposed what is at least a working hypothesis for the rise and function of the book in early Mahāyāna.[30] After a close look at a formula prescribing the copying and worshipping of books that appears in several Mahāyāna scriptures, Schopen suggested that the practice of worshipping books (which usually, as in the *Lotus* passage cited above, included offerings of flowers and incense) began with followers worshipping at the site at which a particular text was recited. Gradually, in order to provide a stable cult, independent of a particular reciter, worshippers of a given text began to copy out the scripture and worship it in the more concrete form of a book. Schopen concludes by

---

[28] Edward Conze, translating from a Sanskrit version of the text. *The Perfection of Wisdom in Eight Thousand Lines and Its Verse Summary*, pp. 104–6. The passage is discussed in Gregory Schopen, "The Phrase 'sa pṛthivīpradeśaś caityabhūto bhavet' in the *Vajracchedikā*: Notes on the Cult of the Book in Mahāyāna," pp. 147–87.

[29] *Miaofa lianhua jing* (Skt. *Saddharmapundarīka*) 4, p. 30c; Hurvitz, *Scripture of the Lotus Blossom of the Fine Dharma*, p. 174.

[30] Schopen, "Notes on the Cult of the Book in Mahāyāna."

suggesting that "since each text placed itself at the center of its own cult, early Mahāyāna (from a sociological point of view), rather than being an identifiable single group, was in the beginning a loose federation of a number of distinct though related cults, all of the same pattern, but each associated with its specific text."[31] If this conjecture is right, then from the first century on, Indian Buddhist books provided not only the doctrinal foundations of particular groups of adherents but also the physical locus of their worship.

Even if we set aside the specific problem of when books first became considered sources of merit and ask the more general question of when books became popular in India, the evidence is still murky. With the exception of inscriptions on metal, clay, or stone, most writings in ancient India were inscribed on pieces of birch bark or palm leaves, which were then bound together. Few such manuscripts survive from ancient and medieval India, owing perhaps more to the ephemerality of palm leaves and birch bark than to disinterest in the medium.[32] References in Mahāyāna texts to copying scriptures tell us at least that although Indian poets and religious leaders were known for their rich store of oral literature, by the first centuries of the Common Era, the written book would not have been foreign to literate Indians.[33]

While the early history of the book in India is poorly documented, the respect and affection of Chinese literati for written books is well attested from very early times. When Buddhism entered China in the first centuries of the Common Era, China already boasted a long history of bookmaking and book lore. In addition to inscriptions on metal or bone, dating back to the beginnings of Chinese writing, various materials were used to produce writings of greater length (i.e., "books"). Slips of bamboo and wood tied together to form scrolled books were in use from the earliest times to the third or fourth centuries A.D. Large numbers of such slips from the Qin-Han period have been discovered in modern times and are an important source for scholars of early Chinese history. Silk too was a popular medium for writing in China from very early on.[34]

---

[31] Ibid., p. 181.

[32] The oldest Buddhist manuscripts identified to date are from the first century A.D. in Gāndhārī language with Kharoṣṭī script on birch bark. See Richard Salomon et al., *Ancient Buddhist Scrolls from Gandhāra: The British Library Kharoṣṭī Fragments*. Another set of early manuscripts, discovered in 1938 in a stupa in Gilgit in present-day Pakistan, dating to between the fourth and ninth centuries, are also of great importance. See Pal and Meech-Pekarik, *Buddhist Book Illuminations*, pp. 41–4.

[33] Later, more easily datable evidence, including the account of the fifth-century Chinese pilgrim Faxian, confirms that Indian monks commonly copied manuscripts on palm leaves circa A.D. 400. This tradition almost certainly began centuries earlier. Pal and Meech-Pekarik, ibid., p. 45.

[34] Tsien, *Paper and Printing*, p. 30. The most famous early silk manuscripts are those discovered at Mawangdui, including the earliest extant version of the *Laozi*.

Along with the custom of manufacturing books written on bamboo strips or silk came the association between knowledge and ownership of books as well as a number of related ideas and practices connected to the habit of book collecting. In ancient China, learned men were known for their libraries, and the state made concerted efforts to control the production and distribution of books—the most famous early example of which was the destruction of books under the reign of Qin Shihuang, first emperor of China. Not only were books respected for their content, but they were also admired for their calligraphy. All of these factors came together in the reading and copying of texts. Manuscript copying in particular was a way to at once read, study, and memorize a text while at the same time practicing the art of calligraphy.[35]

All of this was commonplace in China before the entrance of Buddhism. To continue this sketch of the history of Chinese books beyond the entry of Buddhism, in subsequent centuries bookmaking underwent a number of important technological changes. Paper began to be used for writing in the first century A.D., and by the third century had replaced bamboo and wooden slips as the standard material for making books.[36] Before the Tang (618–907), whether made of bamboo or wooden slips, silk or paper, manuscripts were generally rolled up into scrolls. During the Tang, however, booklets made of bound sheets of paper with individual pages began to appear, and slowly replaced the scroll as the standard format of Chinese books. Also during the Tang, bookmakers began to print books with carved wooden blocks in place of writing them out by hand. Hence, by the tenth century, the basic elements of the modern Chinese book—printed, bound, paper pages—were all in place.

It is one thing to trace the basic outline of these developments; it is another to explain why they took place. Among many other factors driving the evolution of the Chinese book, historians of technology have long recognized that Buddhism played a prominent role. In fact, we can detect a Buddhist influence, over the course of centuries, in all the technological developments I have mentioned. Less attention has been paid to the changes Buddhism introduced in the more abstract attitudes toward books as sources of knowledge and sacred power. Below I will address both the influence of Buddhism on Chinese attitudes toward books and the influence of Buddhism on the technologies related to their production. But before turning to the role of Buddhism in the technological history of bookmaking, let us look first at the most prominent Buddhist notion related to books: that religious merit could be derived from manufacturing Buddhist scriptures.[37] This factor, perhaps more than any other, fueled the

[35] Jean-Pierre Drège, "La lecture et l'écriture en Chine et la xylographie," p. 92.
[36] Tsien, *Paper and Printing*, p. 2.
[37] On the effect of the idea of Buddhist merit on the dissemination of Buddhist texts and

spread and development of Buddhist books in China, which in turn had a profound impact on Chinese book culture in general.

Book Production as a Means for Making Merit

A belief in Buddhist merit lurks behind centuries of prolific book production in China. We have already seen a few examples of Buddhist texts that enjoin their readers to copy them, and assure us that doing so will accrue merit in vast and wondrous quantities. To get a sense of how this notion was received in China, let us focus on one such text, the *Diamond Sutra,* which was probably copied more times than any other book in Chinese history—close to two thousand medieval manuscripts of the text survive from Dunhuang alone.[38]

The *Diamond Sutra,* containing in concise form much of the most influential vocabulary and doctrinal concepts of the voluminous *Perfection of Wisdom* literature, was translated into Chinese at least six times between 402 and 703. The most popular translation of the text was completed by Kumārajīva in 402.[39] The scripture stimulated hundreds of commentaries and was widely read, studied, and memorized.[40] In addition to analysis of the illusory nature of reality and a number of other key Buddhist concepts, a substantial part of the scripture is taken up with passages extolling its own propagation. "In generations to come, if there is a good man or good woman who can keep and recite this scripture, then the Thus-come-Ones, with their Buddha-wisdom, will know this person well and will watch this person well, and this person will obtain merit in inexhaustible measure." In other words, when one recited the *Diamond,* the buddhas were listening. Or again, "To state the matter in brief, this scripture contains an inconceivable, immeasurable, boundless measure of merit." These passages make no mention of writing, and while encouraging readers to read and memorize the text, they do not specifically direct them to reproduce it in writing. For our purposes, another injunction in the *Diamond* especially merits our attention. First the passage describes a devotee who, out of devotion for Buddhism, sacrifices his own body countless times every day for aeons. Even this, the scripture tells us, cannot compare with the merit to be derived from the *Diamond.* For "if there be one who hears this scripture and believes it unfalteringly, his merit will

---

teachings in China, see Stephen F. Teiser, *The Scripture on the Ten Kings and the Making of Purgatory in Medieval Chinese Buddhism* p. 160.

[38] Hirai Yūkei, "*Kongōhannya kyō,*" pp. 20–21.

[39] On the textual history of the *Diamond Sutra,* see Hirai, "*Kongō hannya kyō,*" and Teiser, *The Scripture on the Ten Kings,* pp. 95–7.

[40] According to one Song writer, over eight hundred commentaries to the *Diamond* were in circulation in his day. See Hirai, ibid., p. 19.

be greater than this. How much the more is this the case for one who *copies*, keeps, and recites the scripture, explaining it to others."[41]

Some of the major commentaries to the *Diamond* mention this last line in passing, but while their authors were certainly interested in the mechanism of merit, they do not ascribe any special importance to the idea that merit could be derived from copying a book.[42] In a text filled with difficult, abstract doctrines, the passage was perhaps too straightforward to compete for the commentators' attention. Others, more humble in status and erudition, did, however, notice the phrase and applied it to their own religious practice. This is reflected in any number of miracle stories told, written, and circulated during the medieval period. Several collections of stories of miracles related to the *Diamond Sutra* have come down to us from medieval China. The stories tell of men and women, monks, nuns, and laypeople who are saved from disaster or granted special advantages because they have recited, lectured on, or otherwise propagated the *Diamond Sutra*. In many cases, the method of propagation is to copy the scripture.

The eighth-century *Collection of Miraculous Tales Concerning the Diamond-Prajñā*, for instance, tells of a certain Chen De, who

> [d]evoted himself to copying the [*Diamond*] scripture. Suddenly, he took seriously ill and was taken below the earth by officials from the netherworld. There he saw a platform under construction and asked, "What platform is this?" The official from the netherworld replied, "This is a *prajñā* platform which is being constructed for a certain Mr. Chen who is soon to arrive. We are building the platform in preparation for him." Chen then revived and related these things. People near and far heard of this and hurriedly recited the *Prajñā* [i.e., the *Diamond Sutra*].[43]

Another story tells of a dead woman who speaks through her coffin, telling her sister that, because she ate meat in a monastery and once killed a clam (to apply its juice to a sore), she is now suffering in the "Hell of Knives." Her body is pierced with seven blades. She then instructs her sister to make a donation to a local monastery and ask a certain monk there to make copies of the *Diamond Sutra*. With each roll of the sutra that the monk copies, the dead woman reports that another blade has been removed from her body, until, with the seventh copy of the scripture, all the

---

[41] The quotations are all from Kumārajīva's translation. *Jin'gang banruo boluomi jing*, T no. 235, vol. 8, p. 750c.

[42] Commentaries by the prominent Tang monks Jizang, Kuiji, and Zongmi all give the phrase but do not comment upon it. See *Jin'gang banruo shu*, T no. 1699, vol. 33, p. 103c, *Jin'gang banruo jing zanshu*, p. 139c, and *Jin'gang banruo jing shulun zuanyao*, T no. 1701, vol. 33, p. 163c.

[43] *Jin'gang banruo jiyan ji* C, *Xu zang jing*, vol. 149, p. 49a.

blades are removed and she is released from her suffering.[44] Stories like these could easily be multiplied from this collection and others like it. Even if we do not take such fanciful fictions as factual accounts of actual events, they at the very least reflect the prevalence of the notion that copying scriptures brings merit.

In these tales, as in several of the examples in the introduction to this chapter, production of an object takes the place of knowledge of the scriptures. This point is particularly striking here, since the object in question is itself a scripture. As we have seen, both the *Lotus* and the *Diamond* list copying scriptures among a number of activities that bring merit, including *explaining* the scripture to others. In other words, the injunctions of the scriptures assume the importance of understanding their content. In the Chinese stories, however, the scriptures become the equivalent of Princess Abi Tissā's cave—just another source of merit, no different in nature from buildings, images, or any of the other merit-earning objects discussed in this chapter.

Further, in the story of the Hell of Knives, the sister of the dead woman does not even copy the scripture herself: she pays a monk to do it for her. This tells us, first of all, that the practice of making merit with scriptures was not considered the sole preserve of monks, but extended to laypeople of various social levels, and even, as the last story suggests, to the illiterate, who could derive merit from paying others to copy the scripture for them. Secondly, the story reflects a mentality in which the garnering of merit through copying sacred texts was an economic transaction, rather than a conscious attempt to propagate Buddhist ideas or learn them for oneself by writing out sutras. In this context, the prodigious store of copies of the *Diamond Sutra* at Dunhuang, virtually identical in content and originally belonging to only a few monastic libraries, begins to make sense: for the most part, the texts are "receipts" for merit-giving transactions rather than scriptures that were read.[45]

In the case of the *Diamond Sutra*, we need not rely on such indirect reflections of mentality, but can turn instead to extant medieval manuscripts that provide direct evidence of what individual devotees thought. Manuscripts of the *Diamond Sutra* preserved at Dunhuang often end with brief colophons in which the person who has copied the text or paid for it to be copied includes a prayer stating his or her reasons for doing so. Typically, the colophons end with a formula requesting that the merit derived from copying the scripture be applied to the individuals responsible, to

---

[44] Ibid., B, p. 46a.

[45] It is unlikely that the sutras were used as liturgical handbooks for massive ceremonies, but we know very little about how such Buddhist libraries functioned, and this possibility cannot be ruled out. There were in fact ceremonies at Dunhuang involving thousands of devotees. See Ma, *Dunhuang Mogaokushi yanjiu*, p. 194.

their family, and to "all sentient beings." One manuscript copy of a collection of miracle tales related to the *Diamond,* discovered at Dunhuang, concludes with the remarks of one Di Fengda, who, after noting the date (908), writes, "This scripture praises accounts of miraculous merit. I have contributed to the spread of this scripture for the benefit of devotees of the future and for parents who have already passed away and my living parents, in addition to my community and others."[46] This prayer fits the standard formula for such requests. What is remarkable is that Di Fengda believed not only that one could derive merit for copying the *Diamond,* but that one could even derive merit from copying a collection of stories *about* the *Diamond.*

Di Fengda's request that the merit from copying the text bring benefit to his parents past and present, and to essentially all creatures, is typical, and expresses sentiments that can be found in the formulaic prayers attached to any number of manuscript copies of the *Diamond Sutra* or other scriptures. Such vows extend from the specific and personal (usually parents) to the inclusive and general "all sentient beings." Just how merit was to be parceled out is expressed only vaguely; presumably the vows were directed primarily at specific individuals such as family members, with the more general recipients (all creatures) tacked on as a pious afterthought. Some colophons provide us with rare insights into more individual, specific needs of ordinary people and the ways in which they believed Buddhist merit could assist them. Take, for example, a seventh-century colophon to a copy of the *Diamond Sutra:*

> Twenty-third day of the seventh month of the twelfth year of the Daye era of the Great Sui (616). The devotee and upāsaka Liu Yuanjing has respectfully copied this scripture and hopes that through this meager act of goodness all creatures will read this scripture. May those who hear it respect and believe in it; may all become enlightened to suffering and emptiness; may all who see this scripture keep it and achieve eternal bliss. He also hopes that he personally may leave the frontier region and return quickly to the capital. May his sins be erased, and blessings and joy be forthcoming.[47]

We know nothing more of Liu Yuanjing than what we read here: he was apparently a man of the capital, assigned to the dreary border region of Dunhuang, who wanted to return to the more refined life of the metropolis. A similar colophon by another frustrated official asks bluntly for a promotion.[48] In what is perhaps the most delightful colophon of all from

---

[46] *Chi song jin'gang jing lingyan gongde ji, T* no. 2743, vol. 85, p. 160a (Pelliot no. 2094).

[47] Stein no. 2605, discussed in Hirai, "*Kongō hannya kyō,*" p. 27, and in Fang Guang-chang, "Dunhuang wenxian zhong de *Jin'gang jing* ji qi zhu shu," p. 74.

[48] Stein no. 87, *Jin'gang banruo boluomi jing.*

Dunhuang, a man who has commissioned the copying of a scripture dedicates the merit to a beloved field ox with the following words:

> Presented on behalf of one old plowing ox. The *Diamond* in one scroll and the *Prophecy* in one scroll were reverently written. I pray that this ox may personally receive the merit, be reborn in the Pure Land, and never again receive the body of an animal. May heaven's ministries and earth's prefects understand it clearly and handle it discreetly, so that there be no further enmity or quarrel. The first month of a *xinwei* year [probably 911].[49]

This colophon and the previous ones express the hopes of what appear to be mid-level officials and farmers. If we turn from Dunhuang colophons of the *Diamond Sutra* to references to Buddhist scriptures in secular sources, we find that all manner of people copied Buddhist scriptures in order to derive merit from them, including famous recluses, imperial consorts, and even emperors.[50]

In sum, we have ample evidence from Buddhist and secular accounts as well as from extant medieval manuscripts that the idea that one could derive religious merit from copying Buddhist scriptures was widely accepted in China from the medieval period onward, and that this idea inspired countless people from all walks of life to copy Buddhist texts. This being said, people copied, read, and collected Buddhist scriptures for a variety of reasons, and approached these texts with differing attitudes.

Veneration for Buddhist Books

So far my discussion of Buddhism and books has centered on the belief that one could gain religious merit through reading, reciting, copying, and printing Buddhist scriptures. A broader look at Chinese attitudes toward Buddhist books leads us away from merit and back to the theme of chapter 1—the belief that certain Buddhist objects contained sacred power. From the medieval period to the present day, Chinese Buddhist literature abounds with stories in which Buddhist books saved their owners from calamity, staying the sword of the executioner, warding off demons, or emitting strange and wondrous light.

---

[49] Stein no. 5544. The translation is from Teiser, *The Scripture on the Ten Kings*, p. 136, which includes discussion of the text and of another similar colophon.

[50] For a recluse, see the biography of Liu Huifei in *Liang shu* 51, p. 746. For an imperial consort, see the curious reference by the Song figure Zhang Duanyi, who claims to have seen in a monastic library a manuscript of the *Heart Scripture* copied by no less than Yang Guifei, the most famous imperial consort in Chinese history, for her beloved Emperor Xuanzong. *Guier ji* (CSJC edn.) C, p. 58. Finally, for an account of an emperor copying Buddhist scriptures in order to garner merit, see *Song shi* 242, pp. 8625–6.

The idea that certain texts not only contain sacred wisdom but also hold supernatural power was much less prominent in early China. Certainly one can speak of sacred texts in ancient China, but the reverence of, for instance, Confucius for the *Book of Poetry* or other classics compiled by the sages of antiquity did not entail a belief in the numinous property of books.[51] In the first centuries of the Common Era, as monks, nuns and Buddhist laypeople enthusiastically spread fantastic tales of the miraculous powers of sutras, Daoists also spoke of the miraculous powers of their own scriptures. On occasion, like their Buddhist counterparts, they too entreated followers to light incense and purify themselves with fasts before handling their scriptures,[52] though whether Daoists were directly influenced by the Buddhist conception of scriptures or developed these notions independently is hard to say.

A belief in the numinous power of books does not necessarily follow from the contention that some books contain sacred writing.[53] The sixth-century scholar Yan Zhitui, himself both a knowledgeable scholar of the Chinese classics and a devout Buddhist, may have been influenced by Buddhist attitudes toward books when he wrote that out of respect for the sages of the past, he never used for the toilet "paper on which there are quotations or commentaries from the *Five Classics* or the names of sages."[54] Yet, this seems to be a relatively subdued gesture of respect for the content of the books and those who wrote them; there is no indication that one would risk supernatural punishment for profaning paper inscribed with the words of the sages, as is the case in Buddhist stories of vengeance wreaked on those who desecrate Buddhist scriptures in which

[51] In search of early evidence for this notion, Jean-Pierre Drège has written of the talismantic function of writings in ancient China. Drège, *Les bibliothèques en Chine au temps des manuscrits*, pp. 15–6. The possession of writings and maps, for example, were said to have been partly responsible for the military victories of the founder of the Han, Liu Bang. In this case, as in the other examples Drège cites, writings are important chiefly for the knowledge they contain. They are also important as symbols of the power that possession of this knowledge brings. They do not, however, produce miracles, any more than they improve one's lot in the afterlife. For the pre-Buddhist period in China, we come closer to this idea in early traditions of "revealed charts" sent down by heaven and in writings that, by recording the names of demons, were said to control those demons. See Anna Seidel, "Imperial Treasures and Taoist Sacraments—Taoist Roots in the Apocrypha," pp. 291–371, and Robert F. Campany, *Strange Writing: Anomaly Accounts in Early Medieval China*, pp. 122–4.

[52] Seidel, "Imperial Treasures and Taoist Sacraments," p. 323; Isabelle Robinet, *La révélation du Shangqing dans l'histoire du Taoisme*, vol. 1, pp. 213–14.

[53] In contrast to the Jewish tradition from which they emerged, early Christians did not treat their books with extraordinary reverence. Harry Y. Gamble, *Books and Readers in the Early Church: A History of Early Christian Texts*, p. 78.

[54] *Yan shi jia xun* (SBCK edn.) 5, p. 13b. The passage is discussed in Tsien, *Paper and Printing*, p. 109, and in Drège, *Les bibliothèques en Chine*, p. 162.

the garments a woman has made with the silk of a Buddhist scripture scald her skin or a man is struck dead for burning sutras.[55]

As objects containing sacred power and capable of eliciting miracles, Buddhist scriptures in China, as in India, were worshipped as sacred objects. The sixth-century *Record of Buddhist Monasteries in Luoyang* describes the scriptures housed in the famous Baima Monastery (reputedly the first Buddhist monastery in China) in terms that could only be used to refer to Buddhist texts:

> The scripture cases housed in the temple have survived until this day; to them incense was often burned and good care was given. At times, the scripture cases gave off light that illuminated the room and hall. As a result, both laymen and Buddhist devotees reverently worshipped as if they were facing the real Buddha.[56]

This attitude of veneration for the Buddhist book extended as well to the process of copying scriptures. Various texts describe how copyists are to burn incense, purify their clothing, and even carry out fasts before beginning the solemn task of copying Buddhist scriptures.[57] Here we are well beyond practical concerns for accuracy and even a more abstract sense of respect, and are seeing instead *devotion* for the book that invested the act of copying a scripture with ritual significance. As Stephen Teiser puts it, "[I]n medieval times the making of a book was itself a religious service."[58] In sum, when a monk put brush to paper to copy, say, the *Lotus Sutra*, he was expected to approach his work with the caution reserved for a sacrament; and when readers withdrew such a work from a monastic library, they did so with the knowledge that such books were linked to marvelous, unfathomable powers in a direct, material way.

The ritual nature of the act of copying a Buddhist scripture is perhaps best illustrated by the practice of copying scriptures in one's own blood. A good example of this practice comes from the writings of the prominent Ming monk Hanshan Deqing (1546–1623). In his autobiography, Deqing explains the motivation for copying the *Flower Adornment Sutra* —a mammoth text—in his blood:

> In the Spring of my thirty-second year, I returned from Yanmen. At this time I recalled the benevolence of my parents and the care they had given me. I also thought of all of the obstacles that stood between me and the Dharma.

[55] For examples, see Robert F. Campany, "Notes on the Devotional Uses and Symbolic Functions of Sutra Texts as Depicted in Early Chinese Buddhist Miracle Tales and Hagiographies," pp. 40–43.
[56] *Luoyang jialan ji jiaoshi* 4, p. 151; Wang, *A Record of Buddhist Monasteries in Luoyang*, pp. 173–4.
[57] Drège, *Les bibliothèques en Chine*, p. 204.
[58] Teiser, *The Scripture on the Ten Kings*, p. 10.

On reading the vow of the great master Huisi of Nanyue, I vowed to make a copy of the *Scripture of the Expanse of Buddhas of the Flower Adornment* by mixing my own blood with gold. Above, this would tie me to the karma of *prajñā*, and below it would repay my parents for their benevolence.[59]

Deqing was assisted in this endeavor by the empress who supplied him with the gold leaf he needed for the project. By writing a scripture in a mixture of blood and gold, Deqing was joining two Buddhist scribal traditions of long standing. The vow of Huisi that he refers to in his autobiography is a piece by the eminent sixth-century monk in which he states his vow to copy the *Prajñāpāramitā* with gold leaf, a practice that was often repeated at great expense by devotees of later periods as well.[60] Similarly, the practice of writing scriptures in one's blood also had a lengthy pedigree, finding justification in the *Scripture of Brāhma's Net*—a text probably composed in China in the fifth century but claiming to be a translation from an Indian original—and in the *Avataṃsaka Sutra*.[61]

Frequent references to the practice of blood writing appear from throughout Chinese Buddhist history in biographies of monks, who usually drew blood from a finger or from the tongue and then mixed it with ink and water.[62] The practice was not confined to monks; it was frequently practiced by laypeople, usually (as in Deqing's case) for the sake of a deceased parent. We even have extant copies of the *Diamond Sutra* written in 906 by an eighty-three-year-old man who mixed his blood with ink to copy the scripture.[63] As in the copying of any Buddhist scripture, these curious books were made in part to produce merit. The dedication of merit in the colophons to these manuscripts are curious. In one, the copyist dedicates his merit with the words "May the state and the land be still and peaceful; may the wheel of the Law turn forever. Should I die in writing it, I ask only that I quickly pass out of this world. I have no other prayers." In another, the same man writes that he "is entirely without prayers. [Since] original nature is truly empty, there is no pleasure for which to pray."[64] Evidently, he had taken to heart the doctrine of emptiness preached in the *Diamond* even to the point of denying the ultimate existence of merit, though one suspects a desire for merit lay behind these conspicuous denials.

[59] *Hanshan dashi mengyou quan ji* 53, *Xu zang jing*, vol. 127, p. 479a. I explore the topic at greater length in "Blood Writing in Chinese Buddhism," pp. 177–94.

[60] For Huisi's vow, see *Nanyue Si da chanshi lishi yuanwen*, *T* no. 1933, vol. 46, p. 786c, translated and discussed in Paul Magnin, *La vie et l'oeuvre de Huisi* pp. 192–238.

[61] *Fanwang jing* 10B, p. 1009a19, and *Da fangguang fo huayan jing* (Skt. *Buddhāvataṃsakasūtra*) 40, *T* no. 293, vol. 10, p. 845c.

[62] See Kieschnick, *The Eminent Monk*, pp. 40–41, 49–50, 46.

[63] Pelliot no. 2876, discussed in Teiser, *The Scripture on the Ten Kings*, p. 126.

[64] Stein no. 5669 and Pelliot no. 2876; trans. from Teiser, ibid., pp. 126–7.

It is not surprising that we also have records of such scriptures being worshipped; for if a copy of the *Diamond Sutra* written in ordinary ink was the locus of sacred power, a copy of the scripture in the blood of a devotee was surely even more numinous.[65] A similar custom, especially popular with the *Flower Adornment Scripture,* was to prostrate oneself once for each character of the sutra while chanting it. These practices unite the notions of merit and reverence. It is in part because the scriptures are sources of merit that they are worthy of veneration; and it is through veneration (rather than explanation or understanding) that one gains merit from them.

Buddhist Denigration of Books

In contrast to these attitudes of respect and devotion for Buddhist books—attitudes that often manifested themselves in acts of extreme self-sacrifice and piety—some monks expressed outright disdain for books, Buddhist or otherwise. Perhaps it is not surprising that a culture as steeped in book-learning as China also produced a strong tradition of virulent skepticism for books and writing. Perhaps the most prominent Chinese example of opposition to the book is in the writings of Laozi, who, according to tradition, only allowed his sayings to be copied down when he was forced to do so. Laozi's writings themselves, the famously brief *Way and Its Virtue,* are full of expressions of the inadequacy of language for expressing high truths, beginning with the opening line, "The Way that can be spoken of is not the constant Way."

This same frustration with language was taken up in the late Tang by Chan monks who, at least according to the hagiography, demonstrated their distaste for the written word by burning or otherwise mutilating even the most revered of Buddhist scriptures. For instance, according to a biography of ninth-century monk Zhixian, he was determined to burn all of his books after searching through them in vain for an answer to an enigmatic question his master had asked him. When someone asked if he could take the books instead, Zhixian refused, saying "I have been burdened by these my whole life. What do you want them for?" The account continues, "He refused to give away the books, and burnt them all at once."[66] The burning of Buddhist books never became a common practice among Buddhist believers and did not have an appreciable effect on the volume of Buddhist books circulating, but the attitude such stories represented did play an important role in the minds of Buddhist writers

---

[65] *Song gaoseng zhuan* 25, biography of Hongchu, p. 870b, and 26, biography of Zengren, p. 877b.

[66] *Zu tang ji* 19, p. 415. See also Kieschnick, *The Eminent Monk,* pp. 131–5.

who at least paid lip service to the principle that books cannot fully express the essence of the Buddha's teachings.

Technologies

In addition to interest in the doctrines, imagery, and language of Buddhist scriptures, the belief that on the one hand Buddhist texts could bring merit, and on the other that many of these texts contained sacred power, contributed to the rapid dissemination of Buddhist books on a grand scale. The surge of interest in Buddhist writings from the fifth century on, coupled with the steady flow of new Buddhist texts from India, resulted in the production of countless Buddhist books. While this enthusiasm for Buddhist works was a great source of joy for the faithful, others found their popularity disturbing. In response to the upsurge in the manufacture of Buddhist texts in his day, the author of the bibliographical section of the *Sui History*, compiled in the seventh century, complained bitterly of the rampant proliferation of Buddhist books, fueled, he noted, in part by imperial efforts in the preceding dynasty.[67]

> In the first year of the Kaihuang era (581), Gaozu [aka Sui Wendi] promulgated an edict throughout the empire allowing anyone to become a monk. He also ordered that money be provided according to the number of the population to be used to produce scriptures and images. Official copies of the Buddhist canon were to be made and installed in monasteries in large metropolitan regions such as the capital, Bingzhou, Xiangzhou, and Luozhou. In addition a special copy was to be kept in the imperial library. All in the empire submitted to these orders, competing with one another in the expression of veneration. Buddhist scriptures among the population outnumber the Six Classics by thousands of times![68]

The statement that Buddhist scriptures outnumbered the pre-Buddhist Chinese classics by "thousands of times" at first seems a gross exaggeration until we consider that Sui Wendi was but one among many emperors who ordered the production of multiple copies of the entire Buddhist canon. What is more, imperially sponsored copies of Buddhist scriptures were probably far outnumbered by manuscripts produced privately by individuals.[69] Taken together, the quantity of official and nonofficial Bud-

---

[67] On the composition of this text, see Drège, *Les bibliothèques en Chine au temps des manuscrits*, pp. 120–30.

[68] *Sui shu* 35, p. 1099. The passage is translated and discussed in Drège, ibid., p. 196.

[69] For instance, although the Dunhuang manuscripts do include some copies of scriptures produced by palace artisans and marked by the fine quality of the paper and calligraphy, there are even more manuscripts copied by individuals than there are officially produced manuscripts. See Fang Guangchang, *Fojiao dazangjing shi Ba—shi shiji*, pp. 56–64. Shiga

dhist manuscripts was enormous, dwarfing all other types of Chinese writings. To slake this thirst for Buddhist books, all manner of media and new technology were applied to the task.

The reams of paper used to make these Buddhist books over the course of centuries were doubtless legion. Already in the Han, Buddhist books began to appear in the imperial library.[70] And we know from assorted references that private bibliophiles in the medieval period amassed sizable collections of Buddhist manuscripts as well.[71] Large Buddhist monasteries accumulated large holdings of books, some of which, by the Tang, rivaled the best libraries in the empire. Catalogs of monastic holdings discovered by chance at Dunhuang give us some sense of the massive number of Buddhist manuscripts involved. These catalogs are lists of thousands of titles of books originally contained in several monastic libraries at Dunhuang. Presumably, monastic libraries in the capital and in other cities as well as in wealthy monasteries across medieval China had similar, if not larger, collections of Buddhist manuscripts.[72]

The staggering number of books suggested by such conjectures gives some idea of the heavy demand for raw materials involved in the production of Buddhist books over the centuries. The *Biographies of Eminent Monks* tells the story of a monk whose writings on the monastic regulations were so popular that monks and nuns "competed to copy and propagate them," inspiring a saying at the time that "all the people of the city copy [his book], rendering paper as expensive as jade."[73] In a similar vein, one Six Dynasties critic of Buddhism recommended that the state forbid the copying of Buddhist scriptures so that "brushes and paper would not be so expensive."[74] In fact, despite these claims that the use of paper for Buddhist texts made paper "as expensive as jade," the opposite was probably the case: the demand for paper encouraged the refinement and rationalization of the paper-making process, thus bringing down the price and making paper more readily available. Indeed, one of the chief reasons for the success of paper in China was not only that it was considered more convenient than other materials, but also that it was less expensive.[75]

Takayoshi, on the basis of colophons, divides Dunhuang Buddhist manuscripts into three types: official manuscripts produced in the capital, manuscripts produced in monasteries for liturgical and other monastic purposes, and manuscripts produced by devotees to gain merit. Shiga Takayoshi, "Tonkō shakyō batsubun yori mita bukkyō shinkō," pp. 151–6.

[70] Drège, *Les bibliothèques en Chine*, p. 177.
[71] Ibid., p. 166.
[72] These Dunhuang catalogs have been collected in *Dunhuang fojiao jinglu jijiao*, ed. Fang Guangchang. They are discussed in Drège, ibid., pp. 186–93.
[73] *Gaoseng zhuan* 2, p. 333c, biography of Vimalākṣa.
[74] *Guang hongming ji* 14, p. 188a.
[75] Drège, *Les bibliothèques en Chine*, p. 146.

The complaints of frugal officials notwithstanding, emperors continued to order paper for the making of Buddhist books, whether for new copies of the Buddhist canon or for the needs of the translation center.[76] And there is ample anecdotal evidence of laymen who continued to purchase paper for Buddhist scriptures.[77] Almost all the Buddhist documents found at Dunhuang were made of paper (usually made from hemp and mulberry), and the world's earliest extant example of a complete book on paper (written in A.D. 256) is a Buddhist text: the *Scripture of Parables*.[78] In sum, the need for paper to produce Buddhist manuscripts—a need fueled in part by the belief that the production of Buddhist books garnered merit—was a major contributing factor to the gradual replacement of wood, bamboo, and silk by paper as the standard medium for Chinese books.[79]

It is ironic that texts originating in paperless India encouraged the spread of paper in China. Equally curious is that while Indians (like the rest of the world) learned the art of paper-making from China, the model for binding paper into booklets derived from India, where individual palm leaves were gathered into booklets.[80] By the Tang, monks had been bringing such palm-leaf booklets to China for centuries. Hence, it is not surprising that monks adapted the format to paper.

In China, this new format offered various advantages over the traditional scroll. Several distinct texts could be bound together. Further, once the practice of supplying page numbers was established, the booklet allowed for easier reference to passages buried in the middle of a manuscript. One Song literatus, writing at a time when both the booklet and

[76] For one example of an emperor ordering that paper be provided for a translation center, see *Song gaoseng zhuan* 15, p. 805a, biography of Yuanzhao. The use of paper likely had important implications not only for the *quantity* of translation but also for the *process* of translation. Anthony Pym has argued that the introduction of paper to Islamic Spain allowed for division of labor, multiple drafts, and the formation of translation teams that bear a striking resemblance to those employed in China. Pym, "Translation History and the Manufacture of Paper," pp. 57–71.

[77] See, for instance, *Fayuan zhulin* 18, p. 419c; 71, p. 822c.

[78] *Piyu jing*. See Tsien, *Paper and Printing*, p. 86. On paper at Dunhuang, see Tsien, ibid., p. 47, and Jean-Pierre Drège, "Papiers de Dunhuang: Essai d'analyse morphologique des manuscrits chinois datés," pp. 305–60.

[79] Even after the switch had been made from bamboo, wood, and silk to paper, Buddhism continued to play an important role in the history of Chinese paper. Certain monasteries were famous for the high-quality paper they produced, for the paper dyes they developed, and for the techniques they employed in creating long-lasting paper. Tsien, ibid., pp. 48, 75, 82, 89.

[80] Paper was introduced to India from China in approximately the seventh century, but did not become widespread there until about the twelfth century. Tsien, ibid., pp. 2–3. Both Tsien and Teiser note that the first Chinese booklets were modeled on palm-leaf booklets. Teiser, *The Scripture on the Ten Kings*, pp. 93–4; Tsien, ibid., p. 230.

the scroll were common, commented that he preferred turning pages to the cumbersome process of unrolling and rolling scrolls.[81]

The question of why Buddhism should have offered this innovation to Chinese bookmaking yields interesting answers. When discussing the same development in the West (i.e., the shift from scroll to the booklet, or "codex") in the first centuries of the Common Era, Harry Gamble points out that many of the practical advantages to the booklet, such as ease of reference and slightly less expense (since one could write on both sides of the page) would not have been apparent to the first users of the new format. Binding pages together was at first an expensive process. And before page numbering became common, booklets were not much easier to reference than scrolls. In addition to these practical considerations, the booklet ran against long-established convention. Hence, it is not surprising that the impetus for the change in the West came from a new social movement: Christianity. Less tied to the Roman or Jewish traditions than their contemporaries, the early Christians bound the letters of Paul into a booklet and henceforth came to regard the booklet as the standard format of the Christian book.[82] In the Chinese case, it was not only that monks were less bound to Chinese literary conventions than their non-Buddhist counterparts, but also that they could draw on an Indian tradition that they revered. At first, modeled as it was on the Indian palm-leaf manuscripts from which Chinese Buddhist translations derived, the booklet was seen as a distinctly Buddhist format for a text. In other words, the early owner of a Buddhist booklet could feel that Buddhist books were something entirely different from other, common books, not only in their unusual language, literary style, and sacred content, but even in the way they looked, the way one held them, and the way one turned the pages.

In retrospect, the shift from silk scrolls and bamboo slips to paper booklets seems entirely natural and logical—once the techniques for making paper books were refined, the bound paper book was cheaper to produce and easier to use than its predecessors. But the advantages of paper over silk or booklet over scroll were not so great that the switch was inevitable. Without the persistent demand for Buddhist writings produced in massive quantities, the impetus to experiment with new formats might not have been sufficient to force the change.

We see the same dynamics at work in the birth of printing in China. Various methods were used for duplication in early China, including assorted types of seals and rubbings made from steles. These techniques laid the foundation for the emergence of printing. Yet, even after rudimentary forms of printing appeared, handwritten scrolls were, in general,

---

[81] Jean-Pierre Drège, "Papillons et troubillons," p. 172.
[82] Gamble, *Books and Readers in the Early Church*, pp. 49–66.

sufficient to meet the needs of the average reader, and new techniques of reproduction were not necessary unless a very large number of copies was required.[83] The Buddhist doctrine of merit provided just such an impetus. Most importantly, most Chinese Buddhists did not maintain that mass-producing scriptures through printing diminished the merit due the donors; rather, the more texts produced, the more merit to be won. Hence, if through printing one could produce hundreds of copies of the *Diamond Sutra* in a fraction of the time and at less cost than commissioning hand-written copies of the text, the choice of medium was clear.[84]

As in the case of paper, printing did not rise to prominence with a sin-gle instance of discovery but emerged in a lengthy process of, on the one hand, refinement of techniques and, on the other, of cultural adaptation and familiarization to the idea of printing—the origin of printing cannot be traced to a single inventor. Once we recognize that the emergence of printing was a protracted development, then the connection between Bud-dhism and the birth of the printed book is clear. The earliest extant printed text in the world is a Buddhist charm, discovered in Korea but originally printed from carved wooden blocks in China in the eighth century. The first complete printed book known is a copy of the *Diamond Sutra* from 868, a text that also contains our earliest example of a woodcut illustra-tion in a printed book. Our earliest hand-colored print is an image of the bodhisattva Guanyin dated 947.[85] And so goes the litany of Chinese "firsts" in the history of printing, almost all of which are related directly to Buddhism. Examples of important early printed Buddhist texts such as these could easily be multiplied, demonstrating the important position of Buddhist belief in the early history of printing.

Just as interesting are records of large-scale printing projects dedicated to the production of Buddhist texts. One of the best known such projects was sponsored by Qian Hongchu, prince of the Wu-Yue state (a short-lived kingdom in eastern China), who in the middle of the tenth century commissioned the printing of eighty-four thousand rolls of a *dhāraṇī* scripture.[86] At about the same time, the prominent monk Yanshou over-saw the printing of over four hundred thousand copies of sutras, charms, and pictures.[87] Both of these projects involved the mobilization of a large workforce and the training of craftsmen to cut the blocks and make the prints.

---

[83] Tsien, *Paper and Printing*, p. 136

[84] Drège, *Les bibliothèques en Chine*, p. 266.

[85] Tsien, *Paper and Printing*, pp. 322, 151, 252, 280.

[86] The *Yiqie rulaixin mimi quanshen sheli baoqieyin tuoluoni jing* (Skt. *Sarvatathā-gatādhiṣṭhānahrdayaguhyadhātukaraṇḍamudrādhāraṇī*), *T* no. 1022, vol. 19, translated by Amoghavajra. On this printing, see Tsien, ibid., pp. 157–8.

[87] Tsien, ibid., pp. 158, 255.

These projects paved the way for the large-scale printing projects of the Song. The grandest printing projects of the Song were, once again, printings of Buddhist texts, most notably the five printings of the Buddhist canon. An eleventh-century source notes that one hundred thirty thousand blocks were cut for the first printed edition of the canon, giving us a sense of the massive scale of these projects.[88] When blocks for specific texts were damaged or worn, individuals or groups would solicit funds and have the blocks recut. In extant colophons noting the recutting of such blocks, merit is, as we might expect, again an important theme.[89] And while the motivations for emperors to sponsor large-scale printings of Buddhist texts were no doubt complex and multifaceted—at times involving attempts to assert imperial authority and establish political legitimacy—it is safe to assume that the belief that one could, through such projects, reap enormous benefits for oneself in the afterlife played an important role. Just as the first emperor, Qin Shihuang, buried thousands of terra-cotta soldiers to lead him in a conquest of the next world, emperors of mid and late imperial China could assure for themselves a prominent position in the next world by creating merit on a scale that no other could match.

Who is to say if even without Buddhist influence Chinese bookmakers would not have made the leap from hand-copied bamboo manuscripts to the printed paper book? We can, however, safely assume that even had such leaps been made, they would not have been as fast or as smooth without the pervasive motivating force of the idea of Buddhist merit. Indeed, unlike Buddhist devotees who enthusiastically embraced the new medium, influential Song literati like Su Shi and Zhu Xi grumbled that printing had led to the vulgarization of the book, and that young scholars, accustomed to easily accessible printed texts, no longer showed the same veneration for books (and presumably the learning they contained) that their predecessors in the age of manuscripts had.[90] Buddhist attitudes toward the conventions of bookmaking were less conservative than others—the difference was the overriding Buddhist concern with the spread of vast quantities of Buddhist texts on a massive scale, a project rich in potential merit for all involved.

This is not to say that monks and Buddhist laypeople abandoned the written manuscript entirely for printing in the belief that printing multiple copies of a text was the most efficient means of acquiring merit. Deqing, the Ming monk mentioned above who copied a scripture in his blood,

---

[88] *Bei shan lu* 10, *T* no. 2113, vol. 52, p. 632a. The passage is discussed in Tong Wei, *Bei Song Kaibao Dazangjing diaoyin kaoshi ji mulu huanyuan* pp. 1–3. Tsien Tsuen-hsuin gives the slightly more modest estimate of a total of some sixty thousand to eighty thousand blocks for each of the Song printings of the canon. Tsien, ibid., p. 61.

[89] Luo Zhenyu, "Song Yuan Shizang kanben kao."

[90] Drège, "La lecture et l'écriture en Chine et la xylographie," pp. 101–3.

lived at a time when printing was already well developed. Indeed, he himself once did the proofreading for the printing of a Buddhist treatise.[91] For such men, merit was not so mechanical as it sometimes seems, or they would certainly have opted for printing over written manuscripts, much less manuscripts copied in blood. Sincerity and sacrifice could play as important a role as sheer quantity in the karmic equation. It was, perhaps, because of this flexibility in the notion of merit that it was not overwhelmed by the technologies it helped to create.

Caveats and Speculation

In contrast to accounts linking books to veneration, merit, and miracles, Chan accounts of monks who disparaged books run counter to the general attitudes I have emphasized thus far. What, then, was the overall impact of the Chan critique of books? Stories of seemingly wild, yet highly educated monks who, in search of direct enlightenment, burn their scriptures are a reflection of a rigorous epistemological skepticism and realization of the inadequacies of language. The act of burning a scripture in Chan stories is a self-conscious pose built on a lengthy philosophical tradition prevalent in both Buddhist scriptures and in Chinese classics like the *Laozi* and *Zhuangzi*. In most of these cases, we cannot be sure if actual monks actually burned books or if the stories are meant to be taken as allegorical warnings of the pitfalls of the written word. If we address the more mundane question of how the majority of people treated Buddhist books in general, we must conclude that, as in the case of icons, relics, and robes, the impact of Chan antinomianism on book production was negligible. Monks continued to write books and copy scriptures, and Buddhists never launched a serious campaign to destroy Buddhist writing. To state the obvious: Buddhists generally promoted Buddhist books. This being said, when we look closely at records of the individuals who produced Buddhist texts, the picture I painted above of awesome respect and pious devotion for sacred objects and sources of immeasurable merit gives way to a more mixed assortment of motivations and attitudes.

Not all copied Buddhist scriptures in order to garner merit for deceased relatives or loyal plow oxen. Some were like a certain figure of the Tang named Wang Shaozong, a diligent student with a knack for calligraphy who, because his family was poor, "often hired himself out to copy Buddhist scriptures in order to support himself."[92] Similarly, according to one Tang text, in the eighth century there was a handless beggar of the capital who would copy Buddhist scriptures with his feet in exchange for

---

[91] *Hanshan dashi mengyou quan ji* 53, p. 477b.
[92] *Jiu Tang shu* 189, p. 4963

alms.[93] Or consider the manuscript copy from Dunhuang of a collection of
the sayings of Bodhidharma that ends with a poem appended by the copyist: "Now I have finished copying this book. Why hasn't my payment arrived? What scoundrel has [ordered the copy,] walked away and never since
looked back?"[94] An even more pointed example of one who copied Buddhist scriptures more for profit than for piety is found in a Dunhuang document relating the punishment of one An Hezi, who had been hired to copy
Buddhist scriptures, but "while he wrote of the Great Vehicle with his hand,
from his mouth poured an endless stream of profanities—all of them directed against grandmothers and grandfathers—that were insulting to the
elderly."[95] All of this discloses that the substantial market for Buddhist
books attracted all manner of people to the trade, and at times supported
even those with minimal interest in Buddhist doctrine to work as professional copyists. And as monks were regularly hired to copy scriptures—the
merit of the act going to the patron—the process inevitably became routine, losing much of the sacred character of copying as a devotional act.[96]

More surprising than the fact that not all viewed Buddhist books with
the same sense of reverence are the relative limits of the impact of Buddhist attitudes toward books. Even after centuries of interaction with Buddhism, Daoists, for instance, continued to emphasize esoteric transmission of revealed texts, rather than large-scale, open propagation. As the
prominent Daoist Tao Hongjing (456–536) put it, "[T]hough the Doctrine of the Dao is destined to be promulgated, it is not fitting that its true
subtleties be widely diffused."[97] Even today, Daoist scriptures are not distributed openly in free editions at temples as are many Buddhist texts.
Similarly, even after the impact of Buddhism on Chinese society was felt,
the Confucian classics were not copied out of a desire for religious merit.
And merit was not among the concatenation of motives behind massive
imperial book projects like the hand-copied *Yongle dadian* of the Ming or
the printed *Siku quanshu* of the Qing.[98]

The notion that one could gain merit through the production and dis-

---

[93] *Youyang zazu* 5, p. 34.
[94] *Damo lun.* Peking no. 8374; cited in Faure, *Le traité de Bodhidharma*, pp. 38–9.
[95] Stein no. 5818. Discussed in Fang, *Fojiao dazangjing shi*, p. 60.
[96] Some of the Buddhist scriptures discovered at Dunhuang that were copied by monks
are written in sloppy, poor calligraphy, indicating a less than reverential attitude in the copi-
ests. See Richard Schneider, "Les copies de sūtra défectueuses dans les manuscrits de Touen-
houang" pp. 141–61. Just as in the copying of manuscripts, monks and laypeople who cut
blocks for printing included both those who did so out of piety and those who did so to earn
a living. See Yang Shengxin, "Cong Qishazang keyin kan Song Yuan yinshua gongren de ji
ge wenti," pp. 40–58.
[97] Translated in Michel Strickmann, "The Mao Shan Revelations: Taoism and the Aristocracy," p. 47.
[98] On the compilation of the *Siku quanshu*, see R. Kent Guy, *The Emperor's Four Treasuries: Scholars and the State in the Late Ch'ien-lung Era.*

tribution of books did spread, however, to the literature of popular religion, and in particular to the genre known as "morality books" (*shanshu*). Beginning in the Song, those concerned with the moral fabric of society composed, copied, printed, and distributed moral tracts that usually contain stories of the benefits awarded the good and punishments meted out to the bad. While Buddhist elements are common in such books, they are not distinctively Buddhist—certainly not to the extent that they were entered into the Buddhist canon. Such books, still common today, are almost always distributed free of charge in public places. Among the motivations for producing such texts is the belief that one can gain merit by doing so. The prominent Song figure Zhen Dexiu, for instance, once had printed one of the earliest such books, the *Taishang ganying pian*, in order that the merit so derived would bring him luck in the civil service examination.[99] Throughout late imperial China and up to the present day, individuals have printed morality books to earn merit for themselves or to gain merit for their parents or others.[100]

To turn to another potential offshoot of Buddhist book lore, in late imperial China, many held to a popular belief that all paper containing writing was supernaturally powerful. Many Chinese today can still recall parental warnings not to step on printed sheets of paper, which was thought to bring misfortune. Others believed that merit could be gained by collecting bits of paper containing writing—any writing—off the street. This belief has not been properly studied, but it seems likely that attitudes toward Buddhist scriptures played at least some role in its formation and development.

In sum, despite the caveats, Buddhism not only played a prominent role in the history of the book in the medieval period, but has continued to influence the development of the Chinese book, whether in the massive production of morality books in Taiwan and mainland China or, more directly, in the continued production of printed and now digital Buddhist books today.[101]

MONASTERIES

The Monastery in Chinese Material Culture

Common in the countryside and prominent on city maps, Buddhist monasteries are a persistent presence in the Chinese landscape, as prevalent in

[99] See Song Guangyu (Sung Kuang-yü), "Guanyu shanshu de yanjiu ji qi zhanwang," p. 164.

[100] For an overview of the genre, see Song, ibid., and Cynthia J. Brokaw, *The Ledgers of Merit and Demerit: Social Change and Moral Order in Late Imperial China*.

[101] Many of the projects to produce databases of Buddhist texts are assisted in part by the belief that these projects will reap religious merit for the sponsors.

contemporary China as chapels and cathedrals in Europe. Owing to the difficulty in determining what constitutes a "monastery"—a single building or a large complex, a structure in good repair, or a few dilapidated walls over an old foundation—statistics for the number of monasteries in China are hard to come by, but one estimate puts the number in Beijing alone at more than four hundred, giving some sense of the huge number of monasteries throughout the country.[102] Despite the fact that Chinese monasteries have always been made of wood rather than stone, making them especially susceptible to accidental fire and intentional destruction, they have remained a constituent part of Chinese scenery, even with the persecutions and general neglect of Buddhist institutions in the twentieth century. In addition to serving as a dwelling for monks and nuns—the definition of a monastery—modern monasteries also serve as tourist sites and as devotional, economic, and social centers. None of this is new.

The first Buddhist monasteries in China were probably converted from secular houses with the arrival and growth of the earliest communities of foreign monks in the first centuries of the Common Era. Their expansion in the subsequent centuries with the growth of the Buddhist order is difficult to chart with any accuracy, but certainly by the fifth and sixth centuries, Buddhist monasteries were a common sight, and had begun to play a prominent role in the development of Chinese architecture and civic design.[103]

One modern scholar has estimated the number of monasteries in the capital of the Wei dynasty in the sixth century at well over a thousand.[104] The *Record of Buddhist Monasteries in Luoyang*, a book devoted to the monasteries of the capital at that time, is a good starting point for an understanding of the place of the Buddhist monastery in Chinese society. This concise, elegant book, famous in Chinese history both as a historical document and as a work of literature, reveals the multifaceted social role monasteries played in Chinese society, and demonstrates as well that the monastery had become an important component of Chinese material culture by the sixth century, when the text was composed. Compiled after the once-flourishing capital at Luoyang had been decimated by war and neglect, the *Record of Buddhist Monasteries in Luoyang* is an urbane official's nostalgic look back at a sophisticated, flourishing city rather than the pious record of a Buddhist devotee one might expect from the title.

In his narrative, the author, Yang Xuanzhi, moves from one section of the city to another, describing the most prominent monasteries that had

[102] Wu Yingcai and Guo Juanjie, *Zhongguo de fosi*, p. 3.
[103] For the place of the Buddhist monastery in the history of Chinese architecture, see Liu Dunzhen's survey of Chinese architecture, *Zhongguo gudai jianzhu shi*.
[104] Tang, *Han-Wei Liang Jin Nanbeichao fojiaoshi*, p. 370.

once loomed above a bustling metropolis. He at the same time includes various bits of folklore, history, and gossip in one way or another connected to each monastery. He recounts an emperor held captive in a monastery tower, grand sacrifices to the dead, the Buddhist education of refined ladies, rape and pillage, popular games, magic shows, dancing, singing, and monks engaged in long bouts of meditation—all within the walls of the city's famous monasteries. Taken together, these bits and pieces of urban history give the modern reader some sense of the role of monasteries in medieval Chinese society: from the beginning, monasteries served as sites of lay as well as monastic devotion, for secular entertainment as well as Buddhist ritual.

Beyond even these broad concerns, the text drifts time and again from the monasteries it purports to describe as the author delves into long accounts of political machinations, witty sayings at court parties, and loving descriptions of rare species of fish, succulent fruits, and placid lakes. However frustrating all of this is to the historian of Buddhism who searches in vain for details about monastic life and doctrinal trends, the *Record* teaches us an important lesson about the role of the Buddhist monastery in Chinese material culture. For Yang, monasteries were repositories of memories and associations with unusual events of the past. The mention of the name of one monastery evokes memories of a bandit raid in which all of the normally secluded nuns there were raped by foreigners. Another monastery calls to mind the time a fierce rebel leader quartered his troops on monastic grounds. At a more quotidian level, certain monasteries were connected in the author's mind with particular types of trees or certain sections of the city. In the introduction to the book, Yang laments the destruction of the monasteries he knew in his youth, saying, "Today they are mostly demolished; one cannot hear the tolling of bells at all."[105] For Yang, monastic bells were as much a part of the rhythm of the city as they were calls to devotions. In short, monasteries were linked to various sights, smells, and sounds, regardless of whether or not these were the product of what we would classify as Buddhism. Few other buildings in premodern China could boast this level of social incorporation or general prominence in public life.

In this section I say little more about the social role of monasteries in material culture, choosing instead to focus on the factors that went into building them in the first place and then financing the maintenance and refurbishment of monasteries after they fell into disrepair. This was not a simple matter. Timber had to be cut and delivered, workers recruited, supervised, and paid. While some monks had access to family fortunes, the

[105] *Luoyang jialan ji jiaoshi*, p. 8; Wang, *A Record of Buddhist Monasteries in Luoyang*, p. 7.

vast majority of the funds required to build and restore monasteries had
to come from patrons outside the monastic community. The continued existence of monks and nuns in China depended on their ability to periodically solicit large funds from sympathetic patrons. As in the case of books,
monasteries were made for various reasons, including the desire to propagate Buddhism, to support the sangha, and to earn the respect of the local
community. Among the various factors that went into the decision to donate the huge sums of money and labor necessary to build a monastery,
most prominent was the belief that by building a monastery, one could
acquire merit.

Monasteries as Sources of Merit

As we have seen, this doctrine can be traced to early Buddhist scriptures.
Recall the Buddha's sermon cited earlier in which he details seven acts said
to acquire merit. The first two of these acts are to build and furnish
monasteries.[106] Below, as we follow descriptions of the building of
monasteries from ancient India to early China and up into later times,
merit is invoked consistently as a sound reason for undertaking such
projects.

A brief comparison with a similar Christian concept may help to frame
the discussion that follows. In Europe, the indulgence, a dispensation
granted by the pope guaranteeing its owner the remission of pains in purgatory, was used to fund the construction of cathedrals, most notably
Saint Peter's in Rome at the end of the fifteenth century, a policy that so
infuriated a young Martin Luther that he broke with the Church over it
and accidentally sparked the Reformation.[107] The construction of Saint
Peter's Cathedral and Martin Luther's call for reform involved more than
the theology of indulgences, just as the construction of Buddhist monasteries extended beyond the principles of merit to concerns related to economics, politics, and more nebulous associations with material culture.
Nevertheless, both traditions—Christian and Buddhist—found it necessary to buttress efforts to found religious buildings with complex yet compelling doctrinal support. And in both cases, the doctrine became a point
of contention among critics and even among more thoughtful adherents.
In the case of Buddhism, the strength of this "doctrinal support" is particularly evident when we see how it was consistently applied across
boundaries of space (as we progress from India to China) and time (as we
move from early China to later periods). Throughout, Buddhist material

[106] *Zeng yi ahan jing* (Skt. *Ekottarāgama*) 35, p. 741c.
[107] Owen Chadwick, *The Reformation* pp. 41–3. For a more detailed study of indulgences, see Robert W. Shaffern, "Images, Jurisdiction, and the Treasury of Merit," pp. 237–
47.

culture centered on the monastery, and the monastery depended for its existence on the doctrine of merit.

The Indian Background

Merit crops up in a number of early legends about the founding of the first Buddhist monasteries. The land for what was perhaps the first Buddhist monastery was said to have been donated by King Bimbisāra soon after the Buddha's enlightenment. According to one early text, the *Mahīśāsakavinaya*, when Bimbisāra offered the park known as the Bamboo Grove (Veluvana) near the city of Rājagṛha, the Buddha responded by saying, "'The merit of gifts to the sangha is very great.' The king said again to the Buddha, 'I ask that you deign to accept this gift.' The Buddha replied, 'Only if you make this gift to the sangha of which I am a part.' The king accepted these conditions, making his donations to the monks in all four directions."[108] Throughout, the gift of the monastery was linked not only to the well-being of monks and the propagation of Buddhism but also to the more abstract "merit" that the king would receive in return for his gift.

In another version of the story, in the *Dharmaguptakavinaya*, the Buddha explains to the king that the gift of the park and the objects within it was received by the Buddha alone, and was not shared by other monks, or anyone else, just as a stupa may be the repository of the relics of a Buddha alone.[109] The differences in the two versions of the story probably reflect the doctrines of different Buddhist sects relating to the position of the Buddha: for the Mahīśāsakas, a gift to the Buddha was only worthy of merit insofar as it was also a gift to the sangha as a whole; for the Dharmaguptakas, a gift to the Buddha was superior to a gift to the sangha because of the Buddha's infinitely superior status in comparison to ordinary monks.[110]

For understanding the importance of the concept of merit to monastic construction, the key point in this divergence is that both schools were at pains to ensure their followers of the merit of giving land for a Buddhist monastery. The point of the first position was that even if the Buddha had long since passed into nirvana, one could still gain merit by giving to the

[108] *Mishasaibu wufen jieben* (Skt. *Mahīśāsakavinaya*) T no. 1422, vol. 22, p. 110b. The passage is translated in André Bareau, *Recherches sur la biographie du Buddha dans les sūtrapiṭaka et les vinayapiṭaka anciens: de la quête de léveil à la conversion de Śāriputra et de Maudgalyāyana*, p. 337. See also Thomas, *The Life of Buddha as Legend and History*, p. 92.

[109] *Sifen lü* (Skt. *Dharmaguptakavinaya*) 33, p. 798b.

[110] This is the interpretation of Bareau, *Recherches sur la biographie du Buddha*, pp. 341–2.

monastic community of which he himself had been a part. The thrust of the second was that even after his nirvana, the Buddha remained in a sense *present* in the monastery, and hence a gift of a monastery to any group of Buddhist monks was equivalent to a gift to the Buddha himself.[111]

Perhaps the most famous gift of land for a Buddhist monastery was that of the wealthy layman Anāthapiṇḍika who purchased a park (the Jetavana) from Prince Jeta in order to give it to the Buddha and his disciples. According to the *Dharmaguptakavinaya* version of the story, when Anāthapiṇḍika came across the park of Prince Jeta, he knew at once that this would be the perfect site for a Buddhist monastery. When he offered to buy the park, the prince balked, implying that the park was priceless by setting his price at the amount of gold it would take to cover the grounds in their entirety. To the prince's astonishment, Anāthapiṇḍika accepted the challenge, drawing on his immense wealth to cover the park in gold. When Anāthapiṇḍika had covered all but a small patch of the park, the prince reflected, "This is no ordinary man, and this is no ordinary 'field of merit.'" The prince then told the layman to stop while he himself donated the gold needed to cover the remaining patch.[112] As we have seen, the "field" was a common metaphor for merit. Just as the planting of a seed is later rewarded at harvest, so too are good deeds, such as donating land to monks, rewarded at a later time. In this case, Prince Jeta astutely recognized that the gift of this particular bit of land was an opportunity for merit so great it would be foolish not to give.

Attempts to recover a factual core from such legends, explaining events in the life of the Buddha, are arduous if not impossible: we will probably never acquire solid information on the first Buddhist monastery. We are on firmer ground when we reflect upon what such legends tell us about the monastic community some centuries after its founding, when we know that the legends were widely propagated. To sustain themselves, large groups of monks—led by the erudite monks who compiled the Buddhist scriptures containing the legends we have discussed—needed large plots of land, which could only be acquired from wealthy patrons like the rulers Bimbisāra and Prince Jeta, or the merchant Anāthapiṇḍika. In this world, monks had little to offer such figures in return. But in the other world, through the mechanism of karma and merit, monks were able to offer great rewards to generous donors. In order to ensure that this relationship was well known to potential donors, monks propagated narratives describing gifts of monastic land to the Buddha himself in which the Buddha pronounces in no uncertain terms that the donors will receive im-

---

[111] On this point, see Gregory Schopen, "The Buddha as an Owner of Property and Permanent Resident in Medieval Indian Monasteries," in *Bones, Stones, and Buddhist Monks,* pp. 258–89.

[112] *Sifen lü* 50, p. 939c. See also Thomas, *The Life of Buddha,* pp. 104–5.

mense merit for their gifts—merit that will benefit them in countless lives to come.

Inscriptions tell us that these efforts to garner lay support on a grand scale were remarkably successful. One Indian inscription includes, for instance, a charter issued by a ruler named Dēvapāladēva granting five villages for the upkeep of a monastery built at Nālandā. The villages, he notes, "are granted by us for the increase of the spiritual merit and glory of my parents and of myself."[113] Here we have an actual historical ruler to match the Bimbisāra of Buddhist legend. For a historical equivalent to Anāthapiṇḍika, we can turn to an inscription at Nāgārjunikoṇḍa from approximately the fourth century A.D., in which a laywoman named Bōdhisrī announces the bequeathal of a monastery, dedicating the subsequent merit to various members of her family as well as "for the endless welfare and happiness of the assembly of saints and for that of the whole world."[114] Monastic efforts to promote the idea that building monasteries was a meritorious act were, in short, a great success. The fruits of early monastic propaganda extended even to China, where inscriptions dedicating lands for monasteries or funds to repair monasteries make frequent allusion to Anāthapiṇḍika's gift of the Jetavana.

Merit and Monasteries in China

Many monasteries, throughout Chinese history, were converted from the houses of wealthy individuals that were donated to the monastic community. This accounts in part for the predominantly Chinese style of the architecture of Chinese monasteries; there was no opportunity to begin with a radically different Indian layout of monastic grounds, since the main buildings had been built originally for a Chinese family. Obviously, only the very wealthy could afford to donate an entire residence to the clergy, and to maintain a monastery, donations of large tracts of arable land were also often necessary.

Drawing once again on the *Record of Buddhist Monasteries in Luoyang*, we can quickly gain a sense of the range of people who were moved to make such substantial donations to the sangha. As recorded in this sixth-century text, eunuchs, an assortment of high officials, unidentified "foreigners," generals, aristocrats, emperors, and in one case two prosperous butchers all donated homes to be converted into monasteries. In many cases, the reasons for the donations are not given, but when they are, they almost always relate in some way to merit. The Qin Taishangjun

[113] Hirananda Shastri, "The Nalanda Copper-Plate of Devapaladeva," pp. 310–27.
[114] J. Ph. Vogel, "Prakrit Inscriptions from a Buddhist Site at Nagarjunikonda," pp. 1–37.

Monastery (Grand Duchess of Qin Monastery), founded at the beginning of the sixth century by Empress Dowager Hu, "was built as a means by which posthumous blessings could be offered to the empress dowager's mother."[115] Other monasteries were built to provide merit for the deceased fathers of princes and emperors.

The monastery built by butchers mentioned above illustrates how, in addition to assisting the deceased, Buddhist merit could also serve to alleviate the karmic consequences of one's own actions. According to the text, one Liu Hu and his three brothers "all bound servants to the [Ministry of] Grand Ceremonies" and butchers by trade gave up their house to be converted into the Guijue Monastery when one of their pigs began to plead for mercy in a human voice.[116] Another anecdote tells of a woman "from the Liang clan" who, when her husband died, remarried without first observing the proper mourning rites. After her dead husband reappeared to reprimand her, the terrified woman donated her house for use as a monastery.[117] It is impossible to assess the veracity of such stories. Did Butcher Liu really build a monastery to compensate for the lives of the animals he killed? Did a certain Mrs. Liang really give up her house to placate the spirit of her ex-husband? Or are these stories the product of legends that grew up around the monasteries? Our sources leave such questions hanging. Anecdotes like these can, however, at least tell us that the gift of buildings and land for monasteries was considered a powerful weapon in the battle to control one's destiny. Whatever dark deeds lay in one's past (or the past of an intimate), they could be redeemed by those with the money to pay for it.

In later periods, emperors and their families continued to found large monasteries to assist deceased relatives. In one particularly famous example, Tang Taizong, after founding a monastery and donating the merit for the gift to his mother, is said to have announced that his mother died while he was still young and incapable of caring for her properly, and that his only recourse now was to "assist her in the netherworld through gifts of merit."[118] One of the most ardent supporters of monastic construction in the Tang, Emperor Dezong was said to have first become interested in building monasteries on the advice of three of his ministers, all of them devout Buddhists, who themselves devoted themselves to making monasteries. When the emperor asked them, "Is it really true what the Buddha says about karmic retribution?" they replied,

---

[115] *Luoyang jialan jijiaoshi* 2, p. 84; Wang, *A Record of Buddhist Monasteries*, p. 84.

[116] *Luoyang jialan jijiaoshi* 2, p. 111; Wang, ibid., p. 122.

[117] *Luoyang jialan jijiaoshi* 4, p. 161; Wang, ibid., p. 189.

[118] *Fayuan zhulin* 100, p. 1027a. For further details, see Weinstein, *Buddhism under the T'ang*, pp. 22–3.

The fate of a state depends upon its store of blessings and karma [*fuye*]. Once this store of merit is established, even if there be minor difficulties, in the end the state will come to no harm. It was for this reason [i.e., the good deeds of previous Tang emperors] that when the rebellion of An [Lushan] and Shi [Siming] reached its peak, they were both killed by their own sons, that when [the rebel] Pugu Huai'en raised troops to launch an attack, he suddenly took ill and died, and that while the Uighurs and Tibetans amassed armies and advanced on the interior, in the end they retreated without doing battle. None of this was brought on by human effort. How could anyone say there is no such thing as karmic retribution![119]

These examples from the lives of two Tang emperors underline one of the most appealing aspects of the Buddhist doctrine of merit: on the one hand, merit could be directed toward specific individuals, but at the same time, it was thought to provide more general protection, even extending to one's descendants or the fate of a dynasty. Outside of emperors, few could afford to give on such a lavish scale, particularly as the size of monasteries grew to encompass massive estates housing hundreds of monks. As late as the Song we still have records of individuals donating residences to monasteries in order "to acquire merit for the netherworld."[120] But in general, monasteries were founded by groups of prominent local figures, all of whom could gain some measure of merit from their contribution.

One could also gain merit by contributing to the repair or restoration of a dilapidated monastery. At least one Song writer claimed scriptural support for his view that repairing an old monastery yielded spectacular merit, and in general donors seem to have made no distinction between the merit of founding a monastery and that of restoring an old one.[121] Yet, questions of merit aside, the prospect of building a new monastery was always more exciting than patching up an old one, and the value accorded the wholesale reconstruction of a monastery contributed to the general pattern of Buddhist monasteries in China of neglect or destruction followed by rebuilding. There are remarkably few examples of truly old monastery buildings in China. Monasteries were often destroyed by accidental fire, and occasionally in government persecutions. Just as important, rather than devoting attention to the careful preservation and

[119] *Zizhi tongjian* 224, p. 7196.

[120] The quotation is from a Ming record, relating the history of a monastery founded in the Song from a donated private residence. "Chongfu An," 16, p. 38b.

[121] The writer is Zou Qi, who makes the claim in his "Jingtuyuan Shijiadian ji," in *Liang Zhe jinshi zhi*, pp. 1b–3b. Zou's quotation of an unnamed Buddhist scripture specifically praising the merit of repairing old monasteries seems to be from the *Xiangfa jueyi jing*, T no. 2870, vol. 85, p. 1336a. This text, though claiming to record the words of the Buddha, may in fact have been composed in China. See Kyoko Tokuno, "The Book of Resolving Doubts Concerning the Semblance Dharma," pp. 257–71.

maintenance of monasteries, monks usually allowed the monastery to slowly reach a state of disrepair before launching a serious campaign to solicit funds and rebuild it from scratch.[122] When a monastery was rebuilt or major repair work done, a new record of the monastery was commissioned from a local official or literary figure detailing the efforts along with the names of the contributors. This record was then engraved on stone and displayed at the monastery. Thousands of these records have come down to us preserved in local gazetteers, the collected works of famous writers, and collections of epigraphy, thus providing us with ample material on the history of monasteries and attitudes of local patrons toward them.[123]

Examples of devout patrons linking gifts of funds for monastic construction to the accumulation of merit could easily be multiplied. Records of monasteries at times seem to paint a picture of sweeping success, as the idea of Buddhist merit overwhelmed the Chinese populace and monasteries cropped up in every corner of the empire. "Ever since Buddhism entered China, all the finest scenery is in the possession of Buddhists," writes one Song author, who attributed the popularity of gifts to monasteries in part to the trustworthiness of monks. "In financial matters a follower of the Buddha would not cheat you of so much as a penny, for they believe that every deception has karmic consequences."[124] Others, rather than focusing on the worthiness of monks, credited the continued success of monasteries to a deep and widespread belief in merit, for "while great gifts like cartloads of gold and wagons filled with jade tie one to good karma, even gifts as small as a straw cloak or a felt mat reap great rewards."[125] Another warns that only the "medicine" of charity can cure one of the "sickness" of avarice. "For this reason, masters advise that we must tear out the roots of attachment that men may delight in giving, understand the teachings of the 'field of emotions' and the 'field of merit' and internalize these truths."[126] In this way, monk and donor alike benefited from monastic construction; the Buddhist fields of merit were densely sown. Nevertheless, while most of the faithful continued to preach the doctrine of merit and extol the benefits awaiting the charitable patron, others expressed misgivings about a doctrine so closely tied to material concerns and often applied in a mechanical manner.

[122] See Holmes Welch, The Buddhist Revival in China pp. 87–8.
[123] Two studies in particular have exploited this material: Mark Halperin's "Pieties and Responsibilities: Buddhism and the Chinese Literati, 780–1280," and Timothy Brook, Praying for Power: Buddhism and the Formation of Gentry Society in Late-Ming China.
[124] Nan Linbaosi bei, pp. 35b–37b.
[125] "Chongxiu Ayuwang si muyuan shu," by Tu Long (1542–1605) 4, p. 13b, cited in Brook, Praying for Power, p. 318.
[126] "Donglingsi zhuangtian ji," 34, p. 19b; Halperin, "Pieties and Responsibilities," p. 125.

Merit's Critics

In 767, a powerful court eunuch donated one of his estates to be made into a monastery to "provide merit in the netherworld [*mingfu*] for Empress Zhangjing," the mother of then emperor Daizong.[127] The emperor subsequently agreed to the dismantling of several palace buildings so that their materials could be used in the new monastery. A young, righteous official named Gao Ying, outraged by this decision, immediately remonstrated with a memorial, saying, "The virtues of the deceased Empress Dowager surely do not require the construction of a monastery to be made evident. Rather we must consider the interests of the people first if the future security of the empire is to be achieved. What merit can result from abandoning the people and running off to monasteries?" In another memorial, Gao spoke of the "wise rulers of ancient times," that is, Chinese sages who ruled before Buddhism entered China, who "accumulated goodness in order to elicit blessings,"[128] and concluded by criticizing the emperor for supporting monastic construction, saying, "I think that Your Majesty should not expect to gain merit in this fashion."[129] This critique comes from outside the tradition and seems to reject the value of Buddhist merit altogether. Others turned instead to seeming contradictions in Buddhist doctrine and practice. Reflecting on the lavish buildings of new monasteries freshly painted and stocked with Buddhist sculpture, literate men versed in Buddhist scriptures wondered if all of this was not at odds with Buddhist doctrines of austerity and emptiness. Did provision of timber, paint, and landed estates really warrant the bliss of a Pure Land? What, after all, did the payment of laborers' fees and land contracts have to do with the essence of enlightenment and the truth of emptiness?

When commissioned to write a record for a monastery rebuilt with funds from a patron who bequeathed the merit from his gift to his deceased wife, one Song writer expressed his discomfort with the connection between Buddhism and wealth, saying that, in contrast to such material dealings, he had been led to believe that "Gautama's learning was rooted in suffering and emptiness, tranquility and silence, distancing oneself from material objects and observing the mind in an attempt to achieve perfect and ultimate realization."[130] Such lofty doctrines seemed to him far removed from the mundane attention of monk and patron alike to the

---

[127] *Zizhi tongjian* 224, p. 7195; discussed in Weinstein, *Buddhism under the T'ang*, p. 84.

[128] Probably an allusion to the *Book of Changes* quotation cited in the introduction above.

[129] Both memorials are quoted in *Zizhi tongjian* 224, p. 7196; English trans. from Weinstein, *Buddhism under the T'ang*, p. 84.

[130] "Baoshouyuan ji," 77, pp. 16–17; translated and discussed in Halperin, "Pieties and Responsibilities," p. 153.

exchange value of monastic halls and cash donations in the karmic currency of blessings and good fortune.

These concerns came to the fore with the rise of radical strains of Chan thought at the end of the Tang and into the early Song. It was at this time that a legend of Bodhidharma, said to be the first to bring Chan Buddhism to China, seems to have taken shape. According to this legend, when the great monk once met with Emperor Wu of the Liang dynasty,

> [t]he emperor asked, "Since ascending to the throne, I have had temples built, sutras transcribed, and monks ordained. What merit have I gained?" The master answered: "No merit at all." The emperor replied: "Why no merit at all?" The master said: "All these are but impure motives for merit; they mature the paltry fruit of rebirth as a human being or a deva (a god). They are like shadows that follow the form, having no reality of their own." The emperor said: "Then of what kind is true merit?" He answered: "It is pure knowing, wonderful and perfect. Its essence is emptiness. One cannot gain such merit by worldly means."[131]

We know very little about the obscure historical figure Bodhidharma, but can safely assume that this conversation never took place and was most likely invented in the late Tang. The passage reflects the Chan call for direct enlightenment, unmediated by any practice, whether it be meditation, scripture recitation, or making merit by building a monastery—the same tendency we have already seen challenging the validity of Buddhist icons and symbolic objects. Emperor Wu of the Liang was an obvious choice for the legend not only because he was a contemporary of the historical Bodhidharma but also because of his reputation as the first great imperial patron of Buddhism in China. He did in fact found a number of monasteries, vowing that the merit for at least one of them was to go to his deceased mother.[132] Like Chan stories of monks burning icons and Buddhist books, the legend of Bodhidharma's repudiation of Emperor Wu was no doubt intended to shock, attacking as it does one of the most cherished and fundamental of Buddhist doctrines.

By the Southern Song, this well-known story, already accepted as a factual account of an actual meeting, was the source of much anxiety, and crops up on occasion in monastery records. For instance, in his "Record for the Reconstruction of the Yonglong Cloister," the thirteenth-century figure Lin Xiyi writes:

---

[131] *Jingde chuan deng lu* 3, p. 219a; trans. from Heinrich Dumoulin, *Zen Buddhism: A History,* vol. 1, *India and China,* p. 91. An earlier version of the story can be found in *Zu tang ji* 2, p. 45.

[132] Tang, *Han-Wei Liang Jin Nanbeichao fojiaoshi,* pp. 341–2. The monastery dedicated to Emperor Wu's mother was the Zhidu si. See *Nanchao fosi zhi,* by Sun Wenchuan, 1, p. 20b.

Long ago Bodhidharma said to the Liang [emperor] that to make merit by building monasteries yielded small benefits and was a cause for afflictions. This was intended as criticism. But for all to abandon [the enterprise of building monasteries] in the belief that it yields small benefits would be a mistake. In Fujian, Buddhist temples are most numerous, but have fallen into disrepair over the past several decades while half have been abandoned altogether. When neglecting to repair them, people explain themselves by drawing on Bodhidharma's saying. I smile at this and pity them. How odd that there are people such as this.[133]

For the devout, Chan reservations about the value of contributing toward the construction of monasteries could easily be overcome by the wealth of scriptural passages extolling the virtues of such donations, coupled with the strength of tradition: donating money to a monastery was commonly accepted as something respectable local families did, whether to assert their position in the community or to ensure the well-being of a recently deceased relative.

But for those few who were openly hostile to the Buddhist cause, the Buddhist accumulation of wealth through the doctrine of merit seemed at the least absurd and at the worst invidious. Ouyang Xiu, one of the fiercest critics of Buddhism in the Song, once commented that Buddhists had an unfair advantage over Daoists when soliciting funds for construction.

Both are fond of large, palatial buildings for their dealings with the people of the world. Yet the Buddhists are able to take advantage of people's feelings and stir them up with talk of misfortune and blessings. For this reason people flock to them with great fervor. The Daoists on the other hand speak of purity, serenity, distant isolation and the arts of the sylphs who fly off in transcendence. These are mysterious, profound matters not easily investigated. The Daoists take as their duty untrammeled inaction. Thus, it is an easy matter for Buddhists to move the people to action, while Daoists must depend on the good intentions of a leader of the people.[134]

Ouyang's observation, while certainly biased, is also astute in that he recognizes the importance of the strong connection Buddhist doctrine makes between karmic retribution ("misfortune and blessings") and the construction of Buddhist buildings, an advantage those who solicited money for other types of construction such as Confucian academies and Daoist monasteries lacked. One Ming critic went a step further, not merely lamenting the ability of monks to "stir up the people," but claiming that

[133] "Yong Longyuan," by Lin Xiyi, 79, p. 7; discussed in Halperin, "Pieties and Responsibilities," pp. 162–3.
[134] "Yu Shuge ji," 39, pp. 270–1.

1

98   CHAPTER THREE

attention to such mundane matters was a sign of rank hypocrisy. "Buddhism is hardly worth believing," he wrote,

> [b]ut if you must, then you should enter into the mountain woods, give up desires, eliminate all thoughts and make yourself tolerant, concentrated and tranquil. Only at this point can one see what they call one's "nature" and understand their teaching. But to venerate massive monasteries and reverence fertile fields is to take the path of desire daily. And to make spectacular renovations and prodigious donations for the sake of merit is sheer foolishness.[135]

Specific criticism of the notion of merit was, however, rare, even among the most virulent opponents of Buddhism. In essays criticizing Buddhism, literati preferred instead to focus on philosophical issues of ontology and ethics, castigating monks for abandoning social responsibilities to family and ruler in pursuit of selfish notions of self-cultivation and personal enlightenment.[136] Ironically, it was as much the emphasis on social responsibility expressed through charity and selflessness of patrons as its promotion of a monastic ideal of renunciation that allowed Buddhism to stake out such a firm position for monasteries in Chinese society.

Understanding the Patron

The psychology of the donors who contributed huge sums to the construction or restoration of monasteries is far more complex than I have presented it here. Aside from Buddhist piety, having one's name engraved on a stone tablet and displayed at the local monastery was a means of acquiring prestige. As in the case of funerals, the gift of a monastery in honor of a deceased parent was an important public expression of filial piety and local philanthropy, regardless of one's personal belief or disbelief in the Buddhist doctrine of merit. Families had reputations to build and maintain, often through conventions that did not require extraordinary sincerity. The warp of personal piety was interwoven with the weft of social obligation. It was against this background of prestige, philanthropy, and intricate social relations that Chinese monasteries rose and fell and rose again.

Because a donation to a monastery fulfilled a number of needs, ranging from social responsibilities to familial affection and fear of death, it is no wonder that outside of a few mavericks, few ever questioned the doctrine

---

[135] "Jinxiang yuan" 10, p. 11a–b. Cited in Brook, *Praying for Power*, p. 199. Brook discusses the role of merit (karma) in monastic construction in the Ming on pp. 198–9.

[136] See for instance the passages selected and translated from the *Er Cheng yishu* by Wing-tsit Chan in Wm. Theodore de Bary, ed., *Sources of Chinese Tradition*, vol. 1, pp. 477–8.

of merit. What, after all, was the alternative: to lose an opportunity to improve one's standing among the locals, to risk earning a reputation as a greedy, ungrateful son, and to abandon all hope of influencing one's fate and the fate of one's relations in the afterlife? For all these reasons, Chan misgivings about the ultimate worth of material donations and attacks on merit by the likes of Ouyang Xiu had little discernible impact on the steady growth of monasteries in China. When the call went out for funds to build or restore a local monastery, patrons were usually eager to offer their services. For the rewards to be gained by such a donation were at once tangible and vague enough to respond to a number of emotions, ranging from guilt over past actions to affection for a recently deceased parent.

BRIDGES

Given China's lengthy history of organized labor and unparalleled tradition of accumulating practical experience over vast stretches of time, it should not surprise us that Chinese constructed impressive bridges of various styles over all manner of rivers, ravines, and mountain passes in diverse regions throughout its history. What is surprising is the close connection between many of these bridges and the doctrines and practices of Buddhism. From at least the sixth century to the end of the Qing, monks played a prominent role in building and maintaining Chinese bridges. More generally, the pervasive Buddhist notion of religious merit was a key factor in the construction of any number of bridges—structures that were essential for the transportation, commerce, and communication of the empire. What, then, was the connection between monks, bridges, and the Buddha Dharma?

We begin with a lengthy record of the construction of a bridge in Henan in the sixth century. A large stele titled "Stele for the Stone Images and Righteous Bridge (Constructed by) the Honorable Yu and Others of Wude (Commandery)," inscribed in 549, commemorates the completion of a bridge known only as the "Righteous Bridge" (Yiqiao).[137] The stele says little about the bridge itself and is of only minimal use to scholars interested in the history of engineering or the aesthetics of bridges—the

---

[137] "Wude Yu fujun deng yiqiao shixiang zhi bei." The stele was discovered in 1752. The most complete transcription of the stele's text can be found in *Henei xianzhi*, ed. Yuan Tong and Fang Lüqian, 20, pp. 8a–16b. A more recent transcription of the text can be found in *Lu Xun jijiao shike shougao*, vol. 2, pp. 433–52. Finally, a rubbing of the stele, giving some sense of the Buddhist images on top, can be found in the collection of the Fu Ssu-nien Library. The stele is discussed briefly in Tokiwa Daijō, *Zoku Shina bukkyō no kenkyū*, pp. 486–7.

two chief concerns of modern scholarship on the history of Chinese bridges.[138] The stele does, however, provide interesting information on the construction of public works at the local level at this early date. Determined that a bridge was badly needed at the spot, a group of local officials led by a general named Yu Zijian solicited funds for the bridge, which, given the span of the Qin River it was to cross, was to be of considerable size. The stele begins with a few lines in praise of the project, followed by a brief history of Wude Commandery, the Qin River, and the efforts to build the bridge. The inscription ends with a long list of the names of contributors.

For the history of Buddhism, several aspects of the inscription attract our attention. First of all, at the top of the stele appears a buddha, flanked by two other figures—probably bodhisattvas. Below this, the inscription begins by describing in the ornate language of such epigraphy the arrival of Buddhism to China:

The Brahma-lamp spreads to distant lands, its light piercing the darkest night; the teaching of wisdom breaks through the delusions of the masses, opening their eyes. For this reason, the divine light, not extinguished, was moved to response among the foreigners of the west; the golden one, although he had passed away, appeared in a dream in the Eastern Han.

This last line is an allusion to the legend of the first appearance of Buddhism in China, when Emperor Ming of the Han saw the Buddha in a dream. The text that follows contains a number of Buddhist terms as well, praising this victory of the Buddha over Mara, and noting significantly that when the call went out for help with the project, "[t]hose who assisted in this blessed work stood shoulder to shoulder." All of this suggests that those involved in the project were probably familiar with Buddhist doctrine, or at the least not adverse to being associated with it.

More concrete evidence of the connection between Buddhists and the building of the bridge comes at the bottom of the stele, where a number of lines state the source for the wood needed to build the bridge. They read:

The various masters [i.e., monks] of the Yangying Monastery, Jincheng Monastery, Yongcheng Monastery, Heng'an Monastery, Gaozhong Monastery, Zhuying Monastery and Guanling Monastery were saddened at the

<hr/>

[138] For the history of the engineering of bridge-building in China, see Joseph Needham et al., *Civil Engineering and Nautics*, part 3 of vol. 4, *Physics and Physical Technology*, pp. 145–210, Ronald G. Knapp, *Chinese Bridges*, Tang Huangcheng, *Qiaoliang juan*, and Tang Huancheng, *Zhongguo gudai qiaoliang*. For a study of the cultural significance of the bridge, focusing on contemporary ethnographic data, see Zhou Xing, *Jingjie yu xiangzheng: qiao he minsu*.

sight of a candle in the wind and sighed at the sight of bubbles [symbols of impermanence]. And so they cut off their hair and presented it to the gate of profundity [i.e., Buddhism]. They removed their hairpins [symbol of the gentleman] and searched out the traces of Brahma [i.e., Buddhism]. Sighing at the great difficulties of traversing [the Qin river] and taking pity on the people for the pains they endured to cross it, these monks donated wood and other materials for the construction of the bridge. As Yangying Monastery initiated this good work, it is the keeper of the bridge.

In addition, the list of donors on the back of the stele (containing the names of close to three hundred) includes a number of monks. Why were monks so involved in the project? Why should a record of the construction of a bridge contain a depiction of the Buddha, and why was this record couched in Buddhist terms?

Part of the answer lies in the reference to the bridge as a "blessed work." From very early on in the history of Buddhism, the construction of bridges was said to bring "blessings," that is, merit, to those involved. For instance, the *Scripture of the Field of Blessings and Merit*, translated into Chinese at the end of the third century, states:

> The Buddha announced to Indra, "There are seven types of great donations that are termed 'fields of blessings,' and those who enact them obtain blessings and are reborn in Brahma Heaven. What are these seven? The first is to construct stupas, monastic quarters, halls and buildings. The second is to provide gardens, orchards, pools, woods and cool places. The third is to donate medicine and treat the infirm. The fourth is to maintain boats to help the people cross rivers. *The fifth is to establish bridges so that the ill and the weak can cross rivers.* The sixth is to dig wells close to roads so that the thirsty may drink. And the seventh is to make latrines and places of convenience. Through these seven acts one obtains the blessings required for [rebirth in] Brahma Heaven."[139]

A similar list (of five rather than seven) acts appears in the *Ekottarāgama*, translated at the end of the fourth century, again listing the construction of bridges as a key source of merit.[140] Other scriptures, such as the *Sarvāstivādavinayavibhāṣā*, probably translated into Chinese at the beginning of the fifth century, and the *Scripture of the Place of Concentration of the True Law*, translated in the sixth—just a few years before the construction of the bridge discussed above—also extol the virtues of

---

[139] *Foshuo zhude futian jing, T* no. 683, vol. 16, p. 777b.

[140] *Zeng yi ahan jing* (Skt. *Ekottarāgama*) 27, p. 699a. Preceding this list is a curious list of five gifts that do *not* garner merit, including the gift of a knife, the gift of a prostitute, and so on.

202   CHAPTER THREE

bridge-building, which, they insist, garners merit for those involved.[141] In
short, as in the copying of scriptures, the making of Buddhist images, and
the building of monasteries, the building of bridges was a rich source of
merit, well attested in mainstream Buddhist scriptures that were almost
certainly known to the leading monks who participated in the building of
the sixth-century bridge in Wude.[142]

Yet, the building of a bridge is in many ways different from the types
of activities we have seen so far. Unlike a Buddhist statue, a bridge does
not serve a devotional function. Unlike Buddhist scriptures, a bridge does
little to propagate Buddhist teachings, and unlike the donation of a building for a monastery, a bridge does not necessarily provide benefit for
monks. In Buddhist parlance, a bridge serves none of the Three Jewels
(Buddha, Dharma, Sangha). The personal advantages of acquiring merit
aside, the driving force behind the persistent advocation of bridges in Buddhist scriptures was simple charity: bridges eased the life of the traveler,
making a long journey short and obviating the need for a risky crossing
over dangerous waters.[143] In part because of this distance from strictly
monastic concerns, Buddhist notions of the merit of bridge-building contributed to a curious figuration involving monks, local officials, and local
inhabitants—each with distinct reasons for wanting a bridge and with distinct attitudes toward Buddhism—that consistently provided the impetus
for constructing countless bridges from at least as early as the sixth century to as late as the twentieth.

In a classic of material culture studies, Alan Trachtenberg emphasized

[141] *Sapoduopinipiposha* (Skt. *Sarvāstivādavinayavibhaṣā*) 7, p. 545b; *Zheng fa nian chu
jing* (Skt. *[Saddharma] smrtyupasthānasūtra*) 22, p. 125c. All the four texts I mention here
are cited in the chapter on "Eliciting Merit" (*xingfu*) in the *Fayuan zhulin* (33, pp. 537–42),
completed in 668.

[142] The idea that one received merit for bridge-building was also propagated in a mural
in Cave 296 at Dunhuang. The mural, probably completed in the sixth century, depicts forms
of merit-making, including bridge-building, described in the *Scripture of the Fields of Blessings and Merit*.

[143] Bridge-building was also encouraged as an act of charity under Islamic religious and
administrative systems in medieval times. See Bertold Spuler, "Trade in the Eastern Islamic
Countries in the Early Centuries," p. 15. There are parallels as well in medieval Europe,
where the pope granted indulgences for a host of purposes, including the building of bridges,
in addition to which building a bridge often served as an act of penance. See Paul Sebillot,
"Les ponts du moyen âge et les frères pontifes," pp. 121–140, and Shaffern, "Images, Jurisdiction, and the Treasury of Merit," pp. 237–47. Of more direct relevance for Chinese
Buddhism, bridge-building was encouraged in early Daoism. The biography of Zhang Daoling in the *Shenxian zhuan* states that in addition to encouraging his followers to build roads,
and punishing those who did not by causing them to take ill, he also led them to make
bridges. *Shenxian zhuan* 4, p. 7. Similarly, bridge-building, along with repairing roads, is
listed as a form of penance in the Daoist *Chisongzi zhangli* 2:18. I cannot determine if these
ideas reflect Buddhist influence or an independent development. I owe these references to
Lin Fu-shih.

the important symbolic significance of bridges in the United States, where, from early on, the bridge was a sign of progress, modernity, and the conquest of nature. In addition to more practical concerns of transportation and communication, these abstract ideals also played a key role in the history of the American bridge.[144] In China, the bridge was instead a symbol of charity, compassion, and good governance, ideas that weighed heavily on the minds of various figures on the local scene, including monks, officials, and prominent members of the community, when the need for a bridge became apparent.

Records for bridges in the pre-Song period are scarce, but with the flourishing of local history from the Song to the Qing, we have hundreds if not thousands of records of bridges in which Buddhist monks or Buddhist ideas are mentioned.[145] These records are particularly valuable for what they reveal about the relationship between the material needs of local communities and officials and about Buddhist concepts of material culture. Before turning to the relationship of Buddhism to local elites, officials, and bridges, we look first at the factors that led thousands of monks from at least the sixth century up to the twentieth to invest time, effort, and money in the building of bridges.

Monks and Bridges

The relationship between monks and bridges probably extended back even further than the sixth-century bridge mentioned above, but it is only with the sixth century that we begin to get documentation for the involvement of monks in bridge construction. One of our earliest references to this connection comes in the biography of the sixth-century monk Sengyuan, who, according to the *Further Biographies of Eminent Monks*, built a large bridge with three iron mooring posts of some eighty-nine *chi* (approximately eighty-nine feet) in length and three *chi* (feet) in diameter.[146]

[144] Alan Trachtenberg, *Brooklyn Bridge: Fact and Symbol.*

[145] To be more precise, records of bridges become common with the Southern Song, but are still relatively scarce for the Northern Song. On this point, see Robert P. Hymes, *Statesmen and Gentlemen: The Elite of Fu-Chou, Chiang-Hsi, in Northern and Southern Sung*, p. 332, n. 115. Perhaps the first to emphasize the importance of Buddhism for public works in China was Yang Lien-sheng, *Les aspects économiques des travaux publics dans la Chine impériale*, pp. 13–6. The role of Buddhism in Song-Dynasty Fujian has been particularly well studied. See Cheng Guangyu (Ch'eng Kuang-yü), "Song Yuan shidai Quanzhou zhi qiaoliang yanjiu," vol. 6, pp. 313–34, Fang Hao, "Songdai sengtu dui zao qiao de gongxian," pp. 137–46, Huang, *Songdai fojiao shehui jingjishi lun ji*, pp. 128–37, 413–7, and Masāki Chikusa, *Chūgoku bukkyō shakaishi kenkyū* pp. 169–81.

[146] *Xu gaoseng zhuan* 18, p. 547c. The bridge seems to have been a suspension bridge. This is not surprising, since suspension bridges in China were likely in use at an even earlier date. See Needham et al., *Civil Engineering and Nautics*, pp. 200–1.

Other biographies of monks from the medieval period are silent on the subject of bridges, but two inscriptions from the ninth century note the participation of monks in the projects. In the first, a bridge built in 850 in Zhejiang, a monk named Changya of the Dayun Monastery is credited with raising funds for the bridge.[147] Similarly, an inscription for a bridge built in 868 in Shanxi praises a monk named Puan of the Xiantong Monastery for soliciting the funds necessary for building the bridge.[148]

Already in these three cases we can discern the two basic functions monks fulfilled in bridge construction. First, monks often served as technical specialists who had acquired knowledge in how to build large, durable bridges. Second, monks were specialists in the art of soliciting funds. With the Song we begin to get more extensive records on bridge-building—the modern scholar Huang Min-chih has collected records for the construction of close to a hundred bridges in which monks were involved during the Song dynasty in Fujian alone.[149] In the Ming and Qing periods, the number of documents pertaining to bridges increases exponentially. One can choose from among hundreds of Ming-Qing local gazetteers at random and almost assuredly find references to monks building bridges.

Many of these accounts note briefly that the bridge in question was built in such-and-such a year by such-and-such a monk. Rarely do they give details of how the bridge was constructed or inform us of the precise role the monk played in construction. Nonetheless, the fact that some monks participated in building dozens or even hundreds of bridges suggests that they learned and transmitted specialized technical knowledge of how to construct large bridges that would not collapse with the first heavy rain.[150] The Song monk Puzu (d. 1101), for instance, is credited with building "several tens" of bridges in the Quanzhou region; and the thirteenth-century monk Daoxun, also active in Quanzhou, is said to have built over his lifetime more than two hundred bridges![151] Even without detailed records of exactly what role monks played in the building process, such numbers suggest that these monks must have brought all manner of experience to the task, from technical details of construction, to problems of labor, materials, and financing.

In fact, numerous accounts note the names of monks known specifically for their technical expertise in bridge construction.[152] And some of these

[147] *Wudafu xinqiao ji* 73, pp. 31–4, reproduced in *Shike shiliao xinbian*, series 1, vol. 7, pp. 5182a–5183b.
[148] "Gaobizhen Tongjiqiao bei," by Xiao Gong, 9, pp. 34–6, reproduced in *Shike shiliao xinbian*, series 1, vol. 20, pp. 15125b–7b.
[149] Huang, *Songdai fojiao shehui jingjishi lunji*, p. 135.
[150] On this point see Needham et al., *Civil Engineering and Nautics*, pp. 154–5.
[151] Huang, *Songdai fojiao shehui jingjishi*, pp. 129–30.
[152] Needham et al., *Civil Engineering and Nautics*, p. 154; Mao Yisheng, *Zhongguo guqiao jishushi*, p. 236.

give some sense of the level of expertise such monks possessed. For example, the "Technical Skills" (*fangji*) section of the *Song History* recounts the achievements of a monk named Huaibing.[153] Particularly impressive was his restoration of a pontoon bridge.

> In the Hezhong Superior Prefecture there was a pontoon bridge [*fuqiao*] moored by eight "anchors."[154] Each anchor weighed tens of thousands of catty. Later, when the bridge was swept away in a flood, the anchors were pulled under the water. When the call went out for someone to retrieve them, Huaibing employed two large boats which he filled with earth and then attached to the [submerged] anchors. After hooking large planks of wood like a scale under the anchors, he slowly removed the earth so that the boats floated up and the anchors rose. Transport Commissioner Zhang Tao reported this to the emperor and Huaibing was granted a purple robe.

In addition to restoring old bridges, monks were also active in designing and constructing new ones. In 1574, when the magistrate of Huangyan District in Zhejiang determined to have a bridge built, he

> entrusted the measurements and planning to the monk Xuanyun who was accomplished and reliable. This monk then measured off several feet across the river from north to south which he divided among seven slabs (*liang*). Each slab was four-fifths as broad as it was long. He dove under water to set the [stone] piers, securing them with wooden spikes that they would resist the current. He then ran a rope through a pulley [to set the stone slabs], "using the air to build the solid." He committed himself to making something strong and true that it might serve for eternity.[155]

At the same time, monastic leaders were talented administrators, skilled in the organization of human resources. In 1223, when a minister in Leizhou ordered the monk Miaoying to repair a bridge, the monk is said to have "enlisted others, working hard and eating simply. Laboring during the day and resting during the night, he led more than fifty of his followers, the skilled making plans, and the strong expending their strength."[156] Even allowing for hyperbole, such remarks tell us that it was not considered unusual for monks to engage in the labor of building

---

[153] *Song shi* 462, p. 13519. See also Needham et al., *Civil Engineering and Nautics*, p. 160.

[154] Literally, "iron oxen" (*tieniu*). These were large iron objects shaped like oxen used to secure the bridge to the banks of the river. Several such objects from medieval times are extant. See Tang, *Qiaoliang juan*, pp. 716–7.

[155] "Qin Shangshu Minglei beiji," 1, p. 30. On the use of spikes to secure piers and pulleys to place slabs, see Mao, *Zhongguo guqiao jishushi*, p. 199.

[156] "Baizhangqiao ji," by Li Zhongguang, 10, p. 20, cited in Fang, "Songdai sengtu dui zaoqiao de gongxian," p. 141. Similarly, the famous Song builder Daoxun is said to have constructed a bridge with the assistance of his "followers." See *Quanzhou fuzhi*, 10, p. 25.

bridges, and that at times they drew on their "followers" to help with the project.

An essay by an eighteenth-century traveler, official, and writer named Wang Woshi similarly provides us with another glimpse of a monk at work on a bridge. In the course of a tour of bridges, roads, and various sights in central Sichuan in 1756, Wang came upon a group of laborers at work repairing the Hongta Bridge. "A group of workers were carrying about rocks, the noise and commotion of their efforts resounding in all directions. In their midst stood a monk, bareheaded and barefoot, carrying a staff and directing the work."[157] Curious, Wang asked a local woman what this was all about. She replied that the monk, named Zuyin, was entirely in charge of the project, asking no one else for "so much as a stick of wood or a single rock."

More common than descriptions of monks like Zuyin involved in the physical construction of bridges are references to monks raising funds toward their construction. Occasionally, monks donated their own money, as in the case of a twelfth-century monk named Zhiyuan who contributed ten thousand strings of cash for a bridge in Shaoxing, or the thirteenth-century monk Benyuan who built a bridge with money he earned practicing medicine.[158]

Records of bridges frequently state that once the local magistrate had decided a new bridge was needed, he ordered such-and-such a monk to collect the necessary funds. On occasion we also read of monks who first proposed the idea of building a bridge to a local magistrate and then solicited donations for the project. References to monks collecting funds are so common that we must assume that prominent monks were in the habit of establishing philanthropic networks of potential patrons whose estates they would visit to ask for money when the order came down from a magistrate to gather what were often quite sizable sums in a short amount of time. All of this brings us to the question of why monks, rather than, say, a local official or prominent local literati, were so well suited to the task of getting bridges built.

One Song writer, noting the importance of monks for bridge construction, suggested five reasons why monks were good bridge-builders: monks are devoted to helping others and hence willing to work tirelessly; monks have developed powerful capacities of concentration (through meditation) and hence do not abandon a project before it is completed; a monk is not burdened by wife or children and hence does not keep money for his family; monks believe in the principle of karmic retribution and hence are not corrupt; because the monk is devoted to the task, great men support him and lesser men follow him.[159]

[157] "Wang Woshi chongxiu Hongtaqiao ji" 33, p. 6b.
[158] *Anhai zhi* 3, p. 7; and *Xianchun lin'an zhi*, ed. Zan Shuoyou et al., 21, p. 33.
[159] "Baizhangqiao ji," 10, pp. 20–1.

Some of these points are easier to corroborate than others. Modern scholars have scarcely attempted to assess the impact of regular meditation on a monk's attitudes, beliefs, and working habits, though at least one scholar of Christianity has ventured into this elusive field.[160] More concretely, the fact that monks did not usually have wives or children and were generally perceived to be disinterested in material gain is no doubt one of the reasons for their success at soliciting funds for public works. In a biography of the monk and builder Miaofeng Fudeng, the prominent Ming monk Hanshan Deqing lists the names of a number of bridges built by the monk, and concludes by noting that among the reasons for his success was that "[b]eyond his robe, he owned nothing, and he never had any followers. He carried out all of his works of construction with singleness of mind, and never so much as touched financial contributions."[161] This is of course an idealized characterization of the monk—not all monks were as trustworthy as Fudeng. One eighteenth-century official in Jiangxi complained, for instance, of a "wandering monk" named Haiyun who absconded with funds intended for the reconstruction of a much-needed bridge.[162] And in contrast to the ascetic image of the impoverished, itinerant monk, throughout Chinese history there were always individual monks and monasteries that amassed sizable fortunes. Nonetheless, reality must to a large extent have mirrored the ideal of the monk as a man to be trusted with public funds. For monks consistently played the role of money collector for public works in diverse regions throughout China from the Song to the end of the Qing. Tellingly, on hearing of the news of the renegade monk Haiyun, mentioned above, a local monastery quickly sold off some of its land and donated the money to pay for the bridge. For while a wandering monk could steal from the locals and get away with it, an established monastery depended on a reputation for honesty with prominent local families if it was to thrive—after all, perhaps the next request for a donation would not be for a bridge but for repairs to the monastery itself.

In addition to their reputation for fiscal honesty in society at large, monks were also pulled into bridge projects by their own ideals of compassion and merit. The making of a bridge was considered an act of kindness. References to bridges, usually used as a metaphor for compassion, abound in Buddhist scriptures. "The precepts are a bridge," allowing one to overcome every obstacle. The bodhisattva vows to withstand the trampling of others with forbearance, "like a bridge." The Dharma is a bridge

---

[160] Mary Carruthers, *The Craft of Thought: Meditation, Rhetoric, and the Making of Images, 400–1200.*

[161] "Chi jian Wutaishan Da huguo shengguang si Miaofeng Deng Chanshi zhuan," 30, p. 319b. For more on Fudeng and his building projects, see Else Glahn, "Fu-teng" in L. Carrington Goodrich, ed., *Dictionary of Ming Biography 1368–1644*, pp. 462–6.

[162] "Chongjian Kongmujiangqiao ji," by Zhang Jingcang, 2, p. 45b.

delivering those who follow it to the other bank of the river separating samsara from nirvana. And most important of all, the bodhisattva must, like a bridge, deliver all beings to the other shore.[163] The bridge metaphor was common in basic Buddhist texts in which literate monks were well versed, and it is safe to assume that most of the leading monks who took up the task of building bridges were steeped in such literature. Outside the Buddhist canon, records written by Chinese literati usually ascribe to the monks who built bridges a feeling of "pity for the difficulties of the people" or of compassion for the "people who drowned in boats attempting to cross the river."[164]

As we have seen, Buddhist scriptures buttress pleas for compassion with the carrot and stick of merit and karmic retribution. Not only are those who build bridges promised a place in a heaven (as in the passages cited above), but those who damage bridges are condemned to a "hell of knives," where they are forced to walk along roads made of pointed blades.[165] One record of a bridge makes this connection between merit, compassion, and bridges very clear. The monk responsible for building the bridge explained his motivation for the project as follows: "At first I thought that the greatest source of merit was carving wood [images] and molding clay [icons]. But one day I realized that the true 'ladder and boat of merit' was to help other beings and other people." From that moment, the monk began work on a local bridge.[166] Here we see a monk who links the building of bridges to other merit-making activities like the construction of devotional icons, but who at the same time is particularly attracted to bridges because of the obvious benefit they bring to ordinary people.

While monks at times were able to finance the bridges and carry out the details of their construction, more often they acted with the approval of the local magistrate and with financial support provided by local elites, to whom we now turn.

Magistrates

From early on in Chinese history, bridge construction and maintenance was one of the duties of government. Mencius, for instance, cites bridge-

---

[163] The first two examples are from the *Da zhi du lun* 13, p. 153c (Lamotte, *Le traité*, p. 776) and 52, p. 603c. The "Dharma bridge" (*faqiao*) is a particularly common expression. See, for instance *Changahanjing* (Skt. *Dīrghāgama*) 2, p. 12c. The final example of a bodhisattva acting as a bridge is from *Da fangguang fo huayan jing* (*Buddhāvataṃsaka-sūtra*), 18, p. 96c. These examples could easily be multiplied.

[164] The first quotation is from the "Tongji qiao ji," by Huang Qian, 37, p. 13a. The second reference is to a record contained in *Jiaxing fuzhi*, 5, p. 12a.

[165] *Da zhi du lun* 16, p. 177a; Lamotte, *Le traité*, p. 965.

[166] *Sichuan tongzhi* 33, p. 7a. Like bridges, "ladders and boats" were also used as metaphors for the compassion of the bodhisattva.

building as an example of intelligent, benevolent governance.[167] It is only with the Tang, however, that we begin to get more detail on how the government went about building bridges. According to the *Tang History*, the central government of the Tang dynasty built eleven major bridges (four pontoon bridges, four of stone, and three of wood) and was responsible for their maintenance. Other bridges were the responsibility of local governments. The central government would still provide funding for the building and maintenance of these local bridges, "depending in measure on the size of the bridge and the degree of difficulty in constructing it."[168] The inscriptions we saw above for bridges built in the Tang suggest that in practice, even at that time, funding for bridges often came entirely from local sources, with little or no support from the central government.[169]

From the Song through the Qing, the central government did not even offer theoretical support for bridge-building—funding for such matters was left to the devices of local officials.[170] At the same time, the central government expected the local magistrate to build and maintain bridges in his jurisdiction. Indeed, in the Qing the local magistrate could be punished with a year's loss of salary if an important bridge in his jurisdiction collapsed, and lashed thirty strokes if he failed to repair a dilapidated bridge.[171] Faced with this dilemma, a harried magistrate had no choice but to ask wealthy families in the community to provide funding for local construction.[172] When appealing to prominent local figures for funds for bridges, magistrates frequently turned to monks to handle the details of personal solicitation and collection of moneys. In addition to the reputation of monks for fiscal honesty and the experience many monks had in organizing labor, materials, and funding, it should be remembered that magistrates were usually not members of the community, but were instead

[167] *Mencius* 4B: "When the administration of the state of Zheng was in his hands, Zichan used his own carriage to take people across the Zhen and Wei. 'He was a generous man,' commented Mencius, 'but he did not know how to govern. If the footbridges are built by the eleventh month and the carriage bridges by the twelfth month every year, the people will not suffer the hardship of fording.'" Translation from D. C. Lau, *Mencius*, p. 128. On the political symbolism of the bridge in China, see Zhou, *Jingjie yu xiangzheng*, pp. 145–8.

[168] *Jiu Tang shu* 43, pp. 1841–2.

[169] On government policy toward bridge construction, see Tang Huancheng, *Qiaoliang juan*, pp. 5–7.

[170] This point is made in the introduction to the section on bridges in *Fujian tongzhi*, ed. Chen Shouqi 29, p. 1a. Other scholars have also emphasized the relative weakness of the ties between central and local government in the Song as compared to earlier periods. See, for instance, Qian Mu, *Guoshi dagang*, pp. 409–11, and Hymes, *Statesmen and Gentlemen*, p. 175.

[171] T'ung-tsu Ch'ü, *Local Government in China under the Ch'ing*, p. 156.

[172] For the role of gentry in bridge construction in the nineteenth century, see Chung-li Chang, *The Chinese Gentry: Studies on Their Role in Nineteenth-Century Chinese Society*, pp. 56–7.

appointed to their post from another region, often far away from their hometown. Hence, the magistrate needed the assistance of someone trustworthy and familiar with the local scene to carry out a project that, while clearly an official responsibility, also involved the unofficial but crucial task of raising money. Given these circumstances into which local officials were thrust, it is not surprising that their attitudes toward the monks they employed and the Buddhist beliefs these monks represented were often ambivalent.

Records of bridge construction from before the Song at times employ Buddhist language, suggesting that the officials involved in such projects themselves adhered to Buddhist tenets, or at least did not object strongly to them. A stele from 598, for instance, though containing no references to monks, is sprinkled with Buddhist technical terms, and asks that the merit for building the bridge be distributed to "all beings in the dharmaloka" (i.e., the universe).[173] A record of a bridge from a few years previous (586) is similarly filled with pious Buddhist language and references to the scriptures.[174] This style of writing, so similar to that of Buddhist steles and monastery inscriptions from the Tang and pre-Tang period, changes abruptly in the Song, as authors begin to take a more detached view of Buddhist doctrines.[175]

From the Song on, the local official's appeal to monks seldom took the form of requests; monks were *ordered* to solicit funds. On occasion a magistrate might praise a monk if his service was exceptional, but more frequently the monk's role in soliciting funds is taken for granted and he is compensated for his efforts with little more than a passing reference in the magistrate's record. In inscriptions carved into steles and later copied into local gazetteers, Song and post-Song writers tend to emphasize the importance of sincerity in charitable acts, quoting the Chinese classics and comparing the ideal official, concerned with the welfare of his people, to the sage-king Yu, said to have tamed the rivers in distant antiquity. Gone are references to "Brahma lamps" and the victory of the Buddha over Mara. This is not to say that these authors were not familiar with Buddhist ideas and terminology. Bridge records at times refer to the "immeasurable merit" of building bridges, or lump bridges together with road repair and monastery construction as rich sources of "blessings."[176] In these passages, one detects, however, a detachment from Buddhist doc-

---

[173] See "Mingzhou Nanhexian Lishui shiqiao bei," 40, pp. 1–6, collected in *Shike shiliao*, series 1, vol. 1, pp. 679a–681b.

[174] "Zhong Sina deng zaoqiao bei," vol. 7, pp. 1173–7.

[175] Mark Halperin has documented the same shift in monastery inscriptions. See his "Pieties and Responsibilities."

[176] See, for instance, "Jiaoyu Luo Yuanqi chongjian Yiwenqiao yin," 48, p. 11b, and "Chen Sanke ji" (for the Yuejiang Qiao) p. 61a.

trine not present in pre-Song inscriptions; Buddhist doctrine, like the money-collecting monks, had become more clearly a tool to achieve administrative goals rather than a key ingredient in what was once a quasi-religious activity. One Ming official expressed this sense of distance from the doctrine of merit, so central to efforts to collect funds, when he wrote:

> Strangely, in recent times discussions of merit and compassion are for the most part the provenance of Buddhists, for whom [building] bridges is one of the "eight fields of blessings." Yet, mixing this up perversely, [people] care only for karmic reward (*ganying*), and do good works only in order [to obtain personal benefit]. Further, in years of good harvest, when they have a surplus, they are willing to expend their wealth to sponsor great rituals in an obscene pursuit of "blessings" even to the point of bankrupting themselves. Yet when it comes to a request for a small donation for a bridge, they make gestures of hardship. This is all counter to the spirit of good works.[177]

While the reference to the "eight fields of blessings" indicates at least a passing familiarity with Buddhist doctrine,[178] the author's disdain for "great rituals" and dismissal of "obscene pursuit of blessings" alerts us to his ambivalence for the concept of Buddhist merit. When Buddhist prescriptions for good works overlap with the needs of the magistrate, he accepts them eagerly; but when these prescriptions veer into areas of ritual and devotion unrelated to the magistrate's concerns, and, more importantly, sap away funds that might have been used for public works, he balks.

The same tendency is clear in the piece by Wang Woshi, the Qing official mentioned above who told the story of the monk Zuyin and his dedication to building bridges. According to Wang's essay, the monk originally dedicated himself to gaining merit by making Buddhist icons, and only later gave up this practice in order to devote himself to building a bridge. In general, Buddhist texts would have stressed the continuity between making Buddhist images and building a bridge: both are equally legitimate means of gaining merit. Wang, however, describes the switch as

[177] "Gan Weilin ji" (for the Shuilian Qiao) p. 5b.

[178] The "eight fields of blessings" (*bafutian*), or "eight sources of merit," are usually given as buddhas, holy men, the monastic community, religious teacher (*upādhyāya*), ritual master (*ācārya*), father, mother, and the infirm. See Foguang dacidian bianxiu weiyuan hui, ed., *Foguang da cidian*, p. 305. The list of eight meritorious acts that includes bridges may well be a Chinese innovation. In a commentary to the *Fanwang jing*, the prominent Tang monk Fazang noted, "As for the eight fields of blessings, there are those who give them as (1) making or expanding roads or wells, (2) improving waterways and bridges, (3) leveling dangerous roads, (4) serving ones' parents with filial devotion, (5) supporting sramanas, (6) assisting the infirm, (7) saving the imperiled, and (8) giving 'open religious feasts.' I have not seen this list among any of the sacred teachings." *Fanwang jing pusajieben shu* 5, *T* no. 1813, vol. 40, p. 639a.

a conversion experience, stating that the monk, moved by a local official who attempted to mend a bridge, followed the official's example "like shadow follows form," and proceeded to "abandon the Moists for the Confucians," in other words, giving up his false teachings for true ones.[179] Whether the monk himself would have agreed with this description is impossible to determine. We can say, however, that distinctions between public works intended for the good of the community and more private devotional works intended as offerings to Buddhist deities were for the most part foreign to the Buddhist textual tradition in which such monks were versed.[180] The "utilitarian critique" introduced by outsiders like Wang Woshi and other local officials was something new. But perhaps, rather than "utilitarian," it is more accurate to say that such critiques were based on a different definition of utility. After all, for most devout Buddhists, devotional objects like icons were not only useful, but essential to religious practice.

Donors

When we shift our attention from the local official charged with the construction and upkeep of bridges to those who donated money toward bridge construction, we find more sympathy with Buddhist beliefs. Records occasionally mention the involvement of common people in such projects, as in a reference in one gazetteer to a bridge built by "an old village woman who studied Buddhism."[181] In general, though, the records are dominated by local elites who supplied money for the projects and in many cases initiated them.[182] Such figures engaged in the construction of various public monuments, including monasteries, shrines, and schools. Scholars working on the history of local elites have tended to emphasize the importance of such projects for establishing prestige in the community; just as a local family might prepare a son to pass the civil service examinations more for the prestige it brought back home than for the remote possibility of serving the state abroad, so too prominent families donated toward public works in part for the respect such donations brought to the family. This being said, philanthropy is most always driven by a medley of motives, and when explaining such actions it is as naive to grant exclusive importance to a hunger for prestige as it is to attribute all acts of charity to a selfless desire to do good. Monks experienced in soliciting donations were well aware of the mixed motives of their patrons. One

---

[179] *Sichuan tongzhi*, 33, p. 7.

[180] I will introduce one exception, the apocryphal *Scripture of the Resolution of Doubts in the Age of the Semblance Dharma* (*Xiangfa jueyi jing*) in the conclusion to this chapter.

[181] "Yongjiqiao," in *Nanchang fuzhi* 4, p. 67a.

[182] For the Ming and Qing period, scholars usually refer to local elites as "gentry."

seventeenth-century monk, in a record for a bridge, divided donors into three categories: the selfless who donate only to help others, those who donate to "secure blessings in their future or to redeem a fault in their past," and those who donate to impress others for the good it will do them in this world.[183]

In practice, Buddhist notions of merit and retribution fall somewhere in between the two poles of, on the one hand, disinterested generosity and, on the other, self-serving manipulation of public opinion; a Buddhist devotee was to contribute to the building of bridges with the selfless spirit of a bodhisattva but with the knowledge that such actions would bring him blessings in this life or the next. On rare occasions the rewards for donating to a bridge could be supernatural, as in the case related in one bridge record of a boy of eighteen, silent from birth, who was said to have uttered his first words immediately after his father offered money to a monk at the gate soliciting funds for a local bridge.[184] However much credence we may put in such stories, they reflect a commonly held belief that the good would be rewarded through the Buddhist mechanism of merit of which bridge-building was a part. In general, however, documents refer to merit in less direct terms. When, in 1842, a magistrate asked the leading figures of his community to contribute to a bridge, they replied, "[T]his would reap great merit!"[185] Another Qing figure, writing in praise of three prominent local men who financed a much-needed bridge, exclaimed that they had "planted the seeds of merit and would reap its rewards."[186] In these last two examples, monks played no role whatsoever, and there is no indication that the men involved in the project had any special affinity with Buddhism. Rather, Buddhist notions of merit, and in particular the idea that one could gain merit through the construction of bridges, had become for such people a commonplace element of public works and charitable acts; in bridges as in the making of images and monasteries, the doctrine of merit was well entrenched in the public psyche.[187]

Bridges, Merit, and Material Culture

With this final point—that even bridges built without the help of monks by men with no pretensions to Buddhist piety often involved the Buddhist

[183] "Chong xiu Wan'an qiaoting ji bei," p. 61; discussed in Brook, *Praying for Power*, p. 186.

[184] "Jixiangqiao," in *Jiaxing fuzhi 5*, p. 24a.

[185] "Chongxiu Tongkou Lingguangqiao ji," in *Fujian tongzhi 29*, p. 8b.

[186] "Wanshou Qiao," in *Fujian tongzhi 29*, p. 4b.

[187] For modern examples of the notion of merit in bridge-building without direct reference to Buddhism, see Zhou, *Jingjie yu xiangzheng*, pp. 15-7.

notion of merit—we catch a glimpse of the depths of the impact of merit on Chinese material culture; by the Song, and probably much earlier, the idea of Buddhist merit had become a part of the vocabulary of philanthropy. More specifically, the notion that merit is derived from the construction of bridges—first extolled in India in the sacred scriptures of Buddhism—had become a part of the fabric of everyday life.

In addition to the importance of the doctrine of merit, the active role monks played in designing bridges and overseeing their construction is in large measure the result of a distinctive monastic lifestyle and the place of Buddhist monks in Chinese society. Unburdened with domestic responsibilities and freed from the family farm, monks had the leisure to master the skills necessary to build bridges. The monastic institution supported these efforts both because bridge-building is extolled in Buddhist scriptures as a compassionate act and because building bridges improved the social standing of the monastery in the local community.

Just as important as the building skills of individual monks, however, was the capacity of monks and monasteries to raise funds for bridge construction. Monks had a reputation for honesty and disinterest in personal gain (though at times this reputation proved unfounded), and besides, monasteries depended on a good reputation to secure donations for other projects—graft was not in their long-term interest. At the same time, monks could draw on well-known scriptures, believed to contain the words of the Buddha himself, which explained that the merit gained through donations to bridge construction would improve one's lot as well as the condition of one's intimates in this life and the next.

Local officials were pressured to build and maintain bridges both by a tradition that viewed a well-kept bridge as a sign of good governance and by more direct regulation from the central authorities. Yet, the local official was not supplied with the money or personnel necessary to build bridges and keep them in good repair. This combination of factors led to the formation of what we might term a cultural *figuration,* that is, a cluster of mutually dependent social roles—monk, magistrate, donor—needed to get a large bridge built.[188] The three members of this social triangle did not necessarily respect or even like each other—recall the Ming magistrate's disdain for Buddhist ritual, or the seventeenth-century monk's misgivings about the motivation of his donors. But in the end they all reluctantly acknowledged that they needed each other, at least when it came to building bridges. This particular formation proved remarkably resilient, persisting from as early as the sixth century to the twentieth, and making possible the construction of countless bridges across China.

---

[188] On the term *figuration,* see Norbert Elias, *What is Sociology?* pp. 128–33, and Stephen Mennell, *Norbert Elias: An Introduction,* pp. 251–2.

CONCLUSION

The steady force of merit propelled the history of many of the objects that appear in other chapters of this book. Stupas and icons, robes and alms bowls, were all produced with the support of donors who believed that they would acquire merit by doing so. In each of these cases, the linkage between the particular object and the doctrine of merit can be traced back to India, and seen to run from the earliest period of Chinese Buddhism up to the present day. Inscriptions on steles and monastery bells and drums reveal that there too, merit played a role, though in these cases scriptural support was less direct.

From the fifth century we begin to get records of stone steles, including rubbings from the steles and in many cases extant steles themselves.[189] Typically, a stele is engraved on all four sides, with Buddhist images toward the top and an inscription below. The inscription, in flowery language, dense with metaphor and obscure allusions, extols the virtues of Buddhism and describes the reasons why the donors determined to make the stele. As the production of a stele involved the making of Buddhist images, scriptural support was ready at hand for the idea that erecting a stele was a meritorious act. Invariably, on some part of the inscription appear the names of those who contributed to its manufacture, often including as well a vow directing the merit for the project to a particular recipient. The same holds true for monastic bells and drums: they also typically include inscriptions noting the names of the donors.[190]

As the doctrine of merit persistently proved irresistible to men and women with disposable cash, they not only filled the landscape with objects; they filled it as well with words, above all with their names. Names—some famous, but usually not—clutter countless inscriptions on steles and images from all periods of Chinese history. Walking around monastery grounds in China, one frequently stumbles across broken bits of old, undatable steles covered with the names of people long since forgotten. Why this insistence on recording the names of patrons?

The answer seems at first obvious. As we have seen for books, monasteries, and bridges, such objects represented the wealth and charity of the donor; that is, contributing funds to the construction of a Buddhist object, whether an icon or a bridge, was a means of securing prestige. Peo-

---

[189] On Buddhist steles in China see Kenneth Ch'en, "Inscribed Stelae during the Wei, Chin, and Nan-ch'ao," pp. 75–84, and more recently, Liu Shufen, "Art, Ritual, and Society: Buddhist Practice in Rural China during the Northern Dynasties," pp. 19–46.

[190] In this case, if anyone wished to find scriptural support for the contention that bells and drums too were meritorious acts, they could easily do so, because, as we have seen, the Buddha was quoted as saying that all gifts of "monastic furnishings" rendered merit.

ple of means from various levels of society availed themselves of this method of asserting or improving their social status: from the minor local family who contributed a small amount to have their names added to the list of donors to a stele, to the emperor himself who sponsored the production of thousands of copies of Buddhist texts. At the same time, institutions benefited from association with powerful patrons. A hostile local official would think twice before harassing a monastery that displayed the names of the most prominent local families and perhaps even high generals or officials on a stele before the monastery gates. The name of an emperor stamped on a copy of the Buddhist canon lent authority and majesty to the sacred scriptures. None of this is especially difficult to understand and should no more surprise us than the "King James" Bible or the practice of naming buildings on American college campuses after wealthy patrons.

More curious is the apparent connection between such inscriptions and the operation of merit. It is one thing to expect one's name to appear on the list of donors to a monastery, but why is it necessary to publicly state that one expects to receive Buddhist merit for one's donation? We might attempt to stand on the firm ground of the social function of such acts by pointing out that in the vast majority of such cases, whether for books, steles, or bells, the donor indicates that the merit is to go to a deceased relative. In this way, readers of the inscription are expected to appreciate the selflessness of the donors, their moral rectitude and admirable concern for family members. But this explanation does not always hold true, for at times donors indicate that the merit is for themselves. At other times, the inscription is placed in such an obscure location that we can only conclude that no human was ever intended to read it. In other words, inscriptions describing the donor, the gift, and the donor's wishes for the merit so acquired were intended as well as a contract with forces only dimly understood, broadcasting that the donor had fulfilled his or her side of the bargain and expected to be compensated for it.

Just who was to fulfill the other side of the karmic contract is far from clear. The belief in a bureaucratic order in the netherworld was a prevalent feature of Chinese religion. At death one came before a tribunal of judges who determined one's fate on the basis of ledgers that contained records of one's good and bad deeds.[191] But there is not a whiff of this notion in records that record the merit of donors: the inscriptions are not addressed to the judges of the afterworld. Nor are they addressed to the Buddha or to particular bodhisattvas. This is in keeping with the principles of Buddhist cosmology. Karma does not depend on any particular entity for its administration; it is instead a fundamental part of the natural world, like the movement of the stars or the blooming of flowers. Hence,

---

[191] On the bureaucratic afterlife in China, see Teiser, *The Scripture on the Ten Kings*.

while the need to record one's meritorious deeds implies the belief that there was an arbiter of karmic justice who would consult such records, in practice few donors ever felt it necessary to speculate on this process in any detail.

Donors and monastic thinkers were more concerned with determining the relative value of gifts, which they held depended largely on the state of the donor, the recipient of the gift, and the gift itself. As we have seen, in India different schools held variant positions on the relative merit of gifts to monks as a whole and gifts to the Buddha. *The Scripture of the Resolution of Doubts in the Age of the Semblance Dharma,* a text that purports to record the words of the Buddha but was probably composed in China around the fifth or sixth centuries, in the brief space of a few pages raises most of the chief concerns over the relative merit of various gifts.[192] The text begins with a figure named "Bodhisattva Ever Giving," who asks the Buddha to explain what type of merit is the greatest during the time of the decline of the Buddha Dharma.[193] The Buddha then complains of the insincerity of donors of that future age (which every reader takes to be his own). Laymen host religious feasts, but they station guards at their doors to keep away undesirables. Other patrons insist on being sole contributors to projects, refusing to contribute to any good deeds in which they must share the credit. Others refuse to restore old monasteries or damaged books, insisting on starting from scratch. Finally, some contribute money toward worthy projects only to increase their own fame. All such patrons, the Buddha explains, are terribly deluded. Those who exclude the poor from their religious feasts gain no merit. Those who refuse to cooperate with other donors garner only meager merit. Restoring an old monastery in fact yields much more merit than starting a new one. And to contribute funds only for personal fame yields no merit at all. Finally, at the end of the scripture, the Buddha points out that the donor should give only out of a desire to help those in need rather than in expectation of receiving something in return. "Dharmas contain neither self nor other. When making a donation, one does not hope for a reward in this life, nor does one hope for the joys of paradise in the future. One donates only so that all beings can achieve enlightenment and so that happiness can come to a multitude of beings."

The concern with sincerity as a means of measuring merit is common throughout Chinese Buddhist history. We have seen in the case of books that while devotees believed that the more they made the more merit there was to be gained—a belief that contributed to the spread of printing—at

---

[192] *Xiangfa jueyi jing,* pp. 1335c–8c. On the dating and influence of this text, see Makita Tairyō, *Gikyō kenkyū,* pp. 304–19, and Tokuno, "The *Book of Resolving Doubts Concerning the Semblance Dharma.*"

[193] That is the *xiangfa,* or "semblance Dharma."

the same time, many continued to believe in the superior merit of copying out a Buddhist scripture by hand, especially if the ink was mixed with one's blood, a sign of sincerity that surely counted for something in the complex tabulations of karmic worth. In the cases of monasteries and bridges, we have seen as well that many Chinese were disturbed by the wealth of monks and monasteries, a fact that for them affected the value of the gift. Writers vacillated between enthusiastic praise of the sumptuous majesty of a new monastery or Buddhist statue, and distaste for this betrayal of the monkish ideal of abstinence and humility. Conversely, other writers cited the honest austerity of monks as a primary reason for their success in acquiring wealth for Buddhist causes: patrons could trust monks to apply their money to the cause at hand rather than squander it on decadent treats for themselves.

The final comments of the *Scripture Resolving Doubts* bring us back to the theme of the inherent instability in the relationship between charity and the doctrine of emptiness. If all is ultimately devoid of enduring, independent existence, then what is the point of the flurry of construction and manufacture, promoted by overzealous monks and supported by simple-minded devotees seduced by promises of short-lived pleasures? Aloof literati scoffed at the hypocrisy of it all, while thoughtful laymen and monks looked for solutions—recall the "old gentleman" who donated the merit from his copy of the *Diamond Sutra* to no one at all; for as "original nature is truly empty, there is no pleasure for which to pray."

When we attempt to assess the overall impact of the Buddhist doctrine of merit on Chinese material culture, however, such thoughtful misgivings about the ontology of things quickly fall into the erudite footnotes of a more compelling narrative. Most so took for granted the idea of karmic consequences for making these objects that they gave the mechanism of merit little thought. And the few who openly challenged the notion met with little success. Indeed, even magistrates who thought the idea ridiculous and held monks in contempt still at times found it necessary to employ the doctrine of merit, if indirectly, in order to maintain the bridges and monasteries in their jurisdiction.

I have stressed throughout this chapter that the history of the objects I discuss cannot be reduced to the single motivation of a desire to gain Buddhist merit, whether for oneself or for others. In addition to a wish to garner merit, devotees copied books in order to propagate their contents, in order to memorize them, to practice calligraphy, and even in some cases to make some money. Artisans at Dunhuang believed that they would gain merit for their work, but at the end of the day they also expected to be compensated for their labors with food and ale.[194] Wealthy patrons con-

---

[194] For evidence that Dunhuang artisans believed they would receive merit for their work, see Ma, *Dunhuang Mogaokushi yanjiu*, p. 179, and Ma, *Dunhuang gongjiang shiliao*, p. 21.

tributed to monasteries to raise their standing in the eyes of their neighbors or as an expression of piety for a deceased mother. Magistrates helped monks to solicit funds for bridges in order to satisfy the central authorities and improve transportation. The level of piety in such "charitable" acts ranged from selfless devotion to cynical manipulation. Yet none of these caveats takes away from the impact of merit on Chinese material culture. For from the entry of Buddhism to China up to modern times, the notion of merit was a persistent, persuasive force offering all who would accept it even on the most superficial level a clear course of action for bracing themselves against the caprices of fate, or as the seventeenth-century monk mentioned above put it, "to secure blessings in their future or to redeem a fault in their past."

Chapter Four

ACCIDENTS AND INCIDENTALS

WHEN MODERN scholars attempt to make sense of the spread of Buddhism to China and the rest of Asia, they necessarily arrange the evidence according to sensible patterns, drawing attention to major doctrinal trends, the interaction between important figures, the introduction of influential texts, dominant iconographical motifs, and so on. It is important to note, however, that for those involved in this process of transfer and assimilation, stretching over hundreds of years, the introduction of Buddhism was not so orderly, and hardly any of it was planned. There was no council of Buddhist elders in India dispatching missionaries to China and insisting that they report back to a central authority. During the introduction of Buddhism to China, few if any had an overall grasp of the process in which they were participants. Most of the missionary-monks who arrived in China seem to have come on their own initiative. Buddhist texts came to China in different editions in different conditions and in a haphazard order. In fact, the first few centuries of Buddhist literature in China are the mirror image of their Indian counterpart. Some of the earliest Indian Buddhist texts, the *Āgamas,* were translated latest, while some of the later Mahāyāna works were translated first.

Buddhist ideas and practices developed in China in unpredictable spurts and starts, dependent on a wide variety of factors including individual interests, personalities, and historical accident. The disorderly fashion in which Buddhism spread to China led to much misunderstanding and confusion, but by the same token also inspired innovation as individuals sorted through elements of Buddhism available to them, trying to make sense of what had arrived and adapting it to their own needs.

In part because of the random element in this process, Buddhism sparked changes in China that were only tangentially related to the religion itself, or at least what we normally think of as "the religion itself." Translation of Buddhist scriptures forced Chinese scholars to confront the peculiarities of their own language and develop new ways of analyzing it.[1] Buddhist writings introduced new forms of literature that were later

---

[1] For the impact of Buddhism on Chinese language and linguistics, see Zhu Qingzhi, *Fodian yu zhonggu Hanyu cihui yanjiu,* Liu Jing, "Fanqie yuan yu fojiaoshuo bianxi," pp. 122–7, and Edwin G. Pulleyblank, "Traditional Chinese Phonology," pp. 101–38.

exploited by Chinese writers to express purely secular concerns. The modern Chinese language is filled with commonly used words and proverbs originally coined to represent Buddhist concepts, though the original Buddhist provenance of the bulk of these terms is now known only to philologists.[2] In addition to bringing back scriptures and accounts of monastic life and Buddhist ritual, Buddhist monks from foreign lands and Chinese pilgrims returning from abroad brought Chinese rulers important information about political boundaries, geography, and military affairs. Buddhist liturgy had a profound impact on Chinese music and dance.[3] Such developments—however far removed from Buddhist beliefs, practices, writings, and figures—are all integral parts of the history of Buddhism in China. Hence, if we are to come close to understanding the history of Chinese Buddhism in all of its complexity, we should be willing to follow developments in China sparked by the introduction of Buddhism even when they eventually lead far away from Buddhist ideas and practices; when investigating the history of Buddhism, we should in some way take account of the role of serendipity.

In the realm of material culture, this means that we must on occasion turn our attention from objects the Buddhist tradition specifically venerated as sacred, objects invested by Buddhists with symbolic meaning, or objects championed by Buddhist scriptures as sources of merit, to objects of a less imposing, less *Buddhist,* nature, that nonetheless played influential roles in the development of Chinese culture. Below I focus on three case studies of objects less consciously associated with Buddhism that had important consequences for Chinese material culture. The first is the introduction to China of the chair, an innovation in daily life that contributed to a complex network of adjustments, from the way people sat to the way they built their houses. The second example is of the transfer of a substance, sugar, used in cuisine and medicine, and the technology used to manufacture it. The third example is of the role Buddhism played in the rise of tea, a beverage indigenous to China but spread throughout Chinese society in part through the efforts of monks.

One of the themes tying all three of these case studies together is the role monks played in the propagation of new objects. As we will see, the monastic community served as a conduit along which knowledge of how to manufacture and use these things spread. Monks traveled freely between China and regions abroad, bringing with them ideas, customs, and objects that they had grown up with or adopted somewhere in their travels. Even the voluminous and meticulous compilations of monastic regu-

[2] Chinese proverbs that originated in Buddhist texts are conveniently collected in Zhu Duanwen, *Chengyu yu fojiao.*

[3] For a survey of the impact of Buddhism on Chinese music, see Tian Qing, "Fojiao yinyue de Hua hua," pp. 1–20; for Buddhism and Chinese dance, see Wang Kefen et al., *Fojiao yu Zhongguo wudao.*

lations could not possibly regulate every aspect of a monk's life, leaving room for any number of incidental practices and habits that, while not contradicting Buddhist principles, had little relation to them. The sangha in China was ethnically quite diverse, including monks from India, Ceylon, kingdoms in Central Asia, Japan, and what is today Korea and Vietnam. Just as importantly, monks from various parts of China moved throughout China itself, providing the opportunity for cultural mixes of north, south, east, and west that were unheard of among other social groups in premodern China.

Because the things I discuss in this chapter were not closely associated with Buddhism in the eyes of later scholars, and because they were not specifically championed in Buddhist scriptures, recovering their histories is, for the Buddhologist, more complicated than it is for objects discussed in preceding chapters. Yet, all have attracted scholarly attention, as historians in various fields have attempted to trace the origins and development of Chinese furniture and of eating and drinking habits. In every case, scholars have pointed to a number of elements that contributed to the propagation of the objects; to attribute the success of the chair, sugar, or tea to a single factor—whether it be Buddhism, transportation systems, or geographical constraints—would be a mistake. Nonetheless, the following pages endeavor to convince the reader that Buddhist monks played pivotal roles in all three cases.

The chair, sugar, and tea have all come to take prominent positions in Chinese material culture, and we would be hard-pressed to find a single modern Chinese who does not come into regular contact with all three. In addition to their importance in their own right, the histories of these three things are also important for what they tell us about patterns of change in material culture; for in the course of their development, tea, sugar, and the chair followed different models that can be used to understand the development of other objects, as well as the role of religion in their histories.

THE CHAIR

The Shift in Posture

In the middle of the twelfth century, the prominent thinker Zhu Xi composed a curious essay titled "Kneeling, Sitting, and Bowing," written in response to a friend who asked him for advice on how to construct a Confucian shrine according to proper ritual standards.[4] At first Zhu recommended that if his friend truly wanted to follow classical tradition, he

---

[4] "Gui, zuo, bai shuo," in *Huyan xiansheng Zhu Wengong wenji*, pp. 1a–2b.

should not erect images at all; for, as we saw above, ancient Chinese shrines did not contain images. But when the friend insisted on erecting statues of some sort, Zhu applied his prodigious erudition to determining the form these images should take. Attacking the problem with characteristic enthusiasm, Zhu delved into classical texts and inquired about ancient shrines that survived to his day. In his research, Zhu was impressed by the importance the ancients gave to comportment: invariably, they prescribed kneeling on a mat as the proper posture in formal settings. He at the same time heard of a Han dynasty shrine in Sichuan in which all the sages were depicted kneeling.

In the essay, Zhu describes his findings with the wonder of an archaeologist piecing together the puzzle of a lost civilization. The evidence clearly showed that the ancients did not sit on chairs, but on mats. Further, he discovered that the manner of sitting was in the past much more carefully regulated than in his day, when men and women draped themselves over chairs as they pleased. Zhu confesses that he does not know when this shift from mat to chair took place, but it was clear to him that even in an area as basic as posture, a gulf separated the men of his day from the sages of antiquity. Previous to this, in a similar essay lamenting the loss of ancient sacrificial rites, the eleventh-century figure Su Shi had also observed that the ancients sat on mats, and that ancient ritual vessels were made accordingly low to the ground. "The ancients," Su writes, "sat on mats. Therefore the length of their *bian* and *dou* [vessels], and the height of their *fu* and *gui* [vessels], were all made in accordance with the height at which people sat." Su then goes on to ridicule the shrines of his day, remarking that in these shrines, because ritual vessels were placed on the ground before images of sages on seats, the spirits would either be unable to enjoy the offerings or have to crawl down from their seats to get to them.[5]

Few seem to have heeded Su Shi's remarks, and despite Zhu's learned pleading, his friend ignored his advice and built the shrine in the manner common in his day, with images of the sages sitting on seats rather than kneeling on mats. By the twelfth century, the ancient ways of sitting had been effectively replaced by new ones. Lu You, writing at the end of the twelfth century, quoted a contemporary of his as saying that *in the past, if a woman of a well-bred family sat on a chair, she was ridiculed for her lack of manners.*[6] But by his time all this had changed. Chairs were now a common part of everyday life, used not only in shrines but in teahouses; not only in the performance of reverence to gods and ancestors but even

---

[5] "Sishi ce wen qishon," in *Dongpo wenji* 22, pp. 3b–4a.

[6] *Laoxuean biji* 4, p. 114. The "contemporary" was one Xu Dunli (aka. Xu Du). The passage is cited in Yu Yue's "Songshi yizi wuzi you wei tongxing" in his *Chaxiangshi sanchao* (BJDG edn.) 27, p. 7.

in such basic rituals as weddings and funerals.[7] By the Southern Song, the move from the mat to the chair was complete; like Su Shi before him, Zhu Xi could only lament the "errors borne of a thousand years of separation," and leave a somber essay for the edification of future generations.

As a part of their overall project to reconstruct the ancient world, Qing scholars returned to the question of how Han and pre-Han Chinese sat. In an essay on the "bed" (*chuang*), eighteenth-century scholar Huang Tingjian noted,

> The ancient bed was different from the bed of today. The ancient bed was used primarily for sitting, and only secondarily for lying upon, while today the bed is used primarily for lying upon and only secondarily for sitting. Although [ancient and contemporary beds] share the same name, the method of employing them is somewhat different. Why is this so? It is because the ancients sat and slept on the ground on mats. There were divisions in this regard between noble and commoner. . . . The bed was placed in the bedroom and not in the main room. It was provided for the sake of the old and the sick to sit or sleep on. . . . These were exceptions to custom, and not considered proper. When the ancients slept, it was considered proper to sleep on a mat on the ground.[8]

Similarly, Wang Mingsheng, a contemporary of Huang Tingjian, noted: "The ancients sat on mats spread on the ground. There can be little doubt that they considered sitting on the ground as the most respectful posture. Hence we know that in the Han, chairs were not used."[9]

The observations of these scholars are quickly confirmed by literary and pictorial evidence, which consistently depict people in ancient China sitting on mats on the ground rather than on chairs. The legacy of the ancient practice of sitting on mats has even left traces in the modern language. At the beginning of this century, when confronted with the English word *chairman*, modern Japanese translators drew on the ancient Chinese compound "*zhuxi*," literally meaning "chief mat," to translate the term. Chinese translators then borrowed the word back from the Japanese.[10] Similarly, common modern words such as *chuxi*, which we translate as "to attend" (an important event) but literally means "to come out to the mat," indicate that in ancient China, people of distinction sat on the ground on mats.[11]

---

[7] See "Guitian lu," by Ouyang Xiu, 2, p. 11 in *Ouyang Wenzhong quanji* 27, and Zhu Xi's, *Jiali* (SKQS edn.) 1, p. 2.

[8] "Kao chuang," in *Di liu xianxi wenchao* (CSJC edn.) 1, p. 1.

[9] "Ji ju," in *Shiqishi shangque* 24, p. 2a–b.

[10] Lydia H. Liu, *Translingual Practice: Literature, National Culture and Translated Modernity: China, 1900–1937*, p. 307.

[11] For more on how ancient Chinese sat on mats, see Shang Binghe, *Lidai shehui fengsu*

We have no records at all of Chinese chairs from the Han.[12] But while the chair at that time was not an option, the manner in which one sat on the ground certainly was. In general, the preferred method of sitting was to kneel, especially when wanting to express deference for one's company. When sitting with equals in more casual situations, it was acceptable for men to sit cross-legged. As in the case of clothing and speech, the manner in which one sat was an important component in the syntax of social distinction. One revealing anecdote in the third-century B.C. *Lüshi chunqiu* tells of a tiff between the Warring-States period Marquis Wen of Wei and the official Di Huang sparked by the Marquis's posture:

> When Marquis Wen of Wei went to see Duangan Mu, he stood there until he was quite tired but did not dare rest. Upon returning home, he saw Di Huang and spoke with him squatting [*ju*] in a hall. When Di Huang was displeased, Marquis Wen explained, "If Duangan Mu were offered an official position, he would be unwilling to serve in it, and if given an emolument, would refuse it. Now you desire the position of prime minister as your office, and you want the salary of a senior minister. Having accepted my material gifts, you criticize my manners; what choice have I but to rebuke you?"[13]

For the history of posture, the interesting point here is Di Huang's reaction to his reception by the marquis: it was bad enough to be received by a host who sat squatting rather than kneeling, but it was particularly galling when the same man had just shown deference to another by speaking to him standing.

Even more common than condemnations of squatting in Han and pre-Han texts are illustrations of the impropriety of sitting on one's buttocks with legs in front, which was a sign of either poor breeding or intentional contempt for one's guest.[14] This was especially important when in the

---

shiwu kao, pp. 281–91, Cui Yongxue, *Zhongguo jiajushi—zuojupian*, pp. 15–48, and Yu Yingshi (Yü Ying-shih), "Shuo Hongmenyan de zuoci" in *Shixue yu chuantong*, pp. 184–95.

[12] The evidence Louise Hawley Stone presents for the existence of chairs in the Han in her *The Chair in China* is based on rubbings and a statuette that are not reliably dated. This same statuette (in the Ontario Museum collection) is sometimes cited as evidence for the Han chair in other publications as well. Unfortunately, its origins are unknown, and at least one historian of Chinese furniture has estimated its date as much later. See Cui, *Zhongguo jiajushi*, pls. 4–10.

[13] *Lüshi chunqiu* (SBCK edn.) 15, pp. 9b–10a. The translation is from John Knoblock and Jeffrey Riegel, *The Annals of Lü Buwei: A Complete Translation and Study*, p. 351.

[14] Wang Mingsheng compared ancient proscriptions against sitting on mats with legs extended to the way in which northerners of his day—that is, the end of the eighteenth century—sat on beds. "Jiju," p. 2a. Sitting with the legs out front probably became a sign of ill manners only with the Zhou dynasty; in the Shang, sitting in this way (*jiju*) was apparently common even in ritual settings. See Li Ji, "Gui zuo dun ju yu jiju," pp. 296, 298.

presence of someone deserving respect, like a teacher. When a certain
Yuan Rang sat in the presence of Confucius with his legs before him, Confucius scolded him for his ill manners and then whacked him on the shin
with a stick.[15] It is even said in an early demonography that a sure way
to scare off ghosts is to sit with one's legs spread out.[16] Presumably, any
self-respecting ghost would find this so offensive that it would leave immediately in a huff. In short, in ancient China posture and bearing were
carefully observed for subtle expressions of attitude and intent,[17] and to
sit with one's legs extended was considered extremely impolite. These
rules of etiquette left no room for sitting on chairs even if the ancient
Chinese had had them. Hundreds of Han rubbings and figurines from
throughout China illustrate the prevalence of these notions of proper posture. Seated Han figures are almost always kneeling; we look in vain for
depiction of Han people with legs outstretched, much less sitting on
chairs.

In the Tang, however, all of this begins to change with the introduction
of stools and chairs, and the concomitant change in posture. A mural from
the tomb of the Tang figure Gao Yuangui, completed in 756, includes a
depiction of a man seated on a chair. Textual sources from the Tang also
contain several references to chairs, though use of the chair in the Tang
seems to have been limited: at this time formal affairs, and daily life at
home in general, still took place on mats.[18] By the Song, we can find numerous references to chairs in texts, examples of chairs in datable paint-

[15] *Lunyu zhushu* 14.43, p. 10b.

[16] *Yunmeng Shuihudi Qinmu*, pl. 131, strip nos. 871–2; cited in Donald Harper, "A Chinese Demonography of the Third Century B.C.," p. 483.

[17] As Jean-Claude Schmitt puts it in his study of gestures in medieval Europe, "The monk
had the gestures of the monk, the knight the gestures of the knight. Gestures employed
within communities, as well between them, rendered hierarchies concrete, and brought order
to conflicts over precedence and proximity." This description of medieval Europe could just
as easily apply to medieval China. See *La raison des gestes dans l'Occident médiéval*, p. 19.
For studies of sitting in the Shang, see Li Ji, "Gui zuo dun ju yu jiju," pp. 254–5, and Liu
Huan, "Buci baili shixi" in his *Yin qi xin shi*, pp. 1–51. For posture in the medieval period,
see Zhu Dawei, "Zhonggu Hanren you guizuo dao chuijiao gaozuo," pp. 102–14. Yu Yunhua's, *Gongshou, jugong, guibai: Zhongguo chuantong jiaoji liyi*, may also be consulted.

[18] For the mural image, see He Zicheng, "Tangdai bihua," pp. 31–3. Dai Fu's *Guangyi
ji* contains several references to chairs. See the stories of Chou Jiafu and Li Canjun in *Mingbao ji, Guangyi ji*, Fang Shiming, ed., pp. 58, 201. Chairs appear in the painting *Female Attendants with Fans*, traditionally attributed to the Tang painter Zhou Fang, but this may in
fact be a Song painting. Similarly, the *Six Patriarchs* painting attributed to Lu Lengjia, the
Palace Painting and *Figures in the Lapis Lazuli Hall* attributed to the Tang painter Zhou
Wenju, the *Figure Studying* attributed to the Five Dynasties painter Wang Qihan, and *Han
Xizai's Evening Revelry* attributed to the Five Dynasties painter Gu Hongzhong, though all
containing depictions of chairs, may in fact all be Song paintings. See James Cahill, *An Index
of Early Chinese Painters and Paintings: T'ang, Sung, and Yüan*, pp. 16, 28–30, 50.

ings, and, for the first time, actual chairs unearthed by modern archaeologists.[19] In sum, while the information available to us does not allow for a precise charting of the rise of the chair, scholars from the Song to the present have generally held that sometime between the high Tang and the Northern Song—that is, between the eighth and the eleventh centuries—the chair became a common piece of furniture in the households of the well-to-do.[20]

So now the Chinese sat on chairs. Let us pause for a moment to consider what had happened here. The appearance of the chair on the domestic scene demanded a number of changes in the Chinese household. Household objects are intimately connected. When mats are used as the chief sitting implement, other pieces of furniture must also be low to the ground; conversely, once people began to sit on chairs, other furniture had to rise as well. Wang Mingsheng remarked, for example, that the ancients used small, low tables and had nothing approaching the large, high tables able to seat eight men common in his day.[21] The practice of sitting at table to eat brought with it a number of changes in tableware, not the least of which was that hosts now asked diners to take from common serving dishes, as in modern China, instead of providing each diner with individual servings, as was the practice in ancient times. The size and shape of tableware changed accordingly. Recall Su Shi's comments about ritual vessels: "The ancients sat on mats. Therefore the length of their *bian* and *dou* [vessels], and the height of their *fu* and *gui* [vessels], were all made in accordance with the height at which people sat." Extant Tang bowls and serving dishes point to the recognition that when dining on a mat, tall, larger eating implements are more convenient. In the Song, when eating utensils were placed up on the table, the spatial relationship between one's body and the food before one changed, and for this reason smaller, more delicate bowls, plates, and cups soon became the fashion.[22] After the chair came into use, the position of windows, screens, and ceiling heights all underwent dramatic changes, as did clothing, gestures, and the ways in which people interacted and perceived each other indoors.[23]

Entire industries withered and died with the rise of the chair, while other

[19] For a list of relevant archaeological reports, see Craig Clunas, *Chinese Furniture*, pp. 107–8, n. 21.

[20] This is the position taken, for instance, by Wang Mingsheng, "Jiju," p. 3, Huang Zhengjian, "Tangdai de yizi yu shengchuang," pp. 86–8, and Clunas, *Chinese Furniture*, p. 16, among many.

[21] "Jiju," p. 3b.

[22] See Chen Weiming, *Tang Song yinshi wenhua chutan*, pp. 63–4.

[23] See Sarah Handler, "The Revolution in Chinese Furniture: Moving from Mat to Chair," pp. 9–33. Wu Tung went so far as to suggest that a centralized authoritarian ancient state could not permit the freedom and individualism inherent in the use of the chair. Wu Tung, "From Imported 'Nomadic Seat' to Chinese Folding Armchair," pp. 38–47.

enterprises rose up with it. All of this prompted Donald Holzman to label the introduction of the chair into the Chinese household a domestic revolution of a magnitude even greater than the mechanization of the household in our own century.[24] Numerous paintings testify to the fact that from the Song the chair had become an integral part of the leisured gentleman's life. Even emperors now posed for portraits in chairs. Nor was the chair restricted to the lavish homes of the rich. In the twelfth-century painting *Qingming shanghe tu,* we see that even small shop owners waited on their patrons in chairs, while restaurants now provided their customers with benches. The magnitude of the changes brought about by the chair makes the mystery of its origins all the more intriguing. How had all of this come about?

Four Theories for the Origin of the Chinese Chair

THE INDIGENOUS DEVELOPMENT THEORY

Although people of the Han Dynasty sat on mats, they nonetheless made use of a number of types of furniture. By the end of the Eastern Han, screens, low tables, armrests, and beds were common fixtures in the homes of the upper class.[25] Hence, Han craftsmen undoubtedly possessed the technological capabilities necessary to manufacture chairs, which are not, after all, particularly complicated devices. For this reason, some scholars have suggested that the chair developed independently in China, without the stimulus of foreign influence.

With the exception of the mat, the most important sitting implement in Han Dynasty China was the *ta,* a low, raised platform used by the wealthy and powerful who are depicted in Han and Six Dynasties murals as kneeling on them.[26] Han texts and archaeological evidence reveal that a type of *ta* only large enough to seat one person was quite common during this

---

[24] Donald Holzman, "A propos de l'origine de la chaise en Chine," pp. 279–92. Holzman's article is a review of C. P. FitzGerald's *Barbarian Beds: The Origin of the Chair in China,* which, despite the failings pointed out by Holzman, contains an interesting discussion of the implications to Chinese culture of the introduction of the chair. In his brief review, Holzman mentions almost all the important sources for the history of the Chinese chair, and sketches out the argument that I present in more detail here. I am indebted to this article for much of the material I cite here. Cui Yongxue's *Zhongguo jiajushi* provides the most complete treatment of the historical development of the Chinese chair to date.

[25] For an overview with illustrations, see Sun Ji, *Handai wuzhi wenhua ziliao tushuo,* pp. 216–28.

[26] The stool was not common at this time. During the Six Dynasties period, a kind of stool known as the *quanti* was introduced to China from abroad and in subsequent centuries gradually became a common type of furniture. Buddhism may have played a role in the introduction of at least this type of stool to China. See Sun Ji, *Zhongguo shenghuo,* pp. 198–250.

period.[27] Some were even small enough to be hung on the wall when not in use.[28] It would seem reasonable to assume, then, that such a piece of furniture, with the addition of a back and arms, could easily evolve into a chair, with "chair" defined as a raised sitting implement with a back used to seat a single individual. Qing scholar Zhao Yi proposed just such a solution to the puzzle, outlining the birth of the Chinese chair as follows:

> At that time [that is, the medieval period] when people sat on beds and plat-forms, they did not allow their legs to hang down in front. In the Tang, the wooden platform was adapted by running cords across it. This was called the "corded-chair." ... It was not yet called the *yizi* [the modern word for chair]; the compound *yizi* appeared only in the Song.[29]

Zhao was wrong about a number of details. The word *yizi* appeared already in the Tang,[30] and, more importantly, the corded-chair—about which I will have more to say later—did not derive directly from the platform. Nonetheless, an indigenous origin for the Chinese chair is not out of the question and is probably impossible to disprove.[31] But because of the absence of evidence pointing to a direct line of descent from the platform to the chair, most scholars of Chinese furniture do not hold that the chair was a natural, indigenous outgrowth of the *ta*. Many hold instead to a second theory according to which the impetus for the chair was introduced from outside China in the form of a piece of furniture known as the *huchuang*, or "barbarian stool."[32]

THE HUCHUANG THEORY

Although no medieval *huchuang* has been excavated to date, literary evidence, coupled with a stele dated to 543, a figurine from 547, and a relief on a stone Tang coffin, reveal that the *huchuang* was a foldable stool with a soft seat.[33] The foldable stool has a very respectable pedigree,

[27] See Chen Zengbi, "Han, Wei, Jin duzuoshi xiaota chu lun," pp. 66–71.

[28] See, for example, the anecdote at *Hou Hanshu*, 53, p. 1746.

[29] "Gaozuo yuanqi," by Zhao Yi, in *Gaiyu congkao* 31, pp. 661–2.

[30] The character *yizi*[1], originally written as *yizi*[2], first appears in an inscription completed in 797, the *Jidumiao beihaitan jiqi bei* included in *Jinshi cuipian* 103, p. 42a.

[31] FitzGerald makes this argument, while also permitting for the possibility of foreign influence, in *Barbarian Beds*, pp. 45–9.

[32] Wu Meifeng has drawn attention to another possibility of indigenous influence if not an indigenous source for the Chinese chair by pointing out similarities between early Chinese chairs and the carriages of even earlier Chinese chariots. See her "Song Ming shiqi jiaju xingzhi zhi yanjiu," p. 197. Wu makes the same argument in her more accessible "Zuoyi shengchuang xian zinian—cong Mingshi jiaju kan zuoju zhi yanbian," pp. 59–69.

[33] The earliest and still perhaps best overall study of the *huchuang* is Fujita Toyohachi's "Koshō ni tsuite," pp. 143–85. See also Cui, *Zhongguo jiajushi*, pp. 80–8. Wu Tung's, "From Imported 'Nomadic Seat' to Chinese Folding Armchair," and Yang Hong, "Huchuang," pp. 254–62 (originally published under the pseudonym Yishui in *Wenwu* [1982.10],

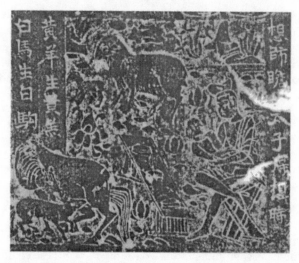

FIG. 13. *Huchuang* in rubbing from stele dated to 534. Photography courtesy of the Fu Ssu-nien Library, Institute of History and Philology, Academia Sinica.

going back to ancient Egypt, where it was a symbol of authority from at least as early as 1500 B.C.[34] The path by which the *huchuang* made its way to China is obscure, but it is likely that it passed from Northern Africa, across Central Asia, and down to China. One of our earliest references to the *huchuang* appears in the *Hou Hanshu*, which states that the Han emperor "Lingdi was fond of foreign clothing, foreign tents, *foreign stools* (*huchuang*), the foreign manner of sitting, foreign foods, the foreign lyre, the foreign flute, and foreign dance. Aristocrats of the capital all indulged in these things."[35] If this passage is accurate, then we know that during Lingdi's reign at the end of the second century, the *huchuang* had already arrived in China and appeared in court settings.[36]

pp. 82–5), discuss archaeological finds. FitzGerald's *Barbarian Beds* is the most comprehensive study of the *huchuang*, but should be read together with Holzman's review, "A propos de l'origine de la chaise en Chine." For reproductions of the 543 stele, see Édouard Chavannes, *Mission archéologique dans la Chine septentrionale*, vol. 2, pt. 1, pl. CCLXXXIV, no. 432, and vol. 1, pt. 2, pp. 589–90; or Nagahiro Toyū, *Rikuchō jidai bijutsu no kenkyū*, pp. 69–92. For the figurine dated to 547, see Cixian Wenhuaguan, "Hebei Cixian Dongchencun Dongweimu," pl. 9. For the coffin, found in the tomb of Li Shou, see Shaanxisheng Bowuguan, "Tang Li Shou mu fajue jianbao" and "Tang Li Shou mu bihua shitan," pp. 71–94, and Sun Ji, *Zhongguo shenghuo*, pp. 198–250.

[34] Ole Wanscher, *Sella Curulis: The Folding Stool, an Ancient Symbol of Dignity*, p. 9. On the following page, Wanscher suggests that the folding stool may have been in use in the ancient Near East a thousand years previous.

[35] *Hou Hanshu* 13, p. 3272.

[36] The *Hou Hanshu* was completed after the Han, but support for the early date of the

Subsequent literary references in a wide variety of sources testify that use of the *huchuang* was not limited to court circles. In addition to emperors and officials, military commanders, teachers, and even peasant women employed the stool. The *huchuang* appeared inside the home, outside the home, in the palace, and on the battlefield.[37]

The *huchuang* played an important role in the shift in posture from kneeling to sitting with the legs hanging down, since it is difficult to kneel on a camp stool. As the legs of the stool would tear a mat beneath them, the *huchuang* may have led to changes in floor covering and consequently footwear as well. Thus the *huchuang* seems a prime candidate for ancestor of the Chinese chair—it was simply a matter of adding a back and replacing the pliant seat with a wooden one. Nonetheless, most scholars, including the Song figures Zhang Duanyi and Cheng Dachang as well as the Ming writer Wang Qi, have taken a more circumspect stance, ascribing the origin of the *jiaoyi*, or "folding chair," to the *huchuang* but remaining silent on the ancestry of the fixed-frame chair.[38]

Thirteenth-century historian Hu Sanxing was perhaps the first to challenge the *huchuang* theory, insisting that the Chinese chair developed independently of the foldable stool. Commenting on a passage in the *Zizhi tongjian*, which states that Tang Emperor Muzong sat on a large "corded-chair" (*shengchuang*) when meeting with his ministers, Hu notes,

> Cheng Dachang, in his *Yanfan lu*, states:
>> The folding-chair of today is of foreign origin. At first it was called a *huchuang*, but Sui [Wendi], displeased by the use of the word *hu* ("barbarian"), changed the name to "folding stool." Muzong of the Tang sat in the Zicheng Hall on a large corded-chair when meeting his ministers. Here we see that the *huchuang* was also called a corded-chair.[39]
>
> At this point I wish to note that today people make use of the folding chair and the corded-chair, and that these are two distinct implements. The folding chair is made with crossing pieces of wood as legs. Pieces of wood are attached horizontally to the front and back legs. . . . [I]t can be folded up and carried, or set down and sat upon. The corded-chair, [on the other hand], is made with a plank for the seat. When sat upon, it is wide enough that one can sit upon it with legs crossed. In addition to a back, it has rests where one may place one's arms. Its four legs rest on the ground.[40]

---

passage can be found in the Song compilation *Taiping yulan*, which quotes the same passage from the Han *Fengsu tongyi*. *Taiping yulan*, "Huchuang" (SBCK edn.) 706, p. 8.

[37] For sources, see Zhu, "Zhonggu Hanren you guizuo dao chuijiao gaozuo," p. 106.

[38] *Guier ji* 3, p. 64; "Huchuang," in *Yanfan luzheng* 10, pp. 3–4; and *Sancai tuhui* 12, p. 14.

[39] Cheng's comments can be found in *Yanfan luzheng* 15, p. 12a.

[40] *Zizhi tongjian* 242, p. 7822.

Thus for Hu, despite its name—literally meaning "corded-chair"—the *shengchuang* was a fixed-frame chair with a plank for a seat, a back, and armrests. I think that Hu was right and will present evidence below that supports his description of the chair.[41] Nonetheless, even if it is possible to show that the *shengchuang* was a fixed-frame chair, and even if we can demonstrate that the ancestor of the modern Chinese chair is the *shengchuang* and not the *huchuang,* the fundamental question of the chair's origins remains: if the *shengchuang* is the ancestor of the modern Chinese chair, where did the *shengchuang* come from? Did it come from abroad like the *huchuang,* and if so, where specifically did it come from? In an attempt to resolve this problem, C. P. FitzGerald placed the Chinese chair in the context of the world history of the chair, to which we now turn.

THE NESTORIAN HYPOTHESIS

As in the case of the folding chair, most of our earliest examples of fixed-frame chairs come from ancient Egypt, where chair design reached great heights of elegance and sophistication. From Egypt the chair spread to Greece, and from Greece to Rome. Of course, at different times and in different places, modifications were made both to the structure of the chair and to the uses to which it was put. Roman citizens, for instance, did not sit on chairs at table when eating. They ate, instead, reclining on couches; only women and slaves sat on chairs when dining.[42] With the expansion of the Roman empire, the chair became firmly established in Constantinople, where it appears frequently in Byzantine art.

To make the connection between the chairs of Constantinople and China, FitzGerald turned to Nestorianism, the most frequently cited link between the Byzantine empire and its Chinese counterpart. Nestorianism emerged in Constantinople in the fifth century. In 635, a group of Nestorian missionaries arrived in the Tang capital of Chang'an, where they began the work of translating scriptures and proselytizing. A few years later, they were permitted to establish a monastery, staffed by twenty-one foreign missionaries. Over the next hundred years, the religion prospered. A stele from 781 states, with what is likely a degree of hyperbole, that Nestorianism "has spread throughout the empire . . . with monasteries in all of our cities." A hundred years after this, in 845, as a part of his anti-Buddhist campaign, Tang Emperor Wuzong ordered the expulsion of more than two thousand Nestorian missionaries, bringing to a close this curious chapter in the history of medieval cultural exchange.[43] In other

[41] On this point, see also Cui, *Zhongguo jiajushi,* p. 88.

[42] Schmitt, *La raison des gestes,* p. 68.

[43] See Zhu Qianzhi, *Zhongguo jingjiao,* and Paul Pelliot, *L'inscription nestorienne de Si-Ngan-Fou.*

words, the period of the most intense Nestorian activity in China roughly corresponds to the period that saw the rise of the Chinese chair. FitzGerald saw a clear connection between these two developments, arguing that the rise of the chair in China can be traced back to Egypt via Byzantium, Rome, and Greece, with Nestorian missionaries playing a key role in the final leg of the chair's journey from Constantinople to Chang'an.[44]

On closer inspection, the Nestorian hypothesis is as unconvincing as it is delightful.[45] As we will see below, there is evidence that the chair had already appeared in China well before the seventh century. In addition, there is no evidence, textual or otherwise, directly linking Nestorian missionaries with the introduction of the chair. More fundamentally, the problem with the Nestorian hypothesis is that it treats the origins of the Chinese chair as a technological rather than a cultural problem: as soon as a handful of foreign craftsmen introduced the techniques necessary for making a chair, the Chinese quickly adopted its use. But as we have seen, from very early on, Chinese craftsmen possessed the skills necessary for making chairs. As the Song thinker Zhang Zai put it, "That the ancients did not employ chairs and tables is not because they were lacking in intelligence; how could the sages [of antiquity] be our inferiors? It was instead because they expressed reverence by sitting on mats, which allowed for bowing and kneeling."[46] In other words, the shift to the chair required a dramatic shift in etiquette, rather than a technological improvement promising obvious and compelling advantages. In search of a cultural force with the power to bring about such a change, at once fundamental and unnecessary, some scholars have looked instead to Buddhism.

MAITREYA'S CHAIR

From the fifth century, two hundred years before our first representations of ordinary Chinese sitting in chairs, we have a large number of sculptures of seated buddhas, both at major cave sites such as Longmen, Yungang, and Dunhuang, and in smaller, portable, freestanding pieces. Whereas Śākyamuni Buddha is usually depicted seated on the ground in the lotus posture, the buddha Maitreya is almost always depicted sitting in the "western posture," with legs in front. Maitreya's posture varies somewhat, from both feet touching the ground, to the right leg crossed over the left, or the left crossed over the right, or at times with ankles crossed.[47]

---

[44] FitzGerald, *Barbarian Beds*, pp. 33–50.

[45] For a critique of FitzGerald's hypothesis, see Holzman, "A propos de l'origine de la chaise en Chine."

[46] *Zhang Zai ji*, p. 265

[47] One common type of seated image is known as the "Pensive Bodhisattva" (Siwei). Determining the identity of these images is complex, and while they are often ascribed to Maitreya, many are clearly not Maitreya. Junghee Lee even goes so far as to suggest that

The reason why Maitreya was depicted in this manner remains obscure and may be tied up with his equally obscure origins. At the beginning of this century, there was some debate over Maitreya's origins, with scholars arguing respectively for Zoroastrian influence, a connection with Mithraism, or an indigenous Indian origin of the deity. More recent scholarship shows little hope for resolving the question of Maitreya's birthplace.[48] Zhou Shaoliang has provided at least a working hypothesis for explaining the motivation behind representing Maitreya in a number of different postures. Zhou argues that the positions of Maitreya's legs were assigned apotropaic, or talismanic functions. That is, certain postures were believed to be effective in fending off evil spirits, while others attracted good fortune. The prevalence of a similar notion in Chinese meditation manuals lends credence to the theory.[49] At the same time, aesthetic considerations probably played a major role in determining Maitreya's posture in different settings.

Considering the prevalence of the image, it would seem reasonable to argue that the first to sit in a Chinese chair was not a noble sitting on a modified platform, a general sitting on a reinforced camp stool, or a Nestorian sitting on an imported Byzantine chair; the first promoter of the chair was instead the buddha Maitreya. But if we look more closely, we see that in the hundreds of images of Maitreya spread throughout China, few can be said with certainty to be sitting on chairs with legs and backs rather than on pedestals or stools. When the image is in a niche in a cave, we cannot of course see behind the buddha to view the back of the chair. But for smaller, freestanding images, we can see behind, and when we do, we see that what appeared from the front to be a solid high-backed chair is in fact not a chair with a back at all, but a pedestal and a halo.

This leads to the question of whether the figures in other sculptures were meant to be sitting on chairs at all. While I have not been able to identify with certainty any early images of buddhas or bodhisattvas sit-

none of these images was intended to represent Maitreya. Nonetheless, for the sake of concision, I here group all these images under the heading of Maitreya. For an overview of the pensive bodhisattva images, see Junghee Lee, "The Origins and Development of the Pensive Bodhisattva Images of Asia," pp. 311–53. Indian art presents a similar problem; for although scholars tend to identify buddhas seated in the "European style" (with legs hanging down) as Maitreya, some of these figures are Śākyamuni rather than Maitreya. See M. G. Bourda, "Quelques réflexions sur la pose assise à l'européenne dans l'art bouddhique," pp. 302–13.

[48] See Jan Nattier, "The Meanings of the Maitreya Myth: A Typological Analysis," pp. 34–6, and Padmanabh S. Jaini, "Stages in the Bodhisattva Career of the Tathāgata Maitreya," p. 54 of the same volume.

[49] For Zhou Shaoliang's article, see "Mile xinyang zai fojiao chu ru Zhongguo de jieduan he qi zaoxiang yiyi," pp. 35–9. For the apotropaic function of posture in meditation manuals, see Carl Bielefeldt, Dōgen's Manuals of Zen Meditation, p. 112, n. 5.

FIG. 14. Front and rear views of seated "meditating bodhisattva," Northern
Wei. Photograph courtesy of Yoshikawa Kobunkan Publishing House.

ting in chairs, buddhas in several sculptures from the eighth century
clearly are.[50] An image that was originally part of the "Tower of Seven
Jewels" (*Qibaotai*), completed in 704, is particularly important. The
Tower of Seven Jewels was commissioned by Empress Wu and displayed
in the capital at Chang'an; it is reasonable to conjecture that an image of
such prominence may have had an impact on the history of Chinese furniture.[51] And the case can be made that at least two earlier representations of seated bodhisattvas may include representations of chairs.[52] At
this point, however, the argument that the chair entered China with Bud-

[50] See the statue from 745 now in the Shanxi Provincial Museum, reproduced in Matsubara Saburō, *Chūgoku bukkyō chōkoku shiron*, vol. 3, p. 723.

[51] For a reconstruction and discussion of the significance of the sculpture, see Yen Chüan-
ying, "The Sculpture from the Tower of Seven Jewels: The Style, Patronage, and Iconography of the Monument."

[52] At Huijian Cave at Longmen, completed in 673, Maitreya may be sitting on a chair
with a back, though it is difficult to determine if the markings behind the bodhisattva are
meant to represent a chair back or merely ornamentation. Cui Yongxue suggests that a
Northern Wei image of a bodhisattva at Cave 254 at Dunhuang is sitting on a chair. *Zhongguo jiajushi*, pl. 4129.

dhist art begins to look strained, for we would have to accept the assumption that a small number of representations of Buddhist figures was sufficient to inspire an empire to change its way of sitting. Fortunately, Buddhist texts and images from both India and China provide us with enough material to propose a more convincing scenario that takes into account not only representations of buddhas and bodhisattvas but also evidence for how ordinary people actually used the chair.

Chairs in Ancient India

Second-century B.C. reliefs at Sañcī and Bharhut reveal that chairs were used in India long before they appeared in China.[53] On the northern gateway of stupa number 1 at Sañcī we can clearly see a man sitting on a fixed-frame chair with back and what appears to be a footstool. The manner and dress of the seated figure suggests that he is probably a person of some note, and at least one scholar has suggested that this may be a depiction of the great Buddhist king Aśoka.[54] In the South Wing of the Bharhut relief we find another figure in a chair. Based on the inscription, the scene has been identified as representing the story of the Buddha in a previous incarnation, before he became Śākyamuni. In this life he was a great king named Maghādeva. One day, when his barber came to cut his hair, the king discovered his first gray hair. At that moment he realized the inevitability of his own demise and the continuing cycle of life and death that would follow it. And so he determined to abandon his kingdom and become a monk.[55]

When the Chinese pilgrim Xuanzang traveled to India in the early seventh century, he noted the continued use of chairs among high-ranking officials and rulers:

> When they sit or rest, they all use corded-chairs (*shengchuang*); the royal family, great personages, officers and local elites use chairs which, though variously ornamented, are of the same size. The throne of the reigning sovereign is high and wide, and much adorned with precious gems: it is called the Lion-throne. It is covered with extremely fine drapery; the footstool is adorned with gems. Officials employ beautifully painted and decorated seats, according to their tastes.[56]

The reliefs at Bharhut and Sañcī, as well as Xuanzang's comments, point to the importance of the chair as a symbol of authority for rulers, an as-

---

[53] See Asha Vishnu, *Material Life of Northern India (3rd century B.C. to 1st Century B.C.)*, pp. 30–2, and Jeannine Auboyer, *Le trône et son symbolisme dans l'Inde ancienne.*

[54] See Itō Shōji, ed., *Genshi bukkyō bijutsu toten*, p. 227.

[55] Ibid., pl. 236.

[56] *Da Tang Xiyu ji* 2, p. 876b. The passage is translated somewhat differently in Beal, *Si-yu-ki: Buddhist Records of the Western World*, p. 75.

FIG. 15. Chair at Sañcī. Photograph by John C. Huntington, compliments of the Huntington Archive.

sociation that is virtually universal in the early history of the chair.[57] Nonetheless, use of the chair was not limited to the wealthy and the powerful; Buddhist texts reveal that chairs were common as well in Indian monasteries. But before turning to the use of chairs in Indian monasteries, a brief excursion into nomenclature is necessary.[58]

In Xuanzang's description we encounter again the compound "*shengchuang*," or "corded-chair," that, as we have seen, crops up later in the thirteenth-century scholar Hu Sanxing's typology of chairs in which Hu states that the *shengchuang* is a fixed-frame chair with a back and armrests. Some modern scholars have argued against Hu, suggesting that the *shengchuang* was simply another name for the *huchuang*, or foldable stool—a usage that by Hu's time had been forgotten.[59] While Chinese fur-

[57] Bourda emphasizes the importance of royal associations with the chair (throne) in Indian depictions of Śākyamuni. "Quelque réflexions sur la pose asise," pp. 307–13. Auboyer discusses the symbolism of the Indian throne at length. After pointing out the associations of the throne with authority, she goes on (drawing on Mus and Przyluski) to argue that the symbolism of the throne derived from sacred stones of a primordial, primitive religion. *Le trône et son symbolisme dans l'Inde ancienne.*

[58] For Indian terms for various types of seats, see Auboyer, ibid.

[59] Fujita, "Koshō ni tsuite," pp. 183–5, and Zhu Dawei, "Zhonggu Hanren you guizuo dao chuijiao gaozuo," p. 106.

niture nomenclature was far from uniform during this transitional period, Buddhist literature supports Hu's interpretation: the term *shengchuang* was generally used to denote a fixed-frame chair and not the foldable stool. In Buddhist texts, monks are sometimes described as sitting on the *shengchuang* cross-legged. The *Zunshang jing,* a Buddhist scripture translated into Chinese in the third century, speaks, for example, of a holy man who "arose one morning, left his cave and placed a *shengchuang* in an open place. Placing a *nīṣīdana* [a carpet] on the *shengchuang,* he sat cross-legged upon it."[60] Similarly, the *Sarvāstivādavinaya,* translated into Chinese at the beginning of the fifth century, relates the story of a monk who meditated cross-legged on a *shengchuang.*[61] It is uncomfortable, if not impossible, to sit cross-legged on a folding stool that, as far as I can tell, was never used by monks for meditation. In a discussion of the use of the corded-chair for meditation, the sixth-century exegete Zhiyi warns the meditator not to "let his ribs touch the chair," and a seventh-century Chinese monk is described as "leaning against the back of his corded-chair," all of which indicates that the *shengchuang* had a back and probably sides.[62] These descriptions jibe well with one of the earliest representations of a monk sitting in a chair: the image in Dunhuang Cave 285, completed in approximately 539, in which we see a monk meditating on a wide chair with a simple, single-pole back and what appears to be a woven seat (figure 16). A similar figure appears in a rubbing from a small votive statue completed in 542.[63] In this image, again we see a monk meditating on a low, wide chair with simple back and sides. The seventh-century Chinese pilgrim to India Yijing left us a brief description of one type of chair used in Indian monasteries in his day, stating that the seat of the chair was made of rattan (*tengsheng*), thus suggesting an explanation for why this type of chair was called a corded-chair (*shengchuang*).[64]

In addition to the corded-chair, Buddhist texts contain numerous references to wooden chairs (*muchuang*), which appear to have been used for more mundane purposes than the corded meditation chairs. The monastic regulations in particular provide hundreds of references to the chair, many of which suggest its prevalence. The *Dharmaguptakavinaya,*

[60] *Foshuo zunshang jing, T* no. 77, vol. 1, p. 886c.

[61] *Shi song lü* (Skt. **Sarvāstivādavinaya*) 39, p. 280b.

[62] *Mohe zhiguan* 2, p. 11b, translated in Neal Donner and Daniel B. Stevenson, *The Great Calming and Contemplation: A Study and Annotated Translation of the First Chapter of Chih-i's Mohe chih-kuan,* p. 222; and *Xu gaoseng zhuan* 20, p. 593a.

[63] A rubbing of the stele is reproduced in *Beijing Tushuguan cang Zhongguo lidai shike taben huibian,* vol. 6, p. 89. Another rubbing of the stele is included in the collection of the Fu Ssu-nien Library, Institute of History and Philology, Academia Sinica.

[64] *Nanhai jigui neifa zhuan* 1, p. 306c; Takakusu, *A Record of the Buddhist Religion,* p. 22. A Chinese stele from 563 includes images of monks meditating on chairs that appear to have flexible seats. "Li Wanhe Li Wenxing deng zao beixiang ji" in the collection of the Fu Ssu-nien Library, Institute of History & Philology, Academia Sinica.

FIG. 16. Dunhuang, Cave 285. Photography courtesy of the Dunhuang
Research Academy.

for example, contains several passages describing how a host monk
should introduce a visiting monk to the monastery. "When a visiting
bhiksu arrives and sees the room of a resident bhiksu, the resident bhiksu
should set out sitting implements like the corded-chair and the wooden
chair, sleeping implements like the mat and quilt, and a basin for wash-
ing the feet."[65] The bulk of references to chairs in the vinaya are to pro-

---

[65] *Sifen lü* (Skt. **Dharmaguptakavinaya*) 36, p. 828b. Similar passages occur at 3, 587b;
38, 842a; and 49, 931c.

scriptions on their construction and use: chairs must be neither too high, nor too low;[66] monks must not use animal skins to cover the seats of their chairs;[67] one should not stand on a chair;[68] silk floss should not be used in the chair cushion, and so forth.[69]

As we have seen, monks used the corded-chair for meditation. According to one account, the Buddha instituted a standard height for such chairs when a monk, meditating on a low corded-chair, fell asleep and was killed by a poisonous snake.[70] This suggests that one of the reasons chairs were used for meditation was to avoid the distraction, not to mention danger, of spiders, snakes, and insects.[71]

In sum, pictorial and textual evidence indicates that the chair was common in ancient India and, in particular, was prevalent in Buddhist monasteries. Further, the painting in Dunhuang Cave 285 indicates that, following the spread of Buddhism, the corded-chair had made its way to Central Asia by at least the sixth century. Other Dunhuang paintings demonstrate monastic use of various other types of chairs in the area in subsequent times.[72]

Monastic Furniture in China

We can to a certain extent trace the progress of the chair from Indian to Chinese monasteries. Already at the beginning of the fourth century, references to the corded-chair begin to appear in Chinese translations of Indian texts.[73] Writing in the seventh century, the prominent monastic historian Daoxuan described the history of the Chinese chair, stating that, during the recitation of the precepts,

[66] There are dozens of such references in the vinayas. See, for instance, *Mishasai wufen jieben*, p. 198b, *Sifen lü* 25, p. 736, and *Shi song lü* 18, p. 127c.

[67] *Sifen lü* 39, p. 846b.

[68] *Mishasaibu hexi wufen lü* (Skt. *Mahīśāsakavinaya*), p. 168a.

[69] *Sifen lü* 19, p. 693b–c; *Mishasaibu hexi* 5, 35a.

[70] *Shi song lü* 39, p. 280b.

[71] The Chinese monk Yuanzhao, writing in the Song, says that the chair was used by monks "to avoid the disturbance and filth brought by wind, dust, insects and birds." *Sifen lü xingshichao zichi ji* B3A, p. 311.

[72] Some discussions of the history of the Chinese chair mention an object discovered by Stein in Niya and tentatively dated to the first to the fourth century A.D. The object, however, is not complete and may not be a chair at all. In contrast to previous scholars who have called the object a chair, Roderick Whitfield has labeled it a "table or altar frame." Whitfield, *The Art of Central Asia: The Stein Collection in the British Museum*, vol. 3, pl. 60, p. 310. Other objects that may have been chair legs were found at the same time, but as they are not connected to backs or seats, it is difficult to determine if they were in fact chairs. For more on furniture at Dunhuang, see Yang Hong, "Dunhuang Mogaoku yu Zhongguo gudai jiajushi yanjiu zhi yi," pp. 520–33.

[73] *Foshuo zunshang jing*, p. 886b22, trans. 266–313, and *Zhong ahan jing* (Skt. *Madhyamāgama*) 41, p. 689, trans. in 398.

[i]n India some employ the corded-chair, but most sit on straw which is spread on the ground. It is for this reason that the *nisīdana* [i.e., carpet], which is rolled out on the straw, is employed. Here in China, in ancient times, seats [*chuang*] were used. People of the rank of *dafu* and above employed them, but in general, people of previous times sat on mats. After the eastern Jin [317–420], use of seats began to spread. The monasteries of today set out many types of seats. The two [seats and mats] are both used. This is the source of much inconvenience during the ordination ceremony.[74]

Daoxuan may have based the date for the spread of the chair to the *Biographies of Eminent Monks,* which comments that the fourth-century monk Fotucheng made use of a corded-chair.[75] Also in the *Biographies of Eminent Monks* is the story of the monk Guṇabhadra, who, at his death in 431, "was seated on a corded-chair. His face had not changed in the least, and he appeared as if he had entered a state of concentration."[76] The *Biographies of Eminent Monks* was compiled in the early part of the sixth century. At approximately the same time (c. 535–40), a stele containing a depiction of a monk seated in a chair was carved in northern China (figure 17).[77] This is our earliest representation of a chair in China. Twenty-some years later, in 566, a stele was engraved, also in northern China, depicting several monks sitting in chairs (figure 18).[78] In sum, while our earliest direct evidence for the use of a chair in a Chinese monastery dates to the sixth century, the chair was probably in use in Chinese monasteries in the fourth century, and perhaps even earlier. Even if we take the later, sixth-century date, this is still a full two centuries before evidence for chairs in China in non-Buddhist sources.[79]

As in India, corded-chairs were used in China for meditation. No less than the Sui monk Zhiyi, one of China's leading authorities on meditation, described the use of the corded-chair in meditation, when he wrote:

[74] *Sifen lü shanfan buque xingshichao* A4, p. 35b.

[75] *Gaoseng zhuan* 9, p. 384a8.

[76] Ibid. 3, p. 341b.

[77] The stele, originally commissioned by one Zhang Xingshuo, was originally discovered in Ruicheng County in 1916 and is now in the collection of the Nelson-Atkins Museum in Kansas City, Missouri. See Niu Zhaozao, ed., *Ruicheng xianzhi,* 13, p. 3b, and Laurence Sickman, "A Sixth-Century Buddhist Stele," pp. 12–7.

[78] One monk appears in a chair on the front of the stele (figure 18), and two more on one of the sides of the stele. A rubbing from this clearly dated stele is in the collection of the Beijing Library and published in *Beijing Tushuguan cang Zhongguo lidai shike taben huibian,* vol. 8, pp. 125–6. The inscription on the front side of the stele is clearer in the rubbing in the collection of the Fu Ssu-nien Library, Institute of History and Philology, Academia Sinica.

[79] In addition to the eighth-century mural cited above, another early non-Buddhist reference to a chair appears in an inscription completed in 797, the *Jidumiao beihaitan jiqi bei,* which lists "ten corded-chairs, including four regular chairs." *Jinshi cuibian* 103, p. 11.

FIG. 17. Detail from stele completed 535–40. The monk sitting in a chair is on the right-hand side of the image. Photograph courtesy of the Nelson-Atkins Museum of Art, Kansas City, Missouri. Nelson Trust, 37–27.

> Find a quiet room or an open space, far from noise and distraction. Place a corded-chair there apart from other seats. Over a period of ninety days, sit upright with legs crossed, and with neck and spine erect. Do not move or sway. Do not slouch or lean to one side. Devote yourself to sitting. Do not allow your ribs to touch [the sides of] the chair.[80]

Zhiyi's disciple Guanding followed suit, recommending the corded-chair for seated meditation in his own writings.[81] In biographies of monks, the corded-chair often appears in descriptions of a monk's moment of death. One account in the *Further Biographies of Eminent Monks* describes the final moments of the sixth-century monk Sengda, saying, "At once he felt weak and unwell. Sitting erectly on a corded-chair, he chanted the *Prajñā[paramitāsūtra]*, calming himself in body and spirit. He then died there

---

[80] *Mohe zhiguan* 2, p. 11b. This passage is translated slightly differently, with notes, in Donner and Stevenson, *The Great Calming and Contemplation*, p. 222. See also Zhiyi's *Xiuxi zhiguan zuochan fayao*, T no. 1915, vol. 46, p. 465c.

[81] *Guanxin lunshu* 3, T no. 1921, vol. 46, p. 600b. In the Tang, Zongmi quoted Zhiyi's comments on the corded-chair in his discussion of seated meditation. See *Yuanjuejing daochang xiuzhengyi, Xu zang jing*, vol. 7, p. 486a.

FIG. 18. Detail from stele in 566. Note old man on chair in upper right-hand corner. Photograph courtesy of the Fu Ssu-nien Library, Institute of History and Philology, Academia Sinica.

at the Honggushan Monastery."[82] Similarly, the *Song Biographies of Eminent Monks* describes the death of eighth-century monk Biancai, saying, "In winter of the thirteenth year [of the Dali era, 778], he took ill. In late winter, on the eighth day, after giving final words of advice to his disciples, he sat calmly on his corded-chair and silently passed into extinction."[83] Passages like these, together with references in the more scholastic literature on meditation, reflect associations between the corded-chair and serenity, whether it be the hard-won tranquility of a disciplined regimen of meditation or the final moment of peace before escaping the world of the living.

Chairs in medieval Chinese monasteries were also put to more mundane uses. In a typically acerbic comment, Yijing complains that Chinese monks do not sit on their chairs properly when eating. In the passage, Yijing claims that chairs were introduced to Chinese monasteries already in the third century, and goes on to complain that Chinese monks do not sit on their chairs properly when eating. In India, he says, when monks eat, they sit on chairs with their knees out front, and their feet on the ground. But in China, Yijing complains, monks sit cross-legged on their chairs, even when eating. For Yijing, Indian monastic practice was always au-

[82] *Xu gaoseng zhuan* 16, p. 553b.
[83] *Song gaoseng zhuan* 16, p. 806c.

thentic, and Chinese deviation from Indian practice always lamentable. Hence, the passage ends with Yijing passionately calling on his brethren back in China to change their ways, and sadly bemoaning the fact that although by his day Indian monks had been coming to China one after the other for seven hundred years, and Chinese monks had been traveling to India for hundreds of years as well, Chinese monks had still not learned to sit properly when having their meals.[84] For our purposes, it is this final line that attracts our attention, for it underlines the strong and continuous line of transmission for the chair (and similar objects) from Indian to Chinese monasteries.

From the Monastery to the Living Room

Although a substantial body of textual and pictorial evidence suggests that the chair was brought to China by monks and used in their monasteries, the process by which the chair spread beyond the monastery to other parts of Chinese society remains obscure. In his classic study of the history of manners in Europe, Norbert Elias demonstrated how new attitudes toward "civilized" behavior—such as table manners, restrictions on spitting, and guidelines for blowing the nose—often spread from court circles to the rest of society. Elias further noted that clerics were key figures in popularizing court customs.[85] Although the nature of the Tang court was considerably different from its medieval European counterparts, the same process of cultural transmission may have been at work in the case of the Chinese chair. The *Zhenyuan lu*, a Buddhist catalog compiled at the end of the eighth century, records that when the Tantric monk Vajrabodhi arrived in China from the West in 719, he brought with him a number of gifts from the king of Malaya, including a Sanskrit edition of the *Mahāprajñāpāramitā*, various precious gems, incense, and a "seven-jewel corded-chair."[86] Recall also the reference in the *Zizhi tongjian* mentioned above, in which Emperor Muzong (r. 821–5) held court seated on a corded-chair. A passage in the travelogue of ninth-century Japanese pilgrim Ennin again makes the connection between monks, the emperor, and chairs. Writing of the events of 844, Ennin states:

> Ever since his accession, the Emperor has enjoyed going out [of the Palace] on trips. . . . Each time he goes out with his retinue, he orders the monasteries to arrange benches, mats, and carpets, to tie flowered curtains to their towers, and to set out cups and saucers, trays, and chairs (*yizi*).[87]

[84] *Nanhai jigui* 1, p. 207a; Takakusu, *A Record of the Buddhist Religion*, pp. 22–4.
[85] Norbert Elias, *The Civilizing Process*, p. 83.
[86] *Zhenyuan xinding shijiao mulu* 14, *T* no. 2157, vol. 55, p. 876a.
[87] *Nittō guhō junrei gyōki* 4, p. 454; Reischauer, *Ennin's Diary*, p. 353.

While the imperial court may have played some role in the spread of the chair from the monastery to society at large, the court was not a necessary link tying monastic society to lay: a more direct path of diffusion is more likely. Laypeople with the means and the leisure to furnish their homes as they pleased often had cause to visit monasteries, either out of personal interest or on official business. At such times, in monasteries throughout the empire, the monastic world met the lay, as poets and officials ventured out of their own cultural environment with its elaborate standards of decorum and etiquette, into a markedly different environment with its own distinct tradition and rules. Ennin describes one such encounter when local officials visited a monastery he was staying at in 838:

> The Minister of State came to the monastery and worshipped the "auspicious images" in the balcony and inspected the newly made image. Presently, his military aide, the Dafu Shen Bian, rushed up to us and said that the Minister of State invited us monks [to join him]. On hearing this, we climbed up to the balcony with the messenger. The Minister of State and the Military Inspector, together with Senior Secretaries, Deputy Secretaries, and Administrative Officers of the prefecture, all were seated on chairs drinking tea. When they saw us monks coming, they all arose and paid us respect by joining their hands and standing. They called out to us to sit down, and we all seated ourselves on the chairs and sipped tea.[88]

Similarly, the accomplished poet Meng Jiao (751–814) wrote of a visit to a monastery in which he saw monks chanting a song in offering to a Chan Master seated on a corded-chair.[89]

As in the case of Buddhist writings, when the chair appears in the works of Tang literati, it is usually associated with serenity and tranquility and linked to the romantic image of the monk as emblem of the antithesis of the vulgar world of intrigue and materialism in which poet-officials lived. Meng Haoran, in a poem written after visiting a monk together with a friend, praises the lofty monk who "[i]n an isolated cave of stone, sits on his corded-chair, sleeping tigers at his side."[90] Or take, for instance, Bai Juyi (772–846), musing over his own affinity for Buddhism in the following lines:

> Sitting back in a corded-chair, I think to myself,
> in a former life, I must have been a poet-monk.[91]

There are dozens of such references in Tang poetry, almost all in some way drawing a link between the corded-chair, Buddhism, and serenity. It was

---

[88] *Nittō guhō junrei gyōki* 1, p. 68; Reischauer, ibid., p. 52.
[89] "Jiaofang ge'er," *Quan Tang shi* 374, p. 4200
[90] "Pei Li Shiyu fang Zong Shangren chanju," *Quan Tang shi* 160, p. 1647.
[91] "Aiyong shi," *Quan Tang shi* 446, p. 5010.

FIG. 19. Detail from *Han Xizai's Night Revelry*. Reproduced with permission of
the National Palace Museum, Beijing.

perhaps a similar ideal of refined detachment that inspired some literati
to attempt to re-create this idealized image of monastic life in their own
homes. The biography in the *Tang History* of Wang Wei (701–761), a
poet and official who modeled himself on the most famous of Buddhist
laymen Vimalikīrti—even taking "Vimalikīrti" as his own style-name—
reports that in his later years, Wang lived a life of simplicity and restraint.
He maintained a vegetarian diet and, after his wife died, did not take a
second wife. "His studio contained nothing save a teapot, a medicine pestle, a table for scriptures, and a corded-chair. After he retired from court,
he burned incense and sat alone, occupying himself with meditation and
chanting."[92]

By the Song dynasty, the relationship between Buddhism and the chair
had been forgotten. The famous painting *Han Xizai's Night Revelry* (figure 19), attributed to Five Dynasties painter Gu Hongzhong, but in all
likelihood a Song copy, contains both a monk and a chair. But far from
drawing a connection between the two, the painting highlights their difference. According to the *Wudai shi bu*, the painting was originally commissioned by the emperor to castigate Han Xizai for choosing to live a life

[92] *Jiu Tang shu* 190b, p. 5052.

of leisure rather than take a position in the government.[93] The painting is a portrait of excess. The scene that surrounds the figure Han Xizai is dotted with signs of his decadence—a gathering of leisured gentlemen, female musicians, dancers, and a hint of sex in the bed at the edge of the painting. By this time, the chair was a part of this world: a symbol of the good life. At least one scholar has argued that the monk, standing behind a musician, hands folded, serves as a foil for his surroundings; a religious devotee dedicated to a spiritual life, he is a man out of place.[94]

Similarly, far from recognizing the role of monks in changing the way Chinese sat, Southern Song writer Zhuang Jiyu suggested that it was only monks who preserved the ancient way of sitting. In an essay on the subject, Zhuang wrote, "Because the ancients sat on mats, they criticized extending the legs as *jiju* [that is, impolite posture]. Today, when sitting on platforms, we consider it proper to sit with the legs hanging down. This does not seem to have been the case in the Tang. . . . The practice of sitting on mats was still common in the Tang. Today, monks are still like the ancients in this respect."[95] In short, by the Song, despite the fact that monks continued to use chairs in the monasteries, people no longer drew a connection between Buddhism and the chair; by this time, the chair had become a part of everyday life, the common cultural heritage of ordinary people.

And so the mystery of the Chinese chair is solved: the chair came to China from India as a form of monastic furniture, made inroads into secular society in the mid-Tang, and finally came to dominate Chinese interiors in the late tenth and early eleventh centuries. The history of the chair, then, is a striking example of the extent of the impact of Buddhism on Chinese society. More than a system of beliefs, Buddhism brought with it any number of objects, practices, and associations that influenced Chinese society in complicated and often unexpected ways.

A quick look at Japan, however, suggests that the process by which Chinese adopted the chair was not as neat as I have presented it here. From very early on, Japanese monks read many of the same texts that Chinese monks read. They read the same descriptions of the proper height for chairs; they read the same accounts of Chinese pilgrims to India; they read stories of Chan masters who "arose from their chairs" before responding to a disciple's question. The Japanese monk Ennin, in the passages cited above, provided a detailed description of the use of chairs in Chinese monasteries. And from a number of medieval Japanese paintings, as well

---

[93] *Wudaishi bu* 5, p. 15.
[94] Wang Bomin, *Zhongguo huihuashi*, p. 224.
[95] *Jilei bian* (SKQS edn.) C, p. 54.

as an actual eighth-century chair, we know that Japanese monks did indeed bring chairs back to Japan.[96]

Nevertheless, we also know that while the chair made some impact on everyday life in Japan, the chair has even now not completely conquered Japan, and may never do so. It takes some effort to find pictures of chairs in medieval Japan, and it was only with European and American influence in modern times that the chair finally became a common fixture in Japanese interiors.[97]

Returning to China, the Japanese case is important because it tells us that there was nothing inevitable about the chair's conquest of China. Use of the chair does not mark the march of progress. In light of the experiences of other cultures that have gotten along quite well without the chair, comments by one modern scholar that the chair "improved the physical fitness of the Chinese people" and that it "was a step up for ancient Chinese civilization" are not convincing.[98] Unlike military technology, which demands acceptance of the latest innovations if a civilization is to compete with its enemies, the chair provides no significant advantages over alternative methods of sitting.[99] Indeed, at least one specialist in chair design and ergonomic theory has recommended that we moderns reduce our dependence on chairs.[100] In short, the decision to adopt the chair is a complicated cultural choice rather than a technological one.

[96] For the chair, in the Shōsōin Collection, see Koizumi Kayuko, "The Furniture of the Shōsōin in Relation to Ancient Chinese and Korean Furniture," pp. 44–51.

[97] Fernand Braudel singled out China as the only civilization that makes use of what he termed "the double pattern of furniture," meaning that Chinese at times sit on chairs, with legs hanging down, and at times sit on the *kang* in a cross-legged position. Actually, Japan, Korea, and India could also be characterized as using this double pattern. More significant is Braudel's formulation of the "rule" that "traditional civilizations remain faithful to their accustomed decor." Since Braudel follows this statement with a summary of the introduction of the chair to China, he must mean that China in the fifteenth to seventeenth centuries was a "traditional civilization," whereas China of the Tang-Song period was not. I leave the validity of his characterization of Ming-Qing culture (including the statement that "[a] Chinese interior of the fifteenth century could equally well date from the eighteenth") to specialists of late imperial China, but the vitality and dynamism of Tang-Song culture, which included the shift in sitting patterns outlined here, is undeniable. See Braudel, *The Structures of Everyday Life*, vol. 1, pp. 285–90.

[98] Zhu Dawei, "Zhonggu Hanren you guizuo dao chuijiao gaozuo," p. 111.

[99] For a good example of the adoption of new military technology, see Albert E. Dien, "The Stirrup and Its Effect on Chinese Military History," pp. 33–56. I do not wish to imply that the diffusion of military technology is a simple matter; on this question, Braudel's comments on oversimplification in some histories of technology are perceptive. See Braudel, *Structures of Everyday Life*, p. 290.

[100] Galen Cranz, *The Chair: Culture, Body, and Design*. In this book, Cranz demonstrates, among other things, that until very recently the history of chair design the world over was driven chiefly by the desire to express status rather than to provide comfort or back support.

For this reason, I have focused on the cultural factors that went into the decision by Chinese to sit in chairs. But all the factors that I have cited as important to the adoption of the chair in China—images of Maitreya on a throne, the prevalence of the chair in monasteries, the association of the chair with meditation and serenity—were equally present in Japan and Korea. Surely there must be more involved in the move to the chair than a handful of cultural and technological factors. Clearly there must be more to the story. That being said, we can at least recognize that the chair played a significant part in the transformation of Chinese sitting habits, and that in the process through which Chinese accepted the chair, Buddhism played a pivotal role.

SUGAR

One of the most curious, if minor, themes in the history of the chair is the transmission from one culture to another of sentiments attached to the object. As we have seen in the case of China, the chair brought with it associations linked on the one hand with authority, and on the other with serenity. The story of the chair illustrates how readily abstract notions become attached even to what may seem to us to be the most mundane of objects, and that these same associations can travel with the object over vast distances, traversing radically different cultures.

Nonetheless, overall, whether in India or China, the chair picked up associations incidentally; it was never considered prime material for the literary imagination. References to the chair in Buddhist literature are almost invariably to the construction and use of the chair as monastic furniture; it was not used to explain doctrine or propel Buddhist narrative. For more fecund sources of simile, metaphor, and hyperbole, we must turn instead to an array of familiar objects employed frequently throughout Buddhist literature for their literary potential. A list of the most common of these things would include the bodhi tree, the lotus blossom, cow's milk, the Ganges river, and—significantly for the history of Chinese medicine and Chinese cuisine—the sugarcane.

One of the most common uses of sugarcane in Buddhist literature is as a symbol of abundance. The *Vimalakīrti,* for instance, describes a spectacular scene in which "the thus-come-ones of three thousand worlds filled the air, as numerous as stalks of sugarcane in a field."[101] In another text, the Buddha tells Ānanda that the world is filled with arhats, in numbers "as dense as stalks of sugarcane, bamboo, reeds, hemp or rice."[102]

---

[101] *Weimojie jing* (Skt. *Vimalakirtinirdeśa*) C, T no. 474, vol. 14, p. 535b.
[102] *Fo benxing ji jing* (Skt. *Abhiniṣkramaṇasūtra*), T no. 190, vol. 3, p. 912a.

Elsewhere bodhisattvas and buddhas appear "as numerous as stalks of sugarcane."[103] These are only a few examples of the use of the image of vast fields of thick and thriving sugarcane as a symbol of abundance. The prevalence of the image reflects the prevalence of the plant itself. Botanists have argued that the sugarcane, which seems to have been first domesticated in New Guinea in 8000 B.C., was carried to India already in 6000 B.C.[104]

When Xuanzang traveled to India in the seventh century, he was struck by the abundance of sugarcane, listing it as a distinguishing characteristic of Gandhāra. He writes, "The country is rich in cereals, and produces a variety of flowers and fruits; it abounds also in sugarcane, from which they prepare *shimi* [i.e., amorphous sugar]. The climate is warm and moist, and in general without ice or snow."[105]

Sugarcane was considered a great delicacy in ancient India, as reflected in numerous prophesies of a harsh, degenerate future age when people will live short, hard lives and be forced to live on bland, tasteless food; for they will be deprived of ghee, honey, oil, salt, and sugarcane.[106] One set of monastic regulations praises the juice of sugarcane as the nectar of the gods, the *Nirvāṇa Sutra* includes sugarcane in a definition of fine foods, and another text includes sugarcane among the "finest tastes in the world."[107] Buddhist similes tell us that Indian sugarcane farmers had already encountered the troubling "red rot" disease (invoked in one text to describe the danger of allowing the ordination of women, who would be to the monastic order what disease is to a field of cane), and even provide information on how sugarcane was irrigated in ancient India.[108] Other anecdotes reveal that in addition to consuming sugarcane for its flavor, sugarcane was also used in medicine.[109]

---

[103] *Shidi jinglun* (Skt. *Daśabhūmikasūtraśāstra*) 12, *T* 1522, vol. 26, p. 199c; *Da zhi du lun* 64, p. 511a.

[104] Sydney Mintz, *Sweetness and Power: The Place of Sugar in Modern History*, p. 19.

[105] *Da Tang Xiyu ji* 2, p. 879b; my translation follows, with minor emendations, Beal, *Buddhist Records*, p. 98. Watters comments briefly on the passage in *On Yuan Chwang's Travels*, pp. 200–201.

[106] See, for example, *Zhong ahan jing* (Skt. *Madhyamāgama*) 15, p. 523a, and *Yujia shidi lun* (*Yogacāryabhūmiśāstra*) 2, *T* no. 1579, vol. 30, p. 286a.

[107] *Sifen lü* (Skt. *Dharmaguptakavinaya*) 42, p. 873c; *Zheng fa nian chu jing* (Skt. *Saddharmasmṛtyupasthānasūtra*) 52, p. 305a; and *Da ban niepan jing* (Skt. *Mahāparinirvāṇasūtra*) 4, *T* 374, vol. 12, p. 386a.

[108] For red-rot disease, see *Genben shuoyiqieyou bu pinaiye za shi* (Skt. *Mūlasarvāstivāda vinayakṣudrakavastu*) 29, p. 350c, and Christian Daniels's comprehensive history of sugar in China, *Science and Civilisation in China*, vol. 6, *Biology and Biological Technology: pt. 3, Agro-Industries and Forestry*, p. 258. On irrigation of sugarcane in India, see *Da fangdeng daji jing* (Skt. *Mahāvaipulyamahāsaṃnipātasūtra*) 11, *T* no. 397, vol. 13, p. 67b, *Haiyi pusa suowen jingyin famen jing* (Skt. *Sāgaramatiparipṛcchā*) 13, *T* no. 400, vol. 13, p. 509b–c, and Daniels, *Agro-Industries and Forestry*, p. 191–2.

[109] *Zhuanji baiyuan jing* (Skt. *Avadānaśataka*) 5, *T* no. 200, vol. 4, p. 222c.

As we attempt to peer into daily life through literary device, more elaborate metaphors provide us with glimpses of how sugarcane was processed.[110] One text likens language to the sugarcane, for just as sugarcane loses its flavor when squeezed, so too do words lose their power when overused.[111] Elsewhere, the bodhisattva is compared to sugarcane: "The great being bodhisattva produces feelings of great compassion, and toils tirelessly for the sake of all beings. He is like sugarcane or sesame which, *when pressed with a device*, give forth juice or oil."[112] References like these make it clear that Indians were accustomed to extracting the sweet juice of sugarcane. Other metaphors and analogies demonstrate that medieval Indians were also aware of the different substances that could be derived from this juice. At one point in the *Nirvāṇa Sutra*, Kāśyapa addresses the Buddha and exclaims, "World-honored-one, like the [juice of the] sugarcane which yields various flavors when boiled various times, I too obtain various senses of the Dharma each time I listen to the Buddha speak."[113] Another text gives names to these "various flavors." The *bodhicitta*, it tells us, yields three types of being (arhat, pratyekabuddha, and buddha), just as the sugarcane yields three types of products: "sugar (*tang*), half-sugar (*bantang*), and syrup (*shimi*)."[114] The relationship between bodhisattva, arhat, and pratyekabuddha "is like the flavor of sugarcane," one text tells us. "Though they are of the same flavor, one who obtains from it white *shimi* is fortunate, while one who derives black *shimi* is less so."[115]

Clearest of all is a passage in the *Saddharmasmṛtyupasthāna Sutra*, translated into Chinese in the early part of the sixth century. The passage compares the cultivation of the monk to the refinement of sugar. A monk's spiritual progress

is like the juice of sugarcane placed in a vessel and boiled over fire. At the initial stage it is separated from impurities. This is called *poniduo* [Skt. *phāṇita*]. At the second boiling, it becomes slightly heavier. This is called *julü* [Skt. *guda*]. When boiled a third time, it becomes white. This is called *shimi* [Skt. *sarkarā*]. In this way, the sugarcane juice is boiled again and again so

[110] Commenting on the use of food in philosophical discourse, David Knechtges noted: "One of the most pervasive uses of food in ancient Chinese literature is as metaphor in political or philosophical discourse. The Chinese alimentary metaphor is quite similar to that of the medieval Christian writer, who equates God with bread, truth with nourishment and food, and Christian doctrine with a meal. In the Chinese classics, the proper seasoning of food is a common analogy for good government." "A Literary Feast: Food in Early Chinese Literature," p. 51.
[111] *Fajue jingxin jing* (Skt. *Adhyāśayasaṃcodana*) C, T no. 327, vol. 12, p. 49b.
[112] *Shouhu guojiezhu tuoluoni jing* 3, T no. 997, vol. 19, p. 537a.
[113] *Da ban niepan jing* 16, p. 461a; Cf. T no. 375, *Da ban niepan jing* (another translation of the *Mahāparinirvāṇasūtra*) vol. 12, p. 703b.
[114] *Baiqian song daji jing Dizang pusa qingwen fashen zan*, T no. 413, vol. 13, p. 791b.
[115] *Da fangdeng daji jing* (Skt. *Mahāvaipulyamahāsaṃnipātasūtra*) 13, p. 87b.

that it is separated from impurities and gradually becomes heavy until it reaches the point where it turns white.

The text continues by making the analogy to the monk who, heated by the "fire of wisdom," refines himself gradually through meditation.[116]

As in the case of furniture, Chinese terminology used to describe sugar in medieval times is frustratingly imprecise. The juice of sugarcane can be used to make a wide variety of products, depending on the degree to which the juice is refined. The term *shimi*, literally, "rock honey," was at times used to refer to a sugar syrup and at other times to a hard crystal.[117] But despite the difficulties in determining the precise nature of sugar referred to in a given text, taken together, evidence from the Buddhist canon and several other early Indian texts has led sugar specialists to conclude that ancient India was "without a doubt the first cultural area to make sugar products."[118] The ancient Greeks learned of the existence of sugarcane and knew something of how sugar was produced in India, but it was not until much later that sugar was manufactured on a wide scale in the West.[119] And as we will see below, China began to produce sugar at a relatively late date as well.

In sum, references in the Buddhist canon indicate that sugar products were well known in ancient India, that they were consumed for pleasure, used in medicine, and employed in ritual,[120] and that knowledge of at least the fundamentals of the process by which various sugar products were derived from sugarcane juice were well enough known that Buddhist writers could draw on sugar manufacture as a rhetorical tool for explaining doctrinal principles, assuming that while some in their audience may have difficulty with Buddhist doctrine, everyone knew the basics of making sugar.

Sugar Production in Indian Monasteries

Sugar production is labor intensive: in drier climates, the sugarcane requires regular irrigation, and once the cane is cut, the juice must be rapidly

---

[116] *Zhengfa nian chu jing* 3, p. 17a–b.

[117] Christian Daniels discusses the Sanskrit, Chinese, and English terminology in detail. See *Agro-Industries and Forestry*, especially pp. 279, 374. See also Li Zhihuan, "Cong zhitangshi tan shimi he bingtang," pp. 146–54, and Li Zhihuan's book-length study of Chinese sugar, *Zhongguo shitangshi gao*, p. 108.

[118] Daniels, *Agro-Industries and Forestry*, p. 367. See also, Mintz, *Sweetness and Power*, pp. 19–20.

[119] For a survey of the place of sugar in antiquity in the West, see R. J. Forbes's chapter on sugar in his *Studies in Ancient Technology*, vol. 5.

[120] Of particular interest are passages referring to the use of sugar in the marriage ceremony. *Genben shuoyiqieyoubu pinaiye* (Skt. *Mūlasarvāstivādavinayavibhaṅga*) 25, T no. 1442, vol. 23, p. 764a; *Genben shuoyiqieyoubu bichuni pinaiye* (Skt. *Mūlasarvāstivādabhikṣuṇīvinayavibhaṅga*), T no. 1443, vol. 23, p. 968c.

extracted and processed to avoid desiccation, rot, or fermentation.[121] Further, while technicians can now measure temperature and density of syrup when preparing sugar, in premodern times this was done with less precision by craftsmen on the basis of approximations of density and color.[122] Monasteries were well equipped to meet both of these demands. Endowed with fields and staffed with a community of monks capable of passing down specialized techniques, monasteries were ideally suited to the task of making sugar.

Textual evidence supports this assumption. The *Saddharmasmṛtyu-pasthāna Sutra,* for instance, mentions the cultivation of sugarcane in monastic fields, as does the *Dharmaguptakavinaya.*[123] One set of monastic regulations describes how monks are to treat sugarcane once it has been harvested: "When monks obtain large quantities of sugarcane, what they cannot eat at once should be pressed into juice which can be consumed in the evening. If this is not consumed completely, it must be boiled and made into syrup (*shimi*) which can be kept for seven days. If the syrup is not consumed in this time, it should be heated until crystals (*hui*) form; this can be kept indefinitely."[124] Another set of monastic regulations refers to a "room for boiling sugar," suggesting that, in addition to fields of sugarcane, some monasteries maintained equipment necessary for producing sugar on a relatively large scale.[125]

The monastic regulations, compiled expressly for monks and at least in principle not to be revealed to the unordained, provide clues to the importance of sugarcane to the monastic community as well as some of the problems sugarcane posed. In theory, strict monks were not to eat after noon, but, according to passages in some monastic regulations, the Buddha made an important exception in the case of certain types of juices, including cane juice.[126] Recall the passage cited above: "When monks obtain large quantities of sugarcane, what they cannot eat at once should be pressed into juice *which can be consumed in the evening.*"[127] Although it

[121] Mintz, *Sweetness and Power,* p. 21.

[122] Li Zhihuan, *Zhongguo shitangshi gao,* p. 113.

[123] The *Saddharmasmṛyupasthāna Sutra* was translated into Chinese in the sixth century. See *Zheng fa nian chu jing* 15, p. 89a, and 24, p. 136c; the *Dharmaguptakavinaya* was translated into Chinese at the beginning of the fifth century; see *Sifen lü* 43, p. 875a.

[124] *Mohe sengqi lü* (Skt. *Mahāsāṃghikavinaya*) 11, p. 317c.

[125] *Genben shuoyiqieyou bu pinaiye yao shi* (Skt. *Mūlasarvāstivādavinayavastu*) 17, T no. 1448, vol. 24, p. 87a.

[126] Daniels, *Agro-Industries and Forestry,* p. 278. There is an interesting parallel in twelfth-century Europe, where a controversy arose as to whether or not consumption of medicinal sugar should be considered a violation of the fast. Thomas Aquinas considered sugar a medicine rather than a food. Mintz, *Sweetness and Power,* p. 99.

[127] *Mohe sengqi lü* (Skt. *Mahāsṃghikavinaya*) 11, p. 317c. Other regulations, however, expressly state that cane juice should not be consumed after noon. See *Shi song lü* (Skt. *Sarvāstivādavinaya*) 53, p. 390c, and *Sapoduobu pinimodelejia* (Skt. *Sarvāstivādavinaya-mātṛkā*), T no. 1441, vol. 23, p. 619c.

is difficult to reconstruct an overall monastic diet from the evidence available to us, cane juice seems to have served in at least some monasteries to fortify monks after noon.[128] Cane juice, while a fine source of nutrition and calories, also presented a problem for the community because of its properties when fermented.[129] The *Mahāprajñāpāramitāśāstra*, for instance, lists cane liquor together with other "medicinal liquors," saying that it should not be consumed, because "for the body it does little benefit and great harm."[130]

Sweeteners in China before the Tang

It would be astonishing if a culture as rich in culinary traditions as early China did not employ a variety of sweeteners. And in fact, honey and maltose were known in China from very early on. Nonetheless, before the Tang, cane sugar consumption was rare, and techniques for producing refined cane sugars scarcely known. Wild honey was no doubt harvested and consumed from an early date in China, and we have records of domesticated bees, raised for their honey, from the end of the second century on. From at least the fourth century, honey was sold on the market in southern China, and by the Tang, documents record tributes of honey to the court from nineteen different regions, indicating that by this time, honey production and consumption were widespread.[131]

Perhaps an even more important sweetener in early China was maltose (*yi*), a sweet substance derived from grain. Maltose may well have been discovered along with fermented grain as far back as the Neolithic period. References to maltose appear in various early Chinese texts, and in the Han maltose was a common product in the markets. Maltose has played a much more important role in the Chinese diet than in the West, and even today, bottles of clear, thick maltose are readily available in Chinese markets.[132]

---

[128] In a similar vein, in a compelling argument in *Sweetness and Power*, Mintz shows how sugar (along with tea) became a key source of calories for the English working class of the nineteenth century. Fortunately for medieval Buddhist monks, cane juice and the sorts of raw sugar that they produced from it are much more nutritionally rich than the highly refined sugar consumed in nineteenth-century England.

[129] For more on how cane juice ferments and the types of liquor that can be produced from it, see Daniels, *Agro-Industries and Forestry*, pp. 81–2; see p. 58 for references to sugarcane wine in early Indian medical treatises.

[130] *Da zhi du lun* (Skt. *Mahāprajñāpāramitāśāstra*) 13, p. 158b; Lamotte, *Le traité de la grande vertu de sagesse*, pp. 816–7.

[131] *Xin Tang shu*, "Dili zhi," *juan* 39. On honey in early China, see Li Zhihuan, *Zhongguo shitangshi gao*, pp. 22–34. The *Song gaoseng zhuan* records an instance of a Tang monastery that offered pear-blossom honey as tribute to the court (16, p. 807c); as in the case of sugar, it is difficult to determine with any precision the extent of honey-making in Tang monasteries throughout the empire.

[132] For a survey of the history of maltose in China, see Li Zhihuan, *Zhongguo shitangshi gao*, pp. 35–59.

Despite the fact that cane sugar was not a common part of the Chinese diet in pre-Tang times, Indian monks cannot be credited with introducing sugarcane to China. Sugarcane appears in the Chinese historical record already in the second century B.C. Christian Daniels has proposed that references to sugarcane begin to appear in Chinese literature at this time because of recent Han Chinese conquests of the southern Yue.[133] Scattered references in Han dynasty texts make it clear that at that time, Chinese were familiar with the sugarcane and had learned of various types of sweeteners derived from its juice. The Han collection of songs *Chuci*, for instance, reveals that sugarcane syrup was used in cooking, and another Han text recommends sugarcane juice as a remedy for hangovers.[134]

The first-century *Yiwuzhi* provides a brief description of how a form of concrete sugar can be made from cane by boiling the juice and then drying it in the sun.[135] Similarly, a gloss in a text by the prominent fifth-century Daoist, alchemist, and pharmacologist Tao Hongjing refers to the product *shatang*, literally "sand sugar," produced from cane in Guangzhou in his time. Tao's comment is confirmed by a gloss in a Buddhist text translated in 488 which also mentions the prevalence of *shatang* in Guangzhou.[136] Judging by the term, scholars have suggested that this was a form of low-grade, dry sugar.[137]

The origin of these techniques for making amorphous sugar are far from clear. Christian Daniels has argued that Han Chinese first learned the techniques for making amorphous sugar from non-Han peoples who lived in south China, which then included the territory of what is now Vietnam.[138] Others have emphasized that at least some of the techniques came from India, citing the *Hou Hanshu*, which in its treatise on India mentions the production of *shimi* there.[139] While the earliest contact of Han Chinese with sugar and sugar production is impossible to determine, a continuous, steady influence from India from the Han through the Tang is undeniable. The very word for sugarcane in Chinese (*ganzhe*) is derived

[133] Daniels, *Agro-Industries and Forestry*, pp. 182–3; on the introduction of sugarcane to China see also, Li Zhihuan, *Zhongguo shitangshi gao*, pp. 66–9.

[134] For some Han references to sugarcane, see Li Zhihuan, *Zhongguo shitangshi gao*, p. 60. For the *Chuci* passage (from the *zhaohun* poem) and the hangover reference (from *Hanshu* 22, p. 1063), see Knechtges, "A Literary Feast," p. 55, and Daniels (*Agro-Industries and Forestry*, p. 59), who notes that modern research has borne out the efficacy of sugarcane juice for metabolizing alcohol.

[135] Daniels, ibid., p. 280.

[136] Tao Hongjing's comment is preserved in the pharmacopia by the Ming writer Li Shizhen, *Ben cao gang mu* 33, p. 12b, under the entry for sugarcane (*ganzhe*). For the Buddhist passage, see *Shanjian lü piposha* (Skt. *Samantapāsādikā*) 17, *T* no. 1462, vol. 24, p. 795b.

[137] Li Zhihuan, *Zhongguo shitangshi gao*, p. 111.

[138] Daniels, *Agro-Industries and Forestry*, p. 88.

[139] *Hou Hanshu* 88, p. 2921.

from the Sanskrit *phāṇita*.[140] And in the Tang, pharmacologists continued to assert that *shimi* from "the West" was the finest available.[141]

In sum, despite scattered references to sugar in the history of Chinese sweeteners, the pre-Tang period was the age of maltose and honey. The chief products derived from sugarcane at this time—amorphous sugar and semisolid types of sugar—degenerated quickly, posing serious problems for storage and transportation.[142] Even into the Tang, more refined types of sugar belonged to the rarefied world of court luxuries and exotics.

Monks and Sugar in China

At one point in his sweeping study of the impact of sugar on the West, Sydney Mintz exclaims, "[W]herever they went, the Arabs brought with them sugar, the product and the technology of its production; sugar, we are told, followed the *Koran*."[143] Asia is perhaps more complicated in that, because of the prevalence of sugarcane, various forms of sugar production existed in areas untouched by Buddhism. Nonetheless, the spread of Buddhist writings throughout Asia doubtless brought news of sugar to many who had never tasted it.

In their commentaries to Indian scriptures, Chinese monks like Huiyuan in the Sui and Kuiji in the Tang, both extremely erudite monks steeped in the classics of Indian Buddhism, explained references to sugar in the original texts, betraying some knowledge of the substance themselves.[144] And one can imagine the discussions at Buddhist translation centers as monks attempted to develop a Chinese vocabulary sufficient to translate references in Indian texts to a wide array of specific types of sugar.[145] Finally, as in India, Chinese writings on the monastic regulations reveal that Chinese monks employed sugarcane in rituals, that they consumed sugarcane for pleasure and as medicine, and that monastic leaders in China were, like their Indian counterparts, concerned with the problem of fermented cane juice.[146]

---

[140] Ji Xianlin, "Yi zhang youguan Yindu zhitangfa chuanru Zhongguo de Dunhuang canjuan," p. 133. Daniels, *Agro-Industries and Forestry*, p. 279.

[141] *Xinxiu bencao*, by Su Jingtang (aka Su Gong), quoted in *Ben cao gang mu* 33, p. 15b s.v. *shimi*.

[142] Daniels, *Agro-Industries and Forestry*, p. 84.

[143] For Mintz's remark, see *Sweetness and Power*, p. 25.

[144] For Huiyuan's comments, see *Da ban niepan jing yiji* 2, *T* no. 1764, vol. 37, pp. 663a, 756c, and 900a. For Kuiji, see *Yujia lun luezuan* 1, *T* no. 1829, vol. 43, p. 14c.

[145] On this point, see Daniels, *Agro-Industries and Forestry*, p. 145.

[146] The evidence for sugarcane and sugar in Chinese monasteries for the medieval period is scant, though a handful of references in Buddhist texts leaves us some clues. For cane consumption, see *Sifen lü biqiu hanzhu jieben*, by Daoxuan, C, *T* no. 1806, vol. 40, p. 459a. Yijing recommends the use of syrup (*shimi*) and dry sugar (*shatang*) in his letter from India,

But if Chinese monks possessed knowledge of sugar-making techniques, they seem to have kept it to themselves, for in the early seventh century the Chinese court deemed it necessary to dispatch envoys to India expressly for the purpose of learning how to make sugar. In an account of the kingdom of Magadha, in what is now northwestern India, the *New Tang History* records:

> In the twenty-first year of the Zhenguan era [647], Magadha for the first time dispatched envoys to establish communication with the Son of Heaven. They presented the *bodhi* tree, a tree resembling the poplar. [Emperor] Taizong then dispatched envoys to obtain the method of boiling sugar. [When this was obtained], he ordered that sugarcane be submitted from Yangzhou. The juice was extracted by pressing [the cane in a mortar] as if [preparing] a dosage [of medicine]. It far surpassed that of the Western regions in color and flavor.[147]

Similar accounts of this event that appear in various historical sources do not tell us with precision who was dispatched to Magadha, what techniques they obtained, and from whom they obtained them.[148] One source, however, does provide answers to some of these questions—answers that square with what we know from the Buddhist canon about sugar in medieval India. In the *Further Biographies of Eminent Monks,* the biography of Xuanzang notes that "[w]hile in India, Xuanzang's fame spread throughout the land. He related the prosperity of the people of China and the abundance of goods there. The great king Harsavardhana [Jieri], as well as the monks at the Bodhi Monastery, had longed to obtain information about China for some time, but in the absence of trustworthy envoys [from China], had no one on whom to rely."[149] Their curiosity piqued by Xuanzang's description,

---

advice which would have been meaningless if sugar was not available for use in Chinese monasteries. *Nanhai jigui,* p. 225b; Takakusu, *A Record of the Buddhist Religion,* p. 140. For the problem of fermented cane, see Daoxuan's, *Sifen lü shanfan buque xingshichao* B2, p. 118, *Seng jiemo,* by Huaisu, A, *T* no. 1809, vol. 40, p. 519b, and *Ni jiemo, T* no. 1810, vol. 40, p. 546b.

[147] *Xin Tangshu* 146a, p. 4239. My translation closely follows that of Daniels, *Agro-Industries and Forestry,* p. 369. Strangely, Li Zhihuan insists that the phrase "like a dosage" (*ru qi qi*) indicates that lime was added, *Zhongguo shitangshi gao,* p. 111. Lime was later used as a reagent when processing sugarcane juice. The lime creates a floc, trapping impurities that can then be scraped off the top of the juice. The use of lime was an important technical innovation in sugar refining, and while we cannot rule out the possibility that, under the influence of India, Chinese were using lime in refining sugar at this time, this passage does not provide clear evidence for it. I follow Daniels's reading of the phrase as likening the sugar-refining process to the making of medicine, since the cane was crushed with a mortar.

[148] Other sources for the mission are *Tang huiyao* 100, p. 1796, *Taiping yulan* 857, p. 2a, and *Cefu yuangui* 970, pp. 11–12.

[149] *Xu gaoseng zhuan* 4, p. 454c.

Harsavardhana and the monks each dispatched emissaries to take scriptures
and treasures to present to China. Thus communications with India were established because of Xuanzang, as they were the result of his proclamations
of imperial intent.

After the envoys returned to the West, an edict ordered Wang Xuance[150]
and others—more than twenty in all—to accompany them to Bactria [and
thence to Magadha]. They were given more than a thousand bolts of silk.
Wang and the monks [who accompanied him] were each given assignments.

Together they approached the monks of the Bodhi Monastery to procure
shimi artisans. The monks then dispatched two artisans and eight monks to
go to China. After their arrival, imperial edict ordered them to Yuezhou,
where they obtained sugarcane and made [*shimi*]. All was accomplished
successfully.

Scholars disagree over the chronology of events described in these documents. Li Zhihuan argues that there were two missions to India to obtain
sugar-refining techniques: the first by Taizong in 647 as described in the
New Tang History, and the second mission—described in the *Further Biographies*—instigated by Gaozong (r. 650–83), with each mission bringing back different techniques for sugar refining. Christian Daniels, on the
other hand, argues that both accounts refer to the same mission, carried
out under Taizong in 647–8.[151]

Whether there was one mission or two, of greatest relevance for the history of Buddhism is the role that monks played in the process. The account in the *Further Biographies* shows once again that Indian monks
were knowledgeable in the craft of sugar refining. It is not clear from the
passage if the "artisans" (*jiang*) were monks or laymen; nonetheless, the
implication is that the artisans at the very least worked in conjunction
with monks. Equally interesting is the role that monks played as cultural-
political emissaries. First, the monk Xuanzang established relations between China and Magadha. Next, the Chinese emperor dispatched Chinese monks to travel to India and make contact with the monks there.
Finally, monks from Magadha were dispatched back to China to complete
the exchange of gifts.

The use here of monks as emissaries will come as no surprise to students of medieval foreign relations. Japanese monks played a prominent
role in relations between the Japanese court and its Chinese counterpart,
from the Tang well into the Ming.[152] Xuanzang too was well aware of

[150] Wang Xuance was dispatched to India by the Tang court on several occasions, and
even composed a lengthy treatise on the "Western Regions," which unfortunately is not extant. See Sun Xiushen, *Wang Xuance shiji gouchen.*

[151] Li Zhihuan, *Zhongguo shitangshi gao,* pp. 123–8; Daniels, *Agro-Industries and
Forestry,* pp. 371–2.

[152] See Wang Zhenping, "Chōnen's Pilgrimage to China, 983–986," pp. 63–4.

the interest Chinese rulers would have in his travels; indeed, the first thing
Xuanzang did on reaching Chinese territory from abroad was to dispatch
a memorial to Emperor Taizong announcing his arrival. And his famous
account of his travels was compiled at the emperor's bidding.[153]

Prominent monks arriving from abroad, whether Chinese or foreign,
often appeared before the court, bringing with them new texts, doctrines,
and rituals. They brought news of military matters and customs and
habits of foreign peoples; along with all the rest, they brought objects and
knowledge of how to make them. In the previous quotation, mention is
made of monks submitting a bodhi tree to the Tang court.[154] We have
also seen the example of the Indian monk Vajrabodhi submitting a gift of
gems, incense, and a jeweled chair to the Chinese emperor. The great pilgrim Yijing submitted a statue and relics, while the Central Asian monk
Nandī brought the Chinese emperor exotic drugs.[155] The motivations of
these monks and the emperors they met were no doubt a complicated mixture of piety, political expedience, and general curiosity. The motivation
of the Chinese emperor for dispatching emissaries to India to learn the art
of sugar-making is not clear from extant documents. The early Tang court
is known to have launched missions for the purpose of procuring foreign
drugs, and hence it may have been the medicinal properties attributed to
sugar that attracted the interest of the emperor. Nor do extant documents
reveal just what techniques these monks brought back from India and presented to the throne. Happily, a chance discovery at Dunhuang provides
us with a clue. The document, provisionally dated to the ninth to tenth
centuries, is the earliest detailed description of the sugar-making process
in China, and perhaps in the world.[156] After listing the best types of sugarcane for making sugar and detailing how they should be cut and crushed
in a large mortar with an ox-driven pestle, the author describes how the
juice is to be treated:

> The juice is received in an earthenware jar and is boiled in fifteen pans. Next
> drain [the boiled syrup] into a [cooling] pan and use chopsticks to add a lit-
> tle [text does not mention of what]. After completely cooled beat [the sugar].
> If it crystallizes it is ready and forms *shatang*. If it does not crystallize it is
> still not ready and is boiled again.[157]

[153] *Da Cien si sanzang fashi zhuan* 6, p. 253b; Li Rongxi, *A Biography of the Tripiṭaka
Master of the Great Ci'en Monastery*, p. 178

[154] See also Schafer, *The Golden Peaches of Samarkand*, pp. 122–3.

[155] For Yijing, see *Song gaoseng zhuan* 1, p. 710b, and Schafer, ibid., p. 266. For Nandī,
see *Xu gaoseng zhuan* 4, p. 458c, and Schafer, ibid., p. 183.

[156] Daniels, *Agro-Industries and Forestry*, p. 373.

[157] Ji Xianlin was the first to draw attention to the document, Pelliot no. 3303, in his article "Yi zhang youguan Yindu zhitangfa chuanru Zhongguo de Dunhuang canjuan," in
which he published a transcription of the document with notes. The document has received
due attention in Li Zhihuan's book and especially in Daniels, ibid., pp. 373–9. Here I quote
from Daniels's annotated translation.

This passage is significant for its mention of how the juice was extracted and for the use of multiple pans for boiling the juice. This method of quickly deriving dry fine-grained sugar from cane juice was in use in various parts of Asia until the nineteenth century. The document continues by describing how to derive an even more refined product from the *shatang*:

> When making *shageling* [i.e., *shimi*] return [the *shatang*] to the pan and after boiling it put it into a bamboo steaming bucket with seven holes in the base, and the molasses drains down into a receiving earthenware jar placed below. Keep the door [of the room in which the sugar in the bamboo steaming buckets are stored] closed for a full fifteen days [before] opening and removing. After the *shageling* has been drained out in the bamboo steaming bucket, bring it together by hand and remove [any remaining molasses] by shaking. [This is] called *shageling*. The molasses that has been drained off is made into wine.

The document discloses a sophisticated knowledge of sugar refining and is particularly significant in the history of sugar for its discussion of drainage techniques. As the document is unsigned, the author of these instructions is unknown. But circumstantial evidence suggests that the piece may have been composed by a monk for monks. First of all, the document was written on the back of a copy of two Buddhist spells (the *Sanshen zhenyan* and the *Qinglingling zhenyan*). Secondly, as in the case of all of the Dunhuang documents, the text probably came from a Buddhist library. Neither of these points rules out the possibility that the document was translated by or for merchants, but a monastic connection seems likely. Since Dunhuang was a common stopover along the silk road, the document probably represented knowledge brought from India that was to be transmitted farther south. In any event, the document suggests that in at least one Chinese monastery, monks were aware of sophisticated techniques for refining sugarcane at a time when, though sugar was highly valued, such techniques were not known in society at large.

The Dunhuang sugar document describes how to make a dry fine-grained sugar by boiling the sugarcane juice repeatedly and beating it as it cools. The text also gives instructions for making an even more refined type of sugar by treating the sugar derived from the first technique. Wang Zhuo's twelfth-century treatise on sugar, the *Tangshuang pu*, traces the origin of yet another type of sugar to a Buddhist monk. According to this treatise, *tangshuang*, literally "sugar frost," a large-grained, hard sugar known variously in the West as sugar candy, coffee crystals, and rock candy, was invented by an enigmatic monk named Zou in a monastery in Sichuan. The account seems as much a fabulous tale as it does an accurate description of fact. It tells us, for instance, that Zou, who lived in an isolated grass hut, would write his needs on a piece of paper and send them into the village on a donkey with money attached. The villagers at the market would then take the money and send the donkey back with the requested goods. Once when the donkey ate the sugarcane of a certain Mr. Huang, Zou as compensation taught the man the process of making sugar candy.[158] The legend of Zou was repeated in a number of sources subsequent to the *Tangshuang pu,* but none provide additional evidence or bring us any closer to the factual core of the legend, if indeed there is a factual core at all.[159] Nonetheless, the fact that our earliest reference to sugar candy comes from India lends credence to an association between Buddhism and the introduction of sugar candy to China.[160] At the very least, the story reflects a general association between sugar-making and monks in the early Song.

In 1072, after a miserable passage from Japan on a rocky boat staffed by drunken sailors, the Japanese monk and pilgrim Jōjin commented on a snack of "sugar cakes" sold to the crew by merchants at the Chinese port of Yuezhou. "They are a sweetmeat," Jōjin explains, "made of wheat flour, shaped like a cake, about three *cun* in width. The round cakes are about five *fen* thick. They are filled with sugar, and are delicious."[161] Throughout his travels in China, which took him as far north as the Wutai mountains in Shanxi, Jōjin repeatedly enjoyed these sweet cakes, often in monasteries. By the eleventh century, refined sugar was common in China, and the techniques for making it were taken for granted. The evidence suggests that the techniques used to make the sugar that went into Jōjin's cakes came originally from India, where sugar-refining techniques early reached an advanced level of sophistication. The Tang court acquired some of these techniques by especially dispatching Chinese monks to an Indian monastery to learn the art of sugar-making; and a document from a Chinese Buddhist library discovered at Dunhuang suggests the degree to which Chinese monks had absorbed these techniques.

As we attempt to assess the role of monasteries in introducing sugar technology to China, comparison with the chair is instructive. Important differences between the two include the fact that, unlike the manufacture

[158] *Tangshuang pu.* The passage is translated in Daniels, ibid., pp. 382–4. It is also discussed in Li Zhihuan, *Zhongguo shitang shigao,* pp. 167–70, which also contains discussion of the textual history of the *Tangshuang pu.* Li provides the complete text with annotation on pp. 216–21.

[159] Song figure Hong Mai included the *Tangshuang pu* in his *Rongzhai wu bi* 6, pp. 2a–2b. Wang Xiangzhi, also of the Song, mentioned the legend in his *Yudi jisheng* 155, 38, p. 5b, as did the Ming scholar Song Yingxing in his *Tian gong kai wu* A, p. 14b. See also Li Zhihuan, *Zhongguo shitang shigao,* p. 167.

[160] Daniels, *Agro-Industries and Forestry,* p. 384.

[161] *San Tendai Godaisan ki* 1, p. 4b.

of chairs, large-scale production of sugar entails substantial capital investment, including the cultivation of cane and the construction of mills for extracting juice from the cane. Large Chinese monasteries possessed both extensive monastic fields and ox-driven edge-runner mills, used in monasteries primarily for crushing oil seeds.[162] Similarities between sugar and the chair are equally instructive. As in the case of the chair, one of the reasons for the successful transfer of sugar technology to China was the steady stream of monks traveling between the two cultures. Historians of technology have pointed out that technology depends upon the movement of populations; even today, technicians are usually dispatched in person to implement new systems rather than relying on blueprints and manuals alone.[163] The sugar mission to India initiated by the Tang court underlines the point; and the court recognized the utility of drawing on the monastic social network for importing new goods and ideas from India.

Whether Indian, Central Asian, or Chinese, monks shared many aspects of a lifestyle that was distinct from that of the laity in any of these regions. Since all monks in these areas practiced—to greater or lesser extents— meditation, the accoutrements of meditation, including the chair, were valued; since all monks in these regions kept—to greater or lesser extents—the rule of eating only before noon, sugarcane juice held a special appeal. By the same token, Chinese monks possessed a higher degree of cultural humility than ordinary Chinese. In other words, because monks participated in the transregional subculture of Buddhist monasticism, Chinese monks identified with Indian monks and considered themselves a part of this larger community. This left them much more open to the habits, customs, foods, and furniture of India than, for instance, the Chinese literati, for whom Chineseness was much more a central part of their identity.

TEA

The Rise of Tea Drinking in China

Unlike most of the objects seen to this point, the relationship between Buddhism and Chinese tea has little to do with India, despite the controversy that raged from the early nineteenth century to the middle of the twentieth over the origins of the tea tree, with British scholars arguing for an Indian origin and Chinese scholars for a Chinese one. Tied as it was to colonialism, the massive international tea market, and national pride, the

---

[162] Daniels, *Agro-Industries and Forestry*, pp. 292–8.
[163] See especially Carlo M. Cipolla, *Before the Industrial Revolution: European Society and Economy 1000–1700*, pp. 137–59.

ACCIDENTS AND INCIDENTALS

debate was a heated one, with more at stake than historical curiosity.[164] The controversy was sparked by the discovery in India of a very old tea tree growing in the wild, suggesting that tea may have been cultivated first in India. But old tea trees have been found in the wild in abundance in various parts of China, providing botanists with at least as much evidence to argue for a Chinese origin of the plant as an Indian one. Although the ultimate origin of the tea tree remains difficult to determine conclusively, most scholars now agree that tea *manufacture*—that is, the cultivation of tea trees for the purpose of using their leaves—originated in China.[165] We cannot rule out the possibility of isolated instances of tea drinking outside of China in ancient times, but regions such as Ceylon and Russia did not begin tea production in earnest until the nineteenth century, when merchants introduced it there from China.[166] And while tea drinking was common in premodern times in other parts of eastern Asia such as Korea and Japan, it was clearly an import there from China. Hence, allowing for scattered and sporadic exceptions, tea cultivation and tea drinking throughout the world can for the most part be traced to China. It has even been argued, on the basis of pronunciations of the word for tea in different Chinese dialects, that words for tea in all modern languages derive ultimately from Chinese.[167]

Just as contentious as the question of the geographic origins of the tea tree has been the question of the earliest use of tea in China. Attempts to trace the early history of tea in China go back at least as far as the *Book of Tea* (*Chajing*) by the eighth-century figure Lu Yu, who drew attention to references to what he identified as tea in the ancient lexicon *Er ya*, and stated that the use of tea in China stretched all the way back to distant antiquity and the mighty Shennong, a figure now considered mythological. Later scholars in the Song and after followed suit, attempting to identify references to tea in ancient texts or, conversely, to refute the identifications of other scholars. As in the case of furniture and sugar, the difficulty in writing the early history of tea on the basis of textual sources is one of nomenclature, for changes in terminology often lag far behind changes in material culture. The modern word for tea, *cha,* did not become the standard word for the plant until the eighth century. But based on context and early word glosses, scholars from Lu Yu on have argued that in ancient texts, various plant names, most importantly *tu,* in fact

---

[164] Chen Chuan describes the debate, vigorously defending the Chinese origin of the tea tree and venomously attacking those who side with India. See his *Chaye tongshi,* pp. 26–8.

[165] See for example, Daniels, *Agro-Industries and Forestry,* pp. 477; Hsing-tsung Huang, *Fermentation and Food Science,* part 5 of vol. 6, *Biology and Biological Technology,* p. 503.

[166] Chen Chuan, *Chaye tongshi,* pp. 91–4.

[167] Chen Chuan traces the word for tea in various languages to two basic pronunciations of the character pronounced *cha* in Cantonese and *te* in Minnanese. Ibid., pp. 18–20.

refer to tea (*Camellia sinensis*). In his history of tea, the modern scholar
Chen Chuan tried to push the history of tea in China back four thousand
years. Others have argued that the early passages in question are not references to tea but to types of grass, or that even if these are references to
tea, there is no evidence that the leaves were used to make a beverage.[168]

The philological record on early tea in China is far from clear, and, barring new archaeological discovery, there will always be room for skepticism about tea drinking in pre-Han China. Fortunately, for our purposes,
we can pick up the history of tea with the earliest conclusive evidence for
tea drinking in China: a passage in the *Contract for a Slave* (*Tong yue*)
composed by one Wang Bao in 59 B.C., in which Wang details a number
of duties to be fulfilled by a slave, including the task of "boiling tea."[169]
After this time, scattered references to tea drinking appear with increasing frequency.   .

During the Six Dynasties period, tea drinking became fashionable
among literati officials in the south, as testified by the numerous references
to tea in the classic compendium of literati anecdotes, *Shishuo xinyu*.
Nonetheless, before the Tang, tea drinking was largely confined to a relatively small group of southern elites. In the north, milk was the drink of
preference, and the tea drinking ways of the southern literati the subject
of ridicule. A story in the sixth-century *Record of Buddhist Monasteries
in Luoyang* vividly illustrates this division in taste:

> When Wang Su first came [from the south] to the [northern] state of Wei, he
> did not take such food as lamb and goat's milk. He often ate carp soup; when
> thirsty he drank tea. Literati of the capital said that he drank one *dou* at a
> gulp; for this he was nicknamed "Leaky Goblet." Several years later, at a
> palace banquet hosted by Emperor Gaozu, Wang Su partook of a large
> amount of lamb and milk curd. Emperor Gaozu found it strange and asked:
> "Among Chinese dishes, how does lamb compare with fish soup and tea with
> milk?" In reply, Wang Su said: "Lamb is the best of land produce, while fish
> leads among seafood. Depending on one's preference, both are considered
> delicacies. In terms of taste, there is a difference between the superior and in-
> ferior. Lamb is comparable to such large states as Qi and Lu; fish, such small
> kingdoms as Zhu and Qu. Only tea is no match; it is a slave of milk."[170]

[168] Ibid., p. 5. Song figure Wang Guangguo, who, as we have seen, commented on the history of the chair, also wrote on the etymologies of words for tea. See his *Xuelin* 4, p. 124;
Qing scholar Gu Yanwu returned to the question in his *Ri zhi lu* 7, pp. 39b–40a, 42a.

[169] A translation of the passage can be found in Martin C. Wilbur, *Slavery in China during the Former Han Dynasty 206 BC–AD 25*, p. 385. The passage is also discussed in Yü
Ying-shih, "Han," in K. C. Chang, ed., *Food in Chinese Culture*, p. 70, Chen Chuan, *Chaye
tongshi*, pp. 272–3, and virtually every other study of the history of Chinese tea.

[170] *Luoyang jialan ji jiaoshi* 3, p. 126; Wang, *A Record of Buddhist Monasteries in Lo-
yang*, p. 142.

In other words, though tea was not unknown to northerners, they thought it inferior to milk and did not as a rule drink it. By the end of the Tang (i.e., the early tenth century), anyone, north or south, claiming that tea was a "slave to milk" would have been considered either barbaric or eccentric, for tea drinking had by that time spread to the north and indeed to all parts of China. By the end of the Tang, tea had become a common feature of court life. Different regions of the empire competed for the emperor's favor by giving him tea as tribute, and the emperor in turn rewarded those who served him faithfully with gifts of tea. The state even made its first attempts to tax tea, indicating that by the end of the Tang, there was a thriving trade in tea leaves. Poets composed hundreds of verses praising the merits of tea, creating what some tea enthusiasts now refer to as a genre of literature: "tea poetry."[171] There is evidence from this period for tea drinking among officials, soldiers, and even peasants. In short, by the tenth century, tea had already become established as the national drink of China, from which it would eventually spread to the rest of the world as one of the most important commodities of the modern era. The transformation of tea from a habit of southern elites in the sixth century, to a drink common to all Chinese by the beginning of the tenth, has received considerable scholarly attention. Specialists have suggested a number of factors that contributed to the rise of tea as a national drink. One of the most important of these was Buddhism.[172]

Lu Yu and the Book of Tea

Undoubtedly the most important single figure in the history of Chinese tea is Lu Yu, the eighth-century author of the *Book of Tea*, a treatise detailing the correct way to cultivate, prepare, and drink tea, including proper selection of water, use of various utensils, citations of references to tea in historical documents, and so forth. Lu Yu's book soon attained enormous popularity among the educated, providing as it did criteria and vocabulary for a new type of connoisseurship. Written at a time in which China enjoyed unprecedented stability, wealth, and rapid communication, the book enjoyed immediate and sustained success. Feng Yan (fl. 742), a contemporary of Lu Yu, commented that after the appearance of Lu's book, "those near and far were enamored [of tea sets], and a set was

[171] Zhu Zizhen, "Zhongguo cha wenhua shi," p. 150.
[172] There are a number of excellent studies on the rise of tea drinking in the Tang. See Zhu Zhongsheng, "Woguo yincha chengfeng zhi yuanyin ji qi dui Tang Song shehui yu guanfu zhi yingxiang," pp. 93–150, Lin Zhengsan, "Tangdai yincha fengqi tantao," pp. 208–28, Nunome Chōfū, "Tōdai no meicha to sono ryūtsū," pp. 255–285, and Ji Yuanzhi, "Tangdai chawenhua de jieduanxing—Dunhuang xieben *Cha jiu lun* yanjiu zhi er," pp. 99–107.

kept in the home of every enthusiast."[173] Tea spread rapidly and Lu Yu's reputation grew with it. By the end of the Tang, images of Lu Yu were worshipped by proprietors of teahouses and others in the tea industry, who themselves attributed the birth of their profession to Lu and his book.[174] In subsequent times, the *Book of Tea* inspired a steady spate of manuals for tea preparation and appreciation.[175]

Lu Yu was ideally suited to bridge gaps between north and south, monk and layman. He was born in 733 in Jiangling, a city in present-day Hubei Province. According to Lu's brief autobiography and a biographical sketch written by an acquaintance of his, he was orphaned at an early age and raised by monks. Much to his master's disapproval, Lu preferred to apply his considerable literary and scholarly talents to secular works rather than to Buddhist scriptures, eventually leaving the monastery and declining to become a monk. Nonetheless, Lu maintained close relationships with monks throughout his life, and on his death was buried by the stupa of his original Buddhist master. Significantly for the history of tea, Lu Yu's life and works disclose a close connection between tea drinking and monks. Lu's most famous friend was the poet-monk Jiaoran, who composed several poems on the subject of drinking tea with Lu Yu. Similarly, Lu's literati friend Huangfu Ran composed a poem on escorting Lu Yu to a monastery to pick tea.[176] The *Book of Tea* itself acclaims the pleasure of picking tea leaves near remote monasteries, and also encourages the use, when making tea, of the "water-strainer," a device brought to China by monks who used it to avoid accidentally killing living creatures in their drinking water.[177] In sum, Lu Yu, the key figure for the rise of tea in the eighth century, maintained close contacts with monks throughout his life and may well have adopted the habit of drinking tea from monks. Other evidence also points to the prevalence of tea drinking in monasteries during this pivotal period for the history of Chinese tea.

Tea in the Monasteries

As we attempt to follow the trail of the rapid spread of tea drinking in the eighth century, we are fortunate to have an account left us by a man who

---

[173] *Fengshi wenjian ji* (BJDG edn.) 6, p. 1.

[174] Lin Zhengsan, "Tangdai yincha fengqi tantao," p. 217.

[175] Twenty-four of these manuals, from the eighth to the eighteenth century, are listed in Huang, *Fermentation and Food Science*, p. 516.

[176] "Song Lu Hongjian Qixiasi cai cha," p. 2808.

[177] The water-strainer (*lushuinang*) appears in the monastic regulations and is described and promoted as well in a number of Yijing's works, including his *Nanhai jigui* 1, p. 208a–b, and Takakusu, *A Record of the Buddhist Religion*, pp. 30–33. See also, Foguang dacidian bianxiu weiyuan hui, ed., *Foguang da cidian*, p. 5825.

witnessed the change. Feng Yan, in addition to noting the popularity of Lu Yu's *Book of Tea* and the passion for tea sets it inspired, also ascribed the rise of tea in the eighth century to another cause. Feng writes:

> [Originally] southerners were fond of drinking tea, but at first few northerners drank it. During the Kaiyuan era [713–41] there was one Master Xiangmo of the Lingyan Monastery at Mount Tai who propagated the teachings of Chan with great success. When practicing meditation he emphasized the importance of staving off sleep. Also, he did not eat in the evening. For this reason, the Master allowed all [of his followers] to drink tea. Everyone then adopted [the habit], and tea was boiled everywhere.[178] From this time on, the custom spread from one to another as it became a fashion. From Qu, Qi, Qiang, and Li [tea drinking] spread eventually to the capital, and tea shops appeared in many cities, where tea was then boiled and sold.[179]

The two reasons given here for drinking tea both stem from distinctly monastic concerns. We have seen that one of the factors behind the monastic use of sugar was the rule that monks should not eat solids after noon, which encouraged the consumption of various sorts of liquids, including sugarcane juice, to satisfy hunger and provide energy in the afternoon and evening. Unlike sugarcane, however, tea drinking was not widespread in India, and hence it is not surprising that we find no references to tea drinking after noon in the canonical monastic regulations. Seventh-century monk Yijing (the same monk who provided such valuable information on the monastic chair), however, mentions just such a use in China. In a work on the proper use of water, Yijing insists on the use of pure water when monks consume boiled herbs, sweetened water, or boiled tea after noon (*feishi*).[180]

The second reason Feng gives for the use of tea in the monasteries is that monks employed tea to stay alert during meditation. In his eloquent yet practical manual for meditation, sixth-century monk Zhiyi addressed the problem of sleep interfering with meditation, and recommended the use of the "meditation staff" (*chanzhenzhang*), a staff employed by a monastic official to arouse meditating monks who had dozed off. Nowhere in this discussion does Zhiyi refer to the use of tea as a stimulant during meditation—this, despite the fact that Chinese had from very early on used tea to stay awake.[181] Tang sources are equally reticent on the use

---

[178] At this time tea leaves were usually ground and boiled, rather than steeped whole in hot water as they are today in China.

[179] *Fengshi wenjian ji* 6, p. 1.

[180] *Shouyong sanshui yaoxingfa*, T no. 1902, vol. 45, p. 903a. In the same work (p. 903c), Yijing, who had lived in India, clearly states that monks in "the West" do not drink tea. Yijing also warns against using impure water to boil tea after noon in his *Shuozui yaoxingfa*, T no. 1903, vol. 45, p. 904a.

[181] The earliest references to tea as a means of staying awake predate the arrival of Bud-

of tea in meditation. Nonetheless, modern monks in China and elsewhere do drink tea in between meditation sessions,[182] and the hypothesis that this practice began, as Feng suggests, during the early Tang seems likely.

Feng's assertion that the spread of tea drinking through monasteries in the early Tang can be attributed to the efforts of Master Xiangmo are just as difficult to corroborate. Although we know that Xiangmo was an influential figure in the Northern Chan lineage, we know little about his life.[183] Biographical material on Xiangmo confirms that he did indeed teach at Mount Tai, where he gathered a large following. But aside from Feng's work, no source makes a connection between Xiangmo and tea. Xiangmo was, however, known for promoting seated meditation, a practice for which he was criticized by the well-known critic of Northern Chan, Shenhui.[184] Hence, Feng's assertion that Xiangmo, determined to propagate the practice of meditation, encouraged the use of tea is reasonable, if difficult to confirm.

If evidence for tea as a tool for meditation is scant, there is ample evidence for monastic use of tea for a variety of other purposes throughout the Tang and beyond, testifying to the importance of tea as an everyday beverage in the monasteries. Seventh-century figure Daoxuan, for example, speaks of the wastefulness of monks who do not finish their tea.[185] In a curious comment in his letter from India, Yijing emphasizes the medicinal properties of tea, when, after describing the medicinal use of ginseng, he writes, "Tea is also good. It is more than twenty years since I left my native country, and this alone as well as the ginseng decoction was the medicament to my body, and I had hardly any serious disease."[186] Since, as Yijing mentioned elsewhere, tea drinking was not common in India at the time,[187] he must have gone to the trouble of bringing tea with him or of obtaining it from other travelers. Elsewhere mention is made of the use of tea in offerings to Buddhist deities.[188] The Lidai fabao ji, compiled at the end of the eighth century in Sichuan, contains several references to monks drinking tea. In one episode, a monk is delighted on receiving a

---

dhism. See Chen Chuan, Chaye tongshi, p. 124; for the Tang, see Schafer, "T'ang," in Chang, Food in Chinese Culture, p. 124.

[182] Holmes Welch, The Practice of Chinese Buddhism 1900–1950, p. 68; Robert E. Buswell, The Zen Monastic Experience: Buddhist Practice in Contemporary Korea, p. 170.

[183] For Xiangmo's biography and his place in Chan history, see John McRae, The Northern School and the Formation of Early Ch'an Buddhism, p. 63, and Faure, The Rhetoric of Immediacy, p. 100.

[184] Putidamo nanzong ding shifei lun, pp. 30–1.

[185] Jiaojie xinxue biqiu xinghu lü yi, T no. 1897, vol. 45, p. 870c.

[186] Nanhai jigui 3, p. 224c; Takakusu, A Record of the Buddhist Religion, p. 135.

[187] Shouyong sanshui yaoxingfa, p. 903c.

[188] Nittō guhō junrei gyōki 2, p. 272; Reischauer, Ennin's Diary, p. 221.

half catty of tea leaves from another monk. At another point in the book, when one monk proclaims his love for tea, a group of monks present him with a poem on the virtues of tea drinking.[189] Late Tang–early Song Chan texts frequently refer in passing to monks drinking tea. And by the early Song there are even references to a "tea hall" in the monastery, as well as a monastic office devoted especially to caring for the tea needs of the monastery.[190] Further, scattered references in Chan texts and Tang poetry indicate that tea was grown in monastic fields, a practice that continued into the Song.[191]

In sum, the evidence suggests that monks began to drink tea in the early Tang—most likely in the seventh century in areas where tea was already popular, such as the region covered by present-day Sichuan Province and in the south. There were a number of reasons for monks to drink tea, including its medicinal properties, its value as a stimulant after noon, and as an aid in staying alert during meditation. By the mid-eighth century, tea drinking seems to have spread to northern monasteries as well. It was perhaps the fact that monks were one of the most mobile segments of the population that allowed the habit to spread so quickly from southern and western monks to the north, well before it spread from southern literati to their northern counterparts. Biographies of monks from all periods of Chinese history are filled with the names of routes taken and places visited. Indeed, from the earliest times up to the present, monks were expected to spend some part of their training wandering from monastery to monastery. It is not surprising, then, that in their travels, monks who had acquired the habit of drinking tea in the south spread it to the north. Extending this hypothesis a step further, once tea was established in northern monasteries, it spread from monks to literati along the same paths of influence we have already examined in the spread of the chair and of sugar.

---

[189] *Lidai fabao ji*, pp. 187b, 159a; there is another poem on tea at p. 193b.

[190] For the use of tea in offerings, see Zhu Zizhen, "Zhongguo cha wenhua shi," p. 177. References to tea appear frequently in various *yulu* and other Chan texts from the late Tang and early Song. For references to the tea hall, see *Jingde chuan deng lu* 8, pp. 256a, 352c, 368a, and a half dozen other places in the text. The monastic office (*chatou*) is mentioned in *Chixiu Baizhang qinggui* 5, *T* no. 2025, vol. 48, pp. 1132c, 1136.

[191] Cultivation of tea by monks near monasteries is mentioned in poems by Zhang Ji (c.776–c.829) and Yuan Zhen (779–831). See "Shanzhong zeng Rinan seng," *Quan Tang shi* 384, p. 4308, and "He you feng ti Kaishansi shi yun," *Quan Tang shi* 408, p. 4541. Chan references to tea trees and fields include *Xutang heshang yulu* 9, *T* no. 2000, vol. 47, p. 1048b, and *Yunzhou Dongshan Wuben chanshi yulu*, *T* no. 1986, vol. 47, p. 509a. On monastic tea cultivation in the Song, see Fang Hao, "Songdai senglü dui yu zai cha zhi gongxian," in *Dalu zazhi*, vol. 29, no. 4 (1964), pp. 124–8, and Zhu Zizhen, "Zhongguo cha wenhua shi," p. 62.

Monks, Tea, and Literati

Among the extant works of the prominent Tang poet Yuan Zhen (779–831) is a clever ode to tea, building from one word to couplets of two characters, then three characters, and so on up to seven characters. The poem begins with the lines

> Tea
> fragrant leaves
> tender shoots
> admired by poets
> loved by monks. . . .[192]

Other poems bear witness to Yuan's claim that poets and monks were the two great champions of tea in the Tang. The *Complete Tang Poems* contains hundreds of references to tea, many if not most of which are also connected in some way to monks. In the preface to a poem on tea, Li Bai describes how on a trip to Jinling (present-day Nanjing), he encountered a monk who showed him a remarkable type of tea leaf that grew to the size of a man's palm and then led him to the place where the tea grew.[193] Similarly, Liu Yuxi (772–842) left a poem in which he describes drinking tea at a monastery. As the tea was grown right behind the monastery, there was "but an instant between the picking and the boiling." Another line in the poem remarks that "[t]he monks say that its numinous flavor suits secluded tranquility. / Bright tiny feathers prepared for fine guests."[194]

The practice of providing tea for guests seems to have originated in southern China during the Eastern Jin (317–420).[195] Sometime during the Tang, the practice spread to monasteries. Yijing commented that after eating or drinking, one must purify oneself before "paying reverence" (*li*) to another. "Even when one has drunk syrup, water, tea, or honey-water, or had ghee or sugar, one is equally unfit before one duly purifies oneself."[196] Although such a practice would seem to make sharing tea with guests impractical, the key term here is "paying reverence," which seems to refer to formal ritual salutation to a master, rather than the day-to-day etiquette of greeting visitors. Slightly later evidence discloses that the practice of offering a cup of tea to a newly arrived guest—now of course common practice in homes throughout China—was accepted custom from the

---

[192] "Cha," *Quan Tang shi*, 423, p. 4632.

[193] "Da Zuzhi seng Zhongfu zeng Yuquan Xianren zhangcha," *Quan Tang shi*, 178, p. 1817.

[194] "Xishan Lanruo shi cha ge," *Quan Tang shi* 356, p. 4000.

[195] Zhu Zizhen, "Zhongguo cha wenhua shi," p. 26.

[196] *Nanhai jigui neifa zhuan*, 2, p. 218; Takakusu, *A Record of the Buddhist Religion*, p. 90.

High Tang on; the frequent references in Tang poetry to tea parties (*chayan*) at monasteries and sharing pots of tea with monks suggest that, certainly by the eighth century, literati had come to expect a cup of tea when they visited a monastery.[197] Ennin's ninth-century diary is filled with references to tea. Recall that when local officials visited the Yang-zhou monastery where Ennin was staying, in addition to being provided with chairs, they were also immediately brought tea.[198] More than a year later, in a monastery in Shandong, Ennin again looked on as visiting officials were provided with tea.[199] The Ming dynasty *Fozu tongzai* records that during the Kaiyuan era (713–41), a monk named Zhichong of the Juelin Monastery made use of three different types of tea: one he drank himself, one he used in offerings to the buddhas, and one he used to provide for guests who would "bring along oil-cloth bags which they would fill to the last drop before returning."[200] It is difficult to determine the origins or historical accuracy of the passage (other sources are silent about Zhichong), but in spirit the passage is quite accurate, reflecting as it does three of the most important uses to which monastic tea was put, not the least of which was in service to visitors to the monasteries.

We saw above how the corded-chair became associated in the literati's minds with the serene mountain life of the tranquil monk. Literati writings reflect an even greater association between tea and the image of the monk. In a poem by Gao Shi (d. 765), for example, written when staying with friends at the Kaishan Monastery, Gao reflected on the advantages of the monastic life over the life of a high official when he wrote, "Reading books cannot compare to reading scriptures, and drinking wine is no match for drinking tea."[201] Other poets wrote of sipping tea at monasteries while sitting on a corded-chair and perusing Buddhist scriptures, or in between discussions of erudite Buddhist doctrines.[202] Buddhist aficionados like Wang Wei and Bai Juyi attempted to re-create this atmosphere of tranquil monastic repose in their own homes. Recall that in the passage I cited earlier from the *Tang History* in connection with the chair, Wang Wei in his later years chose to lead the simple life: "His studio contained nothing save a teapot, a medicine pestle, a table for scriptures, and a corded-chair. After he retired from court, he burned incense and sat

---

[197] Zhu Zizhen, "Zhongguo cha wenhua shi," p. 122.

[198] *Nittō guhō junrei gyōki* 1, p. 68; Reischauer, *Ennin's Diary*, p. 52

[199] *Nittō guhō junrei gyōki* 2, p. 224; Reischauer, ibid., p. 178.

[200] *Fozu lidai tongzai* 14, *T* no. 2036, vol. 49, p. 611c.

[201] "Tong qun gong su Kaishansi zeng Chen Shiliu suoju," *Quan Tang shi*, 212, p. 2206. Zhang Wei, in his "Daolinsi song Mo Shiyu," also speaks of the superiority of tea over wine. *Quan Tang shi* 179, p. 2018.

[202] "Tong Huangfu Shiyu ti Jianfusi Yigong fang," by Li Jiayou, *Quan Tang shi*, 206, p. 2153; "Hanshi su Xiantiansi Wuke Shangren fang," by Fang Gan, *Quan Tang shi*, 649, p. 7459.

FIG. 20. Qiu Ying, Ming dynasty, *Zhao Mengfu Writing the* Heart Sutra *in Exchange for Tea*. Handscroll, ink and color on paper. (Detail). Reproduced with permission from the Cleveland Museum of Art. John L. Severance Fund, 1963.102.

alone, occupying himself with meditation and chanting."[203] Similarly, Bai Juyi writes in one of his poems of recovering from a night of excessive drinking by sitting quietly in a corded-chair and relishing a fragrant pot of fresh-brewed tea.[204]

The relationship between monks, tea, and literati extended beyond abstract associations in the literatus's mind to more practical concerns. Early on in his trip through China, Ennin made a gift of "two large ounces of gold dust and an Ōsaka girdle" to a Korean interpreter who had assisted him with some bureaucratic paperwork after his arrival in China. The

---

[203] *Jiu Tang shu* 190b, p. 5052.
[204] "Shui hou cha xing yi Yang Tongzhou," *Quan Tang shi*, 453, p. 5126.

next day the interpreter returned the favor by offering Ennin ten pounds of powdered tea.[205] Later, when Ennin encountered a particularly stingy host, he was forced to barter for food with a pound of tea (in most of the places he stayed he was offered food for free).[206] Tang poetry also documents a number of such transactions in poems sent along with gifts to monks of tea, or in thanks for gifts of tea from monks.[207] And gifts of tea exchanged between monks and literati were common as well.

Tea served as a sort of monastic currency. As tea grew near mountain monasteries, it was readily available, and because tea was associated with the monastic life, it was useful to monks both for the sorts of material exchanges Ennin used it for when traveling and for more symbolic exchanges as well. One Tang inscription claims that in Yixing District, the practice of submitting tea as tribute to the emperor began with "mountain monks."[208] Emperors, like literati, returned the favor, rewarding monks who served the throne with gifts of tea. The most famous and historically important tea set in China was originally an imperial gift, donated to the Famen Monastery outside Chang'an by Emperor Yizong in 869.[209] Textual evidence buttresses the argument that even emperors associated tea drinking with monastic endeavors. In 788, for instance, when Emperor Daizong called together a conference of monks to compose a new commentary to the *Dharmaguptakavinaya*, he provided them with paper, ink, a ninety-day supply of vegetarian food, and twenty-five strings of tea.[210] Similarly, in 796, Dezong provided monks charged with completing a new translation of the *Avataṃsaka Sutra* with a supply of incense and tea.[211] Apparently, by the end of the eighth century, tea was considered as essential to the scholar-monk's workday as incense and paper.

Sugar is a decidedly ephemeral part of material culture, often contributing only an intangible flavor to the objects (foodstuffs) with which it is combined. Tea has, perhaps, a stronger claim to being an important component in Chinese material culture both because of the more visible, more tangible way in which it was packaged—including ornate tea bricks made with decorative molds—and for the objects that came to be associated

---

[205] *Nittō guhō junrei gyōki* 1, p. 130; Reischauer, *Ennin's Diary,* pp. 94–5.

[206] *Nittō guhō junrei gyōki* 2, p. 239; Reischauer, ibid., p. 191.

[207] Zhu Zizhen, "Zhongguo cha wenhua shi," p. 53.

[208] "Tang Yixingxian chongxiu chashe ji," in *Jinshi lu* 29, p. 2b.

[209] The set was discovered along with various other Buddhist objects in 1987. Han Wei, "Cong yincha fengshang kan Famensi deng di chutu de Tangdai jinyin chaju," pp. 44–56.

[210] *Da Tang Zhenyuan xu Kaiyuan shijiao lu* B, T no. 2156, vol. 55, p. 760b; *Song gaoseng zhuan* 15, p. 805a.

[211] *Zhenyuan xinding shijiao mulu* 17, T no. 2157, vol. 55, p. 895a (see also 892b and 893b for imperial gifts of tea).

with its preparation. The elaborate utensils discovered at Famen Monastery, for instance, illustrate the extraordinary technical sophistication tea utensils attained as well as the social prestige that could be accorded them.[212] But the role Buddhist monks played in altering Chinese material culture through the propagation of a new drink is more ambiguous than that of sugar or the chair, because although monks were instrumental in the transfer of Indian foods and furniture to China, skeptics can reasonably argue that even had Buddhism never entered China, sooner or later tea would have become China's national drink.

Feng Yan's assertion in the mid-eighth century that monks were pivotal in spreading the habit of tea drinking carries much authority as he himself witnessed the transformation of Chinese drinking habits, and virtually every study of the history of Chinese tea cites Feng's claim that the popularity of tea drinking in the north can be traced to monks who began drinking tea to stay alert during meditation and during the afternoon fast. But it would be a mistake to attribute the rise of tea drinking to Buddhism alone, much less to the efforts of a single monk. In addition to the crucial role played by Lu Yu and his influential book, at least as important to the spread of tea was the gradual consolidation of the empire by the Sui and early Tang, and the construction of more reliable systems of transportation that allowed for the rapid dissemination of ideas, habits, and objects throughout China.[213]

Nonetheless, even when we recognize that the reasons for the spread of a particular fashion or taste are often immensely diverse and complex, involving any number of personal interests and historical accidents, it is safe to say that Buddhism played an important role in the rise of tea drinking. As we have seen, the relationship between Lu Yu and Buddhism was a close one, and tea drinking was common in the monasteries in the years before Lu Yu composed his influential book. In addition, perhaps more than any other community in medieval China, monks walked the empire's new roads and enjoyed the increased safety of travel, constantly moving along a network of monasteries that stretched from one end of China to the other. Further, because of the close ties between literati officials and monks, once ideas, habits, and objects spread from one monastery to another, they could quickly spread from these monasteries to the literati cul-

---

[212] The complete Tang tea set included various types of pots used for boiling the water, a pestle for grinding the dried tea leaves to powder, a spoon for measuring the tea into the water, a spoon for beating the tea powder into the water, and so on. Han Wei, "Cong yincha fengshang."

[213] Zhu Zhongsheng gives three main reasons for the spread of tea in the Tang: (1) improved transportation, (2) the efforts of Lu Yu, and (3) the importance of tea for Buddhist monks and Daoist priests. Zhu Zhongsheng, "Woguo yincha fengshang zhi yuanyin ji qi dui Tang Song shehui yu guanfu zhi yingxiang."

ture in the nearest prefecture along well-established, frequently employed social paths.

Beyond the role monks played during the crucial period when tea drinking caught on throughout China, Buddhism continued in later periods to play a prominent role in the development of habits and objects associated with tea. Monks continued to produce tea at their monasteries; in fact, monastic growth of tea in the Song was of a scale that the state (which at this point claimed a monopoly on the sale of tea) found it necessary to insist that monks grow tea only for monastic use and not for sale.[214] Numerous sources make it clear that tea continued to play an important part in the monastic routine through the Ming and into the Qing.[215] In this context, it is not surprising that Ming-era monks are credited with "inventing" Longjing tea, to this day one of the most popular types of Chinese tea grown.[216] Monks are also credited in the Ming with developing what was to become a particularly popular type of teapot, the "purple-clay teapots" of Yixing (Yixing zishahu).[217] In sum, the utensils used in the preparation of tea, the way harvested leaves were treated, the location in which tea plants were grown, and the very habit of tea drinking itself all in some degree owe a debt to the introduction and spread of Buddhism in China.

CONCLUSION

With the three examples discussed in this chapter, we begin to get a sense of the scope and complexity of the Buddhist impact on Chinese material culture. The chair came to China with Buddhism as an incidental accoutrement of the monastic lifestyle, but nonetheless sparked dramatic changes in the arrangement of the Chinese household. The heavy traffic of monks between India and China allowed for the transmission to China of technical knowledge (and probably equipment) for the manufacture of sugar, which, like the chair, quickly spread beyond the monasteries to society at large. Despite the fact that tea drinking was not common in ancient India and had no relation to early Buddhism whatsoever, the adoption of the habit of tea drinking by Chinese monks eventually contributed to the spread of the habit throughout China at all levels of society.

Although from the point of their introduction in medieval times to their

[214] Fang, "Songdai senglü," p. 127.

[215] Zhu Zizhen, "Zhongguo cha wenhua shi," pp. 109, 154.

[216] Ibid., p. 101.

[217] Ibid., pp. 143–4. In addition, Huang Hsing-tsung speculates that the practice of drinking small cups of strong oolong tea, brewed in small pots (gongfu cha), may well have begun with monks. Fermentation and Food Science, p. 561.

present positions as basic commodities in the daily life of virtually all Chinese, none of these objects were especially promoted in Buddhist scriptures; none are the result of pious attempts to inculcate Buddhist values. The meditation chair is referred to in the monastic regulations, but there seems never to have been a concerted effort to promote its use by monks in the monasteries, much less by laymen at home. Cane sugar is used as a metaphor in Buddhist scriptures, but its consumption garners no merit; nor does one achieve merit for sitting on a chair or drinking tea. Although tea may have been used to stay alert during meditation, it is not so much as mentioned in meditation manuals, much less sutras. The chair and tea did at one time carry Buddhist associations, and on one level could even be said to have stood symbolically for the life of the monk. But to a large extent, these associations came about by accident. More precisely, they were formed in literati culture rather than through the efforts of monks in Buddhist writings. Certainly none of the three objects was ever considered to have possessed sacred power. Whatever associations there were between Buddhism and these goods were tenuous and ephemeral—outside a handful of erudite specialists, few from the Song on recognized any connection at all between the chair, sugar, tea, and Buddhism.

A number of other types of goods, of varying levels of importance, followed a similar pattern of diffusion. The *quanti*, a particular kind of stool, narrow in the middle, with top and bottom of equal size, came to China with Buddhism, and for a brief time enjoyed some popularity.[218] A certain type of necklace became popular during the Six Dynasties period when imported, along with Buddhist images, from India.[219] And monks seem to have played a role in the spread of the popularity of the peony in the Tang.[220] More substantially, monks made important contributions to the pharmaceutical repertoire of medieval Chinese medicine by introducing plants from India and elsewhere. Yijing, who was particularly fascinated with medical matters, devoted three sections of his letter from India to medicine. In one of these sections, he notes the different materials available in the two countries. After describing a number of Chinese drugs unavailable in India, he turns to drugs used outside China but unavailable back home:

> Harītaka [yellow myrobalan] is abundant in India; in North [India] there is sometimes the Yujinxiang [Kuṅkuma], and the Awei [assafoetida] is abundant in the western limit of India. The Baroos camphor is found a little in the islands of the Southern Sea, and all the three kinds of cardamoms are found in Dvāra[-vati]; two kinds of cloves grow in Pulo Condore. Only the

---

[218] Sun Ji, *Zhongguo shenghuo*, pp. 198–250.
[219] Ibid., pp. 107–21.
[220] David McMullen, unpublished manuscript.

herbs above mentioned are used in India in the same way [as in China]; all other herbs are not worth gathering.[221]

Aware of the variety of medicinal plants abroad, Emperor Gaozong at approximately the same time dispatched the Central Asian monk Nandī to the Indies and later to Cambodia to collect exotic drugs, suggesting that monks were considered to be among the leading authorities in such matters.[222] Further, several Tang literati commented on the impressive gardens at Buddhist monasteries in China, where exotic medicinal herbs were grown.[223] And a number of poems from the period allude to visits literati made to monks to have various illnesses treated.[224] All of this suggests that monks not only brought new drugs to China from India and elsewhere but were also instrumental in incorporating them into the pharmaceutical repertoire of the Chinese laity.

The history of incense tells a similar story. As in the case of medicine and tea, incense had been in use in China long before the entrance of Buddhism, and probably as early as the late Zhou.[225] Nonetheless, Buddhism, with the avenues of exchange it facilitated between China and the rest of Asia, was instrumental in introducing new fragrances and fueling the demand for these fragrances in China. The most important example of the Buddhist contribution to Chinese incense is aloeswood (*chenxiang*), an incense as central to the fragrances of Asia as frankincense was to the incenses of the West.[226] Mentioned in several Buddhist texts, aloeswood appears to have originated in India, whence it spread to Southeast Asia, entering China in the third century, when we find our first references to aloeswood in Chinese literature. In his detailed study of the history of aloeswood in East Asia, Yamada Kentarō repeatedly warned of the danger of emphasizing the role of Buddhism to the exclusion of other important reasons for the success of this type of incense in China; the appeal of the fragrance itself and its availability in large and relatively inexpensive quantities were also key factors in its incorporation into Chinese ritual

---

[221] *Nanhai jigui* 3, p. 323c; Takakusu, *A Record of the Buddhist Religion*, pp. 128–9.

[222] *Xu gaoseng zhuan* 4, p. 458c; Schafer, *The Golden Peaches of Samarkand*, p. 183.

[223] "Ti Ganlusi," by Xu Tang, *Quan Tang shi* 604, p. 6987; "Chongxuansi Yuanda nian yu ba shi hao zhong ming yao fansuo zhizhe duo zhi Tiantai Siming Baoshan Juqu congcui," by Pi Rixiu, *Quan Tang shi*, 613, p. 7078; "Ji Faqiansi ling Yin Taishi," by Zhang Bin, *Quan Tang shi* 702, p. 8076.

[224] See for instance, "Xun seng Yuanjiao yinbing," by Yang Ning, *Quan Tang shi* 290, p. 3303 (also given under Li Changfu, *Quan Tang shi* 601, p. 6948), and "Wen Zheng Shangren ji," by Huangfu Ran, *Quan Tang shi* 249, p. 2805.

[225] Joseph Needham with Lu Gwei-Djen, *Spagyrical Discovery and Invention: Magisteries of Gold and Immortality,* part 2 of vol. 5, *Chemistry and Chemical Technology in Science and Civilisation in China,* p. 132.

[226] Yamada Kentarō, *Tōa kōryōshi,* p. 195.

and everyday life.[227] Nonetheless, no one would question that Buddhism played an important role in the introduction of aloeswood to China. The same can be said for gum guggal (*anxixiang*), first mentioned in Chinese sources in a biography of the monk Fotucheng.[228]

At least as important as the role monks played in bringing incense to China was the role Buddhism played in encouraging its consumption once it arrived, which, of course, encouraged importation of more incense and eventually domestic production as well.[229] We have records of monastic preparation of incense and ample evidence that huge quantities of incense were burned in the monasteries, prompting one Tang poet to describe the carefree life of the monk with the line "What is there for a monk to do but sweep the ground and burn incense?"[230] As in the case of tea, incense entailed the manufacture of utensils related to its use, most notably the censer. One of the most common objects held by devotees depicted in medieval Chinese Buddhist art is the censer, testifying to both the close connection drawn between Buddhist devotion and incense, and to the popularity of the device, which, in many cases, was manufactured with considerable skill at great expense.[231]

Most curious of all is the apparent connection between monastic ritual use of incense and the use of calibrated incense to keep time. On the basis of several Tang poems that describe the ritual use of calibrated incense by monks, a Tantric text translated in the Tang, and a monastic inventory from Dunhuang, Silvio Bedini has argued plausibly that the "incense seal" (*xiangyin* or *xiangzhuan*), a timekeeping device that eventually became popular in China, originated in Buddhist monasteries.[232]

From furniture and sugar, to medicine and timekeeping devices, in the Chinese context all of these objects were innovations that required to a greater or lesser extent reception by open, tolerant minds before they could be assimilated. Comparison to new ideas in the more rarefied realm of philosophical discourse is instructive. Confronted with the contrast between the flourishing of Buddhist philosophy in the Tang, and the relatively stagnant, cautious classical scholarship of the same period, modern scholars of medieval Chinese thought have argued that while literati-

[227] Ibid., pp. 225–31.

[228] *Gaoseng zhuan* 9, p. 384a; Schafer, *The Golden Peaches of Samarkand*, p. 169.

[229] Production of aloeswood incense in China itself seems to have begun in earnest in the Tang. Yamada, *Tōa kōryōshi*, pp. 232–42.

[230] "Ti Chongfusi Chanyuan," by Cui Tong, *Quan Tang shi*, 294, p. 3343. For a reference to preparing incense in a Tang monastery, see *Xiang pu*, by Hong Chu, "Tang Huadusi xiangfa" (SKQS edn.) C, p. 11b.

[231] Edward Schafer cites a Tang description of an elaborate incense brazier adorned with countless gems. *The Golden Peaches of Samarkand*, p. 161. Just as impressive are the actual Tang censers discovered at Famensi.

[232] Silvio A. Bedini, *The Trail of Time: Time Measurement with Incense in East Asia*, pp. 81–92; Needham et al., *Civil Engineering and Nautics*, pp. 146–7.

officials could express themselves creatively in poetry, the stodgy intellectual environment of the court and the dull weight of tradition stultified attempts at metaphysical inquiry; with the exception of a handful of mavericks like Han Yu, bent on investing new life into what had become a stale tradition of classical exegesis, creative thinkers in medieval China were drawn to Buddhism and the opportunities it provided for new ideas and exploration.[233] The same tendency was at work in the less self-conscious area of daily habits and customs. Many of the most spectacular cultural changes marking the end of the medieval world of the Tang—the introduction of the chair and the consequences this entailed for Chinese interiors in general, marked changes in food, and the adoption of tea as a national drink—were tested and refined in Chinese monasteries. If in medieval Europe the court was a "nursery for good manners,"[234] in medieval China the monastery was a nursery for new forms of material culture.

Had Buddhist monasteries remained aloof from the rest of Chinese society, and had monks come down from their mountain retreats only to preach on Buddhist doctrine, then none of this would have made much difference—monastic innovations in furniture, food and so on could be justly viewed as an exotic aberration, products of the curious habits of a peripheral group of unusual men practicing an isolated, insular lifestyle. But because of the close relationships monks cultivated and maintained with literati and the court, and because of the nature of these relationships in which monks were not only allowed but expected to engage in activities only tangentially related to Buddhist doctrines, practices first developed in the monasteries found their way into other social groups removed from Buddhism, thus allowing for the sort of striking accidents and incidentals discussed in this chapter.[235]

Interaction between monks and court figures, most notably the emperor, were often decisive for key developments in the history of Chinese Buddhism. Tang Taizong's close relationship with the monk Xuanzang and Emperor Xuanzong's relationship with Śubhakarasiṃha, for instance, ensured the great translators of any resources they needed to carry out their projects; and the patronage of emperors such as Liang Wudi, Sui Wendi, and Wu Zetian allowed for the construction of monasteries, stupas, and large-scale works of Buddhist art throughout the empire. The motivations for imperial patronage of Buddhism were complex, involving an easy mixture of personal devotion and political necessity. One of the side

[233] Mou Runsun, "Tangchu nanbei xueren lunxue zhi yiqu yu yingxiang," pp. 50–89; Guo Shaolin, *Tangdai shidafu yu fojiao*, pp. 229–34.

[234] Elias (quoting Erasmus), *The Civilizing Process*, p. 63.

[235] For a detailed study of Chinese monks who mastered specialties only indirectly related to Buddhist doctrines (painting, poetry, medicine, etc.), see Cao Shibang (Tso Sze-Bong), *Zhongguo shamen waixue de yanjiu: Hanmo zhi Wudai*.

effects of this relationship between court and monastery was that monks were common figures at the Chinese court, where they served a number of functions. Most of these functions, in one way or another, called for the exchange of gifts. When foreign monks in need of patronage arrived in the capital, they often submitted gifts from foreign rulers. As we have seen, monks variously submitted everything from jeweled furniture, to trees and medicinal herbs. We have also seen examples of emperors who used monks as emissaries, sending out monks to collect medicine from other countries or to procure foreign techniques for making sugar. Tea and incense fell within the scope of the circuit of gifts as well, as emperors honored monks with gifts of incense, tea, and tea utensils.

In the case of sugar, the court played an active and decisive role in importing the substance from India. Although the relationship between sugar and Buddhism was largely incidental, there was nothing accidental about its transmission to China. Most of the cases we have looked at, however, took place in a much more casual, haphazard way. In most cases, objects that were developed or imported by monks for monastic use were passed on to the rest of Chinese society by literati and local officials with an interest in Buddhism. While many of the literati who maintained close ties with monks and regularly visited monasteries took Buddhist ideas and values very seriously, much of their interaction with monks can, nonetheless, be roughly classified as leisure activity. Literati visited monasteries in part for the scenery, for stimulating conversation with men outside their everyday social and political circles, and out of a vague longing for serenity embodied in romantic associations with monastic life. Specific objects were as much a part of this bundle of associations as doctrines, folklore, and hagiography, stimulating an interest in material aspects of the monk's surroundings and providing motivation to take home some of the objects connected to this lifestyle.

The process of growth and adaptation of new forms of material culture is enormously complex, involving different types of people, an assortment of attitudes, and random historical circumstances. However many ideas and practices we may group under the category of Buddhism, Buddhism alone was not responsible for the success in China of any of the objects discussed above. Nevertheless, Buddhism, and particularly Buddhist monks, played a decisive role in winning a place in Chinese society for each of them. Over the long, varied course of Chinese history, Chinese were exposed to any number of types of food, furniture, and devices, but only a handful of these caught on. In the histories of objects in other places and times, other factors tipped the balance, whether they were new technologies (like the stirrup or the automobile), new beliefs (like Islam or nationalism), or new media (like paper, radio, or television). In the cases discussed above, the key factor that transformed marginal curiosities into staples of everyday life was monastic Buddhism.

CONCLUSION

THE SHEER WEALTH of data relevant
for the study of the impact of Buddhism on Chinese material culture
threatens to overwhelm us in an avalanche of numbing detail that raises
as many questions as it answers. The subject matter ranges from monumental statues that have withstood the elements for centuries and may
well still stand hundreds of years from now, to clumps of sugar that lived
for only a few hours before dissolving in a monk's bowl long ago. It includes straightforward instructions for how to brew a pot of tea, paeans
to the majesty of monastic architecture, and sophisticated treatises on the
nature of material reality.

One way of bringing order to the divergent stories of different objects
is to focus on their beginnings: certain objects originated in India and
came to China with Buddhism. These provide, perhaps, our earliest examples of Buddhism's impact. In each of the preceding chapters, I have
devoted considerable attention to the vexing problem of origins, in most
cases making arguments for the Buddhist roots of objects or of attitudes
and behaviors associated with objects in China. But given the reams of
relevant Chinese textual material and the periodic announcement of
major archaeological finds for all periods of Chinese history, claims for
the Buddhist origins of particular objects and practices are inevitably tem-
pered by caveats and hesitant conjecture. Images of buddhas and bodhisattvas came to China with Buddhism, and the belief that images could
contain sacred power and demand propitiation seems to have come to
China with Buddhism as well, but some day new evidence may show that
ancient Chinese worshipped images long before Buddhism arrived. Indeed, the recent finds at Sanxingdui, as puzzling as they are spectacular,
may represent just such a tradition of image worship in ancient western
China. The same could be true for many of the objects discussed above.
Instances of relic worship, prayer beads, the codex, and the chair in China
independent of Buddhist influence may one day be discovered. Enough is
known, however, that even the uncovering of specific instances of these
objects apart from Buddhist influence would detract little from the determining role Buddhism played in the histories of all these things. While the
genealogy of any object that stretches over centuries always involves a
complex of multiple influences, an overall picture of the prominent role
of Buddhism in shaping the development of Chinese material culture is
clear enough and significant enough to warrant a place in any general history of China.

At the same time, this general picture of the impact of Buddhism on Chinese material culture painted in broad brushstrokes necessarily effaces many motifs, which, though relatively minor players in the grander narrative, are no less important in their own right. While I have, for instance, had much to say about monks, I have said next to nothing about nuns. Although communities of nuns have flourished throughout Chinese Buddhist history, nuns were not a significant force in the formation of the Chinese Buddhist canon, and I have found no writings by nuns on, for example, monastic attire or ritual implements. Nonetheless, nuns do appear on occasion in inscriptions for Buddhist statues and monasteries, and scattered references to connections between nuns and other types of people—figures at court, lay devotees, monks—can be found here and there, suggesting ways in which nuns may have influenced others, perhaps including the way nuns and those who associated with them related to objects. A closer look at this evidence might reveal areas of material culture in which nuns played an important and distinctive role.[1] Moreover, despite the fact that, unlike monks—whose ideas about objects can be studied on the basis of writings as well as material remains—nuns left us little documentation on their attitudes toward things, it may be possible to reconstruct distinctive patterns in the material culture of nuns through careful analysis of artifacts alone.[2] For now, however, I reluctantly leave nuns where the tradition placed them: on the margins of Chinese Buddhist history.

Daoists too have been given short shrift. I have alluded briefly to Daoist attitudes toward books and bridges, but the relationship between the material culture of practitioners of Buddhism and Daoism must have been much richer than such occasional references imply. In this case, the problem was not a dearth of material—the Daoist canon contains an abundance of relevant texts, and there is a substantial body of Daoist archaeological and artistic artifacts as well—but of competence: I am not sufficiently familiar with Daoist writings and objects, and the field of Daoist studies, still in its infancy, tells us too little about Daoist material culture to allow for more general conclusions about how it relates to its Buddhist counterpart.

Another area that will have raised the suspicions of the discriminating reader is my emphasis on India as the sole source of foreign influence on Chinese material culture, as if Buddhism had leaped directly from a uni-

---

[1] Through analysis of Indian inscriptions, Gregory Schopen has argued that nuns played a key role in the introduction of the image cult to Indian Buddhism, since a large number of our earliest inscriptions on Buddha images indicate that they were made with donations from nuns. Similar instances of the influence of Chinese nuns on material culture may one day be demonstrated. See Schopen, *Bones, Stones, and Buddhist Monks*, ch. 11.

[2] Roberta Gilchrist has attempted such a project for medieval English nuns, with mixed results, in her *Gender and Material Culture: The Archaeology of Religious Women*.

form, monolithic India to China without passing through Central or Southeast Asia. In general, the influence of these regions on Chinese Buddhism seems to have been limited, in part because of the Chinese belief that only Indian Buddhism was authentic, and hence that any changes that took place in the process of transmission to China from the holy land of India were to be exposed and rooted out. Perhaps more important still was a conservatism of Buddhism in Central Asia and early Southeast Asia; Buddhists in these areas were much less likely to condone innovation than the more culturally confident Chinese. Here, however, I am limited by the sparse scholarship on Buddhism in these areas, as I am by the absence of detailed work on the influence of Tibetan Buddhism on China in the late Imperial period—all areas in which I lack expertise. More careful attention to interaction between the material cultures of these regions may one day provide us with a more nuanced picture of exchange and influence across what were always porous cultural boundaries.[3]

Within the geographic and temporal boundaries of Chinese history, it would be of great value to refine our picture of the Buddhist impact by assessing the relative importance of Buddhism for Chinese material culture in different time periods. This would allow us to look at other contemporary factors in order to determine why Buddhism had a particularly great influence at a particular time. The word *impact* suggests the meeting of physical objects, with the greatest change at the point of contact—a giant splash in a pond followed by ever-diminishing ripples. But Buddhist influence on Chinese material culture was not greatest in the first century, when our earliest evidence for Buddhism in China begins to surface. In many cases, it took centuries of persistent contact before a Buddhist object or a certain set of Buddhist ideas about objects began to take hold in Chinese society at large. Although textual evidence for monastic use of the chair appears in the third century and in pictorial evidence in the sixth, it was not until the eighth century that the chair began to make inroads into lay society, and not until the tenth that it became common in Chinese interiors. Similarly, while fifth-century texts refer to the rosary, it is only in the seventh that we begin to see references to the use of the rosary among laypeople.

Nor can we trace the point of greatest impact to an era of Buddhism's greatest vigor in India, even were scholars of Indian Buddhism to locate such an era. Significantly for an overall chronology of the impact of Buddhism on Chinese material culture, Buddhism continued to play an important role even after the supply of foreign monks and texts from India withered in the eleventh century. Devotees continued to make Buddhist

---

[3] On the relationship between Central Asian and Chinese Buddhism, see Erik Zürcher, "Han Buddhism and the Western Region," pp. 158–82, and Valerie Hansen, "The Path of Buddhism into China: The View from Turfan," pp. 37–66.

icons, books, and monastic robes long after Indians ceased making these things. And the Buddhist notion of merit continued to play a crucial role in the construction of bridges in China up to modern times. Moreover, Buddhist attitudes toward objects did not remain static once they were established in China. The rosary only became a sign of political status in the seventeenth century, and Buddhist books only began to be printed in the eighth, though the rosary had been brought to China long before and the idea that making Buddhist books in great quantities garnered great merit had been widespread in China for centuries. No period in particular stands out as an era of unequaled influence. Individual objects often followed histories distinct from political and economic developments, and, just as importantly, distinct from each other. That is, the spread of the chair did not follow on the spread of Buddhist art or the increasing popularity of the rosary, and for this reason we cannot easily chart the rise and fall of Buddhist influence in Chinese material culture as a whole. The problem is one of such complexity, involving subjective judgments about what constitutes greater or lesser influence, that it is futile to attempt to assign a golden age to Buddhist material culture in China, or worse, to consign a particular period to an era of decline; for every golden age requires a dark one to lend it luster.

More fruitfully, we might look instead to elements and patterns of Buddhist influence that are repeated in the histories of various objects, each of which proceeded according to its own pace and rhythm. In a few instances, individual events produced dramatic changes, as in the imperial efforts in the Tang to import sugar-refining techniques from Indian monasteries, or the relic campaign of Sui Wendi that sent Buddhist relics to all corners of the empire amidst much pomp and fanfare. More commonly, however, changes happened only very slowly under constant cultural pressure from Buddhist individuals and institutions. In other words, the persistent presence of Buddhist practices and ideas provided the resources as well as the vast stretches of time needed for the spread and development of particular forms of material culture. Unlike the modern era, in which styles of furniture, dress, and architecture can be quickly assigned to a particular decade, material culture was slow to change in premodern times, and often required the long-term overwhelming influence of a powerful cultural force before any change could take hold. Once established in Chinese society, Buddhism provided just such a force.

THE ROLE OF MONKS

While not denying the place of devotees and even non-Buddhists in this long process of acculturation and innovation, the key position of monks in the transformation of Chinese material culture immediately attracts our attention. I have argued at several points for the importance of the cosmopolitan character of monastic culture. We have seen the tendency for monks to transcend social and geographic boundaries on a number of occasions. Monks were willing to adopt a new posture in order to accommodate the chair and readily acquired techniques for making sugar because both were common in Indian monasteries and fit into the routines of monastic life—the chair as an instrument for meditation and sermonizing, sugarcane juice as a dietary supplement during the afternoon fast.

In the same way, monks went to great lengths to emulate the clothing and accoutrements of their Indian counterparts, and felt great uneasiness when they learned that they differed in dress and habit from monks in India. Recall the concerns of leading Chinese monks over the introduction of the sleeved robe or over the way Chinese monks sat at table. In other words, while retaining a decidedly Chinese identity, at the same time Chinese monks felt themselves a part of a distinct community that included Indian monks. In this respect, monks differed from, say, Chinese literati, who did not admire, much less identify with, the educated elites of other cultures. While Chinese poets never expressed interest, much less admiration, for Indian poetry, Chinese monks pored over great Indian Buddhist works with the care and respect of disciples for masters. It was in part this cultural humility that opened Chinese monasticism to certain types of innovation. More precisely, it was the conservative tendency of monks who wished to maintain a way of life they believed had been instituted by the Buddha that allowed them to adopt practices and attitudes unfamiliar to Chinese tradition.

The pull toward uniformity in monastic culture in China went beyond the longing for a pure order conceived in the age of the Buddha. Monks were ready to share habits among themselves that others were reluctant to adopt. We see this dynamic at work within China in the case of tea drinking, which northern monks readily copied from southern monks, while other types of northerners (officials, soldiers, farmers) were slower to accept the southern drink. The distinctive identity of the monk was maintained in part through the accepted tradition of monastic travel: most monks were expected to spend some part of their career traveling about to various monasteries and pilgrim sites. And throughout the history of Buddhism in China, it was common for monks to travel over great distances, meeting along the way with other monks either in their home regions or themselves traveling. The sense of identity reinforced through such repeated, personal interactions was buttressed by the distinctive monastic uniform, comprised of a specified set of ritual and practical implements, including robes, alms bowl, and staff. Whether persecuted on the basis of their clothing or respected because of it, monks wrapped themselves in their identity as a distinctive type of religious professional. In other words, material objects at once reflected a monastic identity that transcended the boundaries confining the behaviors and attitudes of other types of people, and at the same time gradually, persistently, introduced to outsiders new objects and new approaches to them.

Most of the monks in a position to exert influence over the course of material culture were elites within the monastery and in the local community beyond the monastery gates. It required a certain social standing to raise funds for images and monasteries, to organize and propagate the cult of relics to a famous master, to regulate monastic clothing. These same leading monks were those most likely to be well versed in Buddhist texts and doctrines, which at times profess ideas with direct bearing on the use of objects. There is a danger of only noting the influence of monks in cases in which clearly Buddhist ideas are prominent, but in general, monastic contributions to Chinese material culture were in fact closely tied to formal Buddhist doctrines. The practice of worshipping Buddhist images, the cult of relics, and the manufacture of books are well attested in Buddhist scriptures. Although the worship of images and the use of books may have appeared in India only several centuries after the founding of Buddhism, this was not known to Chinese monks, who, on the basis of Indian texts that claimed to represent the authentic word of the Buddha, believed that both practices went back to the Buddha's day and believed that they were solidly based on doctrines established by him. Because of this concern for fidelity to tradition, monks allowed their attitudes toward objects to be shaped by what they perceived to be orthodox Buddhist thought.

While the use of the purple robe as a sign of imperial favor is unrelated to Buddhist doctrine, the symbolism of the monk's robe as a mark of asceticism or, later, as a symbol of Dharma transmission is closely tied to distinctively Buddhist ideas, not only expressed in the robes themselves but also in sophisticated doctrinal treatises by leading Buddhist thinkers. Monastic use of the rosary was usually linked to beliefs in Amitābha's paradise and the notion that one could be reborn there by reciting his name— again, ideas developed and propagated in mainstream Buddhist scriptures. Most prominent of all for the history of material culture was the doctrine of merit, including the belief that one could transfer to one's intimates the merit derived from making certain material objects. Records associated with icons, relics, books, monasteries, and bridges commonly make explicit reference to particular Buddhist scriptures that extol the doctrine of merit. In the creation of all these objects, monks often played leading roles and had ample opportunity to propagate Buddhist principles they had learned in lectures or from reading Buddhist books. And when records of monks who encouraged the use of the rosary, the building of monasteries, or the printing of Buddhist books disclose the monk's motivations, they almost always refer to traditional, canonical Buddhist doctrine.

We have also seen, however, that at times objects operated according to principles of their own, unrelated to formal Buddhist exegesis. We can find some tangential links between the chair, sugar, and tea to the strictures of the monastic way of life that called for certain types of ritual behavior, but for the most part foodstuffs and furniture followed courses independent of formal doctrine: they slipped into the history of Chinese Buddhism almost without notice. With this point we return to one of the issues raised at the beginning of this book: How did doctrines of the evanescence and ultimate lack of inherent existence of the material world affect the way monks related to objects? And what of the austere ideal of restraint and renunciation?

Had these ideas been followed to their extremes, Buddhist material culture would consist of little more than bare walls and drab garments. Although, as we have seen, this is far from the way the story in fact unfolded, both notions did affect the way monks thought about things. For most of the objects discussed above, some monks expressed reservations about their propriety. Monks questioned the ability of images to convey the eternal truths of Buddhism and provocatively suggested that holy relics had nothing to do with enlightenment. They insisted on hard distinctions between the monk's robe as symbol of the Dharma and the Dharma itself, and fought against elaboration in the basic design of the robe. Some monks complained that use of the rosary represented an ostentatious display of piety, and condemned those who mistook the material expression of Buddhist doctrines in books for the more authentic experience of personal awakening, divorced from any form of artificial mediation. The tension between ideals of renunciation and a longing for splendor and concrete expression runs throughout the history of Chinese Buddhism. And well-read, sophisticated monks were always eager to express their misgivings about dealings with the material world, especially while they were engaging in them: noting in an inscription to an image that images are weak approximations of an ineffable reality, and writing books on the futility of pursuing the greatest truths by writing books.

That being said, when we review the development of Buddhist material culture in China, the effects of antimaterialist ideals on behavior prove to have been very limited. For the most part, monastic gowns remain relatively plain and simple—no doubt as a sign of the monk's renunciation of the world—but instances of elaborate, ornate monastic garb are common in depictions of monks from the Tang to the present, and use of the eye-catching purple robe as a sign of monastic attainments died out not because of protests from indignant monks critical of this affront to the traditional ascetic symbolism of the robe but rather because the scramble for the purple robe among prominent monks and their followers reduced its value as a mark of distinction. Few monks ever seriously challenged the construction of large monastic complexes or huge donations to the monastic community. Fund-raising on a grand scale has always been an important part of the monastic institution, whether it meant soliciting donations of cash or land or extracting goods from resources already in a monastery's possession. On a smaller, more personal scale, monks and nuns still make regular use of the rosary and other ritual implements, and the avid worship of relics as material embodiments of sacred power and sources of merit never abated. The same holds true for images, whether we speak of small, humble images or immense, imperially sponsored statuary. The few Chan stories of monks destroying Buddhist icons because of their inadequacies as expressions of profound truths seem all to have been rhetorical parables, rather than records of monks who actually destroyed images. The many cases in which Buddhist images were destroyed, whether in the medieval or modern period, were almost all inspired by economic or political motives and unrelated to Buddhist doctrinal critiques of decadence or of the illusory nature of the material world. Similarly, the few anecdotes we have of monks burning Buddhist books were written to make a lofty philosophical point about the limitations of language and not to encourage others to follow suit with real torches and bonfires. Social movements based on Buddhist doctrine devoted to stripping Buddhism of material expression never materialized in China.

In sum, while Buddhist doctrines that supported the creation and propagation of material things can be clearly shown to have influenced behavior and to have changed the way China looked, the effect of antimaterialist doctrines in Buddhist scriptures was more subtle and for the most part limited to psychology and rhetoric. The case studies above reveal that this tendency toward the material was not a stark sign of hypocrisy or bad faith. The immense repertoire of doctrinal writings available to an erudite monk provided ample justification for the use and elaboration of all manner of objects. The monastic regulations, we are assured, can be altered to adapt to local custom, one can recognize the ultimate emptiness of an object while still employing it provisionally, and so forth. Explanation of actions involving material things was hence more a matter of choosing the appropriate doctrinal principles than it was a question of rigorously applying a standard creed of carefully defined terms and concepts. While the skeptic can read the rich history of Buddhist material culture in China as a sad tale of compromise and ideals unrealized, a more empathetic view sees the story as a victory of subtlety over dogmatism and of active expression over mute resignation.

BEYOND MONKS

Even in the ideal world of the sutras and the monastic regulations, monks were not an insulated social group cut off from the secular world. If they had been, the possessions and habits of monks would have offered only curious but peripheral information on the material culture of China. In fact, because of the integration of monks into Chinese society, monks played a prominent role in the development of Chinese material culture, and in Chinese culture in general. Buddhist scriptures are replete with advice and admonitions on the interaction between the laity and the monastic community, indicating that already in ancient India, monks were expected to maintain contacts of various sorts with people in society at large, ranging from local donors to powerful rulers. From very early on it was assumed that monks would depend upon the support of laypeople, that they would converse with various sorts of people, that they would visit people outside the monastery and be visited by them. Indeed, one of the most prominent characteristics of Buddhist teachings is the emphasis on proselytism; monks were supposed to attempt to change the behavior of the people around them, and a wealth of evidence demonstrates that Buddhist monks everywhere took these admonitions to heart.

Chinese monks interacted with secular figures in various settings, including sermons, public debates, and rituals. On a more personal level, literati, figures with considerable cultural influence, were fond of visiting monasteries and chatting with monks over a cup of tea or sending their sons to the monastery for the libraries and the solitude the monastery provided while they studied for the civil service examinations. In a few instances, most notably the chair, these sorts of private, personal interactions had an impact on the spread of customs and objects from the monasteries to society at large. Conversations between literati and monks, often held in remote monasteries in spectacular mountain settings, involved not only discussion of esoteric Buddhist doctrines but also the vague and romantic longings of local and court officials for a simpler, more serene way of life. These sorts of casual, unselfconscious encounters in the end were just as important for the history of material culture as sweeping imperial edicts and the weighty pronouncements of leading Buddhist thinkers. Material culture was too diffuse and unwieldy to be controlled by any institution, whether monastic or imperial.

In addition to these indirect forces subtly shaping material culture, the production and use of objects often involved cooperation between monks and other types of people. As tokens of friendship or esteem, monks and laypeople exchanged gifts of tea, rosaries, scepters, robes, and other objects thought appropriate in association with Buddhist practitioners. Recall the experience of the ninth-century Japanese monk Ennin, who traveled across China giving and receiving an assortment of "Buddhist" gifts as he asked for and received favors from monks, officials, and other figures who supplied him with food, lodging, travel passes, and conversation during his long and difficult pilgrimage.

While such gifts helped to cement one-to-one relations and to set their tone, at times the creation of objects led more generally to the formation of enduring "figurations." That is, the making of large, complex structures brought people together in relationships of mutual dependency. Buddhist sculpture, for instance, often involved negotiations between prominent patrons, eminent monks, and less visible but nonetheless essential artisans. These three groups had to learn to cooperate with one another— the prominent monk lending his name to a stele erected in part to glorify a group of local families, the craftsman making sure the Buddhist figures he depicted were to the patron's liking, the patrons wanting assurance that the merit for the act would go to their deceased relatives. Similarly, in major ceremonies in which, for instance, the finger relic of the Buddha at Famen Monastery, or the preserved body of the Sixth Patriarch, Huineng, were paraded through the nearby city, monks joined together with high officials and local devotees to ensure that the relic was displayed properly and to maximum effect; all these groups were needed to orchestrate elaborate ceremonies centered on a particular relic. In these instances, objects did not merely facilitate social interactions, as in the case of gifts; rather, objects were the cause and focus of interaction, the thing that brought together people who might otherwise never have exchanged a word.

At times we can discern elements of tension in the figurations that grew up around objects. Recall the medieval monk complaining of foul-mouthed copyists hired to write out sacred Buddhist scriptures. The demand for Buddhist books and the shortage of qualified calligraphers made such compromises inevitable. Perhaps the most interesting such conglomeration of diverse types of people revolved around the construction of bridges. The history of bridges is particularly curious because of the tension between the three types of people needed to make a bridge: the local official, charged by the central authorities with building and maintaining bridges; local elites, who provided the funding for bridge projects; and monks, to whom the local official assigned the task of raising money. In some cases, the local official was ambivalent and even hostile to the Buddhist teachings of merit monks used to solicit funds, but with pressure from his superiors to repair a dilapidated bridge and being short of cash, he had little choice but to turn to the local monastery, the only institution with the experience, social connections, and rhetoric of philanthropy necessary to raise large sums in a hurry. For their part, monks at times expressed disdain for crude donors interested only in personal aggrandizement and the practical benefits that come from meritorious acts and unfamiliar with the sophisticated discussions of the relationship between merit and motivation presented in Buddhist exegetical literature. And one suspects that monks also wearied of orders from the local magistrate, commanding them to raise funds for another bridge, an effort often barely acknowledged once the bridge was built. But a large monastery with complex sources of income depending on various types of social ties relied on good standing in the community, the largesse of local families, and the cooperation of the local magistrate to function smoothly; and so, leading monks had little choice but to accept the magistrate's orders and set to work on the process of raising money for yet another bridge.

The case of bridge-building shows that, far from driving the dynamics of material culture, monks were at times caught up in processes over which they had little control. The same was true not only in communities beyond the monastic compounds but is even reflected in material culture at the heart of monastic life. Chinese monks were from early on profoundly interested in the monastic regulations, and went to great lengths to procure and translate different sets of regulations that had grown up over the course of centuries in different communities of monks in India. Once translated (the sets of the monastic regulations that were to have the greatest effect on Chinese monasticism were translated in the fifth century), these massive, complex works seemed to cover every aspect of monastic life, providing ample material for learned monks to determine the proper stance monks should take on the manufacture and use of various objects. The monastic regulations did not, however, shield monks from external influence, and in many cases we see that rather than monks introducing new objects and their uses to the laity, it was the other way around. The purple monk's robe was first introduced by the emperor as a mark of imperial favor. The *ruyi* scepter seems to have slipped into monastic practice, or at least to have taken on new meaning there, after it was used in debate and "pure conversation" by literati and court figures. Though monks helped to spread the habit of tea drinking to the north, and contributed to the rise of paper production, they invented neither: credit for the "discovery" of tea and paper go to secular Chinese circles untouched by Buddhist influence.

In fact, monks were often peripheral to the use of even Buddhist objects. While some monks engaged in large-scale projects devoted to creating monumental Buddhist art or to organizing the creation of steles made by large communities, monks were not necessary for the creation of countless smaller images, placed in a shrine on the family estate, in the entrance hall of one's home, or in a craftsman's workshop. In the preceding discussion of bridges, I emphasized the importance of monks for raising funds. But there were also many cases of bridges built without the presence of monks, though still for the traditional Buddhist purpose to garner merit, which could then be transferred to recently deceased family members.

Equally important for our understanding of the place of Buddhism in Chinese society, Buddhist elements of material culture not only persisted but often took on new uses and meanings without the intervention of monks. This tendency is particularly evident in the case of the rosary. Ming connoisseurs developed criteria for judging the aesthetic qualities of rosaries without consulting Buddhist scriptures. The rosary could be used as a gift from one layman to another without it entailing any deep religious significance, or even implying that the owners engaged in any of the rituals associated with the rosary and described in Buddhist ritual manuals and writings of leading monks. And there is no evidence that monks played a significant role in the transformation of the rosary into an emblem of court status in the Qing.

With the case of the political symbolism of the rosary, the history of the object reaches the blurry borders of what we term Buddhism; while the court beads clearly derived from Buddhist prayer beads, they were not used to count Buddhist recitations, and in everyday life their original association with Buddhism was lost. The same can be said of the chair, an object whose associations with monks was forgotten soon after it swept into Chinese interiors on a grand scale. In the histories of many objects, Buddhism provides keys to only one segment of a longer, more complex history. Buddhist ideas and practices provided important impetus to the development of bookmaking, bridge-building, and sugar refining in China, but none of these can be said to be strictly Buddhist objects. Yet, rather than excluding such things—as difficult as they may make it for us to precisely define a neatly confined "Buddhist tradition"—they deserve to be considered a part of the story and testimony to the complex string of reactions provoked by the Buddhist impact on Chinese culture.

THE ILLUSION OF IMPACT

For all my hedging and repeated invocations of "complexity" to describe the process of the impact of Buddhism on Chinese material culture, the title of this book suggests a straightforward process of unidirectional influence. I have already noted that when assessing the relative role of Buddhism in material culture at different times in Chinese history, the metaphor of impact does not hold up to scrutiny—there was no single, central moment of greatest impact followed by ever-diminishing influence. Even more fundamentally, the notion of impact may be misleading in that it suggests a passive Chinese culture overwhelmed by a powerful foreign religion. When addressing changes in the material culture of any sophisticated society, one-sided cultural influence is extremely rare: cultures are usually influenced at least in part because they want to be. In areas like Japan and Tibet, where Buddhism entered at an early stage in the formation of their cultures, perhaps one could speak at a high level of generalization of the relatively indiscriminate adoption of Buddhist objects and attitudes toward them, though even in these cases, specialists in Japan and Tibet are sure to bristle at the notion and quickly come to the defense of cultural autonomy. In the history of Chinese Buddhism, selectivity is even more central. For in China, Buddhism encountered a culture with enormous self-confidence and few qualms about pronouncing the foreign inferior.

The titles of two of the most important modern studies of Chinese Buddhism—Erik Zürcher's *The Buddhist Conquest of China,* and Kenneth Chen's *The Chinese Transformation of Buddhism*—frame the problem nicely. The reality, as both authors were no doubt well aware as they wrote their books, was somewhere in between the two models of foreign conquest and local transformation. While foreign missionaries made great efforts to propagate Buddhist teachings, practices, and objects in China, Chinese made equally impressive efforts to acquire the Buddhist objects they found useful. Buddhist relics were not forced upon Chinese devotees; the faithful actively sought them out, whether that meant procuring them from distant India or manufacturing them at home. And once Buddhist objects reached China, they frequently went through changes and transformations to meet the needs of a culture and environment markedly different from India.

Buddhist influence was not all-pervasive in China, and even in some areas in which we might expect a strong Buddhist presence, we find none. For all of the importance of Buddhism in shaping Chinese conceptions of the afterlife, throughout Chinese history the arrangement of tombs and the artifacts placed there show little trace of Buddhist influence. Above ground, in the late Imperial period, while Buddhist motifs and images of various sorts proliferated among ordinary people, the canon of elite painting allowed little room for Buddhism, and one can visit exhibitions or look through catalogs of the most prominent paintings of the Ming-Qing period without finding Buddhist objects. The objects with which the refined literatus of late Imperial China surrounded himself to demonstrate his status and taste—a zither, a landscape painting, servants, and "antiquities"—did not for the most part include any of the Buddhist objects I have discussed; this was an area from which Buddhist influence was forbidden entrance.

But when we leave the rarefied realm of the literatus's studio, Buddhist influence peeps up in every corner. And a closer look at that catalog or museum exhibition of Ming landscapes is likely to yield a stupa or two peeking through the mist. In sum, then, the recognition of the persistent role of Buddhism in the development of Chinese material culture enriches not only our understanding of the history of Buddhism and its function in the societies it entered but also alerts us to the importance of objects in the social interactions of any complex, sophisticated culture, China included.

CHARACTER LIST FOR CHINESE, JAPANESE,

AND KOREAN TERMS

a'nalü—阿那律
Àn Hezi—安和子
An le xing—安樂行
anxixiang—安西香, var. 安息香

bafutian—八福田
Baima Monastery—白馬寺
bainayi—百衲衣
bai nian—百年
Baixing—百姓
Bai Xingjian—白行簡
bantang—半糖
Baoshan—寶山
Baosiwei—寶思惟
beiyun—背雲
Benyuan—本源
bian—籩
Biancai—辯才
Binglingsi—炳靈寺
Biyun Monastery—碧雲寺

Cangyong—藏用
Cao Wangxi—曹望悕
cha—茶
Chajing—茶經
Changjue—常覺
changmingdeng—長明燈
Changya—常雅
chanzhenzhang—禪鎮杖
chaozhu—朝珠
chatou—茶頭
chayan—茶晏
Chenbao—陳寶
Chencang—陳倉
Chen De—陳德
cheng—秤
Cheng Dachang—程大昌
Cheng Duaner—程段兒
Chengguan—澄觀

chenxiang—沈香
chizhu—持珠
Chizhu songfo—持珠誦佛
chuang—床
Chuntuo—純陀
chuxi—出席

Damo lun—達摩論
Danxia Tianran—丹霞天然
Daoan—道岸
Daocheng—道誠
Daochuo—道綽
Daoheng—道恆
Daomi—道密
Daoshi—道世
Daoxin—道信
Daoxuan—道宣
Daoxun—道詢
Dayun Monastery—大雲寺
Di Fengda—翟奉達
digong—地宮
Dihua—地花
Di Huang—翟黃
Dong Wanggong—東王公
dou—豆
Du Guangting—杜廣庭
Du Wenqing—杜文慶

Ennin—圓仁
Er ya—爾雅

Famen Monastery—法門寺
Fang Guan—房琯
fangji—方技
faqiao—法橋
Faxian—法顯
faxiang shuzhu—法相數珠
Fayi—法意
Fazang—法藏

Lanfeng—嵐峰
Leizhou—雷州
li—禮
liang—梁
Lianhua—蓮華
Li Fuguo—李輔國
ling—靈
Lingdi—靈帝
linggu—靈骨
Lingquan Monastery—靈泉寺
lingyan—靈驗
Linji—臨濟
Lin Xiyi—林希逸
Li Shizhen—李時珍
Liu Ding Zixian—劉定子先
Liu Hu—劉胡
Liu Huifei—劉慧斐
Li Xianhui—李仙蕙
Li Xun—李訓
Longjing—龍井
longku—龍窟
Longmen shiku diaosu—龍門石窟
雕塑
Lu Lengjia—盧楞伽
luohan—羅漢
lushuinang—漉水囊
Lu Yu—陸羽

machi—馬齒
Maiji (Mt.)—麥積山
Miaofeng Fudeng—妙峰福登
Miaoying—妙應
mingfu—冥福
Mingxiang ji—冥祥記
mo—貘
Mogaoku—莫高窟
muchuang—木床
Musang—無相
muzhu—母珠

nianzhu—念珠
niaozu—鳥足

Ouyang Xiu—歐陽修

Pan (Lady)—潘夫人

Piyu jing—譬喻經
poniduo—頗尼多
Puan—普安
Puzu—普足

Qian Hongchu—錢弘俶
Qibaotai—七寶臺
Qiju—器具
Qinglingling zhenyan—磬鈴鈴眞言
Qingming shanghe tu—清明上河圖
qingtan—清談
Qin Taishangjun Monastery—秦太
上君寺
Qiu Jun—丘濬
Quanfu—全付
quanti—筌蹄

Ruicheng County—芮城縣
ru qi qi—如其劑
ruyibao—如意寶
ruyi baozhu—如意寶珠
ruyitong—如意通

sanhui—三會
sanjie—三界
Sanshen zhenyan—三身眞言
santai—三台
sanyou—三有
Sengda—僧達
Sengqie—僧伽
Sengyihuan—僧衣環
Sengyuan—僧淵
Shangguan sengdu deng zaoxiang
bei—上官僧度等造像碑
shanshu—善書
Shao Bowen—邵伯溫
shatang—沙糖
sheli—舍利
shelizi—舍利子
shen—神
Shencou—神湊
shengchuang—繩床
Shenhui—神會
Shen Kuo—沈括
Shennong—神農
Shenxiu—神秀

shen yi—甚異
Shimen Monastery—石門寺
shimi—石蜜
shuangxi—雙喜
Shuilian Qiao—水簾橋
shuilu—水陸
Shuiyu shuzhu—水玉數珠
shuzhu—數珠
Sien—四恩
Siku quanshu—四庫全書
Siwei—思惟
Songdai de ziyi shihao—宋代的紫衣
    師號
Su Gong—蘇恭
Su Jingtang—蘇敬唐
Sun Hao—孫皓
Sun Quan—孫權
Su Xiang—塑像

ta (platform)—榻
ta (stupa)—塔
Taishang ganying pian—太上感
    應篇
tanbing—談柄
tang—糖
Tao Hongjing—陶弘景
tapo—塔婆
tengsheng—藤繩
tiao—條
tieniu—鐵牛
Tōdaiji—東大寺
Tongfan Qingzhao—通梵清沼
Tonghui Yunsheng—通慧雲勝
Tong yue—僮約
Tongzi tongshen ji—童子通神集
Tuoshan—駝山

Uisang—義湘

Wang Bao—王豹
Wang Chong—王充
Wang Dun—王敦
Wang Mingsheng—王鳴盛
Wang Pizhi—王闢之
Wang Qihan—王齊翰
Wang Shao—王劭

Wang Shaozong—王紹宗
Wang Woshi—王我師
Wang Xuance—王玄策
Wei Gao—韋皋
Wei Wenhou—魏文侯
Weize—惟則
Wei Zheng—魏徵
Wenyan—文偃
Wofo Monastery—臥佛寺
wu gongyang—五供養
wuweiyin—無畏印
wu xieming—五邪命
Wuzhuo—無著

xiangfa—像法
xiangjiao—像教
Xiangmo (Master)—降魔師
xiangyin—香印
xiangzhuan—香篆
xianlu—仙籙
Xianping—咸平
Xiantong Monastery—咸通寺
Xiaoguo youlou zhi yin—小果有漏
    之因
Xiaowen (Emperor)—孝文帝
Xijing fu—西京賦
xin—心
xingfu—興福
Xing Tipi—幸替否
Xinxiu bencao—新修本草
Xiushan—修善
Xi Wangmu—西王母
xizhang—錫杖
Xuanyun—玄蘊
Xu Du—徐度
Xu Dunli—徐敦立
Xun Ji—荀濟

Yang Guifei—楊貴妃
Yang Jian—楊堅
Yanshou—延壽
Yan Zhitui—顏之推
Yaofang—藥方
yi—飴
Yijing—義淨
yinggu—影骨

Yiqiao—義橋
Yixing District—義興縣
Yixing zishahu—宜興紫砂壺
Yize—遺則
yizi[1]—椅子
yizi[2]—倚子
Yongle dadian—永樂大典
Yongming Yanshou—永明延壽
Yuan Rang—原壤
Yuanshao—圓紹
Yuanzhao (Tang translator)—圓照
Yuanzhao—元照
Yuejiang Qiao—越江橋
Yuezhou—越州
Yu Qing—余靖
Yu Yue—俞樾
Yu Zijian—于子建

Zanning—贊寧
Zengren—增忍
zhaijie—齋潔
Zhang Dai—張岱
Zhang Daoling—張道陵
Zhang Heng—張橫
Zhang Ji—張籍
Zhang Tao—張燾
Zhang Xingshuo—張興碩
Zhanran—湛然
zhaohun—招魂

Zhen Dexiu—眞德秀
Zhengong—甄公
zhengjuexin—正覺心
Zhenjue—眞覺
zhentong—針筒
Zhichong—志崇
Zhi Daolin—支道林
zhiduo—制多
Zhidu si—智度寺
Zhigui—指歸
Zhixi—智晞
Zhixian—智閑
Zhiyi—智顗
Zhiyuan—智淵
Zhou Fang—周昉
Zhou Wenju—周文矩
zhuangyan—莊嚴
Zhu se za huo—諸色雜貨
zhuwei—塵尾
Zhu Xi—朱熹
zhuxi (chairman)—主席
zi—緇
zifu—紫服
Zijue—自覺
ziyi—緇衣
Zongji—總記
Zongmi—宗密
Zou—鄒
Zuyin—祖印

ABBREVIATIONS

CSJC *Congshu jicheng* 叢書集成 (Taipei: Taiwan Shangwu Yinshuguan, 1965).

BJDG *Biji xiaoshuo daguan* 筆記小說大觀 (Taipei: Xinxing Shuju, 1960).

SBBY *Sibu beiyao* 四部備要 (Shanghai: Zhonghua Shuju, 1927–37).

SBCK *Sibu congkan* 四部叢刊 (Shanghai: Shanghai Yinshuguan, 1919).

SKQS *Jingyin wenyuan siku quanshu* 景印文淵四庫全書, ed. Ji Yun 紀昀 et al. (Taipei: Taiwan Shangwu Yinshuguan, 1983–86).

T *Taishō shinshū daizōkyō* 大正新修大藏經, ed. Takakusu Junjirō 高楠順次郎 and Watanabe Kaigyoku 渡邊海旭 (Tokyo: Taishō Issaikyō Kankai, 1924–32).

WORKS CITED

PREMODERN (BEFORE 1900) CHINESE AND JAPANESE WORKS

"Aiyong shi" 愛詠詩, by Bai Juyi 白居易 (772–846), in *Quan Tang shi* 446, p. 5010.

Amituo jing 阿彌陀經 (Skt. *Sukhāvatīamṛtavyūha*), T no. 366, vol. 12.

Anhai zhi 安海志 (Shanghai: Shanghai Shudian, 1992) .

Apidamo jushe lun 阿毗達磨俱舍論 (Skt. *Abhidharmakośaśāstra*), T no. 1558, vol. 29.

Baiqian song daji jing Dizang pusa qingwen fashen zan 百千頌大集經地藏菩薩請問法身讚, T no. 413, vol. 13.

Bai san'gai dafodingwang zuisheng wubi daweide jin'gang wu'ai dadaochang tuoluoni niansong fayao 白傘蓋大佛頂王最勝無比大威德金剛無礙大道場陀羅尼念誦法要, T no. 975, vol. 19.

"Baizhangqiao ji" 百丈橋記, by Li Zhongguang 李仲光 (fl. 1223), in *Leizhou fuzhi* 雷州府志 10, p. 20, in *Xijian Zhongguo di fangzhi huikan* 稀見中國地方志匯刊, ed. Zhongguo Kexueyuan Tushuguan (Beijing: Zhongguo Shudian, 1992), vol. 47.

"Baoshouyuan ji" 保壽院記, *Xianchun Lin'an zhi* 77, pp. 16–7.

Beijing Tushuguan cang Zhongguo lidai shike taben huibian 北京圖書館藏中國歷代石刻拓本彙編, Beijing Tushuguan Jinshi zu 北京圖書館金石組 ed. (Zhengzhou: Zhongzhou Guji Chubanshe, 1989).

Bei shan lu 北山錄, by Shenqing 神清 (d. 814), T no. 2113, vol. 52.

"Bei Wei xiaochang san nian Jiang Boxian zao Mile xiang ji" 北魏孝昌三年蔣伯仙造彌勒像記, rubbing in the collection of the Fu Ssu-nien Library, Institute of History and Philology, Academia Sinica.

Ben cao gang mu 本草綱目, by Li Shizhen 李時珍 (1518–93) (SKQS edn.).

Bie yi za ahan jing 別譯雜阿含經 (Skt. *Saṃyuktāgama*), T no. 100, vol. 2.

Cefu yuangui 冊府元龜, comp. Wang Qinruo 王欽若 (962–1025) et al. (Taipei: Taiwan Zhonghua Shuju, 1972).

"Cha" 茶, by Yuan Zhen 元稹 (779–831), in *Quan Tang shi* 423, p. 4652.

Chang ahan jing 長阿含經 (Skt. *Dīrghāgama*), T no. 1, vol. 1.

Chaxiangshi sanchao 茶香室三鈔, by Yu Yue 俞樾 (1821–1907) (BJDG edn.).

"Chengzi zhi shu: san" 程子之書三, by Zhu Xu 朱熹 (1130–1200), in *Zhuzi yulei* 朱子語類 (Beijing: Zhonghua Shuju, 1986), 97, pp. 2479–505.

"Chen Sanke ji" 陳三恪記 (for the Yuejiang Qiao 越江橋) in *Sichuan tongzhi* 31, p. 64a.

"Chi jian Wutaishan Da huguo shengguang si Miaofeng Deng Chanshi zhuan" 敕建五臺山大護國聖光寺妙峰登禪師傳, by Hanshan Deqing 憨山德清 (1546–1623), in *Hanshan dashi mengyou quan ji* 30, p. 317a–320b.

Chi song jin'gang jing lingyan gongde ji 持誦金剛經靈驗功德記, T no. 2743, vol. 85 (Pelliot no. 2094).

Chisongzi zhangli 赤松子章麗, in *Zhengtong daozang* 正統道藏 (Taipei: Shangwu Yinshuguan, 1923–26), Harvard Yenching no. 615.

Chixiu Baizhang qinggui 敕修百丈清規, comp. Dehui 德輝 (fl. 1338), *T* no. 2025, vol. 48.

"Chongfu An" 崇福庵, in *Changzhao hezhi gao* 常昭合志稿, ed. Wang Jin 王錦, (1797 edn.), 16, pp. 28b–29a.

"Chongjian Kongmujiangqiao ji" 重建孔目江橋記, by Zhang Jingcang 張景蒼, in *Xinyu xianzhi* 新喻縣志, eds. Wen Jukui 文聚奎 and Wu Zengkui 吳增逵 (1873 edn.), 2, pp. 45b–46b.

"Chongxiu Ayuwang si muyuan shu" 重修阿育王寺募緣疏, by Tu Long 屠隆 (1542–1605), in *Ayuwang shan zhi* 阿育王山志, comp. Guo Zizhang 郭子章 (Taipei: Xinwenfeng, 1978), 4, pp. 12a–14a.

"Chongxiu Tongkou Lingguangqiao ji" 重修桐口靈光橋記, in *Fujian tongzhi* 福建通志, comp. Chen Shouqi 陳壽祺 (1771–1834) (1868 edn.) 29, pp. 8b–9a.

"Chong xiu Wan'an qiaoting ji bei" 重修萬安橋亭記碑, by Xingru 行如, in *Shanghai beike ziliao xuanji* 上海碑刻資料選集, ed. Shanghai Bowuguan 上海博物館 (Shanghai: Shanghai Renmin Chubanshe, 1980), pp. 61–3.

"Chongxuansi Yuanda nian yu ba shi hao zhong ming yao fansuo zhizhe duo zhi Tiantai Siming Baoshan Juqu congcui" 重玄寺元達年逾八十好種名藥凡所植者多至自天台四明包山句曲叢翠, by Pi Rixiu 皮日修 (d. 880), *Quan Tang shi* 613, p. 7078

Chu sanzang jiji 出三藏記集, comp. Sengyou 僧祐 (445–518), *T* no. 2145, vol. 55.

Da ban niepan jing 大般涅槃經 (Skt. *Mahāparinirvāṇasūtra*), *T* no. 374, vol. 12.

Da ban niepan jing yiji 大般涅槃經義記, by Huiyuan 慧遠 (523–92), *T* no. 1764, vol. 37.

Da bao ji jing 大寶積經 (Skt. *Mahāratnakūṭa*), *T* no. 310, vol. 11.

Da beikongzhi jin'gang dajiaowang yigui jing 大悲空智金剛大教王儀軌經 (Skt. *Hevajra[dākinījālasambara]tantra*), *T* no. 892, vol. 18.

Da Biluzhe'na jing guangda yigui 大毘盧遮那經廣大儀軌, *T* no. 851, vol. 18.

Da Cien si sanzang fashi zhuan 大慈恩寺三藏法師傳, by Huili 慧立 (b. 614) and Yancong 彥悰 (fl. 649), *T* no. 2053, vol. 50.

Da fangdeng daji jing 大方等大集經 (Skt. **Mahāvaipulyamahāsaṃnipātasūtra*), *T* no. 397, vol. 13.

Da fangguang fo huayan jing 大方廣佛華嚴經 (Skt. *Buddhāvataṃsakasūtra*), *T* no. 278, vol. 9.

Da fangguang fo huayan jing 大方廣佛華嚴經 (Skt. *Gaṇḍavyūha*), *T* no. 293, vol. 10.

Da fangguang pusazang Wenshushili genben yigui jing 大方廣菩薩藏文殊師利根本儀軌經 (*Skt. *Āryamañjuśrīmūlakalpa*), *T* no. 1191, vol. 20.

Damo lun 達摩論 (Dunhuang manuscript), Peking no. 8374.

"Daolinsi song Mo Shiyu" 道林寺送莫侍御, by Zhang Wei 張謂 (fl. 743), *Quan Tang shi*, 197, p. 2018.

Daoxing banruo jing 道行般若經 (Skt. *Aṣṭasāhasrikāprajñāpāramitā*), *T* no. 224, vol. 8.

Daruma no goroku 達摩の語錄. *Zen no goroku* 禪の語錄, ed. Yanagida Seizan 柳田聖山 (Tokyo: Chikuma Shobō, 1969).

Da Song sengshilüe 大宋僧史略, by Zanning 贊寧 (919–1001), *T* no. 2126, vol. 54.

Da Tang Xiyu ji 大唐西域記, by Xuanzang 玄奘 (602–64), *T* no. 2087, vol. 51.

Da Tang Zhenyuan xu Kaiyuan shijiao lu 大唐貞元續開元釋教錄, comp. Yuanzhao 圓照 (fl. 778), *T* no. 2156, vol. 55.

Da zhi du lun 大智度論 (Skt. *Mahāprajñāpāramitāśāstra*), *T* no. 1509, vol. 25.

"Da Zuzhi seng Zhongfu zeng Yuquan Xianren zhangcha" 答族姪僧中孚贈玉泉仙人掌茶, by Li Bai 李白 (699–762), *Quan Tang shi* 178, p. 1817.

Dedao ticheng xizhang jing 得道梯橙錫杖經, *T* no. 785, vol. 17.

Dehu zhangzhe jing 德護長者經 (Skt. *Śrīguptasūtra*), *T* no. 545, vol. 14.

"Donglingsi zhuangtian ji" 東靈寺莊田記, by Lu Huizhi 陸徽之, in *Wudu wencui xuji* 吳都文粹續集, comp. Zheng Huchen 鄭虎臣 (SKQS edn.), 34, pp. 19–20.

Dongpo zhilin 東坡志林, by Su Shi 蘇軾 (1036–1101) (CSJC edn.).

"Dong Wei Tianping er nian Songyang si shamen tonglun Yanzun fashi deng zao qi ji fota tiangong ji baiyu xiang ji" 東魏天平二年嵩陽寺沙門統倫艷遵法師等造七級佛塔天宮及白玉像記, in *Beijing Tushuguan cang Zhongguo lidai shike taben huibian*, vol. 6, p. 28.

Dunhuang fojiao jinglu jijiao 敦煌佛教經錄輯校, ed. Fang Guangchang 方廣錩 (Jiangsu: Jiangsu Guji Chubanshe, 1997).

"Du Wenqing deng zao Tiangong xiang ji" 杜文慶等造天宮象記, in *Lu Xun jijiao shike shougao*, vol. 1, p. 131.

Du xing za zhi 獨醒雜志, by Zeng Minxing 曾敏行 (d. 1175) (SKQS edn.).

Duyang zabian 杜陽雜編, by Su E 蘇鶚 (fl. 890) (CSJC edn.).

"Du zhu seng" 獨住僧, by Xu Ning 徐凝 (fl. 806), *Quan Tang shi* 474, p. 5380.

Fahua zhuanji 法華傳記, by Seng Xiang 僧詳 (fl. 667), *T* no. 2068, vol. 51.

Fajue jingxin jing 發覺淨心經 (Skt. *Adhyāśayasaṃcodana*), *T* no. 327, vol. 12.

Fanwang jing 梵網經, *T* no. 1484, vol. 24.

Fanwang jing pusajieben shu 梵網經菩薩戒本疏, *T* no. 1813, vol. 40.

Faxian zhuan jiaozhu 法顯傳校註, by Faxian 法顯 (f. 399), ed. Zhang Xuan 章巽 (Shanghai: Shanghai Guji Chubanshe, 1985).

Fayuan zhulin 法苑珠林, by Daoshi 道世 (fl. 668), *T* no. 2122, vol. 53.

Fenbie gongde lun 分別功德論, *T* no. 1507, vol. 25.

Fengshi wenjian ji 封氏聞見記, by Feng Yan 封演 (fl. 742) (BJDG edn.).

Fo bannihuan jing 佛般泥洹經 (Skt. *Mahāparinirvāṇasūtra*) *T* no. 5, vol. 1.

Fo benxing ji jing 佛本行集經 (Skt. *Abhiniṣkramaṇasūtra*), *T* no. 190, vol. 3.

Foshuo zhude futian jing 佛說諸德福田經, *T* no. 683, vol. 16.

Foshuo zunshang jing 佛說尊上經, *T* no. 77, vol. 1.

Fozhi biqiu liuwu tu 佛制比丘六物圖, by Yuanzhao 元照 (1049–1116), *T* no. 1900, vol. 45.

Fozu lidai tongzai 佛祖歷代通載, by Nianchang 念常 (b. 1282), *T* no. 2036, vol. 49.

Fujian tongzhi 福建通志, ed. Chen Shouqi 陳壽祺 (1771–1834) (1868 edn.).

Gaiyu congkao 陔餘叢考, by Zhao Yi 趙翼 (1727–1814) (Shanghai: Shangwu Yinshuguan, 1957).

"Gan Weilin ji" 甘爲霖記, by Gan Weilin 甘爲霖, in *Sichuan tongzhi* 32, pp. 4b–6a.

"Gaobizhen Tongjiqiao bei" 高壁鎭通濟橋碑, by Xiao Gong蕭珙 (fl. 868), in *Shanyou shike congbian* 山右石刻叢編, comp. Hu Pinzhi 胡聘之, 9, pp. 34–6, reproduced in *Shike shiliao xinbian*, series 1, vol. 20.

Gaoseng Faxian zhuan 高僧法顯傳, by Faxian 法顯 (fl. 399), *T* no. 2085, vol. 51.

Gaoseng zhuan 高僧傳, by Huijiao 慧皎 (497–554), *T* no. 2059, vol. 50.

Genbenshuo yiqieyoubu bichuni pinaiye 根本說一切有部苾芻尼毘奈耶 (Skt. *Mūlasarvāstivādabhikṣuṇīvinayavibhaṇga*), *T* no. 1443, vol. 23.

*Genben shuoyiqieyou bu pinaiye*根本說一切有部毘奈耶 (*Skt. Mūlasarvāstivā-davinayavibhaṇga*), *T* no. 1442, vol. 23.

Genben shuoyiqieyou bu pinaiye yao shi 根本說一切有部毘奈耶藥事 (*Skt. Mūlasarvāstivādavinayavastu*), *T* no. 1448, vol. 24.

Genben shuoyiqieyou bu pinaiye za shi 根本說一切有部毘奈耶雜事 (*Skt. Mūlasarvāstivādavinayakṣudrakavastu*), *T* no. 1451, vol. 24.

Guangdong xinyu 廣東新語, by Qu Dajun 屈大均 (1630–96), *Qu Dajun quan ji* 屈大均全集 (Beijing: Renmin Wenxue Chuban She, 1996), vol. 4.

Guang hongming ji 廣弘明集, by Daoxuan道宣 (596–667), *T* no. 2103, vol. 52.

Guanxin lun 觀心論, *T* no. 2833, vol. 85.

Guanxin lunshu 觀心論疏, by Guanding 灌頂 (561–632), *T* no. 1921, vol. 46.

Guanzhong chuangli jietan tu jing 關中創立戒壇圖經, by Daoxuan 道宣 (596–667), *T* no. 1892, vol. 45.

Guier ji 貴耳集, by Zhang Duanyi 張端義 (fl. 1234) (CSJC edn.).

"Guitian lu" 歸田錄, by Ouyang Xiu 歐陽修, in *Ouyang Wenzhong quanji* 歐陽文忠全集 127 (SBBY edn).

"Gui, zuo, bai shuo" 跪坐拜說, by Zhuxi 朱熹 (1007–1072), in *Huian xiansheng Zhu Wengong wenji* 晦庵先生朱文公文集 68, pp. 1a–2b (SBCK edn.).

"Haijue Chanshi shanyuan" 海覺禪師山院, by Guanxiu 貫休 (832–912), in *Quan Tang shi* 837, p. 9437.

Haiyi pusa suowen jingyin famen jing 海意菩薩所問淨印法門經 (Skt. *Sāga-ramatipariprcchā*), *T* no. 400, vol. 13.

Hanshan dashi mengyou quan ji 憨山大師夢遊全集, by Hanshan Deqing 憨山德清 (1546–1623), *Xu zang jing*, vol. 127.

"Hanshi su Xiantiansi Wuke Shangren fang" 寒食宿先天寺無可上人房, by Fang Gan 方干 (fl. 860), *Quan Tang shi*, 649, p. 7459.

Hanshu 漢書, by Ban Gu 班固 (32–92) (Beijing: Zhonghua Shuju, 1962).

"He you feng ti Kaishansi shi yun" 和友封題開善寺十韻, by Yuan Zhen 元稹 (779–831), *Quan Tang shi*, 408, p. 4541.

Hongming ji 弘明集, by Sengyou 僧祐 (445–518), *T* no. 2102, vol. 52.

Hou Hanshu 後漢書, by Fan Ye 范曄 (398–445) (Beijing: Zhonghua Shuju, 1965).

Jiali 家禮, by Zhu Xi 朱熹 (1130–1200) (SKQS edn.).

"Jiaofang ge'er" 教坊歌兒, by Meng Jiao 孟郊 (751–814), in *Quan Tang shi* 374, p. 4200.

Jiaojie xinxue biqiu xinghu lü yi 教誡新學比丘行護律儀, by Daoxuan 道宣 (596–667), *T* no. 1897, vol. 45.

Jiaoliang shuzhu gongde jing 校量數珠功德經, *T* no. 788, vol. 17.

"Jiaoyu Luo Yuanqi chongjian Yiwenqiao yin" 教諭羅元琦重建異文橋引, in *Yunnan tongzhi gao* 雲南通志稿, ed. Ruan Yuan 阮元 (1764–1849) (1835 edn.), 48, pp. 11a–12a.

Jiaxing fuzhi 嘉興府志, comp. Xu Yaoguang 許瑤光 (1879 edn.).

Jidumiao beihaitan jiqi bei 濟瀆廟北海壇祭器碑 in *Jinshi cuibian* 103, pp. 40a–45b.

"Ji Faqiansi ling Yin Taishi" 寄法乾寺令諲太師, by Zhang Bin 張蠙 (fl. 895), *Quan Tang shi* 702, p. 8076.

"Ji ju" 箕踞, by Wang Mingsheng 王鳴盛 (1722–97), in *Shiqishi shangque* 十七史商榷 24. 2a–b (1787; rpt. Taipei: Guangwen Shuju, 1960).

Jilei bian 雞肋編, by Zhuang Jiyu 莊季裕 (fl. 1133) (SKQS edn.).

Jin'gang banruo boluomi jing 金剛般若波羅密經 (Skt. *Vajracchedikā*), *T* no. 235, vol. 8.

Jin'gang banruo jing shulun zuanyao 金剛般若經疏論纂要, by Zongmi 宗密 (780–841), *T* no. 1701, vol. 33.

Jin'gang banruo jing zanshu 金剛般若經贊述, by Kuiji 窺基 (632–82), *T* no. 1700, vol. 33.

Jin'gang banruo jiyan ji 金剛般若集驗記, by Meng Xianzhong 孟獻忠, *Xu zang jing*, vol. 149.

Jin'gang banruo shu 金剛般若疏, by Jizang 吉藏 (549–623), *T* no. 1699, vol. 33.

Jin'gangding jing yujia shibahui zhigui 金剛頂經瑜伽十八會指歸, *T* no. 869, vol. 18.

Jin'gangding yizi dinglunwang yujia yiqieshichu niansong chengfo yigui 金剛頂經一字頂輪王瑜伽一切時處念誦成佛儀軌, *T* no. 957, vol. 19.

Jin'gangding yujia nianzhu jing 金剛頂瑜伽念珠經, *T* no. 789, vol. 17.

Jingde chuan deng lu 景得傳燈錄, by Daoyuan 道原 (1200–1253), *T* no. 2076, vol. 51.

"Jingtuyuan Shijiadian ji" 淨土院釋迦殿記, by Zou Qi 鄒起, in *Liang Zhe jinshi zhi*, ed. Ruan Yuan (1890 edn.) 7, pp. 1b–3b.

Jin guang ming jing 金光明經 (Skt. *Suvarṇaprabhāsa[uttamarāja]sūtra*), *T* no. 663, vol. 16.

Jinshi cuibian 金石萃編, by Wang Chang 王昶 (1724–1806), in *Shike shiliao xinbian*, first series, vols. 1–4.

Jinshi lu 金石錄, comp. Zhao Mingcheng 趙明誠 (1081–1129), in *Shike shiliao xinbian*, series 1, vol. 12.

Jin shu 晉書, by Fang Xuanling 房玄齡 (578–648) (Beijing: Zhonghua Shuju, 1974).

"Jinxiang yuan" 金相院, in *Huian xian zhi* 惠安縣志, comp. Mo Shangjian 莫尙
    簡 (Shanghai: Shanghai Guji Shudian, 1963), 10, p. 11a–b.

Ji Shenzhou sanbao gantong lu 集神州三寶感通錄, by Daoxuan 道宣 (596–
    667), *T* no. 2106, vol. 52.

Jiu Tang shu 舊唐書, by Liu Xu 劉昫 (887–946) (1975; rpt. Bejing: Zhonghua
    Shuju, 1987).

"Jixiangqiao" 吉祥橋, in *Jiaxing fuzhi* 嘉興府志, comp. Xu Yaoguang 許瑤光
    (1879 edn.) 5, pp. 24a–b.

Jushe lun ji 俱舍論記, by Puguang 普光 (fl. 660), *T* no. 1821, vol. 41.

"Kao chuang" 考床, in *Di liu xianxi wenchao* 第六絃溪文鈔, by Huang Tingjian
    黃廷鑑, 1, p. 10 (CSJC edn.) .

Kaopan yushi 考槃餘事, by Tu Long 屠隆 (1542–1605) (CSJC edn.).

Laoxuean biji 老學庵筆記, by Lu You 陸游 (1125–1210), in *Lu Fangweng
    quanji* 陸放翁全集 (Taipei: Shijie Shuju, 1961).

Liangchu qingzhong yi 量處輕重儀, by Daoxuan 道宣 (596–667), *T* no. 1895,
    vol. 45.

Liang shu 梁書, by Yao Silian 姚思廉 (557–637) (Beijing: Zhonghua Shuju,
    1973).

Liang Zhe jinshi zhi 兩浙金石志, comp. Ruan Yuan 阮元 (1764–1849) (1890
    edn.).

Lidai fabao ji 歷代法寶記, *T* no. 2075, vol. 51 (Pelliot no. 2125).

"Longfusi changmingdenglou songchuang" 隆福寺長明燈樓頌幢, in *Beijing Tu-
    shuguan cang Zhongguo lidai shike taben huibian*, vol. 17, pp. 87–8.

Lun heng jiaoshi 論衡校釋, by Wang Chong 王充 (27–91), ed. Huang Hui 黃暉
    (Beijing: Zhonghua shuju, 1990).

Lunyu zhushu 論語注疏 (SBBY edn.).

Luoyang jialan ji jiaoshi 洛陽伽藍記校釋, by Yang Xuanzhi 楊衒之 (fl. 547),
    ed. Zhou Zumo 周祖謨 (1963; rpt. Beijing: Zhonghua Shuju, 1987).

Lüshi chunqiu 呂氏春秋, by Lü Buwei 呂不韋 (d. 235 B.C.) (SBCK edn.).

Lüxiang gantong zhuan 律相感通傳, by Daoxuan 道宣 (596–667), *T* no. 1898,
    vol. 45.

Lu Xun jijiao shike shougao 魯迅輯校石刻手稿, comp. Lu Xun 魯迅 (Shanghai:
    Shanghai Shuhua Chubanshe, 1987).

Manshushili zhouzangzhong jiaoliang shuzhu gongde jing 曼殊室利咒藏中校量
    數珠功德經, *T* no. 787, vol. 17.

Meng liang lu 夢梁錄, by Wu Zimu 吳自牧, in *Dongjing menghua lu wai si-
    zhong* 東京夢華錄外四種 (Taipei: Dali Chubanshe, 1980).

Miaofa lianhua jing 妙法蓮華經 (Skt. *Saddharmapuṇḍarīka*), *T* no. 262, vol. 9.

Mingbao ji, Guangyi ji 冥報記 · 廣異記, by Tang Lin 唐臨 and Dai Fu 戴孚 (fl.
    757), ed. Fang Shiming 方詩銘 (Beijing: Zhonghua Shuju, 1992).

"Mingzhou Nanhexian Lishui shiqiao bei" 洺州南和縣灃水石橋碑, in *Jinshi
    cuibian* 40, pp. 1–6.

Mishasaibu hexi wufen lü 彌沙塞部和醯五分律 (Skt. *Mahīśāsakavinaya*), *T* no.
    1421, vol. 22.

Mishasaibu wufen jieben 彌沙塞部五分戒本 (Skt. *Mahīśāsakavinaya*), *T* no.
    1422, vol. 22.

Mohe sengqi lü 摩訶僧祇律 (Skt.* *Mahāsāṃghikavinaya*), *T* no. 1425, vol. 22.

Mohe zhiguan 摩訶止觀, by Zhiyi 智顗 (538–97), *T* no. 1911, vol. 46.

Mozi jiangu 墨子閒詁, ed. Sun Yirang 孫詒讓, Zhuzi jicheng 諸子集成 (Taipei: Shijie Shuju, 1955).

Mu huanzi jing 木槵子經, *T* no. 786, vol. 17.

Mulian wen jielü zhong wu bai qingzhong shi 目連問戒律中五百輕重事, *T* no. 1483, vol. 24.

Nanchang fuzhi 南昌府志, comps. Xu Yingrong 許應鑅 and Zeng Zuozhou 曾作舟 (1873 edn.).

Nanchao fosi zhi 南朝佛寺志, comp. Sun Wenchuan 孫文川, in *Zhongguo fosishi zhi huikan* 中國佛寺史志彙刊, ed. Du Jiexiang 杜潔祥, second series (Taipei: Mingwen, 1980) vol. 2.

Nanhai jigui neifa zhuan 南海寄歸內法傳, by Yijing 義淨 (635–713), *T* no. 2125, vol. 54.

Nan Linbaosi bei 南林報寺碑, in *Liang Zhe jinshi zhi* 11, pp. 35b–37b.

Nan shi 南史, comp. Li Yanshou 李延壽 (fl. 656) (Beijing: Zhonghua Shuju, 1975).

Nanyue Si da chanshi lishi yuanwen 南嶽思大禪師立誓願文, by Huisi 慧思 (515–77), *T* no. 1933, vol. 46.

Nianfo sanmei baowang lun 念佛三昧寶王論, *T* no. 1967, vol. 47.

Ni jiemo 尼羯磨, by Huaisu 懷素 (b. 737), *T* no. 1810, vol. 40.

Nittō guhō junrei gyōki 入唐求法巡禮行記 (*Ru Tang qiufa xunli xingji*), by Ennin 圓仁, ed. Bai Huawen 白化文 (Shijiazhuang: Huashan Wenyi Chubanshe, 1992).

"Pei Li Shiyu fang Zong Shangren chanju" 陪李侍御訪聰上人禪居, by Meng Haoran 孟浩然 (689–740), in *Quan Tang shi*, 160, p. 1647.

Pinimu jing 毘尼母經 (Skt.* *Vinayamātṛkā*), *T* no. 1463, vol. 24.

Putichang suoshuo yizi dinglun wang jing 菩提場所說一字頂輪王經, *T* no. 950, vol. 19.

Putidamo nanzong ding shifei lun 菩提達摩定是非論, by Shenhui 神會 (684–758), in *Shenhui heshang chanhua lu* 神會和尚禪話錄, ed. Yang Zengwen 楊曾文 (Beijing: Zhonghua Shuju, 1996)

Qingchao wenxian tongkao 清朝文獻通考 (Taipei: Taiwan Shangwu Yinshuguan, 1987).

Qing huidian 清會典, comp. Kun Gang 崑岡 (Beijing: Zhonghua Shuju, 1991).

"Qin Shangshu Minglei beiji" 秦尙書鳴雷碑記, by Qin Minglei 秦鳴雷 (fl. 1577), in *Huangyan xianzhi* 黃巖縣志, comp. Yuan Yingqi 遠應祺 (Shanghai: Shanghai guji shudian, 1981), 1, pp. 31a–32a.

Quan Tang shi 全唐詩 (1960; rpt. Beijing: Zhonghua shuju, 1979).

Quanzhou fuzhi 泉州府志, comp. Huai Yinbu 懷蔭布 (Quanzhou: Quanshan Shushe, 1928).

Que shi 闕史, by Gao Yanxiu 高彥休 (fl. 907) (BJDG edn.).

Ri zhi lu 日知錄, by Gu Yanwu 顧炎武 (1613–82) (SKQS edn.).

Rongzhai wu bi 容齋五筆, by Hong Mai 洪邁 (1123–1202) (BJDG edn).

Sancai tuhui 三才圖會, by Wang Qi 王圻 (1530–1615) (Taipei: Chengwen Chubanshe, 1970).

San Tendai Godaisan ki 參天台五臺山記, by Jōjin 成尋 (1011–81), in *Dai Nihon bukkyō zensho*, ed. Takakusu Junjirō (1931; rpt. Tokyo: Kōdansha, 1970–73), vol. 115.

Sapoduobu pinimodelejia 薩婆多部毘尼摩得勒伽 (Skt. *Sarvāstivādavinaya-mātṛkā*) *T* no. 1441, vol. 23.

Sapoduopinipiposha 薩婆多毘尼毘婆沙 (Skt. *Sarvāstivādavinayavibhāṣā*), *T* no. 1440, vol. 23.

Seng jiemo 僧羯磨, by Huaisu 懷素 (b. 737), *T* no. 1809, vol. 40.

Shanjian lü piposha 善見律毘婆沙 (Skt. *Samantapāsādikā*), *T* no. 1462, vol. 24.

"Shanzhong zeng Rinan seng" 山中贈日南僧, by Zhang Ji 張籍 (c. 776–c. 829), *Quan Tang shi* 384, p. 4308.

Shengshui yan tan lu 澠水燕談錄, by Wang Pizhi 王闢之 (fl. 1095) (CSJC edn.).

Shenxian zhuan 神仙傳, by Ge Hong 葛洪 (284–363) (CSJC edn.).

Shidi jinglun 十地經論 (Skt. *Daśabhūmikasūtraśāstra*), *T* no. 1522, vol. 26.

Shiji 史記, by Sima Qian 司馬遷 (145 B.C.–A.D. 86) (Beijing: Zhonghua shuju, 1959).

Shike shiliao xinbian 石刻史料新編 (Taipei: Xinwenfeng Chubanshe, 1978–86).

Shimen zhangfu yi 釋門章服儀, by Daoxuan 道宣 (596–667), *T* no. 1894, vol. 45.

Shishi yaolan 釋氏要覽 (fl. 1019), *T* no. 2127, vol. 54.

Shishuo xinyu jiaojian 世說新語校箋, by Liu Yiqing 劉義慶 (403–44), ed. Xu Zhen'e 徐震堮 (Beijing: Zhonghua Shuju, 1984).

Shisong lü 十誦律 (Skt.*Sarvāstivādavinaya*), *T* no. 1435, vol. 23.

Shi yi ji 拾遺記, by Wang Jia 王嘉 (fl. 385), ed. Qi Zhiping 齊治平 (Beijing: Zhonghua Shuju, 1981).

Shiyimian shenzhou xinjing yishu 十一面神咒心經義疏, *T* no. 1802, vol. 39.

Shouhu guojiezhu tuoluoni jing 守護國界主陀羅尼經, *T* no. 997, vol. 19.

Shouyong sanshui yaoxingfa 受用三水要行法, *T* no. 1902, vol. 45.

"Shui hou cha xing yi Yang Tongzhou" 睡後茶興憶楊同州, by Bai Juyi 白居易 (772–846), *Quan Tang shi* 453, p. 5126.

"Shuijing shuzhu ge" 水精數珠歌, by Jiaoran 皎然 (b. 720), *Quan Tang shi* 821, p. 9265.

Shuozui yaoxingfa 說罪要行法, *T* no. 1903, vol. 45.

Sichuan tongzhi 四川通志, comp. Chang Ming 常明 et al. (1816 edn.)

Sifen lü 四分律 (Skt.*Dharmaguptakavinaya*), *T* no. 1428, vol. 22.

Sifen lü biqiu hanzhu jieben 四分律比丘含注戒本, by Daoxuan 道宣 (596–667), *T* no. 1806, vol. 40.

Sifen lü shanfan buque xingshichao 四分律刪繁補闕行事鈔, by Daoxuan 道宣 (596–667), *T* no. 1804, vol. 40.

Sifen lü xingshichao zichi ji 四分律行事鈔資持記, by Yuanzhao 元照 (1048–1116), *T* no. 1805, vol. 40.

"Sishi ce wen qishou" 私試策問七首, by Su Shi 蘇軾 (1036–1101), in *Dongpo wenji* 東坡文集 22, pp. 2a–5a, in *Dongpo qiji* 東坡七集 (Taipei: Zhonghua Shuju, 1970).

Sita ji 寺塔記, by Duan Chengshi 段成式 (b. 863), *T* no. 2093, vol. 51.

Song gaoseng zhuan 宋高僧傳, by Zanning 贊寧 (919–1001), *T* no. 2061, vol. 50.

Song huiyao jiben 宋會要輯本, ed. Xu Song 徐松 (Taipei: Shijie Shuju, 1964).

"Song Lu Hongjian Qixiasi cai cha" 送陸鴻漸棲霞寺探茶, by Huangfu Ran 皇甫然 (714–67), in *Quan Tang shi* 249, p. 2808.

"Song Min seng" 送閩僧, by Zhang Ji 張籍 (c. 776–c. 829), *Quan Tang shi* 384, p. 4312.

"Song seng gui shan" 送僧歸山, by Liu Yanshi 劉言史, in *Quan Tang shi* 468, p. 5328.

Song shi 宋史, by Tuo Tuo 脫脫 (1238–98) (Beijing: Zhonghua Shuju, 1977).

"Songshi yizi wuzi you wei tongxing" 宋時椅子兀子猶未通行 in *Chaxiangshi sanchao* 27, p. 7.

"Song Xinluo naseng" 宋新羅衲僧, by Guanxiu 貫修 (832–912) in *Quan Tang shi* 836, p. 9418.

Sui shu 隋書, by Wei Zheng 魏徵 (580–643) (Beijing: Zhonghua Shuju, 1973).

Sui Tiantai Zhizhe dashi biezhuan 隋天台智者大師別傳, by Guanding 灌頂 (561–632), *T* no. 2050, vol. 50.

Taiping guangji 太平廣記, comp. Li Fang 李昉 (925–96) (Beijing: Zhonghua Shuju, 1961).

Taiping yulan 太平御覽, comp. Li Fang 李昉 (925–96) (SBCK edn.).

Tang huiyao 唐會要, by Wang Pu 王溥 (922–982) (Beijing: Zhonghua Shuju, 1955).

Tangshuang pu 糖霜譜, by Wang Zhuo 王灼 (1081–1160) (SKQS edn.).

"Tang Yixingxian chongxiu chashe ji" 唐義興縣重修茶舍記, in *Jin shi lu* 29, pp. 2b–3a.

Tanjing jiaoshi 壇經校釋, ed. Guo Peng 郭朋 (Beijing: Zhonghua Shuju, 1983).

Taoan mengyi 陶庵夢憶, by Zhang Dai 張岱 (1597–1685) (CSJC edn.).

"Tian di yinyang jiao huan da le fu" 天地陰陽交歡大樂賦, by Bai Xingjian 白行簡 (d. 826), in *Shuangmei jing'an congshu* 雙梅景闇叢書, ed. Ye Dehui 葉德輝, (1903 edn.) p. 7b.

Tian gong kai wu 天工開物, by Song Yingxing 宋應星 (1587–1666) (1637 edn.).

"Tianzhusi song Jian Shangren gui Lushan" 天竺寺送堅上人歸廬山, by Bai Juyi 白居易 (772–846), in *Quan Tang shi* 446, p. 5006.

"Ti Chongfusi Chanyuan" 題崇福寺禪院, by Cui Tong 崔峒 (fl. 766), in *Quan Tang shi* 294, p. 3343.

"Ti Ganlusi" 題甘露寺, by Xu Tang 許棠 (fl. 862), in *Quan Tang shi* 604, p. 6987.

"Ti Xiushi yingtang" 題秀師影堂, by Zhang Hu 張祜 (fl. 821), in *Quan Tang shi* 511, p. 5837.

Tongdian 通典, by Du You 杜佑 (735–812) (Beijing: Zhonghua Shuju, 1988).

"Tong Huangfu Shiyu ti Jianfusi Yigong fang" 同皇甫侍御題薦福寺一公房, by Li Jiayou 李嘉祐 (fl. 748), in *Quan Tang shi* 206, p. 2153.

"Tongji qiao ji" 通濟橋記, by Huang Qian 黃潛, in *Chixiu Zhejiang tongzhi* 敕修浙江通志, comp. Li Wei 李微 (1812 edn.), 37, p. 13a–b.

"Tong qun gong su Kaishansi zeng Chen Shiliu suoju" 同群公宿開善寺贈陳十六所居, by Gao Shi 高適 (d. 765), in *Quan Tang shi* 212, p. 2206.

Tuoluoni ji jing 陀羅尼集經, *T* no. 901, vol. 18.

"Wang Woshi chongxiu Hongtaqiao ji" 王我師重修洪塔橋記, in *Sichuan tong-zhi* 33, pp. 6b–7b.

"Wanshou Qiao" 萬壽橋, in *Fujian zhi* 29, p. 4b.

Weimojie jing 維摩詰經 (Skt. *Vimalakirtinirdeśa*), *T* no. 474, vol. 14.

Wei shu 魏書, by Wei Shou 魏收 (505–72) (Beijing: Zhonghua Shuju, 1974).

Wenyuan yinghua 文苑英華, by Li Fang 李昉 (925–96) (Beijing: Zhonghua Shuju, 1966).

"Wen Zheng Shangren ji" 問正上人疾, by Huangfu Ran 皇甫冉 (714–67), in *Quan Tang shi* 249, p. 2805.

Wudafu xinqiao ji 五大夫新橋記, in *Ba qiong shi jinshi buzheng* 八瓊室金石補正, comp. Lu Zengxiang 陸增祥 (1816–82), 73, pp. 31–4, in *Shike shiliao xinbian*, series 1, vol. 7.

Wudaishi bu 五代史補, by Tao Yue 陶岳 (fl. 960) (SKQS edn.).

"Wude Yu fujun deng yiqiao shixiang zhi bei" 武德于府君等義橋石像之卑 in *Henei xianzhi* 河內縣志, eds. Yuan Tong 袁通 and Fang Lüqian 方履籛 (1825 edn.), 20, pp. 8a–16b.

Xianchun lin'an zhi 咸淳臨安志, ed. Zan Shuoyou 讚說友 (Beijing: Zhonghua Shuju, 1990).

Xiangfa jueyi jing 像法決疑經, *T* no. 2870, vol. 85.

Xiang pu 香譜, by Hong Chu 洪芻 (fl. 1094) (SKQS edn.).

"Xie si shuang kuai" 謝寺雙檜, by Liu Yuxi 劉禹錫 (772–842), in *Quan Tang shi* 359, p. 4051.

Xin jiaozheng Mengxi bitan 新校正夢溪筆談, by Shen Kuo 沈括 (1029–93), ed. Hu Daojing 胡道靜 (Hong Kong: Zhonghua shuju, 1975).

Xin Tang shu 新唐書, by Ouyang Xiu 歐陽修 (1975: rpt. Beijing: Zhonghua shuju, 1986).

"Xishan Lanruo shi cha ge" 西山蘭若試茶歌, by Liu Yuxi 劉禹錫 (772–842), in *Quan Tang shi* 356, p. 4000.

Xiuxi zhiguan zuochan fayao 修習止觀坐禪法要, by Zhiyi 智顗 (538–597), *T* no. 1915, vol. 46.

Xuelin 學林, by Wang Guanguo 王觀國 (Taipei: Xingwenfeng, 1984).

Xu gaoseng zhuan 續高僧傳, comp. Daoxuan 道宣 (596–667), *T* no. 2060, vol. 50.

"Xun seng Yuanjiao yinbing" 尋僧元皎因病, by Yang Ning 楊凝 (d. 803), in *Quan Tang shi* 290, p. 3303.

Xutang heshang yulu 虛堂和尚語錄, by Xutang 虛堂 (1185–1269), *T* no. 2000, vol. 47.

Xu zang jing 續藏經 (Taipei: Xinwenfeng, 1968–1970), reprint of *Dai Nihon zoku-zōkyō* 大日本續藏經, ed. Nakano Tatsue 中野達慧 (Kyoto: Zōkyō shoin, 1905–1912).

Yanfan luzheng 演繁露正, by Cheng Dachang 程大昌 (1123–95) (Taipei: Xinwenfeng, 1984).

Yanfan lu zhengxu 演繁露正續, by Cheng Dachang 程大昌 (1123–95) (Taipei: Xinwenfeng, 1984).

"Yanqing sita ji" 延慶寺塔記, by Zhu Lin 珠琳, in *Songyang xianzhi* 松陽縣志, ed. Xiu Qingnian 修慶年 (1654 edn.), 7, pp. 11a–12b.

Yan shi jia xun 顏氏家訓, by Yan Zhitui 顏之推 (531–91+) (SBCK edn.) p. 13b.

Yiqie rulai anxiang sanmei yigui jing 一切如來安像三昧儀軌經, *T* no. 1418, vol. 21.

Yiqie rulai wusenisha zuisheng zongchi jing 一切如來烏瑟膩沙最勝總持經 (Skt. *Sarvadurgatipariśodhanauṣṇīṣavijayādhāraṇī*), *T* no. 978, vol. 19.

Yiqie rulaixin mimi quanshen sheli baoqieyin tuoluoni jing 一切如來心祕密全身舍利寶篋印陀羅尼經 (Skt. *Sarvatathāgatādhiṣṭhānahṛdayaguhyadhātukaraṇḍa mudrādhāraṇī*), *T* no. 1022, vol. 19.

"Yong jin'gang" 詠金剛, by Jiang Yigong 蔣貽恭, in *Quan Tang shi* 870, p. 9871.

"Yongjiqiao" 永濟橋, in *Nanchang fuzhi* 南昌府志, comps. Xu Yingrong 許應鑅 and Zeng Zuozhou 曾作舟 (1873 edn.), 4, p. 67a.

"Yong Longyuan" 永隆院, by Lin Xiyi 林希逸, in *Xianchun Lin'an zhi* 79, pp. 7–8.

Youyang zazu 酉陽雜俎, by Duan Chengshi 段成式 (d. 863) (SBCK edn.).

Yuanjuejing daochang xiuzhengyi 圓覺經道場修證義, by Zongmi 宗密 (780–841), *Xu zang jing*, vol. 7.

Yudi jisheng 輿地紀勝, by Wang Xiangzhi 王象之 (1849 edn.).

Yujia lun lüezuan 瑜伽論略纂, by Kuiji 窺基 (632–82), *T* no. 1829, vol. 43.

Yujia shidi lun 瑜伽師地論 (Skt. *Yogacāryabhūmiśāstra*), *T* no. 1579, vol. 30.

Yunmeng Shuihudi Qinmu 雲夢睡虎地秦墓, ed. Yunmeng Shuihudi Qinmu Bianxiezu 雲夢睡虎地秦墓編寫組 (Beijing: Wenwu Chubanshe, 1981).

Yunmen si chongzhuang Kuangzhen zushi jinshen bei ji 雲門寺重裝匡眞祖師金身碑記, by Yuancai 元才 (fl. 1687), in *Yunmen shan zhi* 雲門山志, comp. Cen Xuelü 岑學呂, 9, in *Zhongguo fo si shi zhi huikan* 中國佛寺史志彙刊, ed. Du Jiexiang 杜潔祥 (Taipei: Zongqing tushu, 1994), second series, vol. 6, p. 196.

Yunxian zaji 雲仙雜記, by Feng Zhi 馮贄 (fl. 901) (SBCK edn.).

Yunzhou Dongshan Wuben chanshi yulu 筠州洞山悟本禪師語錄, by Liangjia 良价 (807–69), *T* no. 1986, vol. 47.

"Yu Shuge ji" 御書閣記, by Ouyang Xiu 歐陽修 (1007–72), in *Ouyang Xiu quanji* 歐陽修全集 (Beijing: Zhongguo Shudian, 1986), 39, pp. 270–1.

Za ahan jing 雜阿含經 (Skt. *Saṃyuktāgama*), *T* no. 99, vol. 2.

Za ahan jing 雜阿含經 (Skt. *Saṃyuktāgama*), *T* no. 101, vol. 2.

Zeng yi ahan jing 增一阿含經 (Skt. *Ekottarāgama*), *T* no. 125, vol. 2.

Zhangwuzhi jiaozhu 長物志校注, by 文震亨 (1585–1645), eds. Chen Zhi 陳植 and Yang Chaobo 楊超伯 (Jiangsu: Jiangsu Keji Chubanshe, 1984).

Zhang Zai ji 張載集, by Zhang Zai 張載 (1020–77) (Beijing: Zhonghua Shuju, 1988).

Zheng fa nian chu jing 正法念處經 (Skt. *Saddharmasmṛtyupasthānasūtra*), *T* no. 721, vol. 17.

Zhenyuan xinding shijiao mulu 貞元新定釋教目錄, by Yuanzhao 圓照 (fl. 778), *T* no. 2157, vol. 55.

Zhenzhou Linji Huizhao chanshi yulu 鎮州臨濟慧照禪師語錄, by Huizhao 慧照 (d. 867), *T* no. 1985, vol. 47.

Zhong ahan jing 中阿含經 (Skt. *Madhyamāgama*), *T* no. 26, vol. 1.

Zhongjing mulu 眾經目錄, by Fajing 法經 (fl. 594), *T* no. 2146, vol. 55.

"Zhong Sina deng zaoqiao bei" 仲思那等造橋碑, in *Lu Xun jijiao shike shougao*, vol. 7, pp. 1173–7.

Zhouyi zhengyi 周易正義, in *Shisanjing zhushu* 十三經注疏, ed. Ruan Yuan 阮元 (Beijing: Zhonghua Shuju, 1980).

Zhuangzi jiaozhu 莊子校註, ed. Wang Shumin 王叔岷 (Taipei: Zhongyang Yanjiuyuan Lishiyuyan Yanjiusuo, 1988).

Zhuanji baiyuan jing 撰集百緣經 (Skt. *Avadānaśataka*), *T* no. 200, vol. 4.

Zhufo jingjie shezhenshi jing 諸佛境界攝眞實經, *T* no. 868, vol. 18.

Zizhi tongjian 資治通鑑, by Sima Guang 司馬光 (1019–86) (1956; rpt. Beijing: Zhonghua Shuju, 1987).

Zuofo xingxiang jing 作佛形像經 (*Skt. Thatāgatapratibimbapratiṣṭānuśaṃsā*) *T* no. 692, vol. 16.

Zu tang ji 祖堂集, ed. Wu Zeshun 吳澤順 (Changsha: Yuelu Chubanshe 岳麓出版社, 1996).

MODERN WORKS IN CHINESE AND JAPANESE

Cao Shibang (Tso Sze-Bong) 曹仕邦. *Zhongguo shamen waixue de yanjiu: Hanmo zhi Wudai* 中國沙門外學的研究: 漢末至五代 (Taipei: Dongchu Chubanshe, 1994).

Cao Zhezhi 曹者祉 et al. *Zhongguo gudai yong* 中國古代俑 (Shanghai: Shanghai Wenhua Chubanshe, 1996).

Chang Qing 常青. "Ji Yulin faxian de Liu-Song jintong foxiang" 記榆林發現的劉宋金銅佛像, *Wenwu* 文物 (1995.1), pp. 92–5, 89.

Chang Shuzheng 常叔政, and Zhu Xueshan 朱學山. "Shandong sheng Huimin xian chutu Dingguangfo sheliguan" 山東省惠民縣出土定光佛舍利棺, *Wenwu* 文物 (1987.3), pp. 60–2.

Chen Chuan 陳椽. *Chaye tongshi* 茶葉通史 (Beijing: Nongye Chubanshe, 1984).

Chen Guangzu (Chen Kuang-tsu) 陳光祖. "Foguangshan suoying de bu shi 'di san ke ya'" 佛光山所迎的不是第三顆牙, *Dangdai* 當代 131 (1998.7.1), pp. 88–105.

Chen Weiming 陳偉明. *Tang Song yinshi wenhua chutan* 唐宋飲食文化初探 (Beijing: Zhongguo Shangye Chubanshe, 1993).

Chen Xiasheng (Ch'en Hsia-sheng) 陳夏生. *Jixiang ruyi wenwu tezhan tulu* 吉祥如意文物特展圖錄 (Taipei: National Palace Museum, 1995).

Chen Yuan 陳垣. *Chen Yuan'an xiansheng quanji* 陳援庵先生全集 (Taipei: Xinwenfeng, 1993)

———. "Foya gushi" 佛牙故事 in *Chen Yuan'an xiansheng quanji*, vol. 14, pp. 305–314.

———. "Faxian foya yinxian ji" 法獻佛牙隱現記 in *Chen Yuan'an xiansheng quanji*, vol. 15, pp. 469–71.

Chen Zengbi 陳增弼. "Han, Wei, Jin duzuoshi xiaota chu lun" 漢、魏、晉獨坐式小榻初論, *Wenwu* 文物 (1979.9), pp. 66–71.

Cheng Guangyu (Ch'eng Kuang-yü) 程光裕. "Song Yuan shidai Quanzhou zhi qiaoliang yanjiu" 宋元時代泉州之橋樑研究, in Songshi zuotan hui 宋史座談會 ed., *Songshi yanjiu ji* 宋史研究集 6 (Taipei: Zhonghua congshu bian-shen weiyuanhui, 1958–), pp. 313–34;

Cheng Jizhong 程紀中. "Hebei Gaochengxian faxian yi pi Bei Qi shi zaoxiang" 河北藁城縣發現一批北齊石造像, *Kaogu* 考古 (1980.3), pp. 242–5.

Cheng Ling 陳羚 et al. *Shijiamonifo zhenshen sheli* 釋迦牟尼佛眞身舍利 (I-lan, Taiwan: Foguang Renwen Shehui Xueyuan, 2002), p. 43.

Cixian Wenhuaguan 磁縣文化館. "Hebei Cixian Dongchencun Dongweimu" 河北磁縣東陳村東魏墓, *Kaogu* 考古 (1977.6)

Cui Yongxue 崔詠雪. *Zhongguo jiajushi—zuojupian* 中國家具史——坐具篇 (Taipei: Mingwen Shuju, 1994).

Du Doucheng 杜斗城. *Bei Liang yijing lun* 北涼譯經論 (Lanzhou: Gansu Wen-hua Chubanshe, 1995).

Du Zhengsheng (Tu Cheng-sheng) 杜正勝. "Yu Hua wu ji: ding de lishi yu shen-hua" 與華無極: 鼎的歷史與神話, *Gugong wenwu yuekan* 故宮文物月刊 8.2 (1990), pp. 6–19.

Fang Guangchang 方廣錩. *Fojiao dazangjing shi Ba—shi shiji* 佛教大藏經史八——十世紀 (Beijing: Zhongguo Shehuikexue Chubanshe, 1991).

——. "Dunhuang wenxian zhong de *Jin'gang jing* ji qi zhu shu" 敦煌文獻中的《金剛經》及其注疏, *Shijie zongjiao yanjiu* 世界宗教研究 (1995.1), pp. 73–80.

Fang Hao 方豪. "Songdai senglü dui yu zai cha zhi gongxian" 宋代僧侶對於栽茶之貢獻, *Dalu zazhi* 大陸雜誌, 29.4 (1964), pp. 124–8.

——. "Songdai sengtu dui zao qiao de gongxian" 宋代僧徒對造橋的貢獻, *Fang Hao liushi zhi liushisi zixuan daiding gao* 方豪六十至六十四自選待定稿 (Taipei: Xuesheng Shuju, 1974), pp. 137–46.

Foguang dacidian bianxiu weiyuan hui 佛光大辭典編修委員會 ed. *Foguang da cidian* 佛光大辭典 (Gaoxiong: Foguang Chubanshe, 1988).

Fujita Toyohachi 藤田豐八. "Koshō ni tsuite" 胡床につ︿て, in his *Tōzai kōshō-shi no kenkyū* 東西交涉史の研究 (Tokyo: Kōsho-in, 1934), pp. 143–85.

Gao Gao 高皋, and Yan Jiaqi 嚴家其. *Wenhua dageming shinian shi* 文化大革命十年史 (Tianjin: Tianjin Renmin Chubanshe, 1986).

Guo Shaolin 郭紹林. *Tangdai shidafu yu fojiao* 唐代士大夫與佛教 (Taipei: Wen-shizhe Chubanshe, 1993).

Guoli Gugong Bowuyuan bianji weiyuanhui 國立故宮博物院編輯委員會 ed. *Hai-wai yizhen: Foxiang* 海外遺珍: 佛像 (Taipei: National Palace Museum, 1986).

——. *Qingdai fushi zhanlan tulu* 清代服飾展覽圖錄 (Taipei: National Palace Museum, 1986).

Han Wei 韓偉. "Cong yincha fengshang kan Famensi deng di chutu de Tangdai jinyin chaju" 從飲茶風尚看法門寺等地出土的唐代金銀茶具, *Wenwu* 文物 (1988.10), pp. 44–56.

——. "Famensi digong jinyinqi zanwen kaoshi" 法門寺地宮金銀器鏨文考釋, *Kaogu yu wenwu* 考古與文物 (1995.1), pp. 71–8.

Hanyu dacidian bianzuan chu 漢語大詞典編纂處 ed. *Hanyu dacidian* 漢語大詞典 (Shanghai: Shanghai Cishu Chubanshe, 1991).

He Changjun 賀昌郡, "Shishuo xinyu zhaji," 世說新語札記, *Guoli zhongyang tushuguan guankan* 國立中央圖書館館刊 1 (1947), pp. 1–7.

He Zicheng 賀梓城. "Tangdai bihua" 唐代壁畫, *Wenwu* 文物 (1958), vol. 8, pp. 31–3.

Hebeisheng wenwu guanlichu 河北省文物管理處. "Hebei Yixian Jingjuesi sheli-ta digong qingli ji" 河北易縣淨覺寺舍利塔地宮清理記, *Wenwu* 文物 (1986.9), pp. 76–80.

Henansheng gudai jianzhu baohu yanjiusuo 河南省古代建筑保護研究所 ed. *Baoshan Lingquansi* 寶山靈泉寺 (Henan: Henan Renmin Chubanshe, 1991).

Hirai Yūkei 平井宥慶. "*Kongō hannya kyō*" 金剛般若經. In Makita Tairyō 牧田諦亮 and Fukui Fumimasa 福井文牙 eds., *Tonkō to chūgoku bukkyō* 敦煌と中國佛教. Kōza tonkō 講座敦煌, vol. 7 (Tokyo: Daitō shuppansha, 1984), pp. 17–34.

Hou Xudong 侯旭東. *Wu liu shiji beifang minzhong fojiao xinyang* 五六世紀北方民眾佛教信仰 (Beijing: Zhongguo Shehuikexue Chubanshe, 1998).

Huang Chengzhu 黃成助 ed. *Zhongguo fangzhi congshu: Huazhong difang* 中國方志叢書: 華中地方, no. 892 (Taipei: Chengwen Chubanshe, 1989).

Huang Jinxing (Chin-shing Huang) 黃進興. "Huixiang yu shengshiji" 毀像與聖師祭, *Dalu zazhi* 大陸雜志, vol. 99, no. 5 (1999), pp. 1–8.

Huang Minzhi (Huang Min-chih) 黃敏枝. *Songdai fojiao shehui jingjishi lun ji* 宋代佛教社會經濟史論集 (Taipei: Xuesheng Shuju, 1989).

Huang Zhaohan 黃兆漢. "Muyu kao" 木魚考, *Shijie zongjiao yanjiu* 世界宗教研究 (1987.1), pp. 28–38.

Huang Zhengjian 黃正建. "Tangdai de yizi yu shengchuang" 唐代的椅子與繩床, *Wenwu* 文物 (1990.7), pp. 86–8.

Huang Zi 黃滋. "Zhejiang Songyang Yanqing sita gouzao fenxi" 浙江松陽延慶寺塔構造分析, *Wenwu* 文物 (1991.11), pp. 84–7, 75.

Itō Shōji 伊東照司 ed. *Genshi bukkyō bijutsu toten* 原始佛教美術圖典 (Tokyo: Yūzankaku, 1992).

Ji Xianlin 季羨林. *Yi zhang youguan Yindu zhitangfa chuanru Zhongguo de Dunhuang canjuan* 一張有關印度制糖法傳入中國的敦煌殘卷, *Lishi yanjiu* 歷史研究 (1982.1), pp. 124–36.

Ji Yuanzhi 暨遠志. "Tangdai chawenhua de jieduanxing—Dunhuang xieben *Cha jiu lun* yanjiu zhi er" 唐代茶文化的階段性——敦煌寫本《茶酒論》研究之二, *Dunhuang yanjiu* 敦煌研究 (1991.2), pp. 99–107.

Jiang Canteng (Chiang Ts'an-t'eng) 江燦騰. "Guanyu foya sheli zhenwei zhi bian" 關於佛牙舍利眞僞之辯, *Dangdai* 130 (1998.6.1), pp. 68–73.

Jin Shen 金申 ed. *Zhongguo lidai jinian foxiang tudian* 中國歷代紀年佛像圖典 (Beijing: Wenwu Chubanshe, 1995).

Kawaguchi Kōfū 川口高風. "Kesa-shi ni okeru Dōsen no chii—ryokubutsu o chūshin ni" 袈裟史における道宣の地位——六物を中心に, *Shukyō kenkyū* 宗教研究 47.2 (Jan. 1974), pp. 97–123.

Kawano Satoshi 河野訓 et al. "Sō-i shiryō kenkyū: *Shibunritsu gyōji shō ni-i sōbetsu-hen hombun(shō) narabi ni yakkai*" 僧衣資料研究: 四分律行事鈔二衣總別篇——本文 (抄) 並びに譯解, *Bukkyō bunka* 佛教文化 18 (Jun. 1987), pp. 85–114; 19 (Feb. 1988), pp. 74–86.

Li Ji 李濟. "Gui zuo dun ju yu jiju" 跪坐蹲居與箕距 in *Guoli Zhongyang Yan-jiuyuan Lishi Yuyan Yanjiusuo jikan* 國立中央研究院歷史語言研究所集刊 24 (1954), pp. 283–301.

Li Jianchao 李健超. "Sui Tang Chang'an cheng Shiji si yizhi chutu wenwu" 隋唐長安城實際寺遺址出土文物, *Kaogu* 考古 (1988.4), pp. 314–7.

Li Jianmin 李建民. "Zhongguo gudai yanci lisu kao" 中國古代「掩胔」禮俗考, *Qinghua xue bao* 清華學報 (new series) vol. 24, no. 3 (1994), pp. 319–42.

Li Yumin 李玉珉 (Lee Yumin). "Zhongguo zaoqi fota suyuan" 中國早期佛塔溯源, *Gugong xueshu jikan* 故宮學術季刊, vol. 6, no. 3 (1990), pp. 75–104.

Li Zhihuan 李治寰. "Cong zhitangshi tan shimi he bingtang" 從製糖史談石蜜和冰糖, *Lishi yanjiu* 歷史研究 (1981.2), pp. 146–54.

———. *Zhongguo shitangshi gao* 中國食糖史稿 (Beijing: Nongye Chubanshe, 1990).

Lianyungang shi Bowuguan 連雲港市博物館. "Lianyungang Haiqing si Ayu-wang ta wenwu chutu ji" 連雲港海清寺阿育王塔文物出塔土記, *Wenwu* 文物 (1981.7), pp. 31–8.

Lin Zhengsan 林正三. "Tangdai yincha fengqi tantao" 唐代飲茶風氣探討, *Guoli Bianyiguan guankan* 國立編譯館館刊, vol. 13, no. 2 (Dec. 1984), p. 208–28.

Liu Dunzhen 劉敦楨. *Zhongguo gudai jianzhu shi* 中國古代建築史 (Beijing: Zhongguo Jianzhugongye Chubanshe, 1980).

Liu Huan 劉桓. "Buci baili shixi" 卜辭拜禮試析, in his *Yin qi xin shi* 殷契新釋 (Hebei: Hebei Jiaoyu Chubanshe, 1989), pp. 1–51.

Liu Jing 劉靜. "Fanqie yuan yu fojiaoshuo bianxi" 反切源於佛教說辨析, *Shaanxi Shida xuebao* 陝西師大學報, vol. 22, no. 2 (May 1993), pp. 122–7.

Liu Shanyi 劉善沂. "Shandong Chipingxian Guangping chutu Tangdai shi zao-xiang" 山東荏平縣廣平出土唐代石造像, *Kaogu* 考古 (1983.8), p. 752.

Liu Shufen 劉淑芬. "Wu zhi liu shiji Huabei xiangcun de fojiao xinyang" 五至六世紀華北鄉村的佛教信仰, *Zhongyang yanjiuyuan lishi yuyan yanjiu so ji-kan* 中央研究院歷史語言研究所集刊, 63.3 (1993), pp. 497–544.

Liu Youheng 劉友恒, and Fan Zilin 樊子林. "Hebei Zhengding Tianning si Lingxiao ta digong chutu wenwu" 河北正定天寧寺凌霄塔地宮出土文物, *Wenwu* 文物 (1991.6), pp. 28–37.

Longmen Wenwu Baoguan Suo 龍門文物保管所 et al., eds. *Longmen shiku* 龍門石窟 (Beijing: Wenwu Chubanshe, 1991).

Luo Zhenyu 羅振玉. "*Song Yuan Shizang kanben kao* 宋元釋藏刊本考" in *Yongfeng xiangren zazhu* 永豐鄉人雜著 (1922 edn.).

Luo Zongzhen 羅宗眞. "Tangdai Yangzhou simiao yizhi de chubu kaoxi" 唐代揚州寺廟遺址的初步考析, *Kaogu* 考古 (1981.4), pp. 359–62.

Luoyangshi wenwu gongzuodui 洛陽市文物工作隊. "Luoyang Tang Shenhui heshang shenta taji qingli" 落陽唐神會和尚身塔塔基清理, *Wenwu* 文物 (1992.3), pp. 64–7, 75.

Ma De 馬德. *Dunhuang Mogaokushi yanjiu* 敦煌莫高窟史研究 (Lanzhou: Gansu Jiaoyu Chubanshe, 1996).

———. *Dunhuang gongjiang shiliao* 敦煌工匠史料 (Lanzhou: Gansu Renmin Chubanshe, 1997).

Makita Tairyō 牧田諦亮. *Gikyō kenkyū* 疑經研究 (Kyoto: Kyōto daigaku jinbun kagaku kenkyūjo, 1976).

Maku Takamaro 滿久崇麿. *Butsuden no shokubutsu* 佛典の植物 (Tokyo: Yasaka Shobō, 1985).

Mao Yisheng 矛以升. *Zhongguo guqiao jishushi* 中國古橋技術史 (Beijing: Zhongguo Qingnian Chubanshe, 1986).

Masāki Chikusa 竺沙雅章. *Chūgoku bukkyō shakaishi kenkyū* 中國佛教社會史研究 (Kyoto: Dōhōsha, 1984).

Matsubara Saburō 松原三郎. *Chūgoku bukkyō chōkoku shiron* 中國佛教雕刻史論 (Tokyo: Yoshikawa Kōbunkan, 1995).

Mochizuki Shinkō 望月信亨. *Bukkyō daijiten* 佛教大辭典 (Tokyo: Sekai seiten kankō kyōkai, 1958–63).

Mou Runsun 牟潤孫. "Tangchu nanbei xueren lunxue zhi yiqu yu yingxiang" 唐初南北學人論學之異趣與影響, *Xianggang Zhongwen Daxue Zhongguo wenhua yanjiu xuebao* 香港中文大學中國文化研究學報 1 (Sept. 1968), pp. 50–88.

Nagahiro Toyū 長廣敏雄. *Rikuchō jidai bijutsu no kenkyū* 六朝時代美術の研究 (Tokyo: Bijutsu shuppan-sha, 1969).

Nakamura Hajime 中村元. *Bukkyōgo daijiten* 佛教語大辭典 (Tokyo: Tokyo Shoseki, 1975).

Nie Chongzheng 聶崇正 ed. *Qingdai gongting huihua* 清代宮廷繪畫 (Hong Kong: Shangwu Yinshuguan, 1996).

Niu Zhaozao 牛照藻 ed. *Ruicheng xianzhi* 芮城縣志 (Taipei: Chengwen Chubanshe, 1968).

Nunome Chōfū 布目潮渢. "Tōdai no meicha to sono ryūtsū" 唐代の名茶とその流通. In *Ono Katsutoshi hakase shōju kinen Tōhōgaku ronshū* 小野勝年博士頌壽記年東方學論集 (Kyoto: Ryūkoku Daigaku Tōyō shigaku kenkyūkai, 1982), pp. 255–85.

Ono Genmyō 小野玄妙 ed. *Busshō kaisetsu daijiten* 佛書解說大辭典 (Tokyo: Daitō Shuppansha, 1964–78).

Pan Chonggui 潘重規 ed. *Dunhuang bianwenji xinshu* 敦煌變文集新書 (Taipei: Wenjin Chubanshe, 1994).

Pu Muzhou (Poo Mu-chou) 蒲慕州. *Muzang yu shengsi—Zhongguo gudai zongjiao zhi xingsi* 墓葬與生死——中國古代宗教之省思 (Taipei: Lianjing, 1993).

Qian Mu 錢穆. *Guoshi dagang* 國史大綱 (1931; Taipei: Taiwan Shangwu Yinshuguan, 1984).

Shaanxisheng Bowuguan 陝西省博物館. "Tang Li Shou mu fajue jianbao" 唐李壽墓發掘簡報, *Wenwu* 文物 (1974.9), pp. 71–88.

———. "Tang Li Shou mu bihua shitan" 唐李壽墓壁畫試探, *Wenwu* 文物 (1974.9), pp. 39, 89–94.

Shandong Liaocheng Diqu Bowuguan 山東聊城地區博物館. "Shandong Liaocheng Bei Song tieta" 山東聊城北宋鐵塔, *Kaogu* 考古 (1987.2), pp. 124–30.

Shandongsheng Qingzhoushi Bowuguan 山東省青州市博物館. "Qingzhou Longxingsi fojiao zaoxiang jiaozang qingli jianbao" 青州龍興寺佛教造像窖藏清理簡報, *Wenwu* 文物 (1998.2), pp. 4–15.

Shang Binghe 尚秉和. *Lidai shehui fengsu shiwu kao* 歷代社會風俗事物考 (Taipei: Taiwan Shangwu Yinshuguan, 1985).

Shi Xingbang 石興邦 ed. *Famensi digong zhenbao* 法門寺地宮珍寶 (Xian: Shaanxi Renmin Meishu Chubanshe, 1989).

Shiga Takayoshi 滋賀高義. "Tonkō shakyō batsubun yori mita bukkyō shinkō" 敦煌寫經跋文より見た佛教信仰. In Nogami Shunjō 野上俊靜 ed., *Ōtani daigaku shozo tonko ko shakyō* 大谷大學所藏敦煌古寫經, vol. 1 (Kyoto: Ōtani daigaku tōyōgaku kenkyūshitsu, 1986), pp. 151–6.

Shōsōin Jimusho 正倉院事務所 ed. *Shōsōin hōmotsu, hokusō* 正倉院寶物 (Tokyo: Asahi Shimbunsha, 1987–89).

Sichuansheng Wenwukaogu Yanjiusuo 四川省文物考古研究所 ed. *Sanxingdui jisikeng* 三星堆祭祀坑 (Beijing: Wenwu Chubanshe, 1999).

Song Guangyu (Sung Kuang-yü) 宋光宇. "Guanyu shanshu de yanjiu ji qi zhanwang" 關於善書的研究及其展望, *Xin shixue* 新史學 vol. 5, no. 4 (1994), pp. 163–91.

Sun Ji 孫機. *Handai wuzhi wenhua ziliao tushuo* 漢代物質文化資料圖說 (Beijing: Wenwu Chubanshe, 1991).

———. *Zhongguo shenghuo* 中國聖火 (Liaoning: Liaoning Jiaoyu Chubanshe, 1996).

———, and Yang Hong 楊泓. *Wenwu congtan* 文物叢談 (Beijing: Wenwu Chubanshe, 1991).

Sun Xiushen 孫修身. *Wang Xuance shiji gouchen* 王玄策史跡鉤沉 (Urumuqi: Xinjiang Renmin Chubanshe, 1998).

Tang Huancheng 唐寰澄. *Zhongguo gudai qiaoliang* 中國古代橋梁 (Beijing: Wenwu Chubanshe, 1957).

———. *Qiaoliang juan* 橋樑卷. In Lu Jiaxi 廬嘉錫 ed., *Zhongguo kexue jishushi* 中國科學技術史 (Beijing: Kexue Chubanshe, 2000).

Tang Yongtong 湯用彤. *Han-Wei Liang Jin Nanbeichao fojiaoshi* 漢魏兩晉南北朝佛教史 (1938; rpt. Beijing: Zhonghua Shuju, 1983).

Tian Qing 田青. "Fojiao yinyue de Hua hua" 佛教音樂的華化, *Shijie zongjiao yanjiu* 世界宗教研究 (1985.3), pp. 1–20.

Tianshui Maijishan Shikuyishu Yanjiusuo 天水麥積山石窟藝術研究所 ed. *Chūgoku sekkutsu: Bakusekisan sekkutsu* 中國石窟：麥積山石窟 (Tokyo: Heibonsha, 1987).

Tokiwa Daijō 常盤大定. *Zoku Shina bukkyō no kenkyū* 續支那の研究 (Tokyo: Shunjūsha, 1941).

Tong Wei 童瑋. *Bei Song Kaibao Dazangjing diaoyin kaoshi ji mulu huanyuan* 北宋《開寶大藏經》雕印考釋及目錄還原 (Beijing: Shumu Wenxian Chubanshe, 1991).

Torīmoto Yukiyo 鳥居本幸代. "Nanzan Dōsen no kesha kan ni tsuite 南山道宣の袈裟觀について, *Tendai gakuhō* 天台學報, vol. 25 (1983), pp. 185–8.

Wang Bomin 王伯敏. *Zhongguo huihuashi* 中國繪畫史 (Shanghai: Shanghai Renmin Meishu Chubanshe, 1982).

Wang Jihuai 王吉懷. *Zhongguo yuangu ji sandai zongjiao shi* 中國遠古暨三代宗教史 (Beijing: Renmin chubanshe, 1994).

Wang Kefen 王克芬 et al. *Fojiao yu Zhongguo wudao* 佛教與中國舞蹈 (Tianjin: Tianjin Renmin Chubanshe, 1995).

Wang Nianyi 王年一. *Da dongluan de niandai* 大動亂的年代 (Zhengzhou: Henan Renmin Chubanshe, 1988).

Wang Xixiang 王熙祥, and Zeng Deren 曾德仁. "Sichuan Zizhong Chonglong-shan Moyai zaoxiang" 四川資中重龍山摩崖造像, *Wenwu* 文物 (1988.8), pp. 19–30.

Wang Yong 王勇. "Shubi zakkō" 麈尾雜考, *Bukkyō geijutsu* 佛教藝術 vol. 175 (1987.11), pp. 73–89.

Wang Yunying 王雲英. *Qingdai Manzu fushi* 清代滿族服飾 (Shenyang: Liao-ning Minzu Chubanshe, 1985).

Wenzhoushi Wenwuchu 文州市文物處 et al. "Wenzhoushi Bei Song Baixiangta qingli baogao" 溫州市北宋白象塔清理報告, *Wenwu* 文物 (1987.5), pp. 1–14.

Wu Meifeng 吳美鳳. "Song Ming shiqi jiaju xingzhi zhi yanjiu" 宋明時期家具形制之研究. Taipei: Master's Thesis for Chinese Culture University, 1996.

———. "Zuoyi shengchuang xian zinian—cong Mingshi jiaju kan zuoju zhi yan-bian" 坐椅繩床閑自念——從明式家具看坐具之演變, *Lishi wenwu* 歷史文物 vol. 8, no. 2 (Feb 1998), pp. 59–69.

Wu Xiang 武翔. "Jiangsu Liuchao huaxiangzhuan yanjiu" 江蘇六朝畫像磚研究, *Dongnan wenhua* 東南文化 vol. 115 (1997.1), pp. 72–96.

Wu Yingcai 吳英才, and Guo Juanjie 郭雋杰. *Zhongguo de fosi* 中國的佛寺 (Tianjin: Tianjin Renmin Chubanshe, 1994).

Xiao Fan (Hsiao Fan) 蕭璠. "Changsheng sixiang he yu toufa xiangguan de yang-sheng fangshu" 長生思想和與頭髮相關的養生方術, *Zhongyang yanjiuyuan Lishi yuyan yanjiusuo jikan* 中央研究院歷史語言研究所集刊, vol. 69, no. 4 (1998), pp. 671–726.

Xu Huili 許惠利. "Beijing Zhihuasi faxian Yuandai zangjing" 北京智化寺發現元代藏經, in *Wenwu* 文物 1987.8, pp. 1–7, 29.

Xu Pinfang 徐蘋芳. *Zhongguo lishi kaoguxue luncong* 中國歷史考古學論叢 (Taipei: Yunchen Wenhua Chubanshe, 1995).

Yamada Kentarō 山田憲太朗. *Tōa kōryōshi* 東亞香料史 (1942; rpt. Kyoto: Toyōten, 1979).

Yang Hong 楊泓. "Dunhuang Mogaoku yu Zhongguo gudai jiajushi yanjiu zhi yi" 敦煌莫高窟與中國古代家具史研究之一, in Duan Wenjie 段文杰 ed., *1987 Dunhuang shiku yanjiu guoji taolunhui wenji (Shiku kaogu bian)* 1987 敦煌石窟研究國際討論會文集 (石窟考古編) (Shenyang: Liaoning Meishu Chuban-she, 1990), pp. 520–33.

———. "Huchuang" 胡床. In Sun Ji and Yang Hong eds., *Wenwu congtan*, pp. 254–62.

Yang Shengxin 楊繩信. "Cong *Qishazang* keyin kan Song Yuan yinshua gongren de jige wenti 從磧砂藏刻印看宋元印刷工人的幾個問題, *Zhonghua wenshi luncong* 中華文史論叢, vol. 29, no. 1 (1984), pp. 41–58.

Yin Shengping 尹聖平, and Li Xixing 李西興. *Tangmu bihua zhenpin xuancui* 唐墓壁畫眞品選粹 (Xian: Shaanxi Renmin Meishu Chubanshe, 1991).

Yu Yingshi (Yü Ying-shih) 余英時. "Shuo Hongmenyan de zuoci" 說鴻門宴的坐次. In *Shixue yu chuantong* 史學與傳統 (Taipei: Shibao Wenhua Chuban-she, 1982), pp 184–95.

Yu Yunhua 余雲華. *Gongshou, jugong, guibai—Zhongguo chuantong jiaoji liyi* 拱手、鞠躬、跪拜——中國傳統交際禮儀 (Chengdu: Sichuan Renmin Chu-banshe, 1993).

Zhongguo meishu quanji bianji weiyuanhui 中國美術全集編輯委員會 ed. *Zhongguo meishu quanji* 中國美術全集 (Beijing: Renmin Meishu Chuban-she, 1984–89).

Zhongguo Shehuikexueyuan Kaogu Yanjiuso 中國社會科學院考古研究所 et al. "Hebei Linzhang Yecheng yizhi chutu de Beichao tong zaoxiang" 河北臨漳鄴城遺址出土的北朝銅造像, *Kaogu* 考古 (1992.8), pp. 741–4.

Zhou Shaoliang 周紹良. "Mile xinyang zai fojiao chu ru Zhongguo de jieduan he qi zaoxiang yiyi 彌勒信仰在佛教初入中國的階段和其造像意義, *Shijie zong-jiao yanjiu* 世界宗教研究 (1990.2), pp. 35–9.

Zhou Xing 周星. *Jingjie yu xiangzheng: qiao he minsu* 境界與象徵: 橋和民俗 (Shanghai: Shanghai Wenyi Chubanshe, 1998).

Zhou Zheng 周錚. "Luo Sishen zaoxiang xiaokao" 駱思愼造像小考, *Wenwu* 文物 (1984.12), pp. 23–4.

Zhu Dawei 朱大渭. "Zhonggu Hanren you guizuo dao chuijiao gaozuo" 中古漢人由跪坐到垂腳高坐, *Zhongguoshi yanjiu* 中國史研究 (1994.4), pp. 102–14.

Zhu Duanwen 朱端玟. *Chengyu yu fojiao* 成語與佛教 (Beijing: Beijing Jingji-xueyuan Chubanshe, 1989).

Zhu Qianzhi 朱謙之. *Zhongguo jingjiao* 中國景教 (Beijing: Dongfang Chuban-she, 1993).

Zhu Qingzhi 朱慶之. *Fodian yu zhonggu Hanyu cihui yanjiu* 佛典與中古漢語詞彙研究 (Taipei: Wenjin Chubanshe, 1992).

Zhu Zhongsheng 朱重聖. "Woguo yincha chengfeng zhi yuanyin ji qi dui Tang Song shehui yu guanfu zhi yingxiang" 我國飲茶成風之原因及其對唐宋社會與官府之影響, *Shixue huikan* 史學彙刊, 10 (June 1980), pp. 93–150.

Zhu Zizhen 朱自振. "Zhongguo cha wenhua shi" 中國茶文化史. In Zhu Zi-zhen and Shen Han 沈漢, *Zhongguo chajiu wenhuashi* 中國茶酒文化史 (Tai-pei: Wenjin Chubanshe, 1995).

WORKS IN EUROPEAN LANGUAGES

Abe, Stanley K. "Art and Practice in a Fifth-century Chinese Buddhist Cave Tem-ple," *Ars Orientalis*, vol. 20 (1990), pp. 1–31.

Adamek, Wendi Leigh. "Issues in Chinese Buddhist Transmission as Seen Through the *Lidai Fabao ji (Record of the Dharma)*," Ph.D. dissertation, Stanford Uni-versity, 1997.

———. "Robes Purple and Gold: Transmission of the Robe in the *Lidai fabaoji* (Record of the Dharma-Jewel Through the Ages)," *History of Religions*, vol. 40, no. 1 (August 2000), pp. 58–81.

Aston, William George. *Nihongi: Chronicles of Japan from the Earlist Times to* A.D. *697* (1896; rpt. London: George Allen & Unwin, 1956).

Auboyer, Jeannine. *Le trône et son symbolisme dans l'Inde ancienne* (Paris: Musée Guimet, 1949).

Bareau, André. *Les sectes bouddhiques du petit véhicule* (Paris: École française d'Extrême-Orient, 1955).

———. *Recherches sur la biographie du Buddha dans les sūtrapiṭaka et les vinayapiṭaka anciens: de la quête de l'éveil à la conversion de Śāriputra et de Maudgalyāyana* (Paris: École française d'Extrême-Orient, 1963).

Baxandall, Michael. *Painting and Experience in Fifteenth-Century Italy: A Primer in the Social History of Pictorial Style* (Oxford: Oxford University Press, 1988).

Beal, Samuel. *Si-yu-ki: Buddhist Records of the Western World* (London: K. Paul, Trench, Trubner, 1906).

Bedini, Silvio A. *The Trail of Time: Time Measurement with Incense in East Asia* (Cambridge: Cambridge University Press, 1994).

Belting, Hans. *Likeness and Presence: A History of the Image before the Era of Art,* trans. from the German by Edmund Jephcott (Chicago: University of Chicago Press, 1994).

Benjamin, Walter. *Illuminations: Essays and Reflection,* trans. Hannah Arendt (1955; English trans., New York: Harcourt Brace Jovanovich, 1968).

Bielefeldt, Carl. *Dōgen's Manuals of Zen Meditation* (Berkeley: University of California Press, 1988).

Bourda, M. G. "Quelques réflexions sur la pose assise à l'européenne dans l'art bouddhique," *Artibus Asiae,* vol. 12, no. 4 (1949), pp. 302–13.

Bourdieu, Pierre. *Distinction: A Social Critique of the Judgement of Taste* trans. Richard Nice (Cambridge: Harvard University Press, 1984).

Braudel, Fernand. *The Structures of Everyday Life: Civilization and Capitalism 15th–18th Century* (1979; English trans. by Sian Reynolds, New York: Harper and Row, 1981).

Brekke, Torkel. "Contradiction and the Merit of Giving in Indian Religions," *Numen,* vol. 45, no. 3 (1998), pp. 287–320.

Brokaw, Cynthia J. *The Ledgers of Merit and Demerit: Social Change and Moral Order in Late Imperial China* (Princeton: Princeton University Press, 1991).

Brook, Timothy. *Praying for Power: Buddhism and the Formation of Gentry Society in Late-Ming China* (Cambridge: Harvard University Press, 1993).

Broughton, Jeffrey L. *The Bodhidharma Anthology: The Earliest Records of Zen* (Berkeley: University of California Press, 1999).

Bujard, Marianne. "Le joyau de Chen: culte historique—culte vivant," *Cahiers d'Extrême-Asie,* vol. 10 (1998), pp. 131–81.

Bulliet, Richard W. *The Camel and the Wheel* (New York: Columbia University Press, 1990).

Bunker, Emma C. "Early Chinese Representations of Vimalakīrti," *Artibus Asiae,* vol. 30, no. 1 (1968), pp. 28–52.

Burke, Peter. *The Italian Renaissance: Culture and Society in Italy* (Princeton: Princeton University Press, 1986).

Buswell, Robert E. *The Zen Monastic Experience: Buddhist Practice in Contemporary Korea* (Princeton: Princeton University Press, 1992).

Cahill, James. *Chinese Painting* (New York: Rizzoli International Publications, 1977).

———. *An Index of Early Chinese Painters and Paintings: T'ang, Sung, and Yüan* (Berkeley: University of California Press, 1980).

Cammann, Schuyler V. R. "Ch'ing Dynasty 'Mandarin Chains,'" *Ornament,* vol. 4, no. 1 (1979), pp. 25–9.

Campany, Robert F. "Notes on the Devotional Uses and Symbolic Functions of

Sūtra Texts as Depicted in Early Chinese Buddhist Miracle Tales and Hagiographies," *Journal of the International Association of Buddhist Studies*, vol. 14, no. 1 (1991), pp. 28–72.

———. *Strange Writing: Anomaly Accounts in Early Medieval China* (Albany: State University of New York Press, 1996).

Carruthers, Mary. *The Craft of Thought: Meditation, Rhetoric, and the Making of Images, 400–1200* (Cambridge: Cambridge University Press, 1998).

Chadwick, Owen. *The Reformation* (1964; rpt. Middlesex: Penguin Books, 1972).

Chang, Chung-li. *The Chinese Gentry: Studies on Their Role in Nineteenth-Century Chinese Society* (1955; rpt. Seattle: University of Washington Press, 1970).

Chang, K. C. ed. *Food in Chinese Culture: Anthropological and Historical Perspectives* (New Haven: Yale University Press, 1977).

Chang, Kun. *A Comparative Study of the Kaṭhinavastu* (The Hague: Mouton, 1957).

Chavannes, Édouard. *Mission archéologique dans la Chine septentrionale* (Paris: E. Leroux, 1913–15).

Chen, Kenneth. "Inscribed Stelae During the Wei, Chin, and Nan-ch'ao." In Lawrence G. Thompson, ed., *Studia Asiatica: Essays in Asian Studies in Felicitation of the Seventy-Fifth Anniversary of Professor Ch'en Shou-yi* (San Francisco: Chinese Materials Center, 1975).

———. *The Chinese Transformation of Buddhism* (Princeton: Princeton University Press, 1973).

———. *Buddhism in China: A Historical Survey* (Princeton: Princeton University Press, 1964).

Ch'ü, T'ung-tsu. *Local Government in China under the Ch'ing* (Stanford: Stanford University Press, 1969).

Cipolla, Carlo M. *Before the Industrial Revolution: European Society and Economy 1000–1700*, 3d ed. (London: Routledge, 1993).

Cleuziou, Serge, et al. "The Use of Theory in French Archaeology." In Ian Hodder, ed., *Archaeological Theory in Europe* (New York: Routledge, 1991), pp. 91–128.

Clunas, Craig. *Chinese Furniture* (London: Bamboo Publishing, 1988).

———. *Superfluous Things: Material Culture and Social Status in Early Modern China* (Chicago: University of Illinois Press, 1991).

Conze, Edward. *The Perfection of Wisdom in Eight Thousand Lines and Its Verse Summary* (Bolinas: Four Seasons Foundation, 1973).

Cranz, Galen. *The Chair: Culture, Body, and Design* (New York: W. W. Norton, 1998).

Daniels, Christian. *Science and Civilisation in China, vol. 6, Biology and Biological Technology: part 3, Agro-Industries and Forestry.* (Cambridge: Cambridge University Press, 1995).

Davidson, J. LeRoy. "The Origin and Early Use of the Ju-i," *Artibus Asiae*, vol. 13, no. 4 (1950), pp. 239–49.

de Bary, Wm. Theodore, ed. *Sources of Chinese Tradition*, vol. 1 (New York: Columbia University Press, 1960).

de La Vallée Poussin, Louis, *Abhidharmakośabhāsyam,* trans. Leo M. Pruden (Berkeley: Asian Humanities Press, 1991).

Deetz, James. *In Small Things Forgotten: The Archeology of Early American Life* (New York: Anchor Press, 1977).

Dehejia, Vidya. "Aniconism and the Multivalence of Emblems," *Ars Orientalis,* 21 (1991), pp. 45–66.

Delahaye, Hubert. "Les antécédents magiques des statues chinoises," *Revue d'esthétique,* new series, no. 5 (1983), pp. 45–54.

Demiéville, Paul. "Butzuzō" 佛像. In *Hōbōgirin: dictionnaire encyclopédique du bouddhisme, d'après les sources chinoises et japonaises* (Tokyo: Maison Franco-Japonaise, 1929–84), vol. 3. pp. 210–5.

———. "L'iconoclasme anti-bouddhique en Chine," in *Mélanges d'Histoire des Religions offerts à H. C. Puech* (Paris: Presses Universitaires de France, 1974), pp. 17–25.

Dien, Albert E. "The Stirrup and Its Effect on Chinese Military History," *Ars Orientalis,* 16 (1986), pp. 33–56.

Donner, Neal, and Daniel B. Stevenson. *The Great Calming and Contemplation: A Study and Annotated Translation of the First Chapter of Chih-i's* Mohe chih-kuan (Honolulu: University of Hawaii Press, 1993).

Drège, Jean-Pierre. "Papiers de Dunhuang: essai d'analyse morphologique des manuscrits chinois datés," *T'oung Pao,* 67.3–5 (1981), pp. 305–60.

———. *Les bibliothèques en Chine au temps des manuscrits* (Paris: École française d'Extrême-Orient, 1991).

——— ed. *De Dunhuang au Japon: Études chinoises et bouddhique offertes á Michel Soymié* (Geneva: Librairie Droz, 1996).

———. "La lecture et l'écriture en Chine et la xylographie," *Études chinoises* 10, no. 1–2 (1991), pp. 77–111.

Dubin, Lois Sherr. *The History of Beads* (New York: Abrams, 1987).

Dudbridge, Glen. "Buddhist Images in Action: Five Stories from the Tang," *Cahiers d'Extrême-Asie* 10 (1998), pp. 377–91.

Dumoulin, Heinrich. *Zen Buddhism: A History, vol. 1: India and China* (New York: Macmillan, 1988).

———. *Zen Buddhism: A History, vol. 2: Japan* (New York: Macmillan, 1990).

Dundas, Paul. *The Jains* (London: Routledge, 1992).

Durt, Hubert. "Chōmyōtō" 長明燈, in *Hōbōgirin,* pp. 360–5.

Eliade, Mircea. *Patterns in Comparative Religion,* trans. Rosemary Sheed (London: Sheed and Ward, 1958).

——— ed. *Encyclopedia of Religion* (New York: Macmillan and Free Press, 1987).

Elias, Norbert. *The Civilizing Process,* trans. Edmund Jephcott (Oxford: Basil Blackwell, 1994).

———. *What is Sociology?* (New York: Columbia University Press, 1978).

Eskildsen, Stephen. *Asceticism in Early Taoist Religion* (Albany: State University of New York, 1998).

Faure, Bernard. *Le traité de Bodhidharma: Première anthologie du bouddhisme chan* (Paris: Le Mail, 1986).

———. *The Rhetoric of Immediacy: A Cultural Critique of Chan/Zen Buddhism* (Princeton: Princeton University Press, 1991).

————. "Quand l'habit fait le moine: The Symbolism of the Kāṣāya in Sōtō Zen," *Cahiers d'Extrême-Asie* 8 (1995), pp. 335–69.

————. *Visions of Power: Imagining Medieval Japanese Buddhism* (Princeton: Princeton University Press, 1996).

————. "The Buddhist Icon and the Modern Gaze," *Critical Inquiry* 24 (Spring 1998), pp. 768–813.

Firth, Raymond. *Symbols Public and Private* (London: George Allen and Unwin, 1973).

FitzGerald, C. P. *Barbarian Beds: The Origin of the Chair in China* (London: Cresset Press, 1965).

Forbes, R. J. *Studies in Ancient Technology* (Leiden: E. J. Brill, 1957).

Forke, Alfred. *Lun-heng: Part 1. Philosophical Essays of Wang Ch'ung* (New York: Paragon Book Gallery, 1962).

Forte, Antonino. *Political Propaganda and Ideology in China at the End of the Seventh Century* (Napoli: Istituto Universitario Orientale, 1976).

Foulk, T. Griffith. "Religious Functions of Buddhist Art in China," in Weidner, ed., *Cultural Intersections in Later Chinese Buddhism*, pp. 13–29.

Foulk, T. Griffith, and Robert H. Sharf. "On the Ritual Use of Ch'an Portraiture in Medieval China," *Cahiers d'Extrême-Asie* 7 (1993–94), pp. 149–219.

Frank, Bernard. "Vacuité et corps actualisé: Le problème de la présence des 'Personnages Vénérés' dans leurs images selon la tradition du bouddhisme japonais," *Journal of the International Association of Buddhist Studies,* vol. 11, no. 2 (1988), pp. 53–86.

Franke, Herbert. "Einige Drucke und Handschriften der frühen Ming-Zeit," *Oriens Extremis* 19.1–2 (1972), pp. 55–64.

Fraser, Sarah E. "The Artist's Practice in Tang Dynasty China," Ph.D. dissertation, University of California at Berkeley, 1996.

Frauwallner, Erich. *Studies in Abhidharma Literature and the Origins of Buddhist Philosophical Systems* (Albany: State University of New York, 1995).

Freedberg, David. *The Power of Images: Studies in the History and Theory of Response* (Chicago: University of Chicago Press, 1989).

Gamble, Harry Y. *Books and Readers in the Early Church: A History of Early Christian Texts* (New Haven: Yale University Press, 1995).

Geary, Patrick J. *Furta Sacra: Thefts of Relics in the Central Middle Ages* (Princeton: Princeton University Press, 1990).

Geiger, Wilhelm, ed. *The Mahāvamsa* (Oxford: Pali Text Society, 1912).

Gernet, Jacques. *Buddhism in Chinese Society: An Economic History from the Fifth to the Tenth Centuries,* trans. Franciscus Verellen (New York: Columbia University Press, 1995).

Giebel, Rolf W. "The *Chin-kang-ting ching yü-ch'ieh shih-pa-hui chih-kuei:* An Annotated Translation," *Naritasan Bukkyō kenkyū kiyō* 成田山佛教研究紀要 18 (1995), pp. 107–201.

Gilchrist, Roberta. *Gender and Material Culture: The Archaeology of Religious Women* (London: Routledge, 1994).

Giles, H. A. trans. *The Travels of Fa-hsien (399–414 A.D.), or Record of the Buddhist Kingdoms* (1923; rpt. Westport: Greenwood Press, 1981).

Glahn, Else. "Fu-teng" in L. Carrington Goodrich, ed., *Dictionary of Ming Biography 1368–1644* (New York: Columbia University Press, 1976), pp. 462–6.

Goldziher, Ignaz. "Le rosaire dans l'Islam," *Revue de l'histoire des religions,* vol. 21 (1890), pp. 295–300.

Gombrich, Richard. "The Consecration of a Buddhist Image," *Journal of Asian Studies,* vol. 26, no. 1 (1966), pp. 23–36.

———. *Precept and Practice: Traditional Buddhism in the Rural Highlands of Ceylon* (Oxford: Clarendon Press, 1971).

Gómez, Luis O. *The Land of Bliss: The Paradise of the Buddha of Measureless Light* (Honolulu: University of Hawaii Press, 1996).

Graham, A. C. *Chuang-Tzu: The Inner Chapters* (London: Mandala, 1989).

Gregory, Peter N. *Inquiry into the Origin of Humanity: An Annotated Translation of Tsung-mi's Yüan jen lun with a Modern Commentary* (Honolulu: University of Hawaii Press, 1995).

Griswold, A. B. "Prolegomena to the Study of the Buddha's Dress in Chinese Sculpture," in *Artibus Asiae,* vol. 26, no. 2 (1963), pp. 85–131.

Guy, R. Kent. *The Emperor's Four Treasuries: Scholars and the State in the Late Ch'ien-lung Era* (Cambridge: Harvard University Press, 1987).

Halperin, Mark. "Pieties and Responsibilities: Buddhism and the Chinese Literati, 780–1280," Ph.D. dissertation, University of California at Berkeley, 1997.

Handler, Sarah. "The Revolution in Chinese Furniture: Moving from Mat to Chair," *Asian Art,* vol. 4, no. 3 (Summer 1991), pp. 9–33.

Hansen, Valerie. "The Path of Buddhism into China: The View from Turfan," *Asia Major,* Third Series, vol. 11, part 2 (1998), pp. 37–66.

Harper, Donald. "A Chinese Demonography of the Third Century B.C." *Harvard Journal of Asiatic Studies,* vol. 45, no. 2 (1985), pp. 459–98.

Hawkes, David, trans. *The Story of the Stone,* by Cao Xueqin, (1973; rpt. Middlesex: Penguin Books, 1986).

Herskovits, Melville J. *Man and His Works: The Science of Cultural Anthropology* (New York: Alfred A. Knopf, 1948).

Hevia, James L. *Cherishing Men from Afar: Qing Guest Ritual and the Macartney Embassy of 1793* (Durham: Duke University Press, 1995).

Hirakawa Akira. *A History of Indian Buddhism from Śākyamuni to Early Mahāyāna,* Paul Groner, trans. (Honolulu: University of Hawaii Press, 1990).

Hitchman, F. "Buddhist Symbols on Chinese Ceramics," *Orient Art,* new series, vol. 8, no. 4 (Winter 1962), pp. 15–20; vol. 8, no. 4 (Winter 1962), pp. 207–9.

Hōbōgirin: Dictionnaire encyclopédique du bouddhisme d'après les sources chinoises et japonaises (Paris: Adrien Maisonneuve, 1927–).

Holzman, Donald. "A propos de l'origine de la chaise en Chine," *T'oung Pao* 53 (1967), pp. 279–92.

Honée, Eugène. "Image and Imagination in the Medieval Culture of Prayer: A Historical Perspective." In Hank van Os et al., *The Art of Devotion in the Late Middle Ages in Europe 1300–1500* (Princeton: Princeton University Press, 1994), pp. 157–74.

Hou Ching-lang. "Trésors du monastère Long-hing à Touen-houang: Une étude sur le manuscrit P.3432." In Michel Soymié, ed., *Nouvelles Contributions aux Etudes de Touen-houang* (Geneva: Droz, 1981), pp. 149–68.

Huang Hsing-tsung. *Fermentation and Food Science,* part 5 of vol. 6, *Biology and Biological Technology.* In Joseph Needham, ed., *Science and Civilisation in China* (Cambridge: Cambridge University Press, 2000).

Huizinga, Johan. *The Waning of the Middle Ages: A Study of the Forms of Life, Thought and Art in France and the Netherlands in the Dawn of the Renaissance*, trans. F. Hopman (New York: Doubleday, 1954).

Huntington, Susan L. "Early Buddhist Art and the Theory of Aniconism," *Art Journal*, vol. 49, no. 4 (Winter 1990), pp. 401–8.

———. "Aniconism and the Multivalence of Emblems: Another Look," *Ars Orientalis*, vol. 22 (1992), pp. 111–56.

Hurvitz, Leon. *Scripture of the Lotus Blossom of the Fine Dharma* (New York: Columbia University Press, 1976).

Hymes, Robert P. *Statesmen and Gentlemen: The Elite of Fu-Chou, Chiang-Hsi, in Northern and Southern Sung* (Cambridge: Cambridge University Press, 1986).

Jaini, Padmanabh S. "Stages in the Bodhisattva Career of the Tathāgata Maitreya." In Alan Sponberg and Helen Hardacre, eds., *Maitreya, the Future Buddha* (Cambridge: Cambridge University Press, 1988), pp. 54–90.

Janes, Dominic. *God and Gold in Late Antiquity* (Cambridge: Cambridge University Press, 1998).

Jayawickrama, N. A. *The Inception of Discipline and the Vinaya Nidāna, Being a Translation and Edition of the Bāhiranidāna of Buddhaghosa's Samardapāsādika, the Vinaya Commentary* (London, Luzac, 1962).

Kieschnick, John. *The Eminent Monk: Buddhist Ideals in Medieval Chinese Hagiography* (Honolulu: University of Hawaii Press, 1997).

———. "Blood Writing in Chinese Buddhism," *Journal of the International Association of Buddhist Studies*, vol. 23, no. 2 (2001), pp. 177–94.

Knapp, Ronald G. *Chinese Bridges* (New York: Oxford University Press, 1993).

Knechtges, David. "A Literary Feast: Food in Early Chinese Literature," *Journal of the American Oriental Society*, vol. 106, no. 1 (Jan.–Mar. 1986), pp. 49–63.

Knoblock, John, and Jeffrey Riegel. *The Annals of Lü Buwei: A Complete Translation and Study* (Stanford: Stanford University Press, 2000).

Koizumi Kayuko. "The Furniture of the Shōsōin in Relation to Ancient Chinese and Korean Furniture." In Kimura Norimitsu, ed., *The Treasures of the Shōsōin: Furniture and Interior Furnishings* (Kyoto: Shikosha, 1992), pp. 44–51.

Kopytoff, Igor. "The Cultural Biography of Things: Commoditization as Process." In Arjun Appadurai, ed., *The Social Life of Things: Commodities in Cultural Perspective* (Cambridge: Cambridge University Press, 1986), pp. 64–94.

Kuo Li-ying. *Confession et contrition dans le bouddhisme chinois du Ve au Xe siècle* (Paris: École française d'Extrême-Orient, 1994).

Lamotte, Étienne. *Le traité de la grande vertu de sagesse* (Louvain: Institute Orientaliste Louvain-La-Neuve, 1981).

———. *History of Indian Buddhism: From the Origins to the Saka Era*, trans. Sara Webb-Boin (Louvain: Peeters Press, 1988).

Lau, D. C. *The Analects* (Middlesex: Penguin Books, 1979).

———. *Mencius* (Middlesex: Penguin Books, 1970).

Lee, Junghee. "The Origins and Development of the Pensive Bodhisattva Images of Asia," *Artibus Asiae*, vol. 53, no. 3/4 (1993), pp. 311–53.

Le Roy Ladurie, Emmanuel. *Montaillou. The Promised Land of Error*, trans. Barbara Bray (New York: George Braziller, 1978).

Li Rongxi. *A Biography of the Tripiṭaka Master of the Great Ci'en Monastery of the Great Tang Dynasty* (Berkeley: Numata Center for Buddhist Translation and Research, 1995).

Lin, Fu-shih. "Chinese Shamans and Shamanism in the Chiang-nan Area during the Six Dynasties Period," Ph.D. dissertation, Princeton University, 1994.

Liu, Lydia H. *Translingual Practices: Literature, National Culture and Translated Modernity: China, 1900–1937* (Stanford: Stanford University Press, 1995).

Liu Shufen. "Art, Ritual and Society: Buddhist Practice in Rural China during the Northern Dynasties," *Asia Major,* Third Series, vol. 8, part. 1 (1995), pp. 19–46.

Liu Xinru. *Ancient India and Ancient China: Trade and Religious Exchanges, AD 1–600* (Delhi: Oxford University Press, 1988).

———. *Silk and Religion. An Exploration of Material Life and the Thought of People, AD 600–1200* (Delhi: Oxford University Press, 1996).

Lopez Jr., Donald S., ed. *Religions of China in Practice* (Princeton: Princeton University Press, 1996).

Lowie, Robert H. *The History of Ethnological Theory* (New York: Farrar and Rinehart, 1937).

Ludwig, Alan. *Graven Images: New England Stonecarving and Its Symbols, 1650–1815* (Middletown: Wesleyan University Press, 1966).

Lynn, Richard John. *The Classic of Changes: A New Translation of the I Ching as Interpreted by Wang Bi* (New York: Columbia University Press, 1994).

Macartney, George. *An Embassy to China, Being the Journal Kept by Lord Macartney during His Embassy to the Emperor Ch'ien-lung 1793–1794,* ed. J. L. Cranmer-Byng (London: Longmans, Green, 1961).

Macaulay, Thomas Babington. *The History of England (1848–1861)* (abridged version, London: Penguin Books, 1987).

Magnin, Paul. *La vie et l'oeuvre de Huisi* (Paris: École française d'Extrême-Orient, 1979).

Marett, R. R. *The Threshold of Religion* (1909; 4th ed. London: Methuen, 1929).

Mather, Richard. *A New Account of Tales of the World* (Minneapolis: University of Minnesota Press, 1976).

McDannell, Colleen. "Interpreting Things: Material Culture Studies and American Religion," *Religion* 21 (1991), pp. 371–87.

———. *Material Christianity: Religion and Popular Culture in America* (New Haven: Yale University Press, 1995).

McRae, John. *The Northern School and the Formation of Early Ch'an Buddhism* (Honolulu: University of Hawaii Press, 1986).

Mennell, Stephen. *Norbert Elias: An Introduction* (Oxford: Blackwell, 1989).

Meyer, Birgit. "Christian Mind and Worldly Matters: Religion and Materiality in Nineteenth-Century Gold Coast," *Journal of Material Culture,* vol. 2, no. 3 (1997), pp. 311–37.

Miller, Danny. "Artifacts as Products of Human Categorisation Processes." In Ian Hodder, ed., *Symbolic and Structural Archaeology* (Cambridge: Cambridge University Press, 1982), pp. 17–25.

Mintz, Sydney. *Sweetness and Power: The Place of Sugar in Modern History* (Middlesex: Penguin Books, 1986).

Monier-Williams, Monier. *A Sanskrit-English Dictionary* (1899; rpt. Oxford: Clarendon Press, 1979).

Mote, Frederick W., and Denis Twitchett, eds. *The Cambridge History of China,* vol. 7, *The Ming Dynasty, 1368–1644, Part 1* (Cambridge: Cambridge University Press, 1988).

Murray, Julia M. "Representations of Hārītī, the Mother of Demons, and the Theme of 'Raising the Alms-Bowl' in Chinese Painting," *Artibus Asiae,* vol. 43, no. 4 (1982), pp. 253–84.

Mus, Paul. *Barabudur: Sketch of a History of Buddhism Based on Archaeological Criticism of the Texts,* trans. Alexander W. Macdonald (1933; English trans., New Delhi: Sterling, 1998).

Nattier, Jan. "The Meanings of the Maitreya Myth: A Typological Analysis." In Alan Sponberg and Helen Hardacre, eds., *Maitreya, the Future Buddha* (Cambridge: Cambridge University Press, 1988), pp. 23–50.

Needham, Joseph, et al. *Civil Engineering and Nautics,* part 3 of vol. 4, *Physics and Physical Technology.* In *Science and Civilisation in China* (Cambridge: Cambridge University Press, 1971).

Needham, Joseph, with Lu Gwei-Djen. *Spagyrical Discovery and Invention: Magisteries of Gold and Immortality,* part 2 of vol. 5, *Chemistry and Chemical Technology.* In *Science and Civilisation in China* (Cambridge: Cambridge University Press, 1974).

Nienhauser, William H., ed. *The Grand Scribe's Records* (Bloomington: Indiana University Press, 1994).

Osgood, Cornelius. *Ingalik Material Culture* (New Haven: Yale University Press, 1940).

Otto, Rudolf. *The Idea of the Holy,* trans. John W. Harvey (1923; rpt. Oxford: Oxford University Press, 1958).

Pal, Pratapaditya, and Julia Meech-Pekavik. *Buddhist Book Illuminations* (Hong Kong: Ravi Kumar Publishers, 1988).

Pelliot, Paul. *L'inscription nestorienne de Si-Ngan-Fou,* ed. Antonino Forte (Paris: Collège de France, Institut des Hautes Études Chinoises, 1996).

Poo, Mu-chou. "Ideas Concerning Death and Burial in Pre-Han and Han China," *Asia Major,* Third Series, vol. 3, part. 2, (1990) pp. 25–62.

———. *In Search of Personal Welfare: A View of Ancient Chinese Religion* (Albany: State University of New York Press, 1998).

Prescott, William H. *History of the Conquest of Mexico* (1843; rpt. New York: Random House, 1936).

Przyluski, Jean. "Le partage des reliques du Buddha," *Mélange chinois et bouddhiques,* vol. 4 (1936), pp. 341–67.

Pulleyblank, Edwin G. "Chinese Traditional Phonology," *Asia Major,* Third Series, vol. 12, part 2 (1999), pp. 101–38.

Pym, Anthony. "Translation History and the Manufacture of Paper." In Roger Ellis et al., eds., *The Medieval Translator/ Traduire au Moyen Âge* (Turnhout: Brepols, 1998), vol. 6, pp. 57–71.

Rabe, Michael. Letters to the Editor. *Art Journal,* vol. 51, no. 1 (Spring 1992) pp. 125–7.

Reischauer, Edwin O. *Ennin's Travels in T'ang China* (New York: Ronald Press, 1955).

———. *Ennin's Diary: The Record of a Pilgrimage to China in Search of the Law* (New York: Ronald Press, 1955).

Rhie, Marylin Martin. *Early Buddhist Art of China and Central Asia,* vol. 1 (Leiden: Brill, 1999).

Robinet, Isabelle. *La révélation du Shangqing dans l'histoire du Taoisme,* vol. 1 (Paris: École française d'Extrême-Orient, 1984).

Salomon, Richard, et al. *Ancient Buddhist Scrolls from Gandhāra: The British Library Kharoṣṭī Fragments* (Seattle: University of Washington Press, 1999).

Saunders, E. Dale. *Mudrā: A Study of Symbolic Gestures in Japanese Buddhist Sculpture* (London: Routledge and Kegan Paul, 1960).

Schafer, Edward H. *The Golden Peaches of Samarkand: A Study of T'ang Exotics* (Berkeley: University of California Press, 1963).

———. *Ancient China* (New York: Time-Life Books, 1967).

———. "T'ang." In K'. C. Chang, ed., *Food in Chinese Culture,* pp. 85–140.

Schiffer, Michael Brian. *The Material Life of Human Beings: Artifacts, Behavior, and Communication* (London: Routledge, 1999).

Schlereth, Thomas J. "Material Culture Studies in America, 1876–1976." In Thomas J. Schlereth, ed., *Material Culture Studies in America* (Nashville: American Association for State and Local History, 1982), pp. 1–75.

Schmitt, Jean-Claude. *La raison des gestes dans l'Occident médiéval* (Paris: Gallimard, 1990).

Schneider, Richard. "Les copies de sūtra défectueuses dans les manuscrits de Touen-houang." In Jean-Pierre Drège, ed., *De Dunhuang au Japon,* pp. 141–61.

Schober, Juliane. "Buddhist Just Rule and Burmese National Culture: State Patronage of the Chinese Tooth Relic in Myanma," *History of Religions,* vol. 36, no. 3 (1997), pp. 218–43.

Schopen, Gregory. "The Phrase 'sa pṛthivīpradeśaś caityabhūto bhavet' in the *Vajracchedikā:* Notes on the Cult of the Book in Mahāyāna," *Indo-Iranian Journal,* vol. 17, no. 3/4 (Nov.–Dec. 1975), pp. 147–81.

———. *Bones, Stones, and Buddhist Monks: Collected Papers on the Archaeology, Epigraphy, and Texts of Monastic Buddhism in India* (Honolulu: University of Hawaii Press, 1997).

———. "The Good Monk and His Money in a Buddhist Monasticism of 'The Mahāyāna Period,'" *The Eastern Buddhist,* vol. 32, no. 1 (2000), pp. 85–105.

Sebillot, Paul. "Les ponts du moyen âge et les frères pontifes" in *Les travaux publics et les mines dans les traditions et les superstitions de tous les pays* (1894; rpt. Neuilly, Guy Durier).

Seidel, Anna. "Imperial Treasures and Taoist Sacraments—Taoist Roots in the Apocrypha." In Michel Strickmann, ed., *Tantric and Taoist Studies in Honour of R. A. Stein,* vol. 2, *Mélanges Chinois et bouddhiques,* vol. 21 (Bruxelles: Institute Belge des Hautes Études Chinoises, 1983), pp. 291–371.

———. "Den-e" 傳衣, to appear in *Hōbōgirin.*

Shaffern, Robert W. "Images, Jurisdiction, and the Treasury of Merit," *Journal of Medieval History,* vol. 27, no. 33 (1996), pp. 237–47.

Sharf, Robert H. "The Idolization of Enlightenment: On the Mummification of Ch'an Masters in Medieval China," *History of Religions,* vol. 32, no. 1 (1992), pp. 1–31.

———. "The Scripture on the Production of Buddha Images." In Donald S. Lopez

Jr., ed., *Religions of China in Practice* (Princeton: Princeton University Press, 1996), 261–7.

——. "On the Allure of Buddhist Relics," *Representations* 66 (1999), pp. 75–99.

Sharf, Robert H., and T. Griffith Foulk. "On the Ritual Use of Ch'an Portraiture in Medieval China," *Cahiers d'Extrême-Asie* 7 (1993–94), pp. 149–219.

Shastri, Hirananda. "The Nalanda Copper-Plate of Devapaladeva," *Epigraphia Indica*, vol. 17 (1924), pp. 310–27.

Shinohara, Koichi. "Two Sources of Chinese Buddhist Biographies: Stupa Inscriptions and Miracle Stories." In Phyllis Granoff and Koichi Shinohara, eds., *Monks and Magicians: Religious Biographies in Asia* (Oakville: Mosaic Press, 1988), pp. 119–228.

——. "The Kaṣāya Robe of the Past Buddha Kāśyapa in the Miraculous Instruction Given to the Vinaya Master Daoxuan (596–667)," *Chung-Hwa Buddhist Journal*, vol. 13 (2000), pp. 299–367.

Shiratori Kurakichi. "The Mu-nan-chu of Ta-ch'in and the Cintāmaṇi of India," *Memoirs of the Research Department of the Toyo Bunko*, vol. 11 (1939), pp. 2–54.

Sickman, Laurence. "A Sixth-Century Buddhist Stele," *Apollo* (Mar. 1973), pp. 12–7.

Skilling, Peter. Review of Donald Swearer, *The Buddhist World of Southeast Asia*, *Journal of the American Oriental Society*, vol. 117, no. 3 (1997), pp. 579–80.

Snellgrove, David L., ed. *The Image of the Buddha* (Paris: UNESCO, 1978).

——. *Indo-Tibetan Buddhism: Indian Buddhists and Their Tibetan Successors* (Boston: Shambhala, 1987).

Snodgrass, Adrian. *The Symbolism of the Stupa* (Ithaca: Southeast Asia Program, Cornell University, 1985).

Snyder, Graydon F. *Ante Pacem: Archaeological Evidence of Church Life before Constantine* (Macon: Mercer, 1985).

Sommer, Deborah A. "Images into Words: Ming Confucian Iconoclasm," *National Palace Museum Bulletin*, vol. 29, no. 1–2 (1994), pp. 1–24.

Soper, Alexander. *Literary Evidence for Early Buddhist Art in China* (Ascona: Artibus Asiae Publishers, 1959).

Spuler, Bertold. "Trade in the Eastern Islamic Countries in the Early Centuries." In D. S. Richard, ed., *Islam and the Trade of Asia* (Philadelphia: University of Pennsylvania Press, 1970), pp. 11–20.

Staunton, George. *An Authentic Account of an Embassy from the King of Great Britain to the Emperor of China* (London: W. Bulmer, 1797).

Stcherbatsky, Th. *The Central Conception of Buddhism and the Meaning of the Word "Dharma"* (London: Royal Asiatic Society, 1923).

Stevenson, Daniel B. "Text, Image, and Transformation in the History of the *Shuilu fahui*, the Buddhist Rite for the Deliverance of Creatures of Water and Land." In Marsha Weidner, ed., *Cultural Intersections in Later Chinese Buddhism*, pp. 30–72.

Stiebing Jr., William H. *Uncovering the Past: A History of Archaeology* (Oxford: Oxford University Press, 1993).

Stone, Louise Hawley. *The Chair in China* (Toronto: Royal Ontario Museum of Archaeology, 1952).

Strickmann, Michel. "The Maoshan Revelations: Taoism and the Aristocracy," *T'oung Pao*, vol. 63 (1977), pp. 1–64.

———. *Mantras et mandarins: le bouddhisme tantrique en Chine* (Paris: Gallimard, 1996).

Strong, John S. *The Legend of King Aśoka: A Study and Translation of the Aśokāvadāna* (Princeton: Princeton University Press, 1983).

Takakusu, J. *A Record of the Buddhist Religion as Practiced in India and the Malay Archipelago* (1896; rpt. Delhi: Munshiram Manoharlal, 1966).

Tambiah, Stanley. *The Buddhist Saints of the Forest and the Cult of Amulets* (Cambridge: Cambridge University Press, 1984).

Tanabe Jr., George J. "Telling Beads: The Forms and Functions of the Buddhist Rosary in Japan" (unpublished manuscript).

Teiser, Stephen F. *The Scripture on the Ten Kings and the Making of Purgatory in Medieval Chinese Buddhism* (Honolulu: University of Hawaii Press, 1994).

Thomas, Charles. *The Early Christian Archaeology of North Britain* (London: Oxford University Press, 1971).

Thomas, Edward J. *The Life of Buddha as Legend and History* (3d ed. 1949; rpt. London: Routledge & Kegan Paul, 1975).

Tokuno, Kyoko. "The *Book of Resolving Doubts Concerning the Semblance Dharma*." In Donald S. Lopez Jr., ed., *Buddhism in Practice* (Princeton: Princeton University Press, 1995), pp. 257–71.

Trachtenberg, Alan. *Brooklyn Bridge: Fact and Symbol* (Chicago: University of Chicago Press, 1979).

Trichet, Louis. *Le costume du clergé: ses origines et son évolution en France d'après les réglements de l'Eglise* (Paris: Cerf, 1986).

Trigger, Bruce G. *A History of Archaeological Thought* (Cambridge: Cambridge University Press, 1989).

Trombert, Eric. *Le crédit à Dunhuang: Vie matérielle et société en Chine médiévale* (Paris: Collège de France, Institut des Hautes Études Chinoises, 1995).

Tsien Tsuen-hsuin. *Paper and Printing*, part 1 of vol. 5, *Chemistry and Chemical Technology*. In Joseph Needham, ed., *Science and Civilisation in China* (Cambridge: Cambridge University Press, 1985).

Tylor, Edward B. *Primitive Culture: Researches into the Development of Mythology, Philosophy, Religion, Language, Art, and Custom* (1871; 5th ed., London: John Murray, 1929).

van Os, Henk. *The Art of Devotion in the Later Middle Ages in Europe 1300–1500* (Princeton: Princeton University Press, 1994).

Vishnu, Asha. *Material Life of Northern India (3rd Century B.C. to 1st Century B.C.)* (New Delhi: Mittal Publications, 1993).

Vogel, J. Ph. "Prakrit Inscriptions from a Buddhist Site at Nagarjunikonda," *Epigraphia Indica*, vol. 20 (1929), pp. 1–37.

Walker, William H. "Ceremonial Trash?" In James M. Skibo et al., eds., *Expanding Archaeology* (Salt Lake City: University of Utah Press, 1995), pp. 67–79.

———. "Where Are the Witches of Prehistory?" *Journal of Archaeological Method and Theory*, vol. 5, no. 3 (1998), pp. 245–308.

Wang, Yi-t'ung. *A Record of Buddhist Monasteries in Lo-yang* (Princeton: Princeton University Press, 1984).

Wang-Toutain, Françoise. "Le bol du Buddha. Propagation du bouddhisme et légitimité politique," *Bulletin de l'École française d'Extrême-Orient* vol. 81 (1994), pp. 59–82.

Wang Zhenping. "Chōnen's Pilgrimage to China, 983–986," *Asia Major*, Third Series, vol. 7, no. 2 (1994), pp. 63–97.

Wanscher, Ole. *Sella Curulis: The Folding Stool, an Ancient Symbol of Dignity* (Copenhagen: Rosenkilde and Bagger, 1980).

Watson, Burton. *Records of the Grand Historian of China* (New York: Columbia University Press, 1961).

———. *The Zen Teachings of Master Lin-chi* (Boston: Shambhala, 1993).

Watters, Thomas. *On Yuan Chwang's Travels in India* (1904–5; rpt, New Delhi: Munshiram Manoharlal Publishers Pvt., 1973).

Weidner, Marsha, ed. *Cultural Intersections in Later Chinese Buddhism* (Honolulu: University of Hawaii Press, 2001).

Weinstein, Stanley. *Buddhism under the T'ang* (Cambridge: Cambridge University Press, 1987).

Welch, Holmes. *The Practice of Chinese Buddhism 1900–1950* (Cambridge: Harvard University Press, 1967).

———. *The Buddhist Revival in China* (Cambridge: Harvard University Press, 1968).

———. *Buddhism under Mao* (Cambridge: Harvard University Press, 1972).

Wensinck, A. J. "Subha." In Thomas Patrick Hughes, ed., *A Dictionary of Islam* (Lahore: Premier Book House, 1965), p. 492.

White, Lynn. *Medieval Technology and Social Change* (Oxford: Clarendon Press, 1962).

Whitfield, Roderick. *The Art of Central Asia: The Stein Collection in the British Museum* (Tokyo: Kodansha, 1982).

Wijayaratna, Mohan. *Buddhist Monastic Life According to the Texts of the Theravāda Tradition,* trans. Claude Grangier and Steven Collins (Cambridge: Cambridge University Press, 1990).

Wilbur, Martin C. *Slavery in China during the Former Han Dynasty 206 BC–AD 25* (New York: Russell and Russell, 1943).

Winston-Allen, Anne. *Stories of the Rose: The Making of the Rosary in the Middle Ages* (University Park: Pennsylvania State University Press, 1997).

Wood, Christopher S. "Iconoclasm and Iconophobia." In Michael Kelly, ed., *Encyclopedia of Aesthetics* (Oxford: Oxford University Press, 1998), pp. 450–4.

Wright, Arthur F. *The Sui Dynasty: The Unification of China, A.D. 581–617* (New York: Alfred A. Knopf, 1978).

Wu Hung. "Buddhist Elements in Early Chinese Art," *Artibus Asiae* 47 (1986), pp. 263–352.

Wu Tung. "From Imported 'Nomadic Seat' to Chinese Folding Armchair," *Journal of the Classical Chinese Furniture Society,* vol. 3, no. 2 (Spring 1993), pp. 38–47.

Yampolsky, Philip B. *The Platform Sutra of the Sixth Patriarch* (New York: Columbia University Press, 1967).

Yang Lien-sheng. *Les aspects économiques des travaux publics dans la Chine impériale* (Paris: Collège de France, 1964).

Yen Chüan-ying. "The Sculpture from the Tower of Seven Jewels: The Style, Patronage, and Iconography of the Monument," Ph.D. dissertation, Harvard University, 1986.

Yü Ying-shih. "Han." In K. C. Chang, ed., *Food in Chinese Culture,* pp. 53–83.

Zürcher, Erik. *The Buddhist Conquest of China: The Spread and Adaptation of Buddhism in Early Medieval China* (Leiden: E. J. Brill, 1972).

———. "Han Buddhism and the Western Region." In Wilt Idema and Erik Zürcher, eds., *Thought and Law in Qin and Han China: Studies Dedicated to Anthony Hulsewé on the Occasion of His Eightieth Birthday* (Leiden: E. J. Brill, 1990), pp. 158–82.

———. "Buddhist Art in Medieval China: The Ecclesiastical View." In K. R. van Kooij and H. van der Veere, eds., *Function and Meaning in Buddhist Art* (Groningen: Egbert Forsten, 1995), pp. 1–20.

Zwalf, Wladimir. *Buddhism: Art and Faith* (London: British Museum Publications, 1985).

INDEX

Abhidharmakośaśāstra, 3–4, 10, 158–59
alms bowl: of the Buddha, 111–12; composition of, 108; at Famen Monastery 109; as gift, 109–10; of Shenhui, 111; symbolism of, 107, 110–11
aloeswood, 134, 277–78
Amitābha, 116, 118, 122, 127–28
Amoghavajra, 131
Ānanda, 29, 104, 249
Anāthapiṇḍada, 58
Anāthapiṇḍika, 190
aniconism, 66n, 73
animatism, 80
animism, 25–26, 80
antarvāsa, 90–91
archaeology: in China, 22; of furniture, 227; of icons, 71; and merit, 162–63; and monastic property, 5, 21; of relics, 30, 38; and study of material culture, 16–19; of tombs, 160
arhats, 125n.143
art. *See* Buddhist art
asceticism, 13, 88, 93–100, 108–9, 287.
    See also wealth, renunciation of
Aśoka, 29–30, 33, 41, 236
Avalokiteśvara, 122–23. *See also* Guanyin
Avataṃsaka Sutra, 7, 174–76, 273

Bai Juyi, 271, 272, 245
Baima Monastery, 164
Bai Xingjian, 125–26
Bamboo Grove, 189
Baoshan, 125, 129
Baxandall, Michael, 18
beds, 224
bells, 39, 153, 187
Benyuan, 206
Bharhut, 38, 119n.120, 236
Biancai, 243
Bimbisāra, 189
Binglingsi, 124
Biyun Monastery, 70
blood writing, 174–76
Bodhidharma, 75, 105, 196–97
booklets, 167, 179–80

Book of Changes, 160
Book of Tea, 263, 265–66
books: of bamboo and wood, 166–67; of birch bark and palm leaves, 166; collecting of, 167; destruction of, 167; in India, 164–66; oldest extant Buddhist, 166n.
    See also Buddhist scriptures
Brahmanism, 88, 119
Braudel, Fernand, 19, 248n.97
bridges, 158; in Buddhist scripture, 201–2, 207–8; government policy toward, 209–10; and monks, 203–8; motivation for building, 202; patronage of, 212–13; records of, 204–5, 210–11; scholarship on, 200; symbolism of, 203
Buddha. *See* Śākyamuni
Buddhist art: aniconism in, 66; contrasted to secular art, 56; in Han, 83–84; ideals of, 7; images of lay devotees in, 129; and influence on secular art, 85; rosaries in 124. *See also* icons
Buddhist scriptures: and blood writing, 174–76; burning of, 183; payment for, 183; popularity of, 177–79; translation of, 220
burial, 9, 31, 83–84, 160
Burma, 43

caitya, 158n.7
calligraphy, 167
Cambodia, 277
Cangyong, 110
censer, 147, 278
Central Asia, 283
ceramics, 154
Ceylon, 43, 159
chairs: changes triggered by, 227; in Chinese monasteries, 240–44; and the court, 244–45; definition of, 229; earliest Chinese representations of, 241; in India, 236–40; in pre-Buddhist China, 222–26; terminology for, 229, 237–38; theories for appearance of in China, 228–36; world history of, 232
Chajing, 263, 265–66

336INDEX

opening of the eyes ceremony, 60–62
Ouyang Xiu, 197

paper, 167, 177–79, 185
patronage, 6–7, 157–60, 163–64; of
    bridges, 212–13; in early Buddhist liter-
    ature, 159–60; imperial, 195, 279–80;
    by monks and nuns, 159; motivation for,
    212–13, 215–19; rewards for, 158, 213
Peirce, Charles, 139n.179
peonies, 276
Perfection of Wisdom Scriptures, 30, 74,
    164–66, 168
Platform Scripture, 75, 104–5
posture, 222–28
Prasenajit, 53n
pratiṣṭhā, 59–62
pratyekabuddhas, 34
Prescott, William H., 19
Prince Wusu, 109
printing, 167, 180–83
Pure Land, 123, 161, 163
purple robe, 34, 100–3, 109, 205
Puzu, 204

qi, 27
Qian Hongchu, 181
Qianlong, 140–41
Qibaotai, 235
Qing dynasty: bridges during, 206–7, 209,
    211–13; furniture during, 224; relic
    worship during, 36, 48n.79; rosaries
    during, 116–18, 134–38; *ruyi* during,
    139–41, 152; stupas during, 44n; tea
    during, 275
Qingming shanghe tu, 228
Qingzhao, 150
Qin Shihuang, 58, 143n.190, 167
Qiu Jun, 77
quanti, 276

*Record of Buddhist Monasteries in Lu-
    oyang*, 39, 174, 186, 191–92, 264
*Record of the Jewel of the Law Through-
    out the Ages*, 104–5, 110, 268–69
relics: allure of, 48–52; of Ānanda, 29;
    Aśoka and, 29–30; authenticity of, 41,
    43, 46 nn. 65 and 66, 47, 81; of the
    Buddha, 29–30, 33, 43, 46–47, 49, 51;
    classification of, 36; contention over, 37;

criticism of, 44–48; and cultivation, 35;
    decoy, 46; of Dīpaṃkara, 34; early prop-
    agation of in China, 32; at Famen
    Monastery, 45–46; and geomancy, 44n;
    in the Han, 32, 83; history of, 52; in
    icons, 62–63; in India, 29–30; indige-
    nous to China, 33–36; introduction of
    to China, 31–33; and merit, 30–31, 51;
    and miracles, 32, 42, 46, 49; modern ex-
    cavations of, 30, 38; and monasteries,
    44; of monks, 34; nature of, 80; offer-
    ings to, 37–38; of parrot, 35; and pil-
    grimage, 32–33; political uses of, 40–
    44, 52, 82; of pratyekabuddhas, 34; in
    pre-Buddhist China, 31; as proof of the
    power of Buddhism, 32; provenance of,
    41; skepticism toward, 44–48; and stu-
    pas, 38–39, 189; and success of Bud-
    dhism, 30; Sui Wendi and, 40–43; theft
    of, 37; uses of, 30. *See also* mummies
ringed staff, 113–15
ritual: icons in, 55, 65; implements used in,
    85; use of rosaries in, 121–22; vessels
    used in, 223
rock candy, 260–61
rosaries: aesthetics of, 131, 137–38; in
    Buddhist art, 124; connoisseurship of,
    133–34; consecration of, 121; as a
    counting device, 120; as emblem for the
    monk, 125–26, 128; etymology of,
    118n.116; as gifts, 116, 129–30; in In-
    dian Buddhism, 118–24; introduction of
    to China, 124–29; lay use of, 123, 128–
    29; mother bead of, 122; non-devotional
    uses of, 129–34; number of beads in,
    120–21; at the Qing court, 134–38; re-
    minder of, 122; substances made from,
    121–22; symbolism of, 137; as talis-
    mans, 123
ruyi: aesthetics of, 151–52; connoisseur-
    ship of, 151–52; at court, 143–44; at
    Famen Monastery, 147; as gift, 109,
    116; interpretations of, 148–51; as lec-
    ture baton, 145; origins of, 141–43; use
    by the laity of, 146–47

sacred objects: devotion to, 24–25; as ex-
    otic, 51; icons as, 61–62; nature of, 25,
    81; in pre-Buddhist China, 26–28;
    rosaries as, 123; scholarship on, 25–27;

BUDDHISMS:

A PRINCETON UNIVERSITY PRESS SERIES

CPSIA information can be obtained at www.ICGtesting.com
Printed in the USA
LVOW13s1709090314

376632LV00002B/556/P